CORONATIONS

Published with the cooperation of the
CENTER FOR MEDIEVAL AND RENAISSANCE STUDIES
University of California, Los Angeles

CORONATIONS
Medieval and Early Modern Monarchic Ritual

EDITED BY
János M. Bak

University of California Press

Berkeley · Los Angeles · Oxford

University of California Press
Berkeley and Los Angeles, California
University of California Press, Ltd.
Oxford, England

Copyright © 1990 by The Regents of the University of California

Library of Congress Cataloging-in-Publication Data

Coronations : medieval and early modern monarchic ritual / edited by János M. Bak.
    p. cm.
    Papers originally presented at a conference held February 1985 in Toronto.
    Includes bibliographical references.
    ISBN 0-520-06677-4
    1. Coronations—Europe—Congresses. 2. Europe—Social life and customs—Congresses. I. Bak, János M.
GT5051.E87C67 1990
394'.4—dc20   89-20441
                                                                                 CIP

1 2 3 4 5 6 7 8 9

CONTENTS

PREFACE *vii*

J. M. Bak: Introduction: Coronation Studies—Past, Present, and Future *1*

1. J. L. Nelson: Hincmar of Reims on King-making: The Evidence of the *Annals of St. Bertin*, 861–882 *16*

2. R. E. Giesey: Inaugural Aspects of French Royal Ceremonials *35*

3. J. Le Goff: A Coronation Program for the Age of Saint Louis: The Ordo of 1250 *46*

4. J.-C. Bonne: The Manuscript of the Ordo of 1250 and Its Illuminations *58*

5. A. D. Hedeman: Copies in Context: The Coronation of Charles V in His *Grandes Chroniques de France* *72*

6. L. M. Bryant: The Medieval Entry Ceremony at Paris *88*

7. E. Vestergaard: A Note on Viking Age Inaugurations *119*

8. E. Hoffmann: Coronations and Coronation Ordines in Medieval Scandinavia *125*

9. A. Gieysztor: Gesture in the Coronation Ceremonies of Medieval Poland *152*

10. R. Elze: The Ordo for the Coronation of Roger II of Sicily: An Example of Dating by Internal Evidence *165*

11. B. Schimmelpfennig: Papal Coronations in Avignon *179*

CONTENTS

12. A. Hughes: The Origins and Descent of the Fourth Recension of the English Coronation   *197*

13. R. C. McCoy: "The Wonderfull Spectacle": The Civic Progress of Elizabeth I and the Troublesome Coronation   *217*

14. D. Sturdy: "Continuity" versus "Change": Historians and English Coronations of the Medieval and Early Modern Periods   *228*

CONTRIBUTORS   *247*

GENERAL INDEX   *249*

INDEX OF MANUSCRIPTS   *257*

PREFACE

In memoriam John Brückmann

The majority of the papers in this volume were originally presented at a conference on medieval coronations and related rituals held in February 1985 in Toronto. The meeting was to commemorate the untimely death of John Brückmann, a beloved teacher of medieval history at Glendon College and an original scholar who had concentrated his research on coronation *ordines*. Having studied at Harvard College, the University of Toronto (with Bertie Wilkinson), and the Pontifical Institute for Medieval Studies where he regarded himself a pupil of Father J. R. O'Donnell, C.S.B., Brückmann wrote his doctoral dissertation in 1964 on English coronations between 1213–1318. Besides an article on the "Second Recension" of the royal coronation *ordo*— in the Wilkinson-Festschrift—he also published a checklist of liturgical manuscripts (in *Traditio*), both prolegomena to his great project, the edition of coronation *ordines* of medieval England. This plan remains a desideratum, for John died after a brief illness in December 1983. It is to his memory that this volume is dedicated.

The conference was generously supported by several universities, colleges, and institutes in Toronto and by the Social Sciences and Humanities Research Council of Canada. Without their assistance and the collegial cooperation of the organizers at Glendon College, York University, and the Pontifical Institute it would not have been possible to bring together such an international gathering of like-minded scholars and—ultimately—this volume. It is an honor for us that this volume has been cosponsored by the Center for Medieval and Renaissance Studies at UCLA, which helped to subsidize the cost of the illustrations.

I translated the contributions submitted in German, French, or Italian (with the exception of Professor Le Goff's, which was originally translated by Nora Scott) and wish to acknowledge my debt for assistance in polishing the translations to Professors Idit Dobbs-Weinstein, Diane Owen Hughes, and Margerie Sinel, as well as to Eva Gieysztor-Stucki. I am also grateful for the critical remarks of the anonymous readers and the presenter of the manuscript, and for the expert editorial assistance of the staff of University of California Press. With their help, I have done my best to standardize the many different styles and forms of reference used by the authors who belong to several schools and national conventions. However, just because of this variety of observances, that was not always possible. I also regret that financial considerations forced us to accept the placing of the notes after the single essays and not at the bottom of the pages; I hope that the attentive reader will be able to find them.

Finally, I should like to note that many articles were submitted soon after the meeting in 1985. If some authors may seem not to have taken account of the most recent literature, the fault is mine. Preparing the volume for print took longer than I had anticipated.

Vancouver, Canada
Spring 1989   J. M. B.

Introduction

Coronation Studies—Past, Present, and Future

János M. Bak

This volume of essays offers a survey of the most recent work in "coronation studies" in the widest sense of this term, meaning inquiries into the different symbolic and ritual acts that served both to legitimate and to present monarchical rule in the Middle Ages and the ancien régime.[1] The selection reflects, without claim to be comprehensive, the variety of topics treated by students of rulership and the character of the premodern state, including their different methods of approach and the distinct types of sources used as evidence. The volume contains studies focusing on most of the geographical regions of Europe.[2] There is also a diversity in genre: the essay-type summary of a scholar's many years of thought and research, the initial analysis of a document by a team, the textual study demonstrating a point, the informative survey of development, the brief comment on a controversial issue, and so on. I am pleased to have been able to include authors from various "schools," if they can be called thus,[3] and representatives of several generations, from doyens of the field, such as Reinhard Elze and Ralph Giesey, to a few recently graduated *philosophiae doctores*.

Many of the following articles address an agenda that has been with us for over a century, ever since historians began to scrutinize events surrounding the accession of rulers and the writings associated with it: establishing authentic readings for those liturgical scripts—*ordines*—which guided the actors of the rites; dating these texts; and interpreting their formulae in terms of continuity or change, of native roots and borrowings, of politics, theology, and ritual. Other studies address the general context of the ceremonies, their constitutional, ideological, and propagandistic place in medieval politics. Again, others look at the changes in royal ritual during the early modern centuries, both in form and meaning. One paper explicitly (others more implicitly) explores the historiography of the field, placing it in the context of modern political and intellectual history.

Several authors, moreover, depart from traditional procedures, which were characterized by textual scrutiny and iconographical analysis. By introducing new questions and novel methods their contributions are frequently informed by modes of inquiry elaborated in the social sciences—such as historical anthropology or comparative ethnographical study of gestures, of rites, and of rituals—and apply such sociological terms of analysis as that of legitimation. Many include questions about the relationship of participants and observers, about the relative role of various groups in the events, and about the perception of these acts by eyewitnesses and other contemporaries.

Most of the studies are based primarily on liturgical text (ordines in the wider sense, that include more or less elaborate directions) but confront these with other sources of many types. Often the actual prescription for the rituals is missing, so that reconstructions have to be attempted, based on other contemporary pieces of evidence or on later liturgical writings. It is a tradition in this field to devote as much attention to pictorial evidence as to written sources; in fact, the emancipation of historical images from illustrative decoration to critically evaluated evidence was pioneered in the field of studies on rulership.[4] Authors of this volume remain true to that tradition and refine the modes of interpretation introduced by earlier scholars. The contrasting of image and text (both in liturgical books and chronicles) and precise analysis of relevant illuminations (including colors, dimensions, internal symmetries, and so on) are to a certain extent new directions of inquiry. One pioneering study is based on the musical material of the liturgy: the reconstruction of a ritual's development with the help of the surviving notations of music, an approach novel both in method and in the type of source upon which it is built.

Students of royal ritual have been long aware of the fact that liturgical and ecclesiastical evidence alone is insufficient; only the contrasting of normative prescriptions in ordines and related texts with reports on events can offer valid insights. Several studies in this volume underline the importance of this rule. In particular, the systematic evaluation of a major narrative source, the *Annals of St. Bertin*, written by Hincmar of Reims, sheds unique light on the archbishop's perceptions about kingship. These perceptions are in many respects not consonant with our expectations based on theoretical and liturgical texts of the same age, even of the same author. Even though not discussing ritual in itself, or just because of this, the inquiry into Hincmar's description of "king-making" is an important corrective to one-sided ecclesiastical and liturgical analyses. All in all, this selection of studies attempts to demonstrate that scholars in this field are engaged in completing tasks left unfinished in the past as well as pursuing inquiries of a wider range, based in part on traditional material but also embarking on entirely new avenues of exploration.

INTRODUCTION: CORONATION STUDIES

Critical scholarship on the Middle Ages may be regarded as some three hundred years old if one takes, for example, Mabillon, the father of modern diplomatics, as a point of departure. In contrast, the critical study of royal, imperial, and papal coronations and other rites of accession is much younger: only just over a century old. It is perhaps not merely through central European chauvinism that I date the beginning of historical study of coronations, or more precisely, of their ordines, from the commented edition of texts published by Georg Waitz in 1873 in the proceedings of the Göttingen Academy.[5] To be sure, coronations and related royal ceremonies had been discussed by theologians, lawyers, and royal officers, both during and since their heyday in the medieval centuries. However, those treatises were closely connected to specific inaugrations or to constitutional issues of the day. Their intent was to explain, allegorically or legally, the words, gestures, and precedences within a living practice of royal representation. They are of great value to the historian of kingship, elucidating as they do the perception by contemporaries of the various aspects of the ritual and ceremonial. The allegorical exegesis of events and symbolic objects, as presented by medieval authors, is very significant for the understanding of the sacred character of kingship and of its connections to the liturgy and theology of the Roman Church. The late medieval and early modern changes in interpretation (which can be discovered, for example, by studying the relevant French literature on the *sacre* of the king of France) belong intrinsically to the development of the rituals.[6] It is also true that one of the mottoes of our pursuits, recently quoted by Janet Nelson, originates from the early seventeenth century: John Selden wrote in 1638 that "to know what was generally believed in all ages the way is to consult the liturgies."[7] Yet, I believe that, strictly speaking, the kind of scholarly inquiry which we are still pursuing begins with the study of a closed corpus of past customs, one not immediately connected to legal, political, or constitutional matters.

Naturally, it would be foolish to dismiss the more or less conscious political and ideological implications of such studies, either in the nineteenth century or even in our own day. When Wilhelm Giesebrecht in the late 1860s suggested that the imperial coronation ritual should be studied,[8] his call was surely not unconnected to the imminent "renewal" of the empire. I do not know whether Georg Waitz's presentation of the ordines, the first to be based on extensive manuscript studies, was in any way perceived by the author as related to the inauguration of the Second Reich. The studies that followed were initially also motivated by a combined historical and political interest in the medieval Holy Roman Empire.[9] Later, especially under the impact of *Geistesgeschichte*, partially also in response to the challenging studies of Georg von Below,[10] scholars came to consider a wider question: the structure and form of power in premodern polities and the origin and growth of the modern state in general. Percy Ernst Schramm, whose work is still the most extensive body of inquiry into this field, explained his own approach by pointing to the debate on the character of medieval monarchy, which he saw as "more of a state" than the modern one, precisely because of the religious aura surrounding its rulers. He also admitted, of course, that it was "less of a state" because of the highly personal nature of power in it.[11] Both of these aspects of medieval politics can be studied in an exemplary way in the records of coronations and of related rites and ceremonies.

It would be a worthwhile enterprise—in fact it is a desideratum for coronation studies—to write a pan-European historiography of this field, with a careful eye for the political and ideological implications, along such lines as those sketched by David Sturdy about "continuity" and "change" in English studies of royal ceremonial.[12] Without trying to offer such a historiographical overview of the "long century" since Georg Waitz, or even a bibliographical survey, I shall attempt an outline of a few major approaches to coronation studies in the last sixty-odd years. Chronologically one should start with Marc Bloch, who in *Les rois thaumaturges*,[13] was, I believe, the first to utilize the insights and methods of ethnography and anthropology for the study of medieval monarchical customs. However, he did not pursue this topic any further and, indeed, found no followers till quite recently. Among those who continued the German tradition of Waitz and others, three main concerns seem to stand out which can be more or less connected to three scholars and their "schools." Some historians have looked at medieval coronations in the general context of symbology of kingship (P. E. Schramm, his friends, and his pupils), others have investigated medieval political and legal theory (Walter Ullmann and his students), while a third group has studied "political theology" and the overall perception of the medieval state (Ernst H. Kantorowicz and his pupils). These three major approaches have certainly not been strictly separated, and there have been many other authors who included royal ceremonial in their inquiries.[14]

There were common points of departure in the work of the three German historians who headed these schools, above all the rigorous methods of textual study à l'allemande, but adverse conditions (to put it mildly) reduced contact between Schramm, the Göttingen professor; Ullmann, the Austrian emigré in England; and Kantorowicz, the German exile in America. Yet, students of kingship often consulted more than one of them, and pupils were encouraged to visit other leading scholars. Schramm, for example, corrected a few of his conclusions on Anglo-Saxon orders—albeit only minor ones—after Paul Ward's visit to Göttingen and the publication of his study and accompanying edition.[15] Nevertheless, much work written in Germany and Central Europe did not find its way into English or French scholarship until recently. Most strikingly, Schramm's attempt at a general history of coronations in France was never translated into French. On the other hand, his rather sketchy history of the English coronation was immediately translated for the accession of King George V and is still a point of reference for students of the topic. Bloch's seminal work appeared in English translation as late as 1973 and was thus for half a century accessible only to more learned readers; it was merely noted in Germany, and its innovative methods had no impact on that trend of scholarship either. Quite a few essential issues elaborated upon by German scholars appear occasionally in recent French or English books as new discoveries, and conversely Western European and American scholarship is often overlooked in Central Europe. Such are the vagaries of Western intellectual history.

The three "schools" about which I shall risk saying something may be perhaps called that of Göttingen, that of Cambridge, and that of Berkeley. I have sketched elsewhere the development of Schramm's interest in coronations and their ordines.[16] He started out from the images of medieval kings and was puzzled by the intricate relationship between the classical tradition and medieval accretions. He also felt that Byzantine models are crucial for understanding these developments, without entirely neglecting their partially Germanic, barbarian, or gentile roots.[17] Realizing that the iconography of rulership was closely connected to symbolically relevant objects, he explored the types and history of those objects, parallel with the ritual acts in which they were handed over to the ruler and interpreted politically, theologically, and—above all—allegorically. Challenged by the somewhat one-sided reading of the texts by the canon lawyer Eduard Eichmann,[18] and encouraged in his global approach in terms of the "world of ideas" by the work of Fritz Kern and Carl Erdmann,[19] Schramm began to collect, order, and edit the coronation ordines of the Anglo-Saxon and Frankish realms and of medieval Germany. We know now that many more texts must be considered than those he had in his hands. The more complete editions of the important Roman and Roman-German ceremonial texts subsequently published[20] allow far more precise analyses of borrowing and *imitatio*. Nevertheless, Schramm's "Ordines-Studien" of the 1930s are still bread and butter for our field.

Walter Ullmann's concern for the ordines and royal liturgy originated from his inquiry into ideas of royal and papal sovereignty, the relationship between *regnum* and *sacerdotium*, and those trends that he later called the ascending and descending themes in medieval political thought.[21] While demonstrating his willingness to participate in the continuity of English coronation studies by publishing some of his work with the Henry Bradshaw Society, Ullmann also kept his connections to continental German research: for example, his fine piece on the idea of sovereignty in medieval ordines appeared in the *Festschrift* for Schramm's seventieth birthday. If Schramm's contribution suffered from a certain overreaching and from growing into massive catalogues, Ullmann's seems to be somewhat limited by his primarily legalistic approach, his strong emphasis on the ecclesiastic side, and his almost exclusive reliance on written evidence.

Ernst H. Kantorowicz may have been the scholar who aimed at the widest all-round analysis of those data and ideas on which our present knowledge rests.[22] Having been trained as a classicist, he devoted his academic career to exploring the survival and revival of Antique notions of rulership in the Middle Ages, the Renaissance, and beyond. Already in his work on Frederick II of Sicily Kantorowicz utilized the ritual and iconographical dimensions of the subject.[23] Later he widened his field of research by including liturgical acclamations not studied earlier, the *laudes*, complete with musical analysis contributed by a colleague.[24] Kantorowicz's great summary of the perceptions of medieval kingship, *The King's Two Bodies*,[25] place all these elements, together with coronation rites, ordines, royal funerals (which were extensively studied by his pupil, Ralph Giesey[26]) into the context of the growth of what he called political theology. The progression from Christ-centered kingship to law-centered and man-centered rulership is still one of the most powerful paradigms for the understanding of continuity and change in the medieval state and its symbolic presentation.

In short, one might risk stating that the scholarly "generation" of Schramm-Ullmann-Kantorowicz, together with a few other scholars, such as Marc Bloch, Carl Erdmann, Cornelius Bouman,[27] Paul Ward, Gerhard Ladner,[28] and Reinhard Elze,[29] raised the study of royal ritual from the marginal and illustrative to the paradigmatic, thereby challenging medieval historians to reformulate many tenets about medieval rulership in particular and the state or the structure of power in general.

What is the relevance of this work for our present-day study of history? When some years ago Jacques Le Goff addressed the question whether politics is still a backbone of history, he could only answer it in a qualified affirmative, pointing to the paramount importance of the division and legitimation of power in any society, medieval no less than modern.[30] In that essay Le Goff replied to those who were, not surprisingly, tired of political history cast in terms of battles, dynastic conflicts, and legal quarrels, by pointing to the pioneering work of Bloch, Schramm, and others in exploring the deeper layers of politics by examining the intricacies of power structures. The symbology of rulership and ritual acts, he argued, opens up avenues of inquiry in no way less exciting than the study of other aspects of *mentalité*. And by the mere fact that these ideas and symbolic forms have quite a lot to do with the fate of people, high and low, they are just as relevant to our understanding of medieval life, social change, intellectual growth, and political transformations, as are perceptions of time, space, class, gender, riches, or poverty.

While much remains to be done, the first task in this field (as in any other historical enterprise) was the establishment of solid foundations in textual and pictorial evidence, and that has been to a great extent accomplished by the scholars of the nineteenth and earlier twentieth century. They also delineated the main modes of inquiry and the tools for interpreting liturgical texts, festive presentations, royal and princely iconographies. Above all, they placed the symbolic and ritual expressions of political programs and realities on the map of historical study. Furthermore, they defined various contexts—legal, theological, political, or cultural—in which the texts and images can be analyzed.

The tasks of the present generation of historians—and of future ones—is not necessarily to depart radically from what their teachers and teachers' teachers had pursued. Unedited texts still remain, and published ones also need to be reexamined in the light of new finds and new questions. To begin with, there is still no complete critical edition of the coronation ordines and related texts of any of the kingdoms of medieval Europe. Recent books by Lawrence Bryant, Sarah Hanley, Richard Jackson, and Janet Nelson,[31] as well as articles in this volume on France (by Jacques Le Goff, Jean-Claude Bonne, and Anne Hedeman) demonstrate that well-known texts and images may have to be redated and that even the most studied ones yield new information if scrutinized with an eye for detail, for the implicit meanings of the *mise en scène* of the entire ritual, the significance of color in the images, or bodily movements and gestures (see also Alexander Gieysztor's essay on Poland). The successive redactions of the English ordines, on which so many excellent scholars had worked and debated, among them our late friend John Brückmann, are still not established in a satisfactory way,[32] and Andrew Hughes's study suggests new avenues for dating by using musical as well as textual evidence for the process of change. The very meager textual basis for the history of the coronations in the European North has been only recently explored (presented here by Erich Hoffmann) and, owing to the lack of medieval ordines, much remains conjectural and open to debate (see the comments of Elisabeth Vestergaard). Reinhard Elze offers in this volume an edition of an *ordo* in the best tradition of the *Monumenta*, of which he is part, in order to demonstrate how one of the most difficult questions, the dating of a liturgical text, can be solved when text and circumstances are considered conjointly.

There are, however, directions in which historians now need to depart from the roads trod upon by their predecessors. For example, the study of ordines has been burdened by the fact that, in spite of repeated caveats, the existence of a liturgical script was still often regarded as evidence for the performance of a certain rite or of a certain sequence of rites. Schramm used to joke, "Show me your insignia and I'll tell you who you *want* to be," implying the programmatic rather than descriptive character of many of our sources on royal, imperial, or papal dress, *Herrschaftszeichen*, or gestures. Elze, who keeps emphasizing the dichotomy between prescription and reality, offers in this volume a nice example in which the two can be compared. His dating and interpreting of the Sicilian ordo teaches another very important lesson: changes and continuities in liturgical texts should not be expected to offer proofs for political development as reliable as we would wish, for the inertia of ritual is often greater than the willingness to adapt.[33] In his study of papal consecrations in Avignon, Schimmelpfennig bases his argument for dating late medieval ceremonial not only on liturgical texts, narratives, and accounts, but also on the architecture of the papal palace.

Besides widening the source base and the methods of its scrutiny, there are some new questions to be asked. Even though the scholars of the preceding generation did consider the wider political and social context of royal rituals (Walter Ullmann, for example, in his discussions of the "ascending theme" and the individual), rarely did they study their perception by the "people." The constitutional theme, that is, the place of royal presentation in the context of power sharing (or otherwise) between crown and lords (or estates) was certainly not overlooked, but Schramm, for one, explicitly stated that in the Middle Ages he wished to look at the rulers because they and not the ruled were able to "move" history.[34] As already noted, Marc Bloch was a unique exception in this regard as well. Several studies in this volume demonstrate the considerable importance of participants other than the king and his closest associates in all these symbolic performances. The definition of primary and secondary actors, of stage and audience, and the analysis of interaction between all these in the articles on the ordo of 1250, in the study on gestures in Poland and especially on the elaborate "dialogue" implicit in the entry ceremonies as presented by Larry Bryant are important advances in this direction. There is one further step: Janet Nelson's survey of Hincmar's views on rulership suggests that the archbishop, surely an expert on ritual, placed the greatest importance not on coronations, but on the king's being blessed from on high and accepted by lords and prelates. Her other studies in early medieval politics and ritual underline the need to keep the realities of power as much in mind as the magic and ritual elements of legitimation.

Understandably, the great majority of studies in the preceding generation concentrated on the early and high Middle Ages, that is, on periods when gestures, insignia, and visible ceremonies played a more important role than political tracts or written agreements, if there were any. However, it would be wrong to regard the late developments towards pageantry and festivity as mere "degradations." The early modern centuries witnessed various steps in changing certain functions of the traditional ceremonies. Some of them were replaced by more explicitly contractual and legal enactments, others discarded because their Roman origin was unsuitable for Protestant monarchies. Richard McCoy's study of Queen Elizabeth I's "troublesome" coronation suggests avenues to be explored, while some others have been discussed recently in the Davis Seminar at Princeton and in 1982 at a conference in Mainz.[35]

Future studies will certainly have to address these matters and many others as well. Coronation ritual and royal ceremonial were, of course, parts of a whole world of symbolic action, gesture, and behavior. Le Goff and his colleagues actually came to investigate the ordo, about which they present some preliminary findings here, while studying normative treatises on gestures in general, such as Hugh of St. Victor's *De instructione novitiorum*. In their seminar at the École des Hautes Etudes en Sciences Sociales they chanced upon the ordo of 1250 to discover that it offered unique evidence for gestures—comparable to sculptures on Romanesque tympana or images on gestures of prayer, of marriage, of vassalage—combining, as it does, text and illuminations. Studies on both European and extra-European kingship and state suggest that not all political ritual was concentrated on the major event of accession or funeral of a ruler, moments on which most researchers in this field had usually concentrated their attention. From festive crown wearing through reception of guests, envoys, and vassals, from hunts and feasts to the assembly of the *fideles*, many other occasions were also symbol-laden ritual events and political spectacles.[36]

Exploring harmony and divergence between prescription (ordo, etc.) and actual performance demands research into many hitherto neglected directions. For "reality" is not a one-dimensional matter: even if we can establish what actually transpired, we still need to ask how was it perceived by those present, and furthermore, in what, surely different, ways by contemporaries of various "estates." The mere visual and auditory perception of these events depended on whether one was admitted to a defined sacral or ritual place, or was left outside, whether one belonged to the chosen few in the immediate surrounding of the ruler or to the wider elite, to the secular or the clerical one, or to the *populus*, sometimes present in form of a selected group, at other times serving as mere "extras" in the spectacle. The task becomes very difficult when one must establish how symbolic actions were understood and interpreted by the various persons present or by those informed secondhand about the ceremonies. Since we would have to enter the minds of mostly illiterate laymen and lesser clergy, this will not be an easy task; however, the full weight of the argument about legitimation depends on it.

It is in these spheres of inquiry, where the traditional types of historical record are too thinly spread, that genuine new departures have to be made. One no longer has to defend the legitimacy of comparative and interdisciplinary procedures, which for a long time were regarded as mere auxiliaries admissible in instances where no "better" evidence was available. But it is still not fully agreed to that methods and findings of sister-disciplines, such as ethnography and anthropology, can be properly applied to the interpretation of medieval history. No doubt, there have been foolish and superficial parallels drawn by historians between rituals of "primitive tribes" and the elaborate ecclesiastical and secular festivities of medieval Europe. Such generalizations do not help us in reaching the hidden sides of political symbology. Anthropologists, too, have sometimes made too facile comparisons, often because they had only fragmentary knowledge of the historical material or, more frequently, because they lacked the critical skills and methods of textual interpretation. However, there is no reason to assume that the study of the relations—and the perception of these relations—between ruler and ruled (an essentially nonliterate population, deeply embedded in a fragmented and hybrid magical world view)[37] would not be susceptible to methods applied to recently observed preliterate societies and that certain features of these societies could not help to fill the gaps of our inquiries. The frequency with which anthropologists (A. van Gennep, V. Turner, C. Geertz, E. Leach, M. Fortes, and others) appear in the notes of the studies printed here—and other writings of our authors—suggests that students of medieval and early modern political ritual are well aware of the possibilities of such an exchange of ideas and procedures.

Interest in coronations and related rituals seems to have passed through a period of *baisse* on the stock exchange of historical studies. When Reinhard Elze notes that the edition he presents here was kept for many years in his desk drawer because of obvious lack of interest in this type of text, he is articulating something that many of us have experienced. For the past two or three decades new fields, such as popular ideas, social conditions of the lower classes, and the life of women, have, understandably, occupied the minds of many medievalists and of their readers and students. Kingship and the state appeared to have been studied quite enough and, moreover, seemed not so "relevant," anyhow. However, there seems to be new demand for analyses of power, hierarchy, and rulership, at least for inquiries that are subtle and explain more than what traditional political history of great events had to offer.[38] We hope that our volume reflects this transition from a temporary lull to a new flourishing of coronation studies and that it will also enhance it by encouraging further studies and novel departures.

NOTES

1. In English usage the one word describing the placing of the royal headgear on the new ruler, "coronation," denotes the entire set of rites connected to the ascension to power; from the late Middle Ages the ceremonial beginning of a papal pontificate came also to be called coronatio. In France the anointment (sacre) acquired a central position. In German scholarship both terms *Krönung* and *Weihe* (consecration) are used. However, a proper definition of our interests should include many other symbo-

INTRODUCTION: CORONATION STUDIES   11

lic events and gestures, such as the royal funeral preceding the new king's (or queen's, or pope's) inauguration, the different types of royal festivities, the rulers' entries into their capitals and other cities before and after the coronation, formal first acts of government (such as the *lit de justice* in France, the secular oath and knighting in Poland and Hungary, the general indulgence by a new pope), and so on.

2. I very much regret two obvious gaps: Germany, that is, the medieval empire, and the kingdoms of the Iberian Peninsula. There were plans for papers regarding both, but unfortunately the authors' other obligations prevented them from submitting these in time. Naturally, Byzantium must also be included if any claim to an overview should be valid, for the Greek imperial usage was most a powerful model, at least in the early Middle Ages. However, the extensive coverage of France reflects not only a special interest in French coronation studies both in that country and in North America but also the great number of challenging questions posed by the *religion royale* and its transformations.

3. I add quotation marks because I feel that the vicissitudes of academic life in our hectic age are not exactly conducive to the development of master-pupil relations and schools in the classical sense. As a matter of fact few of the medievalist *doctorandi* and *doctorandae* of the leading scholars mentioned below remained in the field and continued their work, or if they did so, many of them departed from the path of their "fathers."

4. For example, P. E. Schramm, *Die deutschen Kaiser und Könige in Bildern ihrer Zeit*, 1st ed. (Leipzig, 1928), last posthumous ed. by F. Müterich (Munich, 1983); E. H. Kantorowicz, "The 'King's Advent' and Enigmatic Panels in the Doors of S. Sabina," *Art Bulletin* 26 (1944): 207–231, reprinted in *Selected Studies*, ed. M. Cherniavsky and R. E. Giesey (Locust Valley, N.Y.: J. J. Augustin, 1965), 37–75; E. H. Kantorowicz, "The Carolingian King in the Bible of S. Paolo fuori le mura," reprinted in *Selected Studies*, 81–94; G. Ladner's books on the images of the popes, from *I ritratti dei Papi nell'antichità e nel medioevo* 1 (Vatican City, 1941) to *Die Papstbildnisse des Altertums und des Mittelalters* vol. 6 (Vatican City, 1984). The comparable studies for the Eastern Empire include such classics as A. Grabar, *L'empereur dans l'art byzantin. Recherches sur l'art officiel de l'empire d'Orient* (Paris, 1936, reprinted: London, 1971). The overview of the Slavic material, F. Kämpfer, *Das russische Herrscherbild von den Anfängen bis Peter d. Gr.: Studien zur Entwicklung der politischen Ikonographie im byzantinishen Kulturkreis* (Recklinghausen, 1978), with extensive literature, is, as far as I can see, the first attempt to apply modern semiotic analysis to this field (see pp. 17–102).

5. G. Waitz, "Die Formeln der deutschen Königs- und der römischen Kaiserkrönung vom 10. bis zum 12. Jahrhundert," *Abhandlungen der kgl. Gesellschaft der Wissenschaften zu Göttingen*, 18 (1873). There was an earlier dissertation submitted to the University of Halle by Hermann Schreiber ("De ceremoniis conditionibusque, quibus... usi sunt") in 1870, but only a fifty-three page short excerpt (to Berengar, 915 A.D.) was published. Waitz was followed by Joseph Schwarzer in *Forschungen zur deutschen Geschichte* 22 (1882) covering the entire Middle Ages, but too superficially. On the studies of English coronation around the turn of the century, see Sturdy, in this volume; on the relevant French scholarship, see the bibliography in R. A. Jackson, *Vive le Roi! A History of the French Coronations from Charles V to Charles X* (Chapel Hill/London: University of North Carolina Press, 1984), 280–299.

6. Relevant medieval texts include, among other works, the "Libellus de cerimo-

niis aule imperatoris," from the eleventh century, edited as part of the "Graphia auree urbis Roma," with commentary, in vol. 3, pp. 338-352 of Percy E. Schramm's *Kaiser, Könige und Päpste: Gesammelte Abhandlungen*, 4 vols. (Stuttgart, 1968-1971), henceforth referred to as *KKP*; the allegorical interpretations of insignia by Honorius Augustodunensis ("Gemma animae," c. 224-225, Migne PL 172: 612), by Godfrey of Viterbo ("Pantheon," XXVI, MG SS 22: 272ff.), and by Sicardus of Cremona ("Mitrale," II, 6: De regalibus insignis, Migne PL 213: 82), and several others. That these are not reliable sources for the actual appearance of insignia or for events at a ceremony, but rather suggest something about the perception of all these, has been often pointed out; see, e.g., my "Der Reichsapfel," in *Insignia Regni Hungariae* (Budapest, 1986), 193f. The French tracts, beginning with the "Traité du sacre" of Jean Golein, ed. R. A. Jackson, *Proc. of Am. Phil. Soc.* 113 (1969), through the great seventeenth-century edition of ceremonial texts by the two Godefroys to the renewed discussion after the Restoration, are discussed and listed in Jackson, *Vive le Roi*.

7. From his *Table-Talk*, quoted in J. L. Nelson, "Ritual and Reality in Early Medieval ordines," reprinted in her *Politics and Ritual in Early Medieval Europe* (London, 1986), 329.

8. Referred to by E. Eichmann, *Die Kaiserkrönung im Abendland: Ein Beitrag zur Geistesgeschichte des Mittelalters*, 2 vols. (Würzburg, 1942), vii.

9. On the politics of scholarship in this era see E.-W. Beckenförde, *Die deutsche verfassungsgeschichtliche Forschung im 19. Jahrhundert* (Berlin, 1961), and also F. W. Maitland's "Introduction" to the selected English translation of Otto Gierke's *Genossenschaftsrecht: Political Theories of the Middle Ages* (Cambridge, 1900).

10. G. von Below, *Der deutsche Staat des Mittelalters*, 2d ed (Leipzig, 1925), the first hundred pages of which summarize the controversial literature.

11. P. E. Schramm, *Herrschaftszeichen und Staatssymbolik. Beiträge zu ihrer Geschichte vom dritten bis zum sechzehnten Jahrhundert*, 3 vols, (Stuttgart, 1954-1956; MGH Schriften 13: 1-3) I, 1; quoted in English translation in J. M. Bak, "Medieval Symbology of the State: Percy E. Schramm's Contribution," *Viator* 4 (1973): 34.

12. In regard to the political use of royal tradition int the last century, see now also D. Cannadine, "The Context, Performance and Meaning of Ritual: The British Monarchy and the 'Invention of Tradition', c. 1820-1977." In *The Invention of Tradition*, ed. E. Hobsbawm and T. Ranger (London, 1983); reprinted in an abbreviated form in *Rites of Power: Symbolism, Ritual and Politics Since the Middle Ages*, ed. S. Wilentz: (Philadelpia: University of Pennsylvania Press, 1983).

13. First published as *Publications de la faculté des lettres de l'Université de Strasbourg* vol. 19 (Strasbourg, 1924); reprinted Paris, 1961 and now also Paris, 1983, with a preface by J. Le Goff. An English translation was published only in 1973, transl. J. A. Anderson, *The Royal Touch: Sacred Kingship and Scrofula in England and France* (London, 1973).

14. Ecclesiastical historians and students of sacred kingship have also contributed much to our knowledge of monarchical presentations, and so have researchers on Germanic, pre-Christian, and early medieval rulership. A few titles from the many: O. Höfler, *Germanisches Sakralkönigtum* (Tübingen, 1952); H. Wolfram, "Methodische Fragen zur Kritik am 'Sakralen' Königtum," in *Festschrift O. Höfler* (Vienna, 1968); J. M. Wallace-Hadrill, *Early Germanic Kingship in England and the Continent* (Oxford, 1971); W. A. Chaney, *The Cult of Kingship in Anglo-Saxon England* (Manchester, 1970);

and the collective volumes, *Das Königtum: Seine geistigen und rechtlichen Grundlagen. Mainau Voträge 1954*, ed. Th. Mayer (Vorträge und Forschungen 3, 1955; repr. Sigmaringen, 1973); R. Schneider, ed., *Das spätmittelalterliche Königtum in europäischem Vergleich* (Vort. u. Forsch. 32; Sigmaringen, 1986); *The Sacral Kingship: Contributions to the VIIIth International Congress on the History of Religion* (Leiden, 1959); *Early Medieval Kingship*, ed. P. H. Sawyer and I. N. Wood (Leeds, 1977); and so on.

15. See *KKP* 2: 201 ff.; referring to P. L. Ward., "The Coronation Ceremony in Medieval England," *Speculum* 24 (1939): 160–178. See also P. L. Ward, "An Early Version of the Anglo-Saxon Coronation Ceremony," *English Historical Review* 57 (1942): 345–361. Of course, Schramm could not fully accept Ward's findings, because these have essentially proven the weakness of his datings and filiations.

16. See n. 11, above. Most of the "Ordines-studien" are now reprinted in *KKP* 2 and 3. A bibliography of Schramm's work (up to 1963, compiled by A. Ritter) is in the *Festschrift Percy Ernst Schramm: zu seinem siebzigsten Geburtstag*, ed. P. Classen and P. Scheibert, 2 vols. (Wiesbaden, 1964) 2: 291–321. The volumes of *KKP* contain a number of updating comments to earlier studies.

17. See *Viator* 4 (1973): 59, with reference to related works by Treitinger, Deér, Dölger, and others. The landmark articles of A. Alföldi, with whom both Schramm and Kantorowicz held close friendship, on the late Antique models are now collected in his *Die monarchische Repräsentation im römischen Kaiserreich* (Darmstadt, 1970); on the transition period from antiquity to early Middle Ages and Byzantium see now M. McCormick, *Eternal Victory* (Cambridge, 1987) and the excellent overview, with extensive literature by J. L. Nelson, "Symbol in Context: Rulers' Inauguration Rituals in Byzantium and the West in the Early Middle Ages," reprinted in her *Politics and Ritual*, 259–282. Recently A. Cameron has done much in this field, see, e.g., "The Construction of Court Ritual: The Byzantine Book of Ceremonies," *Rituals of Royalty: Power and Ceremonial in Traditional Societies*, ed. D. Cannadine and S. Price (Cambridge, 1987), 106–136.

18. See n. 8, above; a list of his works (most of which are in the field of law and church history) can be found in the *Festschrift Eduard Eichmann zum 70. Geburtstag*, ed. M. Grabmann and K. Hoffman (Paderborn, 1940), 685–687.

19. Fritz Kern, *Gottesgnadentum und Widerstandsrecht im früheren Mittelalter* (c. 1914; rev. ed. by R. Buchner, Münster, 1954; reprinted Darmstadt, 1962); partial English trans. by S. B. Chrimes, as pt. I of *Kingship and Law in the Middle Ages* (Oxford, 1939; reprinted New York: Harper & Row, 1956, 1970); Erdmann's works are reprinted in two posthumous collections: *Forschungen zur politischen Ideenwelt des Frühumittelalters*, ed. F. Baethgen (Berlin, 1951), with bibliography, and *Ottonische Studien*, ed. H. Beumann (Darmstadt, 1968); only his *Origins of the Idea of Crusade* is available in English, trans. M. M. Baldwin and W. Goffart (Princeton: Princeton University Press, 1977).

20. For example: M. Andrieu, *Le pontifical romain au moyen âge*, 6 vols. (Vatican City, 1938–1941, Studi e Testi, 86–88, 99); C. Vogel and R. Elze, *Le pontifical Romano-Germanique du Xe siècle*, 3 vols. (Vatican City, 1963–1972, Studi e Testi, 226–227, 269); see also the titles in the notes to Schimmelpfennig's article in this volume.

21. A bibliography of Ullmann's writings, 1940–1979, compiled by Peter Linehan, is in *Authority and Power: Studies in Medieval Law and Government presented to Walter Ullmann on his Seventieth Birthday*, ed. B. Trieney and P. Linehan (Cambridge, 1980), 225–274; the fullest statements of Ullmann's mature approach to coronation rituals

are *The Carolingian Renaissance and the Idea of Kingship* (London, 1969), lecture IV; and *Law and Politics in the Middle Ages* (London, 1975), 207–208, 263–266. For a critical appreciation of some of his views, see F. Oakley, "Celestial Hierarchies Revisited: Walter Ullmann's Vision of Medieval Politics," *Past & Present* 60 (1975): 3–48; also J. L. Nelson, "The Lord's Anointed and the People's Choice: Carolingian Royal Ritual," in Cannadine and Price, *Rituals*, 137–180, esp. 144–149.

22. An essential bibliography of Kantorowicz's work, complied by himself, is printed in his *Selected Studies*, xi–xiv; cf. also the biography by Eckhart Grünewald, *Ernst Kantorowicz und Stefan George: Beiträge zur Biographie des Historikers bis zum Jahre 1938 und zu seinem Jugendwerk "Kaiser Friedrich der Zweite"* (Wiesbaden, 1982) and the essay by Ralph Giesey, "Ernst Kantorowicz: Scholarly Triumphs and Academic Travails in Weimar Germany and the United States," *Leo Baeck Institute Year Book* 30 (1985): 191–202.

23. *Kaiser Friedrich der Zweite*, 2 vols. (Berlin, 1927–1931), truncated English translation without the essential *Ergänzungsband* by E. O. Lorimer, *Frederick the Second* (London, 1931; reprinted 1957); same in French by A. Kohn (Paris, 1987) and the two Italian ones (by M. Offergeld-Merlo, Milan, 1976, and G. P. Colombo, Milan, 1976), although the last includes some notes from the volume of references.

24. *Laudes Regiae: A Study in Liturgical Acclamations and Medieval Ruler Worship with a Study of the Music of the Laudes and Musical Transcriptions by M. F. Bukofzer* (Berkeley, Los Angeles, University of California Publications in History 33, 1946).

25. *The King's Two Bodies: A Study in Mediaeval Political Theology* (Princeton University Press: Princeton, 1957; reprinted Princeton, 1966); a Spanish translation was published in 1985 in Madrid, a German in 1987 in Munich; an Italian (Milan, 1988) and a French version (Paris, 1988) have just appeared.

26. *The Royal Funeral Ceremony in Renaissance France* (Geneva, 1960; reprinted 1984); in French as *Le roi ne meurt jamais* (Paris, 1987). See also now his *Cérémonial et puissance souveraine: France, XVe—XVIIe siècles* (Paris, 1987).

27. *Sacring and Crowning. The Development of the Latin Ritual for the Anointing of Kings and the Coronation of the Emperor before the XIth Century* (Groningen, 1951, Bijdragen van het Institutt voor Middeleuwse Geschiedenis der Rijksuniversiteit te Utrecht 30).

28. See above, n. 4.

29. Most of his studies are now collected as *Päpste, Kaiser, Könige und die mittelalterliche Herrschersymbolik*, ed. L. Schmugge and B. Schimmelpfennig (London, 1982). Of course, his chef d'oeuvre, so far, is the edition of the imperial coronation ordines in MGH Font. iur. germ. ant. 9 (Hanover, 1960) containing the only complete corpus of such records for any medieval polity.

30. "Is Politics Still the Backbone of History?," *Daedalus* 100 (1971): 1–19. The importance of ritual and symbology for political history is now nicely argued by D. Cannadine in his "Introduction: The Divine Rite of Kings," in Cannadine and Price, *Ritual*, 1–19, with extensive references to the parallel studies in anthropology. See also L. Bryant, *The King and the City in the Parisian Royal Entry Ceremony* (Geneva, 1986); Sarah Hanley, *The Lit de Justice of the Kings of France: Constitutional Ideology in Legend, Ritual and Discourse* (Princeton: Princeton University Press, 1983); for Jackson, see above, n. 5; for Nelson above, n. 7.

32. See J. L. Nelson's paper prepared for the Toronto conference on "The Second English Ordo," printed in her *Politics*, 361–370, with bibliography.

33. On this see also Nelson, "The Rites of the Conqueror," in her *Politics*, 375–401.

34. See *Viator* 4 (1973): 63; some years ago Giesey and I noted that we both have gradually given much more attention also to the other side of the dualist equation in medieval monarchy—diets, parliaments, estates, electors—than our teachers ever did.

35. In 1980–1982 the Shelby Cullom Davis Center for Historical Studies at Princeton University explored in a symposium and in many seminar meetings the problems of "Ideology and power"; the result of these discussions was published in the volume edited by S. Wilentz on *Rites of Power* (see above, n. 10), which contains a 1977 article by Clifford Geertz that was crucial in inspiring this research, papers written by scholars while being fellow-in-residence at the Davis Center (Hanley, Agulhon, Isaac, Lüdtke) and other contributions on topics from the early Middle Ages to our own times. In his introduction (pp. 1–10, "Teufelsröckh's Dilemma: On Symbolism, Politcs, and History"), Sean Wilentz explores the causes of renewed interest in political symbology among American historians. The papers of the 1981 Mainz colloquium were published under the editorship of H. Duchhardt, *Herrscherweihe und Königskrönung im frühneuzeitlichen Europa* (Wiesbaden, 1983). Changes in function and significance of medieval rites were explored, for examples, by Sarah Hanley (see above, n. 30) and by R. Giesey (in this volume) in regard to the French *lit de justice*; similar developments in central Europe toward a more law-oriented symbology were noted both by E. Fügedi, "Coronation in Medieval Hungary," *Studies in Medieval and Renaissance History* NS 2 (1980): 159–189, esp. 179 ff.) and myself, *Königtum und Stände in Ungarn im 14.–16. Jahrhundert* (Wiesbaden, 1973), esp. 79–91.

36. See the wide range of ceremonial events discussed in both Cannadine and Price, *Rituals*, and Wilentz, *Rites of Power*.

37. On these aspects I have learned much from the books of I. A. Gurevich: *Categories of Medieval Culture*, trans. G. L. Campbell (London, 1984), and *Medieval Popular Culture: Problems of Perception and Belief*, trans. J. M. Bak and P. Hollingsworth (Cambridge, 1988).

38. The association founded at the 1985 Toronto conference, *MAJESTAS: Rulership-Souveraineté-Herrschertum*, has sponsored several sessions on different scholarly meetings about relevant subjects and found that interest in these topics is again growing among historians of various orientations.

ONE

Hincmar of Reims on King-making: The Evidence of the *Annals of St. Bertin*, 861–882

Janet L. Nelson

Hincmar of Reims wrote voluminously—on theology, on canon law, and on the conduct of the powerful. Modern historians of medieval political thought have ransacked these works with an energy worthy of the Vikings and have amassed a disparate hoard of fragmentary discussions of how kings ought to act.[1] Among this hacksilver can be found a rare gem of Hincmarian political analysis: a typology of king-making.[2] Its original location was in a series of ripostes to a list of objectionable propositions, which Hincmar appended to his bulky treatise on the divorce of Lothar II and Theutberga. As so often, controversy sharpened Hincmar's cutting edge. "Some wise ones," he noted sardonically, had alleged that Lothar II was "a king, and subject to no human laws or judgements but only those of God, who constituted him king in the realm which his father had left him."[3] Hincmar first tackled the issue of the king's subjection to law: "The law is not laid down for the just man, but for the unjust." Hence a just king would be judged, and rewarded, by Christ alone, but a bad king would be judged by bishops "either secretly or in public."[4] The related, but distinct, proposition that the king was "set up" by God through the workings of filial inheritance then received separate discussion. There were three ways, said Hincmar, that a man could be "set up in rulership": by God, like Moses, Samuel, and Josias; by God through men, like Joshua and David; and by man "but not without the divine nod [of permission]," like Solomon "on the orders of his father David, and by means of Zadoch the prophet and Nathan the priest." Hincmar went on to elaborate further subtypes of the third category: kings constituted "by the support of citizens and soldiers," and kings who succeeded to their fathers, as can be found, said Hincmar, "in the case of all those in the *Histories* and *Chronicles*, and even in the *Lives of the Caesars*."[5] The *Histories* and

Chronicles Hincmar had in mind were presumably Frankish ones; and Lothar II, succeeding his father, thus clearly came into this section of Hincmar's third category. But of the timing or form of Lothar's becoming king, Hincmar said not a word, preferring, instead, to spell out the Biblical lesson that a bad king (and he hastily disclaimed any allegation that Lothar's father had been a bad king) would see the succession depart from his line.[6] In other words, characteristically, Hincmar slid away from analyzing into moralizing.

This passage has been discussed by several modern commentators. It has been excerpted, taken from its immediate context, sometimes misconstrued.[7] Above all, it has not been set against the broader context of Hincmar's own political experience. Yet, as a man who for a generation and more was at the heart of events in the oft-divided Frankish realm, Hincmar observed many settings-up of rulers. His personal interest in the practicalities of royal inauguration is documented in the consecration ordines he himself produced for Carolingian rulers.[8] But most ninth-century Frankish kings received no ecclesiastical consecration. How important was such a ritual in Hincmar's view? How otherwise did a man become a king? Who, other than bishops, could participate? Did Hincmar have consistent criteria for gauging the legitimacy of a king's accession? Given that he regarded "tyrannical usurpers" as divinely ordained ("whether to fill up the number of their own sins, or to allow vengeance on the people's sins"), yet clearly identified the tyrant as one who acquired kingship in a wrongful manner, how did Hincmar distinguish in practice between the usurper and the rightful king? In canonical treatises, and in Mirrors of Princes, such questions could be sidestepped. What forced Hincmar to address them, however briefly and often obliquely, was the writing of contemporary history. His sustained essay in the genre, virtually disregarded by historians who have dealt at length with his political ideas, and even dismissed as "the prelate's most anonymous work," was the last section of the so-called *Annals of St. Bertin*, covering the years 861–882; it was a work that Hincmar himself designated "the Deeds of Our Kings."[9]

In the *AB*, Hincmar mentions some twenty-six acquisitions of regnal power, some abortive, mere attempted coups, some confirming previously established tenure, some inaugurating effective reigns.[10] The twenty years of his authorship of the *AB* were years of unprecedented disruption in the transmission of Carolingian power. A generation of long-lived kings gave way to a series of reigns cut short by illness or accident. Filial succession, whether to a subkingdom during a royal father's lifetime, or to the father's whole kingdom after his death, was no statistical norm, even if contemporaries considered it normal. As frequent as cases of sons succeeding fathers were those where another close kinsman made a bid for the succession.[11] Even where a son was available, the timing of his succession could be problematic: more than one prince was tempted to jump the gun and "usurped part of the realm" as a rebel against his father.[12] The fact that conflict was, with a single exception, contained within the dynastic circle of those descended from Charlemagne in the male line did not remove its intensity. A brother might pit his "hereditary right" against an uncle's claim: the rules of family inheritance in any case allowed room for maneuver.[13]

In the *AB*, Hincmar recorded nearly all of the settings up (successful or otherwise) of rulers known to have occurred during the decades 861–882.[14] Though his accounts were mostly terse, he indicated for some cases distinct elements or stages in the ruler's inauguration. Hereditary right clearly underlay nearly every case, for all save one of the claimants were Carolingians born; yet Hincmar scarcely even mentions it. It was commonplace, uncontroversial: only a Carolingian, and a king's son, was eligible for kingship. By contrast, in nearly all the cases of filial succession not said to involve usurpation of power, Hincmar expressly mentions paternal designation.[15] Still more striking is the stress on the participation of the aristocracy in every type of dynastic succession. The quest of a would-be king for aristocratic support, or aristocratic initiative in inviting a hoped-for king, is mentioned explicitly in well over half the cases Hincmar covered.[16] His silence in certain cases may thus be significant. An elective element could occur, of course, alongside others, such as paternal designation or fraternal division. But rarely was it wholly absent. In fact, Hincmar presents nearly every king-to-be, or would-be king, whatever his position in the dynasty, as dependent on the support of aristocrats for the timing, course, and outcome of his bid for rulership.[17] The emphasis is worth noting, since it has been argued on the basis of Hincmar's ordines that his basic view was hierocratic—that he was trying to establish the authority of bishops, and especially the archbishop of Reims, as king-makers. The performance of royal consecration rites, on this argument, gave Hincmar the means to control the king. But Hincmar the recorder of royal *Gesta* expresses no such view and is, as we shall see, capable of realism about the political forces that could underlie, and belie, episcopal role-playing.[18]

The status of the *AB* as evidence of Hincmar's opinions is also worth noting. This was an "unofficial," private work in which Hincmar gave vent to some very personal views on, for example, the interventions of Pope Nicholas I in the affairs of the Frankish Church, or the promotion of the archbishop of Sens to the primacy of Gaul.[19] For Hincmar, perhaps even more than for any of his contemporaries, the writing of royal *Gesta* was a self-conscious and subjective business: it involved selectivity and (in both senses of the word) discrimination.[20] In the *AB*, Hincmar did not seek anonymity: his own preferences, and prejudices, shine through almost every page. Hence, if we want to know what Hincmar "really" thought about king-making, his section of the *AB* seems a good place to look. A brief examination of four cases follows.

THE ATTEMPTED SETTING UP OF CARLOMAN AS KING IN 873

This is Hincmar's account of the final phase in the rebellion of Charles the Bald's son Carloman. Three years before Carloman was first alleged to have been "plotting against his father, thereby breaching his fidelity."[21] He had been put into the Church as a child of five or six and tonsured as a cleric, subsequently receiving minor orders as a deacon. He had then been given several abbacies, which he held in the manner of a lay abbot, having a regular abbot in office alongside to supervise the monasteries' religious life. In 868, Hincmar records Charles the Bald's sending of Carloman "with a crack force of household troops" to Neustria to fight the Vikings on the Loire.[22] In 869, when Charles made a strong bid for the succession to his nephew Lothar II, he endowed Carloman with further abbacies in the newly acquired western part of Lothar's kingdom. But the new situation had evoked a new ambition in Carloman: his rebellion was surely a response to the potential availability of a Lotharingian kingdom for himself. Though Hincmar does not say that Carloman aspired to kingship in 870 or 871, his record of Carloman's activities in these years strongly suggests such an ambition. The annal for 873 makes this explicit. Life imprisonment was the punishment intended by Charles for his faithless son. But when the bishop had

> deposed Carloman from all ecclesiastical rank, and left him only the communion of a layman, . . . the ancient cunning Enemy incited Carloman and his accomplices to exploit another argument, namely, that because he no longer held any ecclesiastical orders, he could be all the more free to assume the title and power of a king. . . So it came about that, following his deposition, his former accomplices began to rally to him again, more enthusiastically than ever. . . : their plan was that, as soon as they got the chance, they would snatch him out of the prison where he was being held, and set him up as their king.[23]

Charles the Bald then had Carloman hailed before a secular court and condemned to death for his crimes—a sentence commuted to blinding "in order to deceive the pernicious hope in him on the part of those men who hated peace."[24]

There are two implications here for Hincmar's view of ninth-century Frankish king-making. First, however much Hincmar disapproved of Carloman's supporters, he did not challenge their capacity to "set up a king."[25] It was Carloman's personal ineligibility that made his elevation to kingship impossible: the would-be king-makers' qualifications for their role were implicitly accepted. Significantly, there is no hint here or in Hincmar's letters that Carloman's supporters included any bishop. Second, in affirming here Charles's right to override filial claims in making his arrangements for the future, Hincmar was asserting (and perhaps wished to assure Charles the Bald) that the Church could offer a workable method for excluding a legitimate son from a share in the royal succession. Consecration to holy orders, was indelible: hence Carloman, by receiving tonsure as a cleric, had been removed permanently from the ranks of those eligible for kingship.[26] Carloman's supporters sinned in ignoring this. In the end, the Church's rule was vindicated, even if secular power and a secular judgment were needed to enforce it.[27] Thus the Church, which increasingly stressed the obligations of Christian marriage, and hence, by implication, the claims of all legitimate sons, was offering at the same time an escape route from the ensuing intensification of problems arising from partible inheritance. In practice, previous kings too had recognized that partibility had limits: the kingdom of the Franks had never been treated just like a family holding. But the Carolingian dynasty in the middle decades of the ninth century seemed to risk a crisis of overproduction. Hincmar was clearsighted about the threat further partition might pose to royal power in a kingdom reduced to a mere "fragment."[28] Carloman could, perhaps should, receive *honores* that would enable him to maintain high social status. But the "title and power of a king" would be denied him. Hincmar was no less clearsighted about Charles's need to buttress the new method of exclusion by a traditional one. Only by blinding was Carloman's fate sealed, and his supporters' hopes thereby finally dashed. Hincmar recorded the sentence without comment. In his view, it was justified by Carloman's faithlessness towards his father and by the overriding need to forestall any further partition of the Frankish heartlands.[29]

The rest of the 873 annal sets Carloman's story in a context that also suggests its meaning for Hincmar. Alongside it is placed the story of the East Frankish prince Charles the Fat, tempted doubly by the devil, on the one hand, to rebellion against his father, and on the other, to renounce the world. Both temptations had to be spurned, in Hincmar's view: royal power must be transmitted legitimately, from father to son, and, thus acquired, must be used.[30] The annal goes on to highlight Charles the Bald's success in defeating the Vikings at Angers. Here was a king acting "manfully and strenuously," and carrying out his royal function to the full. His judgment on his faithless son was amply vindicated in a triumphant affirmation at once of his paternal and regal authority, and of the integrity of his realm.

THE ROYAL CONSECRATIONS OF LOUIS III AND CARLOMAN

Another view of Hincmar on king-making can be noted in the consecration of Louis III and Carloman, sons of Louis the Stammerer at Ferrières in 879. The context of this event was the complex situation that arose in the West Frankish kingdom after the death of Louis the Stammerer at Compiègne on 10 April. Hincmar began the 879 annal with an account of the arrangements made by Louis during his final illness for the sole succession of his elder son, the future Louis III. Though the boy was already of age, a sort of regency council was set up for him. Then the dying father sent his son "crown and sword and the rest of the royal gear, and ordered those who were with his son to have him consecrated and crowned king."[31] According to Hincmar, these paternal plans were blocked by the interests of two powerful factions, the one inviting the intervention of the East Frankish king Louis the Younger to take over the West Frankish realm, the other wishing to see the realm divided between the Stammerer's two sons.[32] To avert the former's success, "Abbot Hugh and the other magnates who were with the sons of their late lord Louis (the Stammerer) . . . , namely, Louis and Carloman, sent certain bishops, Ansegis and others, to the monastery of Ferrières, and there had Louis and Carloman consecrated and crowned kings."[33]

The tone of this account is markedly reserved, as if Hincmar were detaching himself from proceedings that constituted a plain violation of Louis the Stammerer's plans for the single succession of his eldest son; the consequence would be a new division of the realm, as described in the next annal.[34] Note the pointed reminder that the magnates who acted were with "the sons of their late lord," whose last wishes they were disregarding. No doubt Hincmar was motivated by personal rancor: his deepest hostility was to Louis the Younger's main partisan, Abbot Gauzlin, whose motives and support he blatantly misrepresents; but Abbot Hugh and Archbishop Ansegis of Sens were also his rivals and supplanters in influence at court.[35] Hincmar may well have thought that he, if anyone, ought to have performed the consecrations of the Stammerer's sons, as he had their father's.[36] Nevertheless, the *AB*'s account stresses the need for haste. For Hincmar (unlike the other main source for these events) records the impending invasion of Louis the Younger, which justified the action of Abbot Hugh and the other magnates. Further, Hincmar, though absent from the consecrations, sent envoys to convey his consent to what was done.[37] In the *AB* thereafter, the Stammerer's sons are referred to as kings. The king-makings at Ferrières were valid, then, in Hincmar's eyes; and his account indicates that their validity derived from the magnates' initiative and role therein. They are the subjects of the two main verbs of Hincmar's key sentence: they "sent" the bishops, and they "caused" the late king's sons to be consecrated and crowned. Hincmar seems to be suggesting that when paternal designation and aristocratic choice did not coincide, in the last resort the latter sufficed to authorize the setting up of king's sons as kings. Again, his prime concern was to preserve the separate existence of a West Frankish realm.

BOSO'S CONSECRATION, 879

Hincmar sets the scene for his account of Boso's king-making by another explicit attribution of initiative: Boso was "persuaded by his wife, who kept on saying that she no longer wanted to live if, daughter as she was of the emperor of Italy, and former betrothed of the emperor of Greece, she did not make her husband a king."[38] The statement gains its point from the account that immediately precedes it in Hincmar's annal (and the word "meanwhile" signals the synchronicity of the two events) of the king-making of the Stammerer's sons. There the subject of the verb (regem) *facere* was the *primores*; here the subject is Boso's wife! After this travesty of correct proceedings, we are not surprised to read that Boso "persuaded the bishops of those regions, who had in part been constrained by threats, in part drawn in by greed for the abbacies and estates promised them and later given them, to anoint and crown him king."[39] Hincmar's single long sentence is carefully constructed: the final verbs "anoint and crown" are drained of their usual meaning, and rendered positively ironic, by what precedes them.

Further, as in the case of Carloman's fate in 873, the Boso episode needs to be read in the context of a whole annal. In fact it is framed by accounts of two other king-makings. Not only is it immediately preceded by the description of the consecrations at Ferrières, as we have seen, but it is immediately followed by this statement: "And also Hugh, son of Lothar II by Waldrada, collected a great gang of brigands and tried to seize the realm of his father."[40] The use of the words "meanwhile" and "also" to introduce the successive sentences dealing with Boso and Hugh suggests that Hincmar means us to link these episodes. Boso's attempted coup "in those parts" has as complement the bastard Hugh's abortive "invasion" of Lotharingia. Only in the next sentence, with its neutral statement that Charles the Fat "obtained the kingdom" of Lombardy, does Hincmar recover his composure; he can go on to conclude this annal with an upbeat account of the young West Frankish kings' encounter with the Vikings, "and the army of the Franks, by God's will, returned home safe with victory."[41]

Both in his record of Boso's consecration, and in his setting of it, Hincmar has packed a judgment. The omission of reference to primores (though other sources imply just such backing for Boso) is surely deliberate. For a man who lacked any hereditary right, only aristocratic invitation could have supplied legitimacy. A consecration performed by bishops under such circumstances was inoperative as far as Hincmar was concerned: in his remaining annals, he pointedly denies Boso the title of king. Far from elevating episcopal consecration to the cardinal constitutive act of king-making, Hincmar shows here his contempt for what the relationship of king to bishops could all too easily become: a mere matter of bribes and threats. By juxtaposing this to the very different case of the Stammerer's sons, Hincmar highlights the absence of the primores from Boso's inauguration and hence implies that no true king-making was effected.

THE KING-MAKING OF CHARLES THE BALD IN LOTHARINGIA, 869

Hincmar's account of Charles the Bald's assumption of power in the Middle Kingdom is the great set-piece of the *AB*. It occupies more space than almost any other single episode. This is not only because Hincmar here quotes more texts in full than elsewhere; nor does Hincmar give this event such prominence simply because he himself had "stage-managed" it. In fact, the theatrical metaphor diverts us from Hincmar's purpose in writing up these events as he does: precisely what he seeks to emphasize are the spontaneous actions of many powerful men, clerical and lay.[42]

Hincmar acknowledges that the news of Lothar II's death in Italy without a legitimate heir produced divergent responses among the Lotharingian aristocracy. Two sets of envoys, he says, came to Charles at Attigny: a minority of the bishops and magnates (primores) of the late Lothar's kingdom sent word that Charles should await his brother Louis the German's agreement to a partition of Lotharingia before himself advancing into that kingdom; but a majority invitied Charles to move into Lotharingia as swiftly as possible, promising to meet him either en route to Metz or on his arrival at that city. Hincmar reveals his own preference: the latter counsel was "sounder" (sanior), and Charles thought it "more acceptable and healthier [salubrius] for him."[43] These adjectives are redolent of the language of church councils, and evoke the role of consensus therein.[44] Sounder, healthier proposals naturally prevail: a vote carried by the part that is greater both in quantity and quality entails unanimous compliance.

Charler's calculation, so Hincmar wishes to imply, proved correct: at Verdun, Charles was met by "many men" from Lotharingia, and at Metz received "many others" into his lordship. All these persons participated in the ensuing rituals (cohibentibus omnibus) in the church of St. Stephen at Metz. Hincmar gives the full texts of two speeches. The first was by Bishop Adventius of Metz. His theme was the divinely inspired unanimity that activated all present. He quoted St. Paul: "[God] hath made us to live of one mind in one house, and broken down the middle wall of partition between us."[45] Adventius also stressed the hereditary right by which Charles succeeded as "legitimate heir" to his nephew's kingdom. Now therefore, he said, it was "worthy for Charles and necessary for us" that the "faithful people" should hear what was fitting from "the most Christian king." Charles responded with the desired assurances: "You know that I will keep for each his due law and justice, as long as each of you offers the royal honour due obedience and subjection.[46]

Hincmar now addressed the Lotharingian bishops present, to justify his officiating at Metz, which was outside his province. He could advance good canonical reasons for an archbishop of Reims to act during a vacancy in the neighboring province "in his Belgic region." On receiving the bishops' collective assent, Hincmar proceeded to a second, general speech. Charles, he said, who had "usefully been in charge of and benefited" his people in the West Frankish kingdom, has come to Metz "led by God" (deo ducente). Like Adventius, Hincmar stressed unanimity. But his accent was not just on the support of the Lotharingians, but on its voluntary, spontaneous character:

"Just as all the animals came together into Noah's ark, with no one compelling them," so "you have flowed together here by divine inspiration." What men could perceive as an unforced, collective assembling ("you have come together on your own volition") signified the action of God through them.[47]

Hincmar invoked two earlier occasions. One was in the remote past, when Clovis, "famous king of the Franks," converted by St. Remigius, "apostle of the Franks," with "his whole people," was baptized "with 3000 Franks (not counting their women and children)," and was anointed king with oil brought from heaven. The other occasion was within living memory, when Clovis's "descendant" and namesake, Louis the Pious, Charles's own father, was "restored to rulership and crowned with the crown of the realm by the priests of the Lord with the acclamation of the faithful people in this very church, as we saw who were present there!"[48] Hincmar could telescope the whole of Frankish history: the same heavenly oil "of which we still have some" was to be used for Charles as had been divinely supplied for Clovis, while Charles's coronation recalled that of his father in the same place a generation before. Both models, of oiling and of crowning, were to be taken up and fused in the ritual that followed.[49] The common factor linking the three occasions was the manifestation of God's will through the participation of the Franks, "the faithful people," as well of Frankish bishops, in the elevation of their rulers.

Hincmar ended by letting the "people" speak for themselves:

> "If this pleases you, make a noise together with your own voices." And at this all shouted out together. The bishop [i.e. Hincmar] then said: "Let us give thanks with one mind to the Lord, singing 'Te deum laudamus.'" And after this [Charles] was crowned king by the bishops.[50]

In thus allowing us to "hear" the aristocracy's consent to Charles's kingmaking, Hincmar conveys the indispensability of their collaboration with the bishops. Louis the Pious's restoration, still vivid in Hincmar's memory, Clovis's anointing, no less vivid in Hincmar's historical imagination, both seemed to him to show God working through the Franks to give them the rulers that were good for them. The king-making of 869 too represented, for Hincmar, a Judgment of God.

In his section of the *AB*, Hincmar supplied his contemporary audience with something other than objective reporting. What they could perceive as apologia or propaganda or self-conscious myth-making, we modern historians tend to read as a genre familiar to us: history as fact. This short paper's sampling of just one theme has suggested that each annal may be a more skillful literary construct than hitherto suspected and would thus repay careful textual analysis.[51] But the historian's further aim must be to get behind the text to ninth-century political realities. The more closely we scrutinize the *AB* in the light of other literary sources of the period, the stronger our impression that its "facts" are refracted—that inconvenient realities have been distorted, even obscured altogether. This is clear, for instance, in the case of the *AB*'s presentation of Charles's inauguration at Metz: where the *AB* shows unanimity, divisions remained; where spontaneity is depicted, political pressures were rife; where the historic unity of the Frankish *gens* is evoked, only a localized fraction of that people were involved; where Charles's success is implied, in fact only months later, Metz, and much of Lotharingia, were in the hands of his rival Louis the German.[52]

But we need not give up the quest for truth of a kind in the *AB*. Hincmar's original audience, a coterie of sympathizers sharing his local concerns, would have expected bias, but not cynicism. For them, the writing of *Gesta*, based, so to speak, on "real life" details, was an opportunity to express, and evoke, more general assumptions and values. Hincmar's accounts of king-makings are evidence of consistent views as to how power might legitimately be acquired in the Frankish realm. The *AB* is a work of ideology. The power to shape the past is itself an historical fact. In the case of the *AB*, the early medieval historian can know more than usual of the wielder of this power, his methods and his purposes.

The political ideas of the mature Hincmar touched his theological views at a crucial point. He had fought hard, and successfully, against the predestinarian teachings of Gottschalk: "How could it be that each will receive according to his works on the day of Judgement, if there were no Free Will?"[53] Hincmar wanted to affirm the responsibility of individuals for their own actions, hence for their own salvation. The alternative, as Hincmar saw it, was social disintegration. Hincmar was "above all a pastor."[54] Like Gottschalk, he was acutely aware of the ubiquity of coercion in the temporal world: unlike Gottschalk, he could conceive of truly voluntary human actions and understood divine grace as enabling rather than constraining. Hence Hincmar could set a high value on decision-making that was unforced. Of course, he was no egalitarian democrat: those directly involved in the choosing of Frankish kings were the leaders of the Franks, the aristocracy, to which Hincmar himself belonged. Nevertheless the assumption was that they spoke for the rest.[55] Hincmar has been regarded as a less true Augustinian than Gottschalk; but his appreciation of the role of consensus as the expression of the community of faithful men accords with Augustine's definition of the commonwealth as an association of wills.[56] For Hincmar, God worked through the church and its sacraments, but he could also work "through soldiers and citizens." In old age, responding to what he perceived as new threats both to the kingdom that he had struggled so long to defend, and to his personal influence in its government, Hincmar laid new stress on the politics of consensus. His annals (and he was nearly sixty when he took up the job of writing them) convey, intermittently, the same message as his revision of the *de Ordine Palatii*, or the letter written in 879 to a great lay magnate reminding him that "the general disposition of the realm" must depend, not on any one man, but on "the judgement and consent of many."[57] Such ideas had long underlain the political practice of the Franks. Hincmar gave them clearer expression and a new coherence and social force: "The Deeds of Our Kings" were the pastor's teaching aid. Whether addressing his intimates at Reims, in the *AB*, or reaching out in capitularies and manifestos to a wider audience, Hincmar had a very clear perception of "the useful past."[58]

Hincmar saw in the Carolingian dynasty a divinely placed bulwark of social order for the Franks. Boso, the non-Carolingian, was to be rejected. The dynasty's discarded members deserved some sympathy and some share in its *honores*. But discarded they must be. The overriding problem of past and present was to transmit the dynasty's power safely over time. In a letter to Charles the Bald, Hincmar pointed anxiously to "the loss of many capital places as a result of the multiple divisions of the Frankish realm. For the sake of the royal *honor*, there must be no diminution of the resources your predecessors used to be able to have from those places." The king and the faithful men in his household needed those *portiuncula* for their upkeep.[59] The solution was to avoid further division of the Frankish heartlands (the tripartite arrangement agreed at Verdun by the leading men of the Franks along with their kings became for Hincmar both model and limiting case), and if possible to reintegrate what had previously been divided.[60] Hincmar supported Charles the Bald's efforts in this direction, opposing distractions in far-off Italy; he supported Louis the Stammerer's plan for an undivided succession in 879. But another equally urgent requirement had to be set alongside this one: namely, to maintain the aristocratic support on which the dynasty's power depended. Hincmar sought to square these imperatives, presenting Charles in 869 as having such support, Boso in 879 as lacking it. But in the last resort, as in the case of the Stammerer's sons, or as in 876 when Charles sought to acquire his nephew's inherited kingdom, it was the expressed will of the local *primores* that must prevail. Without their consent, Hincmar implied, no realm could be acquired, in fact or in right. Contemporary history taught prudence, recognition of the fundamental reality of aristocratic power. But for Hincmar, it also showed the role of the faithful men in king-making, not opposed to, but the vehicle of, God's intervention in the world.

NOTES

1. See H. H. Anton, *Fürstenspiegel und Herrscherethos in der Karolingerzeit* (Bonn, 1968), 281–356; U. Penndorf, *Das Problem des "Reichseinheitsidee" nach der Teilung von Verdun (843)* (Munich, 1974), 77–88; J. Devisse, *Hincmar archevêque de Reims, 845–882*, 3 vols. (Geneva, 1975–1976) 2: 671–723; J. L. Nelson, "Kingship, Law and Liturgy in

the Political Thought of Hincmar of Rheims," *English Historical Review* 92 (1977): 241–279 (reprinted in Nelson, *Politics and Ritual in Early Medieval Europe* (London, 1986), chap. 7); J. M. Wallace-Hadrill, "History in the Mind of Archbishop Hincmar," in *The Writing of History in the Middle Ages. Essays Presented to R. W. Southern*, ed. R. H. C. Davis and J. M. Wallace-Hadrill (Oxford, 1981), 43–70.

2. Cf. Anton, *Fürstenspiegel*, 295–296, with references at n. 756 to earlier literature; Wallace-Hadrill, "History in the Mind of Hincmar," 57.

3. *De Divortio Lotharii regis et Tetbergae reginae*, quaestio vi, PL 125, col. 756.

4. The reference here is clearly to the imposition of penance on the king as an individual, rather than to deposition from office: see Nelson, "Kingship, Law and Liturgy," 243–245.

5. PL 125, col. 758 "... sicut de his omnibus in historiis et chronicis et etiam in libro qui inscribitur Vita Caesarum invenitur." Tyrannical usurpers constituted a third subgroup.

6. Ibid.: "Non sufficit ad suffragium liberis paterna nobilitas. Vitia siquidem vicerunt naturae privilegia." To the Biblical exempla mentioned by Hincmar here may be added the influence of Pseudo-Cyprian, *De XII abusivis saeculi*, chap. 9, ed. S. Hellmann, *Texte und Untersuchungen* 34 (Leipzig, 1910), 52: "... regis iniustitia non solum praesentis imperii faciem fuscat, sed etiam filios suos et nepotes ne post se regni hereditatem teneant obscurat." (The text goes on to cite the case of Solomon.) Lothar II's inauguration occurred, curiously, under his uncle's auspices, outside his own kingdom, but with the support of its *principes* and *optimates*; see *Annales Fuldenses*, ed. F. Kurze, MGH Scriptores rerum Germanicarum in usum scholarum 7 (Hanover, 1891), s.a. 855, 46.

7. Cf. above, n. 2 (followed by Wallace-Hadrill) claims that Hincmar distinguished "six types of ruler," when in fact the distinction is between three types of ruler-making.

8. Anton and Devisse say very little about these. But see. C. A. Bouman, *Sacring and Crowning* (Groningen, 1957), 103, 112–114; see also Nelson, "Kingship, Law and Liturgy," 246 and nn. 1 and 4.

9. Ep. 187, MGH Epp. KA VI, i, p. 196. The *Annals of St. Bertin* are referred to below as the *AB* and cited in the edition of F. Grat, J. Vielliard and S. Clemencet (Paris, 1964). The comment quoted is that of Devisse, vol. 2: 1054.

10. See Appendix. Cf. the list of "coronations" in C. R. Bruhl, "Fränkischer Krönungsbrauch," *Historische Zeitschrift* 194 (1962): 265–326, at 321–326.

11. Filial succession: see Appendix, items 1, 4, 5, 6, 13, 14, 16, 18, 19, 21; succession to brother, uncle, nephew, or cousin: see items 2, 3, 7, 8, 9, 10, 12, 17, 22, 25, 26.

12. See Appendix, items 1, 10. Cf. the case of Louis the Stammerer in 862, *AB*, s.a., p. 88, where Hincmar hints at, but does not specify, the aim of usurping royal power; and the sons of Louis the German, *Annales Fuldenses*, s.a. 861, 863, 866, 871, 873, pp. 55, 56, 64, 72–73, 77–78. See K. Bund, *Thronsturz und Herrscherabsetzung im Frühmittelalter* (Bonn, 1979), 469–470, 528–529.

13. See Appendix, item 8. On family inheritance, see J. L. Nelson, "Public Histories and Private History in the Work of Nithard," *Speculum* 60 (1985): 251–293, at 264, 272–273 (reprinted in *Politics and Ritual*, chap. 9).

14. Among the few not mentioned by Hincmar are some of the East Frankish cases listed above, n. 11. Hincmar may not have taken the unrest of Louis the Ger-

man's sons as seriously as the authors of the East Frankish *Annals of Fulda*. It is of course not always easy to distinguish usurpation from a ritual of rebellion, in the case of kings' sons, nor from a probing-exercise, such as Louis the German's attack on West Francia in 875; see Bund, *Thronsturz*, 467-468. My list in the Appendix follow Hincmar's interpretation, with all the possibilities of arbitrariness that implies.

15. See Appendix, items 4, 5, 6, 13, 14, 16.

16. See Appendix, items 2, 3, 4, 7, 9, 12, 13, 14, 16, 17, 19, 23, 25, 26. Excluding the three papally performed coronations (two of them involving emperors), the figures are thus 14/23. Note that Hincmar does not mention aristocratic support for filial usurpations: See Appendix items 1, 10, 18, 21, though he does talk of "accomplices" (item 10) and "brigands" (item 21).

17. A helpful survey of such situations in the ninth century can be found in W. Schlesinger, "Karlingische Königswahlen," in his *Beiträge zur deutschen Verfassungsgeschichte des Mittelalters*, 2 vols. (Göttingen, 1963), 1: 88-138. But whereas Schlesinger, pp. 97, 132, sees a "winning-back" of aristocratic influence after 814, I would see expectations as constant throughout the period. Cf. K. Brunner, *Oppositionelle Gruppen im Karolingerreich* (Vienna-Cologne-Graz, 1979). G. Tellenbach, "Die geistigen und politischen Grundlagen der karolingischen Thronfolge," *Frühmittelalterliche Studien* 13 (1979): 184-302, offers penetrating observations on the creation of consensus between king and aristocracy, esp. at pp. 253-257, despite the unpleasant ring of some of his terminology. (The first part of this study was written in 1944/1945.)

18. For the view that Hincmar expounded hierocracy or episcopalism, see W. Ullmann, *The Carolingian Renaissance and the Idea of Kingship* (London, 1979), 82-124.

19. *AB*, s.a. 865, p. 118-119, 121; 866, pp. 128-129; 876, pp. 201-202. Cf. J. L. Nelson, "The Annals of St. Bertin," in M. Gibson and J. L. Nelson, *Charles the Bald: Court and Kingdom* (B.A.R., International Series 101, Oxford, 1981), 15-36 (reprinted in *Politics and Ritual*, chap. 8, pp. 24-29).

20. Cf. Wallace-Hadrill, "History in the Mind of Hincmar," [54: ". . . the entire account of public life as he sees it over more than twenty years betrays the historian's instinctive control of material"]. For some reservations about Hincmar the historian, see below.

21. *AB*, s.a. 870, p. 171: ". . . reputatus quoniam insidias erga patrem suum infideliter moliebatur . . ." On the revolt of Carloman, E. Dümmler, *Geschichte des ostfränkischen Reiches*, 2d ed., 3 vols. (Leipzig, 1888) 2: 320-323, 337-338, 356-359 remains fundamental. See also P. McKeon, *Hincmar of Laon and Carolingian Politics* (Urbana, 1978), chap. 7, and J. L. Nelson, "A Tale of Two Princes: Politics, Text and Ideology in a Carolingian Annal," *Studies in Medieval and Renaissance History* 10(1988): 105-141. Hincmar left three different types of information on Carloman's revolt: the *AB*; references in letters, excerpted by Flodoard; and the Capitulary of Quierzy (January, 873). A hint in a letter, Flodoard, *Historia Ecclesiae Remensis* iii, chap. 18, MGH Scriptores XIII, p. 508, indicates that Hincmar attempted to negotiate with Carloman on Charles's behalf in 871.

22. *AB*, s.a. 868, p. 151: "Karlomannum filium suum, diaconum et abbatem, cum scara e vestigio . . . [Karolus] misit . . ." Carloman's abbacies included St. Médard, Soissons, St. Germain, Auxerre, and St. Amand: lucrative *honores*.

23. *AB*, s.a. 873, pp. 189-190: ". . . antiquus et callidus Adversarius [Karloman-

num] et suos complices ad argumentum aliud excitavit, videlicet quia liberius ad nomen et potentiam regiam conscendere posset quia ordinem ecclesiasticam non haberet. . . . Unde post depositionem eius complices illius ardentius coeperunt se ei iterum reconiugere et alios quos valebant in societatem suam abducere, quatenus, mox ut locum invenire possent, illum a custodia in qua servabatur educerent et sibi regem constituerent . . ."

24. *AB*, s.a. 873, p. 180: "quatenus pernitiosa spes pacem odientium de illo frustraretur."

25. The location of Carloman's supporters is indicated by his itinerary: *AB*, s.a. 870, p. 178; 871, pp. 179, 182–183; and by several of Hincmar's letters: Flodoard, iii, chap. 21, p. 515; chap. 26, p. 543. On the difficulty of identifying these supporters, see Nelson, "Tale of Two Princes," p. 112 Pope Hadrian II's interventions (probably at the instance of the Emperor Louis) are in MGH Epp. VI, nos. 32, 33, pp. 736, 737.

26. For earlier use of similar strategies in 849 and 852 for Charles's nephews, see *AB*, s.a., pp. 58, 65. See. T. Schieffer, "Karl von Aquitanien. Der Weg eines karolingischen Prinzen auf den Stuhl des heiligen Bonifatius," in *Universitas. Festschrift für A. Stohr*, ed. L. Lenhart, 2 vols. (Mainz, 1960) 2: 42–54, at 47–48. Before the ninth century, of course, as during it, kings' illegitimate sons were often put into the Church.

27. As Hincmar recognized in Flodoard, iii, chap. 26, MGH SS XIII, p. 543: ecclesiastical sanctions would need backing by *alia* (i.e., royal) *potestas*.

28. Letter to King Carloman (881), PL 125, col. 1045: "particula regni." Cf. below, n. 58. On earlier attempts to limit partibility, see J. L. Nelson, "Queens as Jezebels" in *Medieval Women*, ed. D. Baker (Oxford: Blackwell, 1977), 45, 48 (reprinted in Nelson, *Politics and Ritual*, chap. 1). Cf. Schlesinger, "Karlingische Königswahlen," 95, 101.

29. Blinding, widely used as a punishment for political crimes in the early Middle Ages, had special consequences in the case of royals: generally it removed them definitively from the circle of eligibles. (The dissertation of M. Schaab has unfortunately been inaccessible.)

30. For the structure of the rest of the 873 annal, and the story of Charles the Fat, see Nelson, "Tale of Two Princes."

31. *AB*, s.a. 879, pp. 234–235: ". . . coronam et spatam ac reliquum regium apparatum filio suo Hludouuico misit, mandans illis qui cum eo erant ut eum in regem sacrari ac coronari facerent." The political conflicts following Louis the Stammerer's death are lucidly examined by K. F. Werner, "Gauzlin von Saint-Denis und die westfränkische Reichsteilung von Amiens (880)," *Deutsches Archiv* 35 (1979): 395–462. Hincmar's stance is discussed by Penndorf, *Das Problem des "Reichseinheitsidee,"* pp. 77–88.

32. *AB*, s.a. 879, pp. 236, 239. See J. Fried, "König Ludwig der Jüngere in seiner Zeit," *Geschichtsblätter für den Kreis Bergstrasse* 16 (1983): 5–32, at 15–17.

33. *AB*, s.a. 879, pp. 238–239: ". . . Hugo abbas et ceteri primores, qui cum filiis quondam senioris sui Hludouuici . . . agebant, . . . quosdam episcopos, Ansegisum et alios, miserunt ad Ferrarias monasterium, et ibi eos consecrari ac coronari in reges fecerunt."

34. *AB*, s.a. 880, pp. 241–242. Hincmar had also recorded the agreement made

with Louis the Younger at Fouron in November 878, when Louis the Stammerer had apparently envisaged a divided succession between his sons: *AB*, s.a. 878, pp. 230–234, esp. chap. 3, p. 232. But it is not clear that Hincmar himself approved this plan.

35. See Werner, "Gauzlin," pp. 426, 449–450; also G. Schmitz, "Hinkmar von Reims, die Synode von Fismes (881) und der Streit um das Bistum Beauvais," *Deutsches Archiv* 35 (1979): 463–486, at 471, n. 31, 478, n. 51. It may have been Hincmar's resentment of Abbots Hugh and (especially) Gauzlin which occasioned his new emphasis on episcopal authority in writings of these last years, e.g., the decrees of the Synod of Fismes, PL 125, cols. 1071, 1087–1088; and letter to Louis III, PL 126, col. 119. Bishops (and not abbots) could consecrate kings.

36. Hincmar's ordo for Louis the Stammerer: MGH Capitularia II, no. 304, pp. 461–462.

37. Flodoard, iii, chap. 23. MGH SS XIII, p. 532: Hincmar to the bishop of Soissons. Evidently the initiative had come from the magnates with the young kings, however. Hincmar later had to protest his support for the "election" of Louis III and Carloman: ibid., chap. 19, p. 510. The differing accounts of the *AB* and the *Annals of St. Vaast* are discussed by Werner, "Gauzlin," pp. 428–431. The problem of dating and placing the "electoral assembly" implied by Hincmar disappears if his reference is seen as ideological rather than literal.

38. *AB*, s.a. 879, p. 239: "Interea Boso, persuadente uxore sua, quae nolle vivere se dicebat, si filia imperatoris Italiae et desponsata imperatori Greciae, maritum suum regem non faceret..." This is often taken as a statement of fact: cf. W. Mohr, "Boso von Vienne und die Nachfolgerfrage," *Archivum Latinitatis Medii Aevi* 26 (1956): 141–165, at 158–160; but for an alternative view, see P. Stafford, *Queens, Concubines and Dowagers* (Athens, 1983), p. 24.

39. *AB*, s.a. 879, p. 239: "... partim comminatione constrictis, partim cupiditate illectis pro abbatiis et villis eis promissis et postea datis, episcopis illarum partium persuasit ut eum in regem ungerent et coronarent." On Boso's installation, see R. H. Bautier, "Aux origines du royaume de Provence. De la sédition avortée de Boso à la royauté légitime de Louis," *Provence Historique* 23 (1973): 41–68; See also Bund, *Thronsturz*, 499–503.

40. *AB*, s.a. 879, p. 239: "Hugo etiam, filius iunioris Hlotharii ex Vualdrada, collecta praedonum multitudine, regnum patris sui est molitus invadere." For other sources, see Bund, *Thronsturz*, 447–478. Hincmar's attitude is further revealed in Flodoard, iii chap. 26, pp. 545–546, where he warns Hugh against "any flatterer who urges him to attempt the usurpation of a realm" (*pervasio regni*), but also recalls his friendship with Hugh's father and grandfather, and urges Hugh to accept the honores promised him by Charles the Fat.

41. *AB*, s.a. 879, p. 240. The structure of this annal shows some parallels to that of 873; see n. 23 above.

42. *AB*, s.a. 869, pp. 157–164. See W. Schlesinger, "Zur Erhebung Karls des Kahlen zum König von Lothringen," in *Festschrift für F. Petri* (Bonn, 1970), 454–475; and N. Staubach, "Das Herrscherbild Karls des Kahlen. Formen und Funktionen monarchischer Repräsentation im früheren Mittelalter" (diss. Münster, 1982), 239–271. Staubach, p. 555, n. 672, stresses that the rituals of 869 should also be looked at from Charles's standpoint as having "die Funktion herrscherlicher Selbstdarstellung." Thus the *AB* account can be seen as the representation of a representation, in

another medium. (L. Riefenstahl's film of the 1936 Olympics comes to mind as a modern parallel.)

43. *AB*, s.a. 869, p. 157: "...plures autem saniore consilio illi mandaverunt ut quantotius commode posset usque Mettis properare satageret.... Quorum consilium Karolus acceptabilius et sibi salubrius esse intellegens...festinavit." Cf. the prologue to the *Ordinatio imperii* of 817, MGH Capitularia I, no. 136, p. 270: "hi qui sanum sapiunt."

44. J. Hannig, *Consensus Fidelium* (Stuttgart, 1982).

45. *AB*, s.a. 869, pp. 158–159, quoting Eph. 2: 14.

46. Ibid., p. 160: "...sciatis me...unicuique in suo ordine secundum sibi competentem leges...legem et iustitiam conservare." This echoes the promise of Coulaine (843): see Nelson, "Kingship, Law and Liturgy," 255–256.

47. *AB*, s.a. 869, pp. 162–164: "...quo etiam vos eius inspiratione confluxistis et ipsi vos sponte commendastis, cuius instinctu animata omnia in arcam Noe...nullo cogente convenerunt." (The allusion is to Gen. 7: 8–9, but the idea of the animals moving without human compulsion is Hincmar's own.) "...non incongruum videtur...ut in obtentu regni, unde vos ad illum sponte convenistis...coronetur."

48. *AB*, s.a. 869, pp. 162–163. The two precedents are described in a single lengthy clause, beginning with "because" (quia) and covering nineteen lines of the printed text! The second "cause" adduced is the Biblical precedent of I Macc. 2: 13, for a repeated coronation when a king acquires a second kingdom. P. E. Schramm, "Die Krönung bei den Westfranken und den Franzosen," *Archiv für Urkundenforschung* 15 (1938): 3–55, at 13, n. 6, noted that seven bishops officiated both in 835 and in 869. On the myth of Carolingian descent from Clovis, see O. G. Oexle, "Die Karolinger und die Stadt des heiligen Arnulf," *Frühmittelalterliche Studien* 1 (1967): 250–364; on the holy oil, see Ullmann, *Carolingian Renaissance*, p. 92; and on the meaning of all this for Hincmar, see Wallace-Hadrill, "History in the Mind of Hincmar," 54–55.

49. The prayers for the anointing and the crowning both begin with same phrase, "Coronet te dominus corona gloriae": MGH Capitularia II, no. 302, p. 457. Hincmar's personal involvement in the two rituals, of 835 and 869, partly explains this association. For some further considerations, see J. L. Nelson, "The Lord's Anointed and the People's Choice: Carolingian Royal Ritual," in *Rituals of Royalty*, ed. D. Cannadine and S. Price (Cambridge, 1987), 137–180.

50. *AB*, s.a. 869, p. 164.

51. I have attempted this for the 873 annals in "Tale of Two Princes." For some suggestions about the original audience of Hincmar's *AB*, see Nelson, "Annals of St. Bertin," pp. 24, 28.

52. The evidence is sensitively discussed by Schlesinger, "Zur Erhebung," 460–464, and Staubach, *Herrscherbild*, 252–253. In this case, other contemporary annals have little to say. For 873, the *Annuals of Fulda* and other evidence can be set against the *AB*: see Nelson, "Tale of Two Princes." For 879, the Annals of St. Vaast give a very different picture from the *AB*'s, while papal letters offer a corrective to the *AB* on both Carloman and Boso: see references above, notes 24, 36, 37.

53. Hincmar, *Third Treatise on Predestination*, PL 125, col. 191, quoting the *Hypomnesticon* which he believed to be by Augustine (iii, chap. 10, PL 45, col. 1631): "...quomodo autem unicuique secundum opera sua redderetur in die iudicii nisi liberum esset arbitrium?" For Hincmar's use of this probably fifth-century work, see

Devisse, *Hincmar* 1: 234-236.

54. Devisse, *Hincmar* 1: 256; and see also the thought-provoking comparison between the psychologies of Gottschalk and Hincmar, pp. 265-268.

55. *De Ordine Palatii*, ed. T. Gross and R. Schieffer, MGH Fontes Iuris Germanici Antiqui (Hanover, 1980), chap. 29, pp. 84-85. See J. L. Nelson, "Legislation and Consensus in the Reign of Charles the Bald," in *Ideals and Reality. Studies in Frankish and Anglo-Saxon Society presented to J. M. Wallace-Hadrill*, ed. P. Wormald (Oxford, 1983), 202-227 (reprinted in *Politics and Ritual*, chap. 5).

56. See P. Brown, "St. Augustine," in *Trends in Medieval Political Thought*, ed. B. Smalley (Oxford, 1965), 1-21, at 12-16; R. Markus, *Saeculum* (Cambridge, 1970), 59-71.

57. Flodoard, iii, chap. 26, MGH SS XIII, p. 545 (to Count Theuderic): "... ne moleste acciperet si eum commoneret ... quia non solum grandis presumptio, sed etiam magnum periculum est, uni soli generalem regni dispositionem tractare sine consultu et consensu plurimorum ..." Cf. *De Ordine Palatii*, chaps. 29-34, pp. 82-93; *Instruction to Louis the Stammerer*, chap. 8, PL 125, col. 987-988; *Acta* of Syond of Fismes, PL 125, cols. 1085-1086. Note that the letter of warning to Theuderic ends by harking back to the three-fold division of 843. On Theuderic's role in the late 870s, see Werner, "Gauzlin," 416, n. 74. The *primores*' "utilitarian" values are given particularly clear expression in Hincmar's very first annal: *AB* 861, p. 87.

58. Wallace-Hadrill, "History in the Mind of Hincmar," 58-59, also noting the appeal to dynastic history, and to Verdun as a model settlement, in the *Instruction to Louis the Stammerer*, PL 125, chap. 4, col. 986.

59. MGH Epp. KA VI, no. 126, p. 65.

60. Cf. Hincmar's letters cited above, notes 56, 57; and note the regretful tone of *AB*, s.a. 880, p. 241: in the division of Amiens, Louis III received "quod de Francia residuum erat ex paterno regno ..."

Appendix

The following is a list of acquisitions of rulership (claimed or achieved) mentioned in Hincmar's section of the *Annals of St. Bertin*. (Page references are to the edition of F. Grat, J. Vielliard, and S. Clemencet, Paris, 1964.) Note: Consecrations of consorts are not included in this list.

1. 861, p. 85: Karlmann, son of Louis the German "magnam sibi partem... paterni regni praesumit."
2. 861, p. 87: Charles the Bald "a quibusdam invitatus quasi regnum Provintiae adepturus."
3. 863, p. 96: Louis II "Provintiam venit et quos potuit ipsius regni primores sibi conciliavit."
4. 865, pp. 117–118: Charles the Bald "Aquitaniae primores suscepit. Ad quorum multam petitionem filium suum Karolum... in Aquitaniam cum regio nomine ac potestate redire permittit."
5. 865, p. 123: Charles the Bald "Hludouuicum filium suum in Neustraim dirigit, nec reddito nec interdicto sibi nomine regio."
6. 867, p. 135: Charles the Bald "primores Aquitaniorum sibi obviam accersivit et filium suum Hludouuicum... eisdem Aquitanis regem praefecit."
7. 869, pp. 106–111: Charles the Bald in Lotharingia.
8. 869, pp. 167–168: Louis II "regnum quondam regis Hlotharii... Hludouuico imperatori... hereditario iure debetur."
9. 870, pp. 169, 172: Louis the German/Charles the Bald "talem portionem de regno Hlotharii regis consensit habere, qualem aut ipsi iustiorem et aequiorem aut communes fideles eorum inter se invenerint... Reges... convenerunt, et... regnum Hlotharii inter se diviserunt."
10. 873, p. 190: Carloman's bid for a kingdom.

11. 875–876, pp. 199–200: Charles the Bald "quibusdam de primoribus ex Italia ad se non venientibus, pluribus autem receptis, Roman invitante papa Iohanne perrexit et... in imperatorem unctus et coronatus atque imperator Romanorum est appellatus."

12. 876, pp. 206–207: Charles the Bald "dispositum habens... episcopos et primores regni quondam fratris sui ad se venientes recipere."

13. 876, p. 207: Louis the Younger uses Judgment of God to assert "plus per rectum ille habere deberet portionem de regno [Hlotharii] quam pater suus dimisit."

14. 877, pp. 218–221: Louis the Stammerer's accession to West Frankish kingdom, receiving "praeceptum per quod pater suus illi regnum ante mortem suum tradiderat," and *regalia*; "coronatus est"; *promissio* to bishops; *professio* to clergy and people.

15. 878, p. 227: Louis the Stammerer "coronatus Hluduuicus a papa Iohanne" at Troyes.

16. 879, pp. 234–235: Louis the Stammerer designates Louis III.

17. 879, p. 236: Gauzlin and others persuade "potentes homines... ut Hludouuicum Germaniae rege, in hoc regno convocarent."

18. 879, p. 238: Louis the Younger hears that his late brother's illegitimate son Arnulf "partem regni illius occupasse."

19. 879, p. 239: The consecrations of Louis III and Carloman.

20. 879, p. 239: Boso's consecration.

21. 879, p. 239: Hugh's bid for Lotharingia.

22. 879, p. 240: Charles the Fat "in Longobardiam perrexit et ipsum regnum obtinuit."

23. 880, p. 241: Louis III and Carloman "sicut fideles illorum invenerunt regnum paternum inter se diviserunt."

24. 880, p. 243: Charles the Fat "a Iohanne papa se... in imperatorem consecrari obtinuit."

25. 882, p. 245: "Venientes autem primores partis illius regni [Lotharingia] voluerunt se [to Louis III] commendare. Sed... non eos in commendatione suscepit."

26. 882, pp. 246–247: "Primores autem regni [of Louis III] nuntium miserunt ad Karlomannum, mandantes ut... ipse quantotius ad eos venire festinaret.... Ipsi autem parati erant illum recipere et se illi commendare, sicut et fecerunt."

TWO

Inaugural Aspects of French Royal Ceremonials

Ralph E. Giesey

In all the years (now decades) of my devotion to the study of royal ceremonial in France, I have been concerned almost exclusively with just one aspect, the "constitutional"—that is, with what in France during the old regime was called *droit public* or *loi fondamentale*. Among royal ceremonials in France during the 1300-plus years from Clovis to Charles X, the coronation holds the preeminent place. For the first half of that period—until the late thirteenth century—the coronation seems to have enjoyed a monopoly of the ceremonial side of constitutional matters. Embodied in it were the answers to three critical aspects of rulership: "who, when, and how." Only one of these three, the "when," the precise moment of beginning of rule, is the proper subject of this essay. My main purpose here is to show how other royal ceremonials came to share this "inaugural aspect" with the coronation. It will help, however, to set the context of the "when" by considering, very briefly, the "how" and the "who" as they relate to the coronation.

The "how" of the constitutional issue—that is, prescriptions of the manner in which the king is to rule—are embodied in the coronation oath. Quite rightly this has been the object of intensive research—most recently by Richard Jackson in his recent book on the royal coronation[1] and in a special study of late medieval oaths that he is preparing. I shall not be concerned here with the oaths, except coincidentally on one occasion.

The "who" of the constitutional issue is regulated overall by juristic principles, and the importance of the coronation as a ritual confirmation varies according to the nature of the monarchy being considered. If we consider the two extremes, the truly elective monarchy and the fully dynastic one, we find a considerable difference: in the former, the coronation invests power in someone who until very shortly beforehand had had no royal rights whatever; in the latter, the coronation confirms in power someone who from birth had had a preemptive right to the throne. In France, if anywhere, the latter was the case during the eight hundred and forty-three years from Hugh Capet's accession (987) to Charles X's deposition (1830). The Capetian dynasty experienced perturbations to be sure—challenges to its right to rule by the English in the fourteenth and fifteenth centuries and by the Catholic Ligue in the sixteenth. The dynasty was even suspended for twenty-two years during the French Revolution and Napoleonic era. Still, I do not find in all of monarchic history any equal to the Capetian dynasty in longevity and stability, even if you count female and not just male transmission of successive right.

Such uncontested dynastic succession had both pluses and minuses for the performance of the coronation. On the plus side, the ceremonial would almost always be conducted in peaceful circumstances, its planning and staging undisturbed by political exigencies. The substance of the ceremonial could also be infused meaningfully (not just hopefully) with notions of dynastic grandeur. On the minus side, however, one has to ponder the extent to which uncontested dynastic succession weakened the constitutional significance of the French coronation by making it appear less as an elevation to power than as a confirmation of a preexistent right to rule. On the face of things, therefore, if he "who" is being crowned enjoys dynastic right to the throne, then the coronation's power over "when" royal status is achieved is seriously preempted. In this respect the "who" directly affects the "when," to which I now turn.

I shall be dealing here with "state ceremonials," those in which the king personifies the Crown, or State. The late medieval and Renaissance times are rich in such ceremonials, befitting the fact that the modern state came into being during that era. Besides the coronation, these state ceremonials are the funeral, the entry, and the *lit de justice*. Each of the last three developed a distinctive way of sharing the inaugural principle, the "when" of exercising royal power, with its erstwhile exclusive exponent, the coronation. They did this sometimes by articulating a trait of inauguration they possessed by nature; sometimes they did it by what is best left called "coincidence"; and sometimes they did it by outright usurpation. As I proceed to deal with these ceremonials seriatim, I shall try to show how each's inaugural elements were related to those of others. I shall not hesitate to push the inaugural element to the limit, to go beyond the mode of analysis into that of interpretation and even of imaginatively reconstructing what might have been.

CORONATION

The Capetian dynasty was blessed for over three hundred years by always having the sons of previous kings to succeed to the throne, a fact of life that allowed the principle of primogenitary right to prosper. For the first two hundred years, however, from Hugh Capet through Louis VII, every king found it prudent during his own lifetime to secure the crowning of his heir apparent—even, on two occasions, of having him also consecrated. These presuccession rites usually took place somewhere other than Reims, and they did not preclude the need later, after the king-father died, to perform the full consecration and coronation rites at Reims.[2]

During the course of the twelfth century, the use of a premature *sacre* and/or *couronnement* to strengthen the successive right of the heir-apparent was complemented, and then replaced, by the device of naming him in official documents as *rex designatus*. At least for the first of the *reges designati*, Louis VI, consecration was still urgently needed to overcome baronial opposition when he succeeded to the throne in 1108. His grandson then, Philip II (1180–1223), was the first Capetian who, during his lifetime, did not have his son either crowned or consecrated—or designated.[3]

These diverse ways of initiating kings prematurely cannot be considered truly inaugural. In every case, the commencement of the reign was officially reckoned in documents only from the date of the final sacre and couronnement. Rather than the "when" of rulership, presuccession rites served the "who." They were essentially dynastic devices, and they were abandoned when the Capetians' dynastic claim became secure. From a logical point of view, it could even be argued that presuccession initiations diminished the efficacy of the ceremonials as such. For if it was considered necessary for a king to be crowned and consecrated twice during his lifetime, then either one or the other of the performances had to be regarded as superfluous or else neither one of them was constitutive all by itself. Furthermore, since presuccession crownings and consecrations were as often as not performed separately, the interplay between their respective principles of rulership—secular choice operating concomitantly with divine grace—was obfuscated. Only in 1223 was the optimal situation achieved (and observed ever thereafter) of having the sacre and couronnement performed only conjointly and only on one occasion for each king.

One could extend the last sentence to read, "... and only at Reims," if one excepted the instance of Henry IV in 1593. The status of Reims is so firmly established in our perception of the cult of the French monarchy that it seems almost perverse to point out that Reims' unassailable claim to be the locus of the *sacre et couronnement* proved to be, almost inevitably, the cardinal flaw in that ceremony's claim to be the true inaugural event. Sooner or later the successor to the throne would find himself so far from Reims when his predecessor died that even a hurried trip thence would take such a long time to accomplish that the principle of maintaining a reasonable propinquity between the demise of one king and the coronation of the next would break down. That is what happened in 1270, when the heir apparent, Philip III, was with his father, Louis IX, when the latter died on a crusade in North

Africa. We are not told of any ceremonial that was performed, just that Philip was recognized as king of France by the barons who were there. It had to be done: the exigencies of governance had to come before the proprieties of the ceremonial at Reims.[4]

It has occurred to me, speculating upon the possibilities that presented themselves in Tunisia in 1270, that crowning and sacring might have been separated then. That is, the coronation might have taken place at once, investing Philip with essential powers of command, but the rites of consecration withheld until it was possible to perform them at Reims. The presuccession rites of the not-too-distant past, which had often separated crowning and sacring, could have provided a precedent of sorts. But, as mentioned above, such separation had the flaw of not allowing the secular and sacred principles of rulership to reinforce each other by being acted out simultaneously. Keeping the ceremonials together—that is, heeding Reims' geographical prerogative, which it is difficult to imagine not having been done—did mean, however, that both of them were separated in time from rulership itself. The official dating of the new reign now—and ever after—began from the time of the old king's demise. The traditional rites at Reims were left intact, to be performed when feasible. Philip III did not get to Reims until over a year later, but all that was added to the actuality of royal power by the ceremonials performed there was the power to cure the king's evil.

Not to have given Philip royal powers at once would have been to suggest the existence of an interregnal period. Such was intolerable from a constitutional point of view. There was created, however, what I call a ceremonial interregnum, that is, a hiatus in the rule of properly crowned and sacred kings. Other state ceremonials, to which I now turn, would subsequently enter the inaugural picture. Reims will, however, return to the scene when the time comes to consider how its ritual program was modified to keep step with those other ceremonials. Indeed, nothing shows better the ingenuity of the French in ceremonial matters than their effort to maintain the standing of the oldest of the inaugural rites in the face of new ones that arose.

FUNERAL

Compelled as I am on this occasion to regard "state" ceremonials exclusively in light of their inaugural aspects, the shape of the French royal funeral in my mind changes somewhat from the way I described it twenty-five years ago. I have to say that right now I see the royal funeral serving an explicitly inaugural purpose only very briefly, in the fifteenth century, well before the full bloom of the Renaissance ceremonial. That occurred at the graveside scene, just before the coffin was finally interred. The household officers' batons, along with the sword and banner of France, were lowered and raised in accompaniment to the cries for the old and the new kings. In the early stage of elaboration of this ritual, the cries contained the Christian names of the dead and the living kings, as for example: *Le roi Charles est mort! Vive le Roi Louis!* In effect, I would argue, the beginning of the reign of a specific king was fictively embedded in the ceremonial obsequies of his predecessor. This was enhanced considerably by the fact that up to the moment of those funerary cries the new king's name was never mentioned—indeed, his very existence was not recognized since he was required by custom to absent himself from the ceremony and be out of the public eye.[5]

Early in the sixteenth century, however, the Christian names were dropped, giving us the classic expression *Le roi est mort! Vive le roi!*[6] I do not regard this as inaugural, for the reference is not to Charles or Louis or Francis but to that one fictional King with a capital "K"—the body corporate, the *Dignitas regiae*—who never dies. No king is being inaugurated: kingship itself its being acclaimed perpetual. The royal officials who stood over the mortal remains of the king's body natural while they proclaimed the instantaneous renewal of the King's body corporate were dramatizing the concept of the "King's two bodies" as well as any jurisconsult of the time was able to express it in words. The best I can come up with, in truly inaugural terms, is to say that the classic, anonymous version of the funeral cries, by their announcing that kingship is ever alive, provide a fictional legitimacy for the fact that the new king had been exercising the full powers of royal office from the moment his predecessor had died—that is, the graveside cries reinforced the principle begun in 1270 that effective rulership should never cease.

The lifelike funeral effigy of the dead king, around which grew up the grandest display of the king's corporate self, was never displayed at the graveside ritual in St. Denis. It had been carried, triumphally displayed, separately from the encoffined body on a shrouded wagon during the funeral cortège within Paris and out to St. Denis, but then was retired.[7] During the final interment the ritual was entirely liturgical, focused upon the dead king, until the spell was broken by the final half of the graveside cries by hailing the new king: *Vive le roi!*

Allowing fancy free reign, one could imagine some representation of the new king being introduced at that moment, or even the new king himself appearing. But the new king was prohibited by custom from appearing at his predecessor's funeral. Such was not the case at ducal funerals, however, and here we do find that the *mise au tombeau* could be structured as a truly inaugural event. The House of Lorraine, which copied the French royal funeral ceremony over the span of a century, shows this most clearly. At the beginning, in 1508, the deceased prince, René II, happened to claim the Kingdom of Sicily in addition to his fundamental dignity as Duke of Lorraine. His successor, his son Antoine, did not claim Sicily, however, and this led to the following oddity at the climax of René's funeral. The herald-at-arms began the ritual with the cry: *Le tres hault, tres puissant et tres illustre roy, nostre souverain seigneur et maitre, est mort, le roy est mort! le roy est mort!* He then called for the various ducal and royal emblems, batons, and so forth to be deposited in the grave. Finally, the master of the horse, who had deposited the royal sword, descended into the grave and recovered it, raised it on high and cried out: *Vive nostre souverain seigneur et maitre le duc de Lorraine! Vive le duc! vive le duc!*[8]

There are no Christian names attached to the old and new princes, but since the deceased was a king but his successor only a duke, the necessity to formulate the graveside cries as *Le roy est mort! Vive le duc!* makes it clear that no one undying office is being referred to. The new duke was probably there, and it is even possible that the sword emblemizing his power was carried before him as he left the church.

Such was surely done a century later, in 1608, when Charles III, Grand Duke of Lorraine, was buried at Nancy. He had an effigy ritual that copied the French royal practice in details and perhaps exceeded it in splendor. On the other hand, the graveside ritual, close as it appears to the French formulation in style, embodied elements of constitutional significance that the French royal model could not. Not only was the grand duke's son present but also the sword and other emblems of sovereign power were carried before him in a most pompous fashion as he left the funeral. It was a veritable ceremonial of inauguration, the likes of which were quite impossible in the French royal counterpart: the new king was barred from attending his predecessor's funeral in the first place, and, even if he had been allowed to be there, any form of inaugural ceremonial would have been forestalled by Reims' exclusive claim to inaugural prerogatives. Ironically, therefore, dukes could borrow royal ceremonial apparatus and do with it things the kings could not. In the case at hand, the dukes were freer because they had no proper coronation rite and, in general, did not have a *two bodies* theory to contend with.[9]

ENTRÉE

The triumphal entry of the new king of France into Paris usually took place not long after the coronation. From the point of view of Parisians (then as now I daresay) nothing that happened out in the provinces really counted until its impact was felt in Paris. For Parisians the royal entry was the ultimate phase of the inauguration process in terms both of time and significance. The crowned king was coming for the first time into the capital city to exercise his sovereign powers. The pageantry was splendid. The people of Paris welcoming the king was all France welcoming him.[10]

Porte Saint-Denis was always the entry point, and the route through the city to Notre Dame was absolutely traditional. It happens that the same route in the other direction is the one always taken by the royal funeral cortège on its way to the royal necropolis in St. Denis. Therefore, the last crowned king the Parisians had seen before the new king made his first entry was his predecessor (in effigy) making his final exit. Did the Parisians appreciate this symmetry between the funeral and the entry? Were the masters of ceremony trying to convey the notion of continuity, or renewal, of rulership? Alas there is no evidence.

It needs to be mentioned that the entry of a prince into his capital could be an explicitly inaugural event in the fourteenth century. I refer to the famous *Entrée-joyeuse* of the Duke of Brabant into Brussels, when the ruler and the ruled performed a ceremonial of great constitutional import: he got keys to the city; they got confirmation of rights. Something of this is evident in the later fourteenth- and fifteenth-century royal entries into Paris, as the kings stopped at Châtelet and vowed to maintain certain established privileges, but in general this element tended to fade away as the aspects of pageantry grew more abundant.

The full-blown Renaissance royal entry consisted much less of acts performed by the king than of acts—*tableaux vivants* especially—performed *for* him as he rode from station to station. The guilds and other corporations of the city that prepared the station tried to flatter and to edify the king. The theme of royal continuity was a mainstay. Having the live new king gaze upon representations of his illustrious forebears supplied an historicizing counterpart to the royal funeral's acting out of the juristic abstraction that the king never died.

Other cities offered the king formal ceremonies of entry upon the occasion of his first visit. Lyons and Rouen excelled in magnificence, but for our present concern the most important—perhaps more important than the Parisian entry—was Reims. Since this entry was made *before* the king was crowned, its iconographical aspects had to be (or so it seems to me) carefully scrutinized. I am not aware of any comprehensive study of these entries, or whether a complete series of them was performed and has survived. The few I do know about have very interesting pictoral tableaux relevant for the inauguration.[11] (We shall look at one of them at the end.) Indeed, was not the entry into Reims the first stage of the "official" inauguration?

LIT DE JUSTICE

If I had been the master of ceremonies in the later sixteenth century, after the *lit de justice* had achieved its splendid ceremonial status during the reign of Francis I, I would have tacked that royal enthronement in Parlement onto the king's entry into Paris. In my ceremonial *livret* I would have explained the event in this way.

> The new king has exercised royal power from the moment his father died; indeed, he had issued many edicts already. The ultimate demonstration of the kingly power, however, is his personal enthronement in Parlement at a lit de

justice. When the king makes his joyous entry into Paris after being crowned at Reims, he reveals to his people the sanctified nature of the royal power he has exercised heretofore out of necessity. The climactic event of the entry, of this revelation of royal power, is most rightfully found in the king's enthroning himself at the head of Parlement. The scepter and the *main de justice* exchange places in the king's hands, from how they had been held at Reims, for at the lit de justice it is only fitting that the main de justice have the dominant place, held in the right hand.

I might even have insinuated that the lit de justice was to couronnement what curing the king's evil was to the sacre.

There is a hint that a faint version of this scenario was carried out in 1549, when Henry II enthroned himself in Parlement just sixteen days after his formal entry into Paris. The event was not, however, entered into the registers of Parlement as a lit de justice but only as a royal *séance*. And we cannot suspect that this was an error of the clerk of Parlement, for that clerk was Jean Du Tillet, the person in all of France most learned in royal ceremonial and who had been a prime mover in shaping the lit de justice.[12]

Michel de l'Hôpital, chancellor of France, was responsible for the first use of the lit de justice for inaugural purposes—the pronouncement of the majority of the king, Charles IX, in 1563.[13] I see here, too, something of the spirit of legitimizing royal power I earlier in my ceremonial fantasizing. Charles's "majority *lit*" rectifies a flaw in the royal power up to 1563; for, although he had been crowned as a minor in 1561 he had had to have a regent rule for him until he came of age. Still, France had been ruled in the name of King Charles IX for two years, under whatever auspices you choose, and that was enough to render the "majority *lit*" a weak instance of inauguration. L' Hôpital's power politics was more to the point. In the long run, constitutionally, the "majority *lit*" was clearly an ad hoc arrangement necessitated by the fact that the king was a minor; a ceremonial nicety to be sure, but (one surely hoped) not something that would often be necessary.

Fate dictated, however, that three successive kings of France would accede as minors in later times, in 1610, 1643, and 1715. Each of them had to have a regency government, and each held a lit de justice when he came of age. In these instances, however, the "majority *lit*" that was performed contained the merest token of inaugural significance compared with an earlier lit de justice that each of these kings had performed, the explicitly "inaugural lit de justice."

Only a matter of hours after Henry IV was assassinated in 1610 his eight-year-old son Louis, dressed in regal attire, was lifted onto the royal seat at the head of the Parlement of Paris and the regency of his mother, Marie de Médicis, promulgated in his name.[14] Political exigency was obviously the motive: Marie was by no means everyone's choice for regent. No one, I daresay, gave any thought at that time to what this revelation of the new ruler, presiding at a state ceremonial that expressed the royal power most awesomely—one reporter designated the event as literally the inauguration of the king[15]—would mean for the traditional symbolism of the other state ceremonials. Indeed, all three of them would be performed within six months.

Before considering that question, however, let me put in simple terms what this "inaugural *lit*" meant for the basic inaugural principle I have been considering: in Paris in 1610 there was terminated a 340-year estrangement between the exercise of royal power and its ceremonial inauguration that had begun in Tunisia in 1270. I don't believe anyone in 1610 would have seen it that way. Even I today find it hard to regard the metaphor of estrangement as much more than a pedant's delight. It is, however, more worthwhile than the position that positivist-minded historians would be likely to take, which is that the events of 1270 and 1610 both show nothing of interest beyond the fact that political exigency always causes ceremonial proprieties to be treated slightingly, sometimes by disuse and other times by abuse.

Let us consider the abuse. It could be argued that the lit de justice was debased by its hasty and improvised utilization in 1610. On the other hand the lit de justice, unlike the other state ceremonials, was not a once-in-a-lifetime proposition for any king. Had it not already shown its versatility as an instrument of propagating (propagandizing?) royal authority in 1563? Was the lit de justice not the obvious means at hand to resolve the crisis of regency in 1610? If Charles IX could use one to end a regency why couldn't Louis XIII do the same to begin one? In short, the constitutional character of the lit de justice did not limit its ceremonial prospects.

The funeral ceremony, however, suffered irreparable damage in 1610. One of its cardinal rules was that the new king should stay out of the public eye until his predecessor's lifelike effigy had had its allotted weeks to make visible the marvel that the *K*ing lived on although the *k*ing had died. Louis XIII's inaugural lit vitiated the purpose of his father's effigy before the effigy was even made. No one at the time seems to have noticed this, and Henry IV's funeral was conducted in the traditional fashion. But never again after 1610.[16]

The inaugural lit of 1610 also preempted whatever notion tradition had implanted that a fully ceremonious entry of the new king into Paris should be the first public manifestation of royal power in the capital city. I pushed that idea to the limit in an earlier section, especially in my fantasy that the king's first lit de justice should have been celebrated as the climax of the entrée. In 1610 it came first. The fact is that the entrée was very flexible. The one into Paris might enjoy the status of a state ceremonial but entrées into provincial cities could be just as grand, even grander because nothing in those cities' experience was likely to equal the king's coming, Not so in Reims, of course, where the king's entry, however great its pomp, could be just a prelude to the most sublime of all French royal ceremonials. Looked at another way, however, whatever pomp attended the king's precoronation arrival at Reims was sure to involve the entrée per se with the inaugural principle at large.

Louis XIII's coronation took place in mid-October of 1610. During the six months that had elapsed since he had become king, those responsible to stage his entrée into the city of Reims and ordain his sacre et couronnement in Reims' Cathedral gave considerable thought to the question of how their ceremonials could be made to jibe with the inaugural lit de justice performed the day after Henry IV died in mid-May. What they accomplished shows that ceremonial exigencies could be just as great as political ones. Their deeds have been analyzed keenly from two different points of view, by Richard Jackson as they influenced the sacre, by Sarah Hanley as they reflected awareness of the lit de justice.[17]

The most inspired innovation was the ritual of the "sleeping king" performed in an antechamber of the cathedral when two archbishops came to fetch Louis for his coronation. By a series of three knockings on the door and callings out of his name they insinuated that Henry IV's son was still asleep while the god-given King of France was fully awake. This skit brought to perfection an earlier form of precoronation ritual for a minor king that intimated (and resolved) the tension between the want of years and the wearing of the crown, but in 1610 it also linked the wide-awake kin about to be crowned with the king who had already been "inaugurated" at a lit de justice.[18]

The stage for the "sleeping king" had already been set when Louis entered Reims the day before. One tableau juxtaposed the lit de justice of May with the sacre et couronnement of October in terms of designating the king (Rege designato) and receiving the kingdom (Regno suscepto), and another linked the two ceremonials as the king's betrothal, then marriage, to the kingdom. The theme "the King never dies" also received considerable attention, but only as found in writings of jurists (the entry's director was a legist) and not with reference to its ceremonial expression in the royal funeral where it had first been articulated a century before and last performed just a few months earlier.[19]

The inaugural aspects of French royal ceremonial had never before been as conscientiously unified as they were in 1610. Ad hoc as the arrangements surely were on that occasion, they provided the format for the inauguration of the next two kings because they too acceded as minors and had to hold inaugural lits to establish regencies. For a very long period during the ancien régime—150 years if one counts the time until the next adult king acceded, in 1760—the sacre-coronation found itself at the tail end (the inaugural lit being at the head) of the inaugural ceremonies. Yet another irony, for getting crowned had been during all the early centuries of the monarchy the exclusive terminus a quo for dating the reign and acting like a king. But yet, it was not anomalous in the context of the new order of things. The perpetuity of royal power, or (as well) of the nation itself, had become the salient component of fundamental law. The inaugural principle as such was essentially superannuated. Perfect kingly status was achieved by the first breath the new king drew in after his predecessor had breathed his last. The sacre et couronnement was needed in order to dramatize this new theory of royalty as much as it had been required in times past to initiate the reign of every new king.

NOTES

1. R. A. Jackson, *Vive le Roi! A History of the French Coronation from Charles V to Charles X* (Chapel Hill: University of North Carolina Press, 1984); also in French as *Vivat Rex* (Strasbourg, 1984).

2. Percy E. Schramm, *Der König von Frankreich* (Weimar, 1960) 1: 97–103; Robert Holtzmann, *Französische Verfassungsgeschichte* (Munich, 1910), 112–113.

3. Schramm, *Frankreich* 1: 104–111.

4. Ibid., 1: 226.

5. Ralph E. Giesey, *The Royal Funeral Ceremony in Renaissance France* (Geneva, 1960; reprinted 1984), 41–50.

6. Ibid., 125–144.

7. Ibid., 105–124.

8. See the chapter "Le Roi est mort! Vive le Duc!" in my forthcoming monograph, *Le Cérémonial royal en France à l'époque de la Renaissance* (Editions de l'Ecole des Hautes Études Sciences Sociales, Paris, 1987), where the Lorraine and other ducal rituals of *mis au tombeau* are compared with the French royal custom.

9. Ibid., and also the chapter "Effigies Royales et Effigies Ducale."

10. I draw freely in this section upon the new work by Lawrence M. Bryant, *The King and the City in the Parisian Royal Entry Ceremony* (Geneva, 1986).

11. See, e.g., my *Juristic Basis of Dynastic Right to the Throne* (Transactions of the American Philosophical Society, vol. 51, part 5; Philadelphia, 1961), 18.

12. Sarah Hanley, *The Lit de Justice of the Kings of France* (Princeton: Princeton University Press, 1983), 127–133.

13. Ibid., 160–172.

14. Ibid., 231–253.

15. This is stated explicitly in the title of a contemporary pamphlet: *Les cérémonies et ordre tenu au sacre et couronnement de la royne Marie de Médicis, Royne de France et de Navarre... Ensemble la mort du roy & Comme Monsieur le Dauphin a esté declaré Roy, et la Royne Régente par la Cour de Parlement* (S.1., 1610) B.N. Lb^{35}. 870; see p. 13 for some details.

16. See my *Royal Funeral*, 122–124, 190–192; also "The Presidente of Parlement at the Royal Funeral," *Sixteenth-Century Journal*, VII (1976): 25–34.

17. Jackson, *Vive le Roi*, 131–154; Hanley, *Lit de Justice*, 254–280.

18. Jackson, *Vive le Roi*, esp. 145.

19. Nicolas Bergier, *Le Bouquet Royal, ou le parterre des riches inventions qui servy a l'Entrée du Roy Louis le Juste en sa Ville de Reims* (Reims, 1637), 54–57.

THREE

A Coronation Program for the Age of Saint Louis: The Ordo of 1250

Jacques Le Goff

In memoriam Pierre Fénot

This essay is one of two contributions in this volume discussing the Latin manuscript no. 1246 of the Bibliothèque Nationale in Paris, containing a liturgical text of great importance. As mentioned in the preface, in our seminar devoted to the problem of medieval systems of gestures and rituals, three of us worked as a team on this manuscript, which has the unique quality of containing a description of a ceremony accompanied by a series of images. But alas, the part that would have been the contribution of our colleague, Pierre Fénot, will never be written: he was struck down by a cruel illness a few months ago; it is to his memory that we dedicate our essays.

Jean-Claude Bonne will discuss the text and illuminations and provide a codicological analysis, as far as it relates to our interests. My study emphasizes the unity of the manuscript in form, in content, and the ideological themes that underlie all other elements. This unity reflects that precarious balance between royal and ecclesiastical power achieved in the kingdom of France under Saint Louis which came to benefit both the monarchy and the church, and for which this ordo is a prime symbolic piece of evidence.

We have little new to say about when and where the manuscript was made. Although the style of the miniatures is almost certainly Parisian, as Robert Branner and François Avril have indicated,[1] the manuscript's presence in Reims for many centuries permits us to assume that it was produced in that city. Its dating still depends essentially on that of the miniatures, because the reference to the Fourth Lateran Council (1215) in the ordo of Reims,[2] certainly preceding our ordo, gives only a *terminus post quem*. François Avril, who is a leading expert on French miniatures of the thirteenth and fourteenth centuries, dates the pictorial cycle around (probably before) 1250; we accept this dating, as does Richard Jackson.[3] Finally, the book was certainly made for the bishop of Châlons-sur-Marne, suffragan of the archbishop of Reims and one of the ecclesiastical peers, but, contrary to the opinion of Leroquais,[4] it cannot have been part of a pontifical from Châlons. J.-C. Bonne will present our arguments for this decision. Although we had originally called it "the ordo of Châlons," since it exists only in the sole manuscript that was made for Châlons, we now agree with the name that Jackson has given it: the "ordo of 1250." Both the Godefroys' title, "ordo of Louis VIII,"[5] and Schramm's, "Compilation of 1300,"[6] are to be rejected in the light of recent study.

As Richard Jackson recently summed up in his *Vive le Roi!*, there are three types of documents that inform us about consecrations and coronations: ordines, that is, liturgical works containing the text of prayers, hymns, and antiphons for the office connected to the consecration and coronation of a ruler; directories, which are normative works prescribing what is to be done in such a ceremony; and narrative records describing actual ceremonies. Paris, B.N., ms. lat. 1246 is closely related to a slightly older text, most probably dating from the first years of the reign of Saint Louis. That text, the so-called ordo of Reims (in fact a directory) is, despite its brevity, an important piece of evidence, for we find in it the earliest references to certain innovations of ritual and to some kings of France which also appear in our text. Paris, B.N., ms. lat. 1246 adds the liturgical texts to the "ordo of Reims" and thus constitutes a true ordo. This ordo of 1250 is an heir to the western Frankish ordines, with borrowings from and allusions to the European corpus of ordines from the early Middle Ages, both Anglo-Saxon and Continental. We see it as a dossier, just as Schramm called it, a compilation, a document that not only marks a stage in the evolution of a ceremony, but one that others later built upon.

Jackson also reminds us of another important rule: unless there is explicit proof, an ordo should not be too closely linked to the actual coronation of any particular king. The ordo of 1250 probably never served as the sole or even the preferred text for any one consecration. It was certainly not used for that of Louis VIII in 1223 or for that of Saint Louis in 1226, but in all likelihood it was influenced by these ceremonies. It was not employed for the consecration of Philip III in 1271, since for that the "last Capetian ordo" must have been used; however, the ritual in our ordo and the spirit of its ideology had a strong impact on the coronation ceremonies of subsequent French kings, expressing a program as well as containing a "mirror for the prince."

My commentary on the ceremony described in Paris, B.N., ms. lat. 1246 will be organized around two ideas. The first is that the structure of the ceremony should be read as the unfolding of a definite rite. I prefer to liken it to a rite of passage[7] rather than to an "inauguration ritual," which, of course it is also. (Therefore, references that Ralph Giesey, Janet Nelson, and Sarah Hanley, among others, make to Meyer Fortes and Clifford Geertz are pertinent.) The second idea is that whereas one of the major concerns of the two protagonists of the ceremony, the king and the clergy—standing for royal and ecclesiastical power, was to establish between them a balance as near perfect as possible, at the end of the ceremony the advantage shifted to the king.

First, let us consider the elements of this rite of passage: the subjects, the place, the time, and the procedure. Who plays a role in the ritual? The hero of the ceremony is, of course, the king, who in the course of the ceremony will pass from one state to another. (I leave aside the queen, whose coronation is described at the end of the ordo. Although the king is the main hero of the ceremony, the normal royal coronation in medieval France applied to a couple, including a queen and future mother.)

At the beginning of the ceremony the king is already king, but not yet entirely king. When he arrives at Reims, the king is king because he has already satisfied two of three conditions. First of all, he has been chosen by God. This is made clear from the beginning of the opening prayer of our ordo, which is pronounced by one of the two bishops who goes to fetch the king from his bed: *Omnipotens sempiterne Deus, qui famulum tuum N. regni fastigio dignatus es sublimare....* As the king enters the cathedral, the antiphon *Domine salvum fac regem...* is sung. The second condition, succession by birthright, necessary in the thirteenth century, is only suggested in our ordo through the words spoken by the archbishop of Reims before the throne, between the coronation and enthronization: *Sta et retine locum amodo quem hucusque paterna successione tenuisti haereditario iure tibi delegatum.* To these words is added a reminder of the king's divine election, *per auctoritatem Dei omnipotentis.* But it is the third step in the ritual that makes the prince truly king. At the anointing, the archbishop says *ungo te in regem.* Now, *in* with the accusative indicates an action toward a goal, but also and especially, a consequence, the end of a transformation. Finally the third condition is spelled out when the text of the ordo states: *et per praesentem traditionem nostram, omnium scilicet episcoporum, caeterorumque Dei servorum.*

Opposite the king stand the clergy. Their role is a complex one. The clergy are a collective personage who hold a sacred power giving them the monopoly to transform the king and with that transformation grant him access to a portion of sacred power. Although our ordo says nothing of this, it is from the anointment that the magical power of the king to cure the King's Evil proceeds. But the clergy also negotiate with the king in their own interests, those of the Church and the ministry. They propose or even impose a contract, that in exchange for his anointment and coronation, the king must swear to protect the Church and his people and to be a good Christian king. Contracts often accompany rites of passage, for example engagements and marriages. In another respect, the clergy are also regarded as spokesmen for the sovereign people and as such grant the king political power that emanated from the *populus* in Roman tradition. Finally, the clergy, mediators between God and man, constitute the king as mediator between themselves and the people: *Quatenus mediator Dei et homimum te mediatorem cleri et plebis constituat.*

The clergy are not a homogeneous group. The ceremony of the ordo of 1250 (and its predecessor, the ordo of Reims) sets up a subtle balance among the various ecclesiastical participants. To begin with, there are the cathedral clergy, those, so to speak, on home ground. The clerical protagonist as *coronator* and principal partner in dialogue with the king is the archbishop of Reims. After him come the bishops according to rank: the six ecclesiastical peers, then the archbishop's suffragans, and finally the rest of the bishops. Next, and yet to one side in this complex hierarchy, come the canons of the cathedral chapter; they are not bishops but are "at home" in the church. On another level, there are the regular clergy, represented by two groups: the abbot of St. Rémi, guardian and bearer of the Holy Ampulla, together with his monks; and the abbot of St. Denis, guardian and bearer of the royal insignia. At the outset of the ceremony the archbishop must promise them to return the borrowed objects necessary for the rite. The attempt at a triple equilibrium is noteworthy: between secular and regular clergy; between the two kinds of representatives of Reims, archbishop and the cathedral clergy on the one hand, abbot and monks of St. Rémi on the other; and between the two monasteries so intimately linked to the French monarchy, St. Rémi of Reims and St. Denis. The former was the church of that holy bishop who had consecrated Clovis, the first Christian king of France, whose baptism was subsequently interpreted as the first royal anointing. The relics of St. Remigius and the most important object used in the royal consecration, the Holy Ampulla, were kept in the abbey. The other monastery, St. Denis, had become the necropolis of the dynasty, its historical focal point and memorial. Its abbot was the guardian of the royal insignia, the most significant of which was the sword and crown. Although our text says nothing on this, the insignia might have already been attributed to Charlemagne.

The third protagonist, after the king and the clergy, were the peers of France. After the ordo of Reims, our document is the second to mention the involvement of the peers in the coronation. The notion of the peers was a relatively recent one, dating, at the earliest, from the end of the twelfth century. They were the incarnation of a literary creation, as Ferdinand Lot has shown, of the imaginary peers of Charlemagne in the chansons de geste.[8] Their first participation in a royal inauguration might have been at the coronation of Louis VIII in 1223, or perhaps only that of Louis IX in 1226. The peers, who help support the crown after the coronation and who accompany the crowned king to his throne, express in this ceremony the participation of the feudal lords and their submission to the royal power. This feature is demonstrated immediately after the coronation proper in the rite of the kiss of peace which is related to the kiss of homage and fealty. Once again there is a conspicuous numerical balance between six ecclesiastical and six lay peers, however, the former have the advantage of being on the right-hand side of the king, the place of privilege.

Secondary figures are the feudal lords and the high officers of the crown. (For now "historical" problems connected with the person of the duke of Burgundy and with the disappearance of the seneschal in the thirteenth century should be put aside.) These important lay personages feature in that part of the ceremony, which is, in fact, the rite of knighting, inserted between the royal promises and the crowning. The grand chamberlain (*magnus camerarius*) puts the sandals embroidered with golden fleurs-de-lis on the king's feet; the duke of Burgundy fits him with the golden spurs, the seneschal (or his representative) receives the sword once it has been conferred on the king. He bears it unsheathed before the king for the rest of the ceremony, during the mass, and finally in the procession returning to the palace which marks the end of the rite of passage.

Finally, there are those whom one might think should be the most important participants, but whose presence is marginal: the people. Several allusions are made to them in the king's oaths and in certain prayers, but the people's actual presence is only fleeting. At the very beginning of the ceremony, after the king's first oath, two bishops ask for their assent: (postea inquirant alii duo episcopi assensum populi). After the king's third promise, a bishop (or archbishop) asks the people whether they want to be the subjects of this very prince (ipse episcopus affatur populum, si tali Principi ac rectori se subjicere, ipsiusque Regnum forma fide stabilire atque iussionibus illius obtemperare velint), to which clergy and people are to respond unanimously: *Fiat, fiat*. The final promise of the king in front of his throne is made "before God, the clergy, and the people" (coram Deo, clero et populo). And last, during the closing *Te Deum*, the people are to sing *Kyrie eleison* while all the bells are ringing. Thus the people's presence is mostly passive, a mere symbol of the masses; probably only a few lay nobles and burghers were admitted into the nave of the church, while the rest crowded the entrance of the cathedral, as is suggested in the preamble of the ordo of Reims.

The second consideration is: where does the rite take place? Here, the significance of the rite's location, the cathedral of Reims, must be stressed. It does not matter that at the time of the three ordines—the ordo of Reims, the ordo of 1250, and the last Capetian ordo—the actual church in which the consecration of Louis VIII in 1223, Louis IX in 1226, and Philip II in 1271 occurred was still unfinished. The cathedral is more than a locale for the ceremony: it plays a large part in determining the topography of its phases; it participates actively in the ceremony in that (although this is not mentioned in the text) it is dressed up, walls, pillars, and floor covered with tapestries, drapery, and carpets in the same way as the king himself will be clothed in new robes. The church space is neither static nor homogeneous. Certain parts of the church are more important than others: the choir and especially the altar, the sacred (though not the topographical) center. It is here that the royal insignia are laid out, where they take on the sacred power that will be transmitted to the king upon receiving them, where the principal actors in the ritual, the main transmitters of the religious power, the archbishop and the prelates, are seated (et debent esse sedes dispositae circa altare ubi honorifice sedeant ad oppositum altaris). It is before the altar that the king will prostrate himself and be anointed, and where he will receive the royal insignia, in particular, the crown. For the most part, the king will be seated in a prominent position that the ordo of Reims alone describes in detail: a slightly elevated platform, accessible by a few steps, situated in the center, reaching the edge of the choir, that is, touching the line that separates the laity from the clergy (paratur primo solium in modum eschafeudi aliquantulum eminens, contiguum exterius choro ecclesie inter utrumque chorum in quod per gradus ascenditur). The ordo of 1250 indicates that, when the king has received his insignia and has been crowned, the archbishop is to install him on the throne placed on the platform "in a prominent seat where he may be seen by all" (in sede eminente unde ab omnibus possit videri). The desire to exhibit the king was finally fulfilled after the construction in 1416 of a jube on which the throne could be mounted.

The ordo of 1250 mentions, besides the cathedral, another essential locus and within it a particular space. On the day of his consecration, the king leaves from his palace (palatium), and he returns to it after the ceremony. The palatium is, of course, the archbishop's palace where the king resides when he is in Reims. He is, however, not the guest of the archbishop. By virtue of the right of purveyance, he is "at home." At the beginning of the ceremonies, he is in his bed: *exeunte autem rege de thalamo*. For once I disagree with Jackson, who maintains that "before the ordo of Charles V, none contains any hint of a bed."[9] But the bed is here, for *thalamus* means "bed" rather than "bedroom," and in fact, there is also mention of two bishops who, according to the ordo of Charles V, take hold of the king, one on the right, one on the left. True, the ordo of 1250 says nothing of the king sleeping or being seized by two bishops, but it does say that when the king quits his bed, one of the bishops (not "a bishop," but "one of the bishops") is to say a prayer: *dicitur haec oratio ab uno episcoporum*. It seems reasonable to advance the hypothesis that the system of the two bishops—if not as rousers, at least as witnesses to the rising—was already in place.

I do not know whether Jackson is correct in saying that the rite of the sleeping king, which is documented for the fourteenth century, originated in the use of a bed in the knightly initiation ceremony and that the two bishops who wake and rouse the king are like the two godparents in the baptismal ceremony. It seems important to me not to construct an interpretation of the coronation which, through too rigid a logic and false historicism, makes of it a "combination of three ceremonies: coronation, baptism, and knighting."[10]

One could, after all, add an even more similar fourth ceremony: the ordination of a priest, or a bishop. Although it is true that the royal consecration owes something to each of these rites, I think that these analogies stem from the necessary resemblance between different rites of passage—such as baptism or knighting, as well as marriage, ordination, and, of course, funeral—and royal consecration.

Let me argue here why do I not like the term inauguration. Royal consecration is much more than mere inauguration, for it implies a change, more precisely, an increase, in status and power. If we need comparisons, then the wide category of rites of passage appears to be the most suitable, with many parallels to the royal accession ceremony. In the latter there is, for example, if not sleep, at least an awakening. Sleep is one of the rites of purification in preparation for a passage; and awakening is one of the rites of separation that is a prelude to passage, as Arnold Van Gennep has shown. Better yet, it is one of those "liminal" stages that Victor Turner defined so well. As for the two bishops, they are among the helpers in separation rites who take on many different forms, including the perverted ones, such as the mock rape of the bride in her bed practiced among certain peoples on the wedding morning by two men to whom tradition has allotted this role. The rising of the king is, compared to a rising of a cadaver, an inverted rite of the funeral. The rising is not that of a corpse going to its last resting place, but of a body awakened to a new life.

In a rite of passage there are not only fixed loci—the one where one comes from in the separation phase, the one where the transformation takes place, and the one where one goes to assume the new and higher power that one has received. There are also the movements from one place to another or within a defined space: from the palace to the cathedral; in slow motion within the cathedral from the door (a "liminal" point par excellence, the threshold of the sacred space where the king and his retinue pause) to the choir and the altar; and finally from the cathedral to the palace. One word comes up again and again in text and image: *processionaliter*. The circuits are processions, cortèges that are religious if not sacred. The space and the movements within it are, if not religious, like the altar, certainly magical. All these features resemble elements of rites of passage rather than inaugurations in the simple sense of the opening of a building or unveiling a monument.

The question "when?" is easy to answer. The ordo says that the ceremony should be celebrated preferably on a Sunday, clearly to reinforce the religious and sacred character of the ceremony.

The question "how?" is best answered by analyzing the structure of the ceremony in respect to the objects used and the different rites performed in its successive phases. While there is no allusion to a watch or a vigil or to early morning preparations, as in the ordo of Reims, there are brief references to two preparatory phases of the rite of passage. First, there is the setting up of the *sedes* in the church in order to mark the achievement of the king's transformation, placing him on a special seat, "both sign and repository of the magico-religious royal power."[11] This seat, as a symbol, can be compared to the empty throne in ancient India, or to the *hetimasia* (empty seat of God or of the cross) in early Christian and Byzantine art. Second, the acts of waking the king, helping him out of bed, and leaving the palace demonstrate a separation from the profane and, with the procession to the cathedral, a movement toward the sacred.

The ceremony inside the church can be broken down into eight phases, not equal in significance.

1. *Entry*. The king, with the two bishops, enters into the church after a pause on the threshold; there is a procession up to the choir; the king makes contact with the most sacred part of this holy space reserved for the altar; and the important secondary agents of the ritual (bishops and peers) are seated.
2. *Holly Ampulla*. Next is the processional delivery of the Holy Ampulla carried by abbot and monks of St. Rémi; their solemn procession continues within the church with the holy oil under the canopy—in other words, this phase is the arrival of the holiest object of the ceremony. This is the culmination of the sacralizing process; the Holy Chrism, its vessel, and the relic of the Holy Ampulla, also emphasize the national character of the cult of St. Remigius.[12] (The ordo of Reims and the ordo of 1250 mark the promotion of this relic within the ritual of the anointing and coronation.)
3. *Contracts*. Royal promises and oaths to the clergy[13] from formulae used in royal consecration ceremonies in Anglo-Saxon England, in Germany, and in the imperial coronations are made.

   a. The king first pronounces the *petitio-promissio*, which is addressed directly to the church, and reinforces it with an oath. The formula of the promise is the one of the *Erdmann-ordo* (c. 900) that was used in the consecration of Philip I in 1059.
   b. After they have asked the people for assent and *Te Deum* has been sung, the two bishops help the king to his feet in order for him to pronounce the *tria precepta*,[14] peace, justice, and mercy, which directly concern the people. Their text is quite similar to the promises included in the ritual of the consecration for bishops and to the *scrutinium* in the German coronations in Aachen/Aix-la-Chapelle ever since the late tenth century. The ordo of 1250 did not retain the fourth *praeceptum* that had been added to the ordo of Reims after the Fourth Lateran Council about the prosecution of heretics.
   c. After the king, the bishops, and the priests have prostrated themselves (note the dialectic of seated, standing, kneeling, prostrate!) and a litany has been sung, a bishop asks the people whether they accept this prince, which they affirm. He then asks the king, back on his feet, to swear an oath concerning

God (to defend holy Catholic faith), the Church (to uphold and defend the churches and their ministers), and the people (to govern and defend the *regnum* granted him by God according to the tradition of justice of his fathers). The assent of the clergy and the people (by *Fiat! fiat!*) seals this pact between the king and the clergy, who are also seen as acting on behalf of the *populus*.

At this point the first phase of the ritual proper is virtually completed. The objects that will grant the king his true status and power have been placed by the abbot of St. Denis on the altar, the physical contact of which confers sacred power on them. The king, standing before the altar, takes off his old outer robes: this act marks the end of the separation rite.

4. *Knighting*. The king receives from the grand chamberlain the sandals on which, for the first time, the fleurs-de-lis, characteristic of the French monarchy, appear. From the Duke of Burgundy, the king receives the golden spurs; from the archbishop, he receives, in a complex rite involving the altar and the scabbard, the sword that makes him the secular arm of the Church and which he entrusts to be borne unsheathed by the seneschal of France.

5. *Unction*. The anointing is performed by the archbishop, upon the head (as in the case of the high priest and the king in ancient Israel, and of bishops), on the chest, between the shoulders, on the shoulders, at the elbows, and, finally, somewhat later, on the hands. The commentary of the ordo points out that of all the kings on earth the king of France alone has the glorious privilege of being anointed with an oil from heaven. Although, as the title of the manuscript indicates, the ordo of 1250 contains the ritual of the consecration and coronation of the king, the emphasis in this part of the rite of passage is placed on the procession of the Holy Ampulla and on the anointing. As the archbishop states, the king, after his hands have been anointed, has become like the kings and prophets of the Old Testament, like David anointed by Samuel (*benedictus et constitutus Rex in regno isto, super populum istum*). He then asks God to look with equanimity upon *hunc gloriosum regem N*.

6. *Conferring the insignia*.[15] The grand chamberlain drapes the king in the hyacintine tunic, the color worn by the high priests of Israel which became the color of the kings of France, (making blue the color of power, of the sacred, and, along with pastel blue, the color à la mode). Above the tunic he places a cloak or surcoat, turned up on the left arm like a priest's chasuble. Next, the archbishop puts the ring on the king's finger, symbol of royal dignity, the Catholic faith, and perhaps the marriage that God contracts with his people. Into his right hand the king receives the scepter and into his left the rod, which represents— this document offers the oldest evidence for this interpretation—"a

hand of justice" (*virga ad mensuram unius cubiti vel amplius habente disuper manum eburneam*); and justice, of course, is the most sacred of all royal duties. At the end follow the two principal insignia of power: the crown, which the peers are called upon to place on the king's head, and the throne, on which he is seated, thereby establishing the fullness of his dignity and power. The king pronounces a last vow, which he speaks as a sort of collective address, *coram Deo, clero et populo*, following the German imperial *formula professionis*, by which, even without reference to the pope or the Roman Church, the king of France takes upon himself the commitments of the emperors. The last phase of the rite of consecration and coronation ends with the kiss of peace and fealty given to the king by the archbishop and by the peers. Now, the bells are rung, the clergy sings the *Te Deum*, and the people reply with *Kyrie eleison*.

7. *Mass.* The high mass that follows seems to have been an appendage tacked on to the principal rite of anointment and coronation (as was later the case with marriage). It contains however, one important event that is indicative of the king's new state and his passage into an estate in which the royal office takes on a priestly character: the king partakes of the communion under both kinds as would a cleric.

8. *Final "rites of aggregation."*[16] The king, now wholly king, leaves the sacred place, having exchanged the heavy ceremonial crown for a lighter one, and returns to the palace; but he returns with a greater dignity with new powers embodied in the unsheathed sword that precedes him. The ordo does not tell us whether the day ends with a ritual banquet, but it is quite likely. It would be fittingly one of those communal meals, which, as Van Gennep pointed out, frequently end rites of passage.

Although it has borrowed much from Christian traditions of the early Middle Ages and bears the basic imprint of the Old Testament model revived in 751 and 754 for the two consecrations of Pepin the Short, the ordo of 1250, as a successor of the ordo of Reims, marks the beginning of a series of ordines and coronation ceremonies that were thoroughly French. The emphasis on the Holy Ampulla, the display of the fleurs-de-lis, and the appearance of the main de justice—all innovations of the French court—as well as the harmonious collaboration of the catherdral clergy of Reims and the abbots of St. Rémi and St. Denis and the specific role of the peers of France indicate in ritual and liturgical language that the ideology of French monarchy became autonomous and even contained a certain claim of superiority over all other Christian rulers.

These ceremonies expressed the equilibrium between king and church achieved by the kingdom of France under Saint Louis. By reexamining step by step the ceremony it can be demonstrated how carefully—through the places occupied by the participants, the rites, the texts of the royal oaths, the prayers and songs, the processions, the movements from place to place, and the gestures—these rites avoided placing one power higher than the other; each time one of the two seems to dominate, there is an effort to reestablish the balance. Only at the moment when the king takes his place on the throne does he finally outweigh the prelates and lay lords. The archbishop doffs his miter before the crowned king and respectfully kisses him, and the peers follow suit. When the king leaves the church, the unsheathed sword borne before him overshadows the croziers of the bishops and abbots.

NOTES

1. Our thanks go to François Avril for his generous and illuminating help.

2. The text of the ordo of Reims can be found in U. Chevalier, *Sacramentaire et martyrologie de l'abbaye de Saint Remy. Martyrologie, calendriers, ordinaires et prosaire de la métropole de Reims (VIIIe–XIIIe siècles)* (Paris, 1900), 22–26. The text of the ordo of 1250 has been published by Theodore et Denis Godefroy, *Le ceremonial français* (Paris, 1619) 1: 13–25 (Latin text) and 26–30 (French translation from the end of the thirteenth century).

3. We are greatly indebted to Richard A. Jackson for his general study of French royal ordines: *Vive le Roi! A History of the French coronation ceremony from Charles V to Charles X* (Chapel Hill, London: University of North Carolina Press, 1984) which contains the indispensible bibliography.

4. V. Leroquais, *Les pontificaux manuscrits des bibliothèques publiques de France* (Paris, 1937) 2: 145 ff.; see Bonne, in this volume.

5. See above, n. 2.

6. The works of the great German historian Percy Ernst Schramm remain fundamental, although the manuscript datings are dubious and the orientation is somewhat outdated (he pays too much attention to insignia, to the detriment of the rituals, and fails to recognize the specific character of the liturgical texts): *Der König von Frankreich. Das Wesen der Monarchie vom 9. bis zum 16. Jahrhundert* (Weimar, 1939); "Ordines-Studien II" in *Archiv für Urkundenforschung* 15 (1938): 3–55.

7. On rites of passage: Arnold van Gennep, *Les rites de passage* (Paris, 1909), 2d ed. (Paris, 1969); Robert Hertz, *Sociologie religieuse et folklore* (Paris, 1928), 2d ed. (Paris, 1970); Victor Turner, *Ritual Process: Structure and Anti-Structure*, (Chicago: University of Chicago Press, 1969); Edmund Leach, *Culture and Communication: the logic by which Symbols are Connected. An Introduction to the Use of Structuralist Analysis in Social Anthropology*, (Cambridge, 1976), esp. 77–79. The best thinking on the liturgical character of the ordines and on the possibilities of comparing them with inauguration rituals studied by anthropologists can be found in the work of Janet L. Nelson, especially her article "Inauguration Rituals," now in her *Politics and Ritual in Early Medieval Europe* (London, 1986). The most useful work concerning comparable African rituals is M. Fortes, "Of Installation Ceremonies," in *Proceedings of the Royal Anthropological Institute for 1967*, 5–20.

8. F. Lot, "Quelques mots sur l'origine des pairs de France", *Revue historique* 104 (1894): 34-59.
9. Jackson, *Vive le Roi*, 134.
10. Ibid., 135.
11. Van Gennep, *Les rites*, 156.
12. Jean Beleth (Parisian master of the end of the twelveth century), *Summa de ecclesiasticis officiis,* CC Cont. Med. CLI/A, p. 297: "De sancto Remigio: Sanctus Remigius Gallorum dicitur pontifex, quoniam primus regem Gallorum inunxit, atque ideo in tanto honore et veneratione habetur in Francia, ut festum illud obfuscet festum beati Michaelis."
13. Cf. M. David, *Le serment du sacre du IXe au XVe siècle. Contribution à l'étude des limites juridiques de la souveraineté,* (Strasbourg, 1951), first published in *Revue du Moyen Age latin* 6 (1950): 5-272).
14. These come from the Anglo-Saxon ritual (consecration of Edgar in 973 where they were pronounced before the anointing) and were introduced into the French ritual through the ordo of Fulrad (*c*. 980), which was used for the first time at the consecration of Louis VI (1108), but they were pronounced at the end of the ceremony. The people (populus) were added for the consecration of Philip I (1059).
15. Cf. Hervé Pinoteau, "La tenue de sacre de Saint Louis IX, roi de France. Son arrière-plan symbolique et la 'renovatio regni Juda,'" *Itinéraires* 162: 120-166; reprinted in his *Vingt-cing ans d'études dynastiques* (Paris, 1982), 447-504.
16. Of course, the parallel to rites of passage, where there is a place to "assemble" or "aggregate" (in Van Gennep's word) for the initiated, can be drawn only metaphorically, for the king is the only one of his kind in any society.

FOUR

The Manuscript of the Ordo of 1250 and Its Illuminations

Jean-Claude Bonne

An all-round assessment of the ordo of 1250 can be achieved only when it is placed in the context of the manuscript that contains it and when it is studied in relation to the images that illustrate it. A consideration of the text alone—or especially of the isolated text in the printed edition—tends to obscure both the ambitious nature of the work and its considerable symbolic importance. Even though it is something of a dossier about a ceremony in the process of evolution with concomitant imperfections, the ordo of 1250 contributed greatly to the form of the idea of royal consecration by emphasizing its specifically French characteristics. The attention devoted to the miniatures and, more generally, to the manuscript itself, which was clearly conceived as a sort of prototype or ideal model, is an indication of the significance of the whole enterprise.

The inclusion of the ordo among the litanies of Châlons-sur-Marne suggests that its compiler or patron may have been the bishop of Châlons, suffragan of the archbishop of Reims, peer of France, and officiant in the coronation ceremony, but by no means proves that it ever formed part of a fuller manuscript of a pontifical, as Canon Leroquais believed.[1] There are, in fact, three signs that point in the opposite direction, that is, that it was an autonomous text, produced for a specific circumstance: first, the perfect arrangement of the quires, and especially the completeness of the first and last; second, the fact that the last original folio was left blank until another hand added to its recto a slightly later illumination (an indication that the parchment was not intended to be used as part of a larger, continuing manuscript); third, the small format (215 × 150 millimeters), which led to the extension of the ordo over forty-two folios and which hardly seems compatible with the typically larger liturgical manuscripts containing numerous other episcopal services. The autonomy and particularity of the manuscript's design are most convincingly indicated by the elaborate connections between its four components: rubrics, prayers, "notated" chants, and illuminations. Before turning to the last, the focus of this paper, a few remarks on the first three are in order.

The rubrics, conspicuous by their color, not only fill their usual role of providing ceremonial direction but also offer occasional commentary, for example, on the nature of the Holy Ampulla, or on the priestly connotation of a royal vestment. More fully developed and more precise than those of earlier ordines, the rubrics of the ordo of 1250 offered the illuminator material that he could manipulate more easily than the liturgical texts.

The prayers are written in black, their sections and subsections indicated by the use of large and small initials. These filigreed letters, alternately blue and red, serve as guides and prompts to the brief responses. Other elements of page design, such as the subtle balance between rubrics, prayers, and chants further attest to the care given to the ordo's appearance. If there is nothing exceptional in this, it does nevertheless suggest the considerable pains that were taken to give the ordo the quality of a good liturgical manuscript. We might note, in contrast, that in the oldest known version of the "last Capetian ordo" (in the pontifical Paris, B.N., ms. nouv. acq. lat. 1202), which is probably slightly later than the ordo of 1250, such elements are less fully apparent.

A consideration of the chants adds to the sense of the manuscript's importance and refinement. That notation was added to chants newly introduced into the service while the more familiar were left unnotated, indicates, as Pierre Fénot had suggested, the participation of a specialist and adduces further proof for the care taken in the orchestration.

The fifteen illuminations (approximately one for every three folios) are distributed according to their relation to the text and to the space required by their size (varying from a third to the whole of the page). The important thing is that they are not conceived as separate, isolated pictures but rather constitute a whole set designed to throw into relief, through the illustration of over twenty steps of his consecration, the politico-religious image of the king of France. This cycle, although neither as continuous nor as detailed as the miniatures in the ordo of Charles V,[2] selects and orders a series of distinct and essential stages of the consecration that transforms the status of the king. The illuminations thus lend themselves to analysis in terms of a rite of passage. Perhaps we should think of the manuscript as a kind of double ordo in which the images go their own way, as a sort of summary, parallel to the text.

The relation between text and illumination, and particularly their discrepancies, can be treated here only in the most perfunctory way. The problem of consistency of the images still deserves some discussion since certain factors—particularly the handling of color—tend to negate a person's pictorial identity. Thus the features of the king, the color of his dress or of the seat on which he sits change from one illustration to another without its being justified by the demands of the coronation ceremony. However, the prevalence of the rhythmical or "musical" effects over the descriptive ones, such as the alternating blue and red backgrounds, has certain relevance to the importance of chant within the ceremony. One might say that color is to the figural meaning of the image what psalmody is to the semantic meaning of the prayers and *formulae* recited in the ceremony. Thus color, an element that historians too often neglect because they cannot assign it a documentary value, is actually fundamental to an understanding of the tone of these ceremonies. For it is color that, in a typically medieval way, "musicalizes" the image and integrates it organically into the ritual.[3]

There is obvious difference between two types of illumination. The nine largest of the fifteen pictures, each in its own frame, depict, separately or together, on one or two levels, one or more phases of the ceremony. The six others are smaller, placed in initials to illustrate a single scene. The difference between the two groups is, to a certain extent, functional: the illuminator chose the smaller format of the initial when he sensed incoherence or awkwardness in the text. When, for example, a long rubric describes a sequence of distinct ceremonial steps for which the accompanying prayers appear only some pages later, the illuminator chose to place certain of his illustrations in the initials of the relevant prayers. This procedure, which creates a definite visual hierarchy and gradation between the two sets of images, provided an ingenious way to accomodate and contain, if not completely to resolve, textual incoherence: the figurative initials make it easy to find the relevant prayers.

Images of royal or imperial investiture prior to the manuscript of 1250 reflect entirely different concepts, essentially of three kinds: biblical, "mythical," and historical. To begin with, there are those that refer to the unction of Old Testament kings, above all David, illustrating the Book of Kings or Psalm 26. Their political importance might be investigated through a study of iconographic change,[4] but it is hard to be precise about their implications, which remain relatively limited. Then there are images of investiture that one might term mythical because they attempt to establish or reaffirm the legitimacy of a ruler or dynasty through direct divine intervention. Those miniatures in Carolingian, Ottonian, and Salian manuscripts of the ninth through eleventh centuries that show investiture by the hand of God, Christ, the Virgin, or an angel come immediately to mind. In contrast to these, the images of the ordo of 1250 deliberately avoid all such "supernaturalism," a fact of considerable importance in understanding the place of the Holy Ampulla in them, the heavenly origin of which is emphasized in the text. The third category of images (to which those of our ordo belong) might be called historical because they try to evoke the sense of an actual ceremony, whether real or idealized. They begin to appear toward the end of the tenth century (Pontifical of Mainz, 960 A.D.; Ivrea Sacramentary, around 1000 A.D.), but the images do not become widespread in historical or liturgical manuscripts until the thirteenth century, and even at that date remain isolated collages that cannot escape supernaturalism or marked biblical allusion. And so far as I know, very few of the older liturgical manuscripts, including richly illustrated sacramentaries and pontificals, offer a sequence of images for one specific religious rite as long and complete as that supplied by the ordo of 1250.

All these factors taken together make the originality of this extensive and homogenous cycle of images particularly striking. A new concern for the sequential ordering of the illustrations of a rite—illustrations that are themselves largely new and fresh—reflects, in turn, a need to order, institutionalize, and promote the renewal of that very rite. The illustrations strengthen Le Goff's assertion that the elaboration of the rite served to demonstrate that balance of powers established in France during the reign of St. Louis between the feudal monarchy and the ecclesiastical aristocracy—a point that brings us to the question of the manuscript's date.

The two leading experts on Gothic manuscript illumination, R. Branner and F. Avril, date this manuscript, on the basis of its miniatures, around 1250, the latter pushing it back closer to 1240; and Branner has also identified the Paris workshop and two hands that may have produced them.[5] The date neatly tallies, as François Avril has pointed out to me, with the period between 1243 and 1248 when St. Louis decided to take the Cross and make meticulous arrangements for the governance of the realm during his absence. Given the precarious conditions of his own coronation and his desire to sacralize the image of the king of France, the achievement of an ordo focusing on these concerns fits neatly into the context of Louis's ordering of royal affairs to avoid crises that might be occasioned by his departure, including his death as a martyr of the Crusade. The image of unction on the king's forehead in the form of a red cross might very well be interpreted in this sense (see fig. 4.1).

A detailed analysis of the illustrations, which will appear elsewhere, will consider a number of factors which I can merely list here to suggest their significance. Apart from color, which has already been discussed, one should consider the following:

1. *Format.* The horizontal rectangle favors the lateral or simply "earthly" aspects of the stages of the ceremony at the expense of vertical relations, which, especially in "mythical" images of investiture, emphasize relations with the divinity.
2. *Internal frame.* Except for the initials and the very last miniature, it consists of trifoil arches, which suggest more the sacredness of the place where the ceremony is held, than the solid architecture of the building.

Figure 4.1. Paris, B.N., ms. lat. 1246, fol. 17r. (Photo Michel Pastoureau)

This type of frame serves to establish rhythmic parallels to those of color, presents topographical patterns affirming hierarchic positions carefully distributed among the participants, and posits syntactic patterns articulating the successive or simultaneous moments of the action.

3. *Figure and background.* The way in which figures are inscribed on the background and on the different superimposed planes establishes another hierarchy of places and persons and an inherent relationship between the figure and its place, as is typical of medieval images.

4. *Corporality.* The striking whiteness of unmodeled flesh turns the bodies of the various figures into a kind of blank space to be inscribed or invested with Christian signs—particularly the bare chest of the king during unction with the Holy Oil (see fig. 4.1).

5. *Vestments and other regalia.* The manipulation of ordered sequences (such as dressing, undressing, dressing again) is at least as important as the appearance of the objects themselves.

6. *Gesture.* This is the means through which the symbolic and ideological content of the portrayed ritual becomes most explicit. Gestures include several relevant features, such as:

   a. *Place.* Place and change of place (less realistic than symbolic), are always precisely indicated for the three main poles of the ceremony, that is, the king, the officiating person, and the altar.
   b. *Posture.* The illuminator carefully presented all the figures in a standing position, except the king, who is depicted in four possible positions, standing, sitting, kneeling, and prostrate, a clear and significant contrast, particularly noteworthy because the images do not exactly follow the text on this point.
   c. *Positioning of head, arms, and legs.* These are also elements in a system in which everything signifies something. The king can be recognized through three gestures reserved to him: his hand (usually the left) placed at the cords of his mantle, or his right hand on his hip with the elbow bent (a traditional gesture of authority), or his legs crossed; at the end of the ceremony, these three positions of his are combined (see no. 14, below, fol. 37v).
   d. *Orientation.* Since we are looking at a "narrative" of the consecration, lateral relations are stressed by three-quarter face, following medieval iconographic practice.[6] Since the progress of the action and its "earthly" character are emphasized, frontal figures gazing directly at the spectator in a "timeless" pose of majesty are avoided.

To demonstrate, at least in outline, what is meant, I describe summarily the fifteen illuminations and elaborate on those three that appear most important for my argument.

1 (fol. 1). (a) Reception of the king and his entourage by the archbishop and clergy at the threshold of the church. (b) The king, seated, surrounded by standing clergy, prays, turned toward the altar.

uobis perdonari petimus ut nobis 7 ecclesijs n̄ris canonicū priuilegium ac debitā legem atq̢ iusticiā consecuturis 7 defensuris. Responsio regis·

Figure 4.2. Paris, B.N., ms. lat. 1246, fol. 4r. (Photo Michel Pastoureau)

2 (fol. 4). Processional arrival of the Holy Ampulla (see fig. 4.2). This is one of the largest illustrations and the only one that depicts a single event, as in the smaller initials. This important stage of the ceremony brings together three groups. On the left, the king at the head of his entourage makes a gesture of assent in the direction of the cortège which fills the central space of the picture: the solemn transfer of the gilded Holy Ampulla by the abbot of St. Rémi under a golden canopy borne by four acolytes dressed in white albs. Movement is stressed by the fact that this central group infringes upon both the compartments behind and in front of it. The abbot carries the Holy Ampulla in his outstretched hands, as though he were presenting a chalice, not on a chain around his neck, as in the ordo of Charles V where one occasionally sees relics and the Holy Ampulla furnished with their hanging chains. This method of transferral seems all the more unlikely since the so-called ordo of Reims contains several measures aimed at protecting the procession of the Holy Ampulla from overly enthusiastic crowds. The cortège is seen to reach the altar on the right where a monk, also dressed entirely in white, turns toward it, holding a vase before him. This object may be the vessel containing the holy chrism, to which only a drop of the precious Holy Oil will be added. Near the altar, the archbishop and a group of bishops face the procession, while the king and his entourage are placed in the position of spectators and followers. R. Branner noted that the head of the abbot of St. Rémi had been redrawn by the same hand that painted the last illumination. One should also note the preponderance of the color white—a symbol, among others, of the Holy Spirit—in the procession of the Holy Ampulla; it is, of course, the heavenly relic that explains the white attire, otherwise inexplicable on so considerable a figure as the abbot of St. Rémi.

All these elements underline the importance of this moment and the exceptional reverence paid to the Holy Ampulla. Compared with this solemn *adventus*, the king's entry into the cathedral is a rather modest affair—although his return to the palace is another matter (see no. 15b below). What is remarkable in this miniature is the total absence of any "supernaturalism" in the sense described above. In contrast to the text and to certain earlier and later images—such as the ivory plaque with scenes from the life of St. Rémi, where the dove brings down the oil for Clovis's royal baptism,[7] or the ordo of Charles IV, where the dove supplies the vial for the royal unction[8]—this illustration makes no reference to the heavenly origin of the Holy Ampulla. We should further note that no picture illustrates the transfer of regalia from St. Denis, a less significant event than the transfer of that miraculous object that would serve as the high point of the consecration.

3 (fol. 4v). (a) Two bishops ask the people's assent; (b) & (c) The king, led by two bishops, goes to kneel at the altar, while the prelates chant the *Te Deum*.

4 (fol. 5v). The king lies prostrate before the altar while clergy chant the litanies in responding choirs.

5 (fol. 15v). (a) The lord chamberlain puts the slippers on the king's feet; (b) The Duke of Burgundy attaches the golden spurs.

6 (fol. 17r). The rite of the sword and the king's unction on the head (cf. fig. 4.1).

These two distinct phases of the ceremony are here combined in one image. In the left section a bishop, accompanied by a group of clergy, carries the naked sword upright in his left hand, looking to the right. The sword reappears in the center, placed on the altar from which it is supposed to acquire holiness, along with the two other metal regalia: crown and ring. On the right, the seneschal of France, surrounded by a group of laymen, has received the sword, which he holds in his bent right hand, turning right toward the center. (Note the different gesture of the two swordbearers!) The complex ceremonial handling of the sword by archbishop and king, as described in the ordo, is not depicted; rather, the king is shown kneeling at the altar, his hands joined before him in a gesture that suggests the offering of the sword at the altar, as the rubric prescribes. The principal action in the center is the anointing of the king on the forehead. The archbishop does not do this with his thumb, as prescribed in the ceremony, but with a golden nail. In fact, two distinct steps are condensed here: the extraction with the nail of a drop of Holy Oil from the Holy Ampulla to be mixed with the chrism and the anointing. Moreover, the metropolitan does not hold in his left hand a paten in which the mixing would be done, but rather a vial, as though the unction were to be accomplished with the pure and untouchable oil. Furthermore, he is accompanied, so to say doubled, by a monk in white, who recalls the procession from St. Rémi and attests, in a sense, to the nature of the liquid used. All these traits serve to emphasize the extraordinary sacredness of the oil with which the king of France was anointed. Without being able to discuss here at length the iconography of royal unction, which is sometimes represented as done directly with a vase or horn, sometimes with the thumb, let me note that to my knowledge only a few liturgical manuscripts containing the consecration of a king of France show anointing with a nail. In all likelihood, that iconography was pioneered by our manuscript.

We should also note that the unction, the oil of which is normally invisible, has gained substance on the forehead of the king in the form of a red cross, as though traced with the blood of Christ by a symbolic scarification into the king's flesh.[9] In sum, there is a distinct sacerdotal and christological connotation to the unction. The combination within the same image of the rite of the sword (an instrument for drawing blood) with the anointing is not mere iconographic fancy but a significant association. It might be interpreted in terms of a contract: in exchange for unction, which grants sacredness to the king, the Church receives his promise to protect her (sealed by taking the cross) and to administer justice.

7 (fol. 19r, historiated initial to the word *Unguantur*). Anointing of the king's hands.

8 (fol. 22v, initial of V in *Vere*). The traditional image of a priest praying in front of the altar.

9 (fol. 26r, whole page). (a) The ties of the king's tunic are fastened; (b) The king receives the mantle (*soccus*); (c) The lay and spiritual peers hold the crown above the head of the seated king; (d) The king, standing, crowned, and surrounded by the peers, receives the kiss of the (bare-headed) archbishop.

10 (fol. 26v, historiated initial of *Accipe*). The standing king receives his sword.

11 (fol. 27v, same form). The seated king is given the ring.

12 (fol. 28r, same form). The scepter is handed to the seated king.

13 (fol. 29r, the fourth historiated initial to an *Accipe*). Coronation of the standing king.

14 (fol. 37v). (a) The crown of the king and queen, seated, are exchanged for a less ceremonial diadem; (b) The king and queen take communion.

15 (fol. 42, cf. fig. 4.3; illumination by another, perhaps somewhat later, hand). (a) The crown of the standing king and queen are replaced by other ones; (b) The royal procession returns from the church to the palace.

The organization of this last miniature differs in many ways from all the preceding ones. The heads are more powerful, their physiognomy more elongated and sinuous, the drapery more developed; the groups are less compact and their relations more transitive. In the upper register the columns of the arched background are hidden by figures so that the partition is weakened; in the lower, the tripartite architectural frame disappears altogether to give way to an architecture that refers to the subject of the image. On the left there is the portal of a church which the royal procession is seen leaving; and on the right, where the altar had usually been placed, stands a fortified double arch, through which the procession enters. The palace is much larger than the church, and its two crenellated towers are higher than the spires of the bell-towers. The central scene takes place under an open sky, suggested by the empty space left on the parchment above the background in the middle. The cortège is led by the seneschal, who holds the sword aloft. His figure is painted entirely over the palace, as though he were about to defend it or take possession of it. The palace portal above the swordbearer corresponds, in a sense, to the canopy over the bearers of the Holy Ampulla. No banner is depicted (nor is there a reference to one in the ordo), but the mantles of the seneschal and queen, who stand before and behind the king, are lined with ermine, which suggests the coat of arms of the royal house.

Figure 4.3. Paris, B.N., ms. lat. 1246, fol. 42r. (Photo Michel Pastoureau)

Several other features distinguish this royal procession from the preceding illuminations. The king's silhouette is more subtle, more "aestheticized," particularly the position of his head and arms. A woman, recognizable by her coiffure, can be seen in the royal entourage, while all the clergy have disappeared. This procession, a lay counterpart of the one accompanying the Holy Ampulla on fol. 4r, implies a wish on the part of a king (who does not yet bear the physiognomy of a particular ruler) to be seen in person by his people. The people, who are almost totally missing from the other images (with the pale exception of 3a on fol. 4v), are here referred to in an implicit but nevertheless definite way, as the royal cortège crosses the town on foot, after the consecration, in order to be seen. Ceremony turns into spectacle.

What political significance can be attached to the fact that the consecration of the Capetian kings of France was deemed worthy of a cycle of such elaborate images in a liturgical manuscript?

These illuminations confirm in a striking way Jacques Le Goff's proposition that the supreme political project of Saint Louis—whose ideal of kingship lies, beyond doubt, at the basis of these miniatures—was to elevate the image of the Capetian monarchy and to develop its national and international prestige by pushing to its limits the religious and sacred character of the king, and using his paradoxical status of an anointed layman for political ends. It is important to notice the particular emphasis, both institutional and spectacular, placed by the illuminations on the sacredness of the king. The retelling of the consecration in images produces, among other effects, an intense historicization of the rite. Even the processional transfer of the Holy Ampulla and the very special way in which the king's body is anointed—to take only two highly characteristic acts—imply that the intervention of the supernatural, that is, the only means to sacralization, is conceived of as mediated by a liturgical action and by an object of a specifically national character. Although the ecclesiastical establishment kept real control over the sacred, in this affair it was portrayed only in the role of mediator. It could not use the Holy Ampulla for its own ends, for that vial was destined by God for the French kingship and accorded special honor for sacralizing the Capetian monarchy.

At the end of the ceremony, as it is depicted in the last miniature, the king makes use of his new sacrality to gain recognition by the people. The access of the French high clergy to the Holy Ampulla and the immanence of the supernatural in the liturgy is paralleled by a feeling of a quasi-immanence of the sacred in the Capetian dynasty. In fact, the vertical, or supernatural relationship—according to Luc de Heusch, the essence of any ritual[10]—is not particularly explicit in our set of images. Even if it is suggested by such features as the king's prostration before the altar, the cross on his forehead or the whiteness associated with the Holy Ampulla, the relationship with the supernatural is much less explicit in this cycle of images than in other works of a similar genre. It is the horizontal references and "earthly" relationships that are underlined making rather those transactions explicit that are strictly ceremonial.[11] They are performed by those who represented power in thirteenth–century France: the high clergy as lords spiritual, the secular magnates of the realm, the still rather anonymous members of the court, and the king and queen themselves. The ordo's cycle of illuminations implies that the consecration can no longer be seen as only a mythical foundation of kingship or as the continuance of some immortal rite. It is rather intended to bestow official character on a national tradition by embedding it in a ceremony that was common throughout the West.

If the ordo of 1250 in its entirety succeeds in demonstrating a remarkable balance between the different modes—sacred ritual versus spectacular ceremony, ecclesiastical authority versus royal power on the path to autonomy, national spirit versus shared ideas of Christendom—the images also contain hints at the source of future tensions between these poles by placing value on the earthly, the spectacular, the French, and the powerfully royal aspects. Rarely does an illuminated manuscript of the high Middle Ages offer the historian of politics and ideology and the anthropologist of symbols and rites of power such a complex and enlightening document.

NOTES

1. V. Leroquais, *Les Pontificaux manuscrits des biblithèques publiques de France* (Paris, 1937), 2:145f.

2. On this ordo see E. S. Dewick, *The Coronation Book of Charles V of France (Cottonian MS Tiberius B. VIII)* (London, 1899).

3. See J.-Cl. Bonne, "Rituel de la couleur," in *Image et signification. Rencontres de l'Ecole du Louvre* (Paris, 1983), 129f.

4. Robert Benson discussed these aspects eloquently at the Toronto Conference; it is to be hoped that he will publish his comments.

5. R. Branner, *Manuscript Painting in Paris During the Reign of Saint Louis: A Study of Styles* (Berkeley, Los Angeles, London: University of California Press, 1977), 69, 87–91; F. Avril, annotation no. 216, in *La France de Saint Louis: Catalogue de l'exposition Paris, Octobre 1970-Janvier 1971*. I express my gratitude to François Avril for his invaluable codicological information and suggestions in connection with my study of the manuscript.

6. Cf. M. Schapiro, *Words and Pictures* (The Hague-Paris, 1973), 38.

7. D. Gaborit-Chopin, *Ivoires du Moyen Age* (Fribourg, 1978), 68, pl. 83: Reims, last quarter of the ninth century, Amiens, Musée de Picardie.

8. H. Bober, "The Coronation Book of Charles IV and Jeanne d'Evreux," *Rare Books* 8 (November 1985): 4, fig. 4.

9. From a symboligical perspective it is worth noting that it was precisely between 1243–1248 that St. Lous had the Sainte-Chapelle built to house the relic of the Crown of Thorns.

10. Luc de Heusch, "Introduction à une ritologie générale," in *L'Unité de l'homme:*

Pour une anthropolgie fondamentale, ed. E. Morin, and M. Piatelli-Palmarini (Paris, 1974); cf. also R. Giesey's article in this volume.

11. This distinction between rite and ceremony has been worked out by Luc de Heusch, as above, n. 10.

FIVE

Copies in Context: The Coronation of Charles V in His *Grandes Chroniques de France*

Anne D. Hedeman

Until recently, scholars studying the French coronation concentrated for the most part on textual problems posed by the ordines and discussed representations of the ceremony only in passing.[1] Art historians have begun to fill that lacuna by focusing on two areas of research. Claire Sherman's masterful analysis of the pictures and text of the queen's ordo in Charles V's *Coronation Book* (London, B.L., Ms. Cotton Tiberius B. VIII) exemplifies the first, which could be termed a monographic approach. Sherman took as a point of departure an analysis of the relationship between text and image of the ordo in Charles V's *Coronation Book*. This analysis enabled her to demonstrate ways in which themes that were sharpened in the revised text of the ordo were supported and strengthened in the pictorial cycle that decorated the king's copy of the text. She broadened her study to show that the emphasis on fertility and stress on the importance of the French house that shaped the text and illustrations of the *Coronation Book* had a place within the broader context of Charles V's commissions and responded to contemporary historical events.[2] Robert Scheller's study of narrative genres in representations of the French coronation exemplifies a second, synthetic approach to the study of images of coronation. In his study, Scheller, through an analysis of pictures of French coronations from such diverse sources as ordines and histories, isolated three broad genres of illustration: factually narrative, condensed, and emblematic images. He defined factually narrative illustrations as those that isolate each ceremonial moment of the coronation in an individual scene. Cycles containing these pictures are rare; the most elaborate example is Charles V's *Coronation Book*. More common are condensed scenes that encapsulate the ceremony in a single image that represents such easily recognized features of the ceremony as the presence of the peers, or emblematic scenes that represent the coronation in the guise of symbols of the monarchy.

Scheller cautioned that the selection of a narrative, condensed, or emblematic representation was independent of the decision to paint the scene in a particular artistic style. Increased naturalism of representation would not necessarily guarantee increased historical accuracy; thus condensed scenes could be painted in the highly naturalistic style of Jean Fouquet, and detailed factually narrative scenes in the less naturalistic style of the master of Charles V's *Coronation Book*.[3]

A major strength of Scheller's and Sherman's studies lies in the care with which they establish a context for the image. Sherman considered the illustrations of the *Coronation Book* within the narrow framework of the book itself and then within the broader cultural context of the court of Charles V, whereas Scheller analyzed representations of coronations within the dual contexts of genres of narrative and of artistic styles. In some ways their approaches seem to be mutually exclusive—Sherman's grounded in the analysis of one book and Scheller's in a comparative examination of many books. However their methods can—and, I hope to demonstrate, must—be united in order to deal with a particular class of images: medieval copies. To show how these approaches can be blended I will analyze one copy of the *Coronation Book*, a manuscript that both Scheller and Sherman found to be exceptional. Among questions to consider are the following. What happens when illustrations of an important text like the *Coronation Book* are copied? Do pictures that imitate images from the *Coronation Book* have the same historical content that Sherman described for the prototype? If the original image is, as Scheller suggested, factually narrative, would the copy be as well? Or might the copy be a condensed or emblematic scene belonging to a different narrative genre? To what extent would a scene based on a picture from the *Coronation Book* illustrate the ordo, and to what degree would it illustrate the new text? To explore some of these questions, I will consider as a case study one of the better-known copies after Charles V's *Coronation Book*—the illustration selected to represent Charles V's coronation in his personal copy of the *Grandes Chroniques de France* (Paris, B.N. ms. fr. 2813). An analysis of this picture suggests that copies do form a special class of image which often functions in a different narrative genre and which must be considered within the dual contexts of the text that generated it and the text that it accompanies.

The scene that introduces the narrative of Charles V's life is one of the most perplexing miniatures in his *Grandes Chroniques de France* (fig. 5.1).[4] Historians and art historians alike have dismissed the double miniature of the king and queen enthroned from serious consideration because it copied earlier images.[5] Paradoxically, it is precisely this dependence that makes the scene representing Charles's coronation special. Of the 175 pictures in this manuscript, it is the only derivative miniature, a status that raises questions about its function in the *Grandes Chroniques*.

Figure 5.1. Peers supporting the crowns at the coronations of Charles V and Jeanne of Bourbon, *Grandes Chroniques de France*, Paris, B.N., ms. fr. 2813, fol. 439, c. 1375–1377.

In order to understand its importance, the picture of Charles V and Jeanne of Bourbon must be considered within the specific context of Charles V's manuscript. This image was painted between 1375 and 1377 to decorate a continuation of the *Grandes Chroniques* which was written at court. The continuation updated a previously completed manuscript that contained texts written at the monastery of St. Denis chronicling the history of the French kings from their Trojan origins through the reign of Philip of Valois.[6] The new continuation, describing the reign of John the Good and part of Charles V's reign, ended in a chapter that discussed two events of 1375: the publication in Parlement of the ordinance regulating the majority of the French kings and the forging of a treaty with the English at Bruges. Charles V's *Grandes Chroniques* did not exist long in this form; in 1379 or 1380 the manuscript was updated by a second continuation and by illustrated substitutions that replaced select older texts. With these changes the manuscript effectively took the shape it has today.

These circumstances of production make Charles V's book unique among copies of the *Grandes Chroniques*. Twice it was finished and presumably placed in the royal library, and twice it was removed so that texts and pictures could be added in order to update the history of the Valois dynasty and the reigning king.[7] Many of the images that decorate these added texts are large in scale and particularly detailed. Most of them are unique to Charles V's manuscript and respond closely to contemporary politics and to Charles's concern with the legitimacy and the continuity of his line in the face of a rival claim to the throne by the king of England supported by the king of Navarre.[8]

The first continuation written at court between 1375 and 1377 provides the specific context for the miniature of Charles V and Jeanne of Bourbon (fig. 5.1). This image introduces the account of Charles V's reign and draws special attention to that king and to his queen. The ceremony portrayed here differs in detail from those in the manuscript that mark the commencement of other kings' reigns, exemplified here by the Coronation of John the Good (fig. 5.2), a miniature painted in the same campaign as the double scene of Charles V and Jeanne of Bourbon. Thus Charles grasps a scepter representing Charlemagne enthroned that is still preserved in the Louvre, and Jeanne of Bourbon holds in her right hand the scepter of Dagobert, now lost but known from eighteenth-century drawings by Montfaucon.[9]

Scholars have explained the specificity of this particular picture by citing its models—images from Charles V's commemorative *Coronation Book* (figs. 5.3 and 5.4).[10] The *Coronation Book*, produced in 1365 under Charles V's direct supervision, was decorated by the same workshop that later painted the double picture in the *Grandes Chroniques*. Because it formed part of the royal library, the *Coronation Book* was an authoritative and convenient model for the images in the *Grandes Chroniques*. The relationship to the *Coronation Book* provides a plausible explanation for the compositional similarity between these images, but it makes their differences in heraldry, to be discussed below, even more problematic.

Also puzzling is the moment chosen to illustrate the beginning of Charles V's reign. Instead of the moment of coronation, the picture represents a portion of the ceremony that occurred after the coronation proper—a symbolic expression of support for the new king and queen by the clerical and lay peers. The text of the chronicle does not describe the ceremony of coronation in sufficient detail to mention this action by the peers of France. Indeed, the *Grandes Chroniques* recounts simply that the king and queen were crowned, and it lists some of the nobles in attendance.[11] Strictly speaking, the miniatures of the coronations of Charles V and of Jeanne of Bourbon from the *Coronation Book* would have been more appropriate models if the only goal of this picture in the *Grandes Chroniques* were commemoration.[12]

The placement of the queen next to the king in the chronicle suggests that these images played a fundamentally different role in Charles V's *Grandes Chroniques* than they did in his *Coronation Book*. The double miniature in the *Grandes Chroniques* juxtaposes two pictures that were separated by eleven folios and by as many miniatures in the *Coronation Book*. In reality, the ceremony of the queen's coronation was begun only after that of the king was

Figure 5.2. Coronation of John the Good, *Grandes Chroniques de France*, Paris, B.N., ms. fr. 2813, fol. 393, c. 1375–1377.

Figure 5.3. Peers supporting the crown of Charles V, *Coronation Book*, London, B.L., Cottonian Ms. Tiberius B. VIII, fol. 59v, c. 1365.

Figure 5.4. Peers supporting the crown of Jeanne of Bourbon, *Coronation Book*, London, B.L., Cottonian Ms. Tiberius B. VIII, fol. 70, c. 1365.

finished. The representation in the *Grandes Chroniques* of parallel moments from two ceremonies glosses over the temporal separation between them. This telescoping of two distinct events gives more prominence to the queen; it presents her on an almost-equal footing with the king.

Compositional changes also transcend the specific historical events of the coronation of 1364. The double miniature of the *Grandes Chroniques* does not contain the altars that established in the *Coronation Book* that the ceremony took place in an ecclesiastical setting. This change makes the double miniature from the *Grandes Chroniques* more secular than its model from the *Coronation Book*.[13]

This comparison of the double miniature of support in the *Grandes Chroniques* with its text and with the illustrations of the *Coronation Book* raises three basic questions. Why was the heraldry changed? Why was the queen included in Charles's book? And what significance does the selection of the moment of support have, considering that a model depicting the precise moment of coronation was also available?

As will become clear, a consideration of the double image within the specific context of Charles V's manuscript and the more generalized context of contemporary historical events provides answers for some of these questions. Such a consideration demonstrates that the change of heraldry between the model of 1365 and the copy of 1375–1377, the inclusion of the queen, and the choice of a moment of support rather than coronation reflect the dual function of the picture: it was both a commemoration of the events of 1364 and an expression of Charles V's concerns for a smooth transition of power upon his death.

The double miniature in Charles V's chronicle combines into one image two scenes from the *Coronation Book*. In the first, an image from the sequence of pictures dedicated to the king's coronation (fig. 5.3), the king is flanked by the count of Flanders, the duke of Bourbon, the count of Toulouse, the duke of Anjou, the archbishop of Reims, and the bishop of Beauvais. In the second, a miniature from the ceremony of the queen's coronation (fig. 5.4), the queen is flanked by the count of Toulouse, the count of Étampes, the bishop of Beauvais, and the archbishop of Reims.[14]

The positions of three people changed when these scenes were copied in the *Grandes Chroniques* (fig. 5.1). In the scene showing the peers supporting the crown after the coronation of the queen, the duke of Burgundy replaced the count of Flanders and the duke of Bourbon replaced the count of Étampes.[15] In the scene with the king, the count of Étampes takes the position near the king that the duke of Bourbon held in the *Coronation Book*.

These careful heraldic changes do not increase the historical accuracy of the picture. Of the peers distinguished by heraldry in the miniatures, the *Grandes Chroniques* describe as present only the archbishop of Reims; the bishop of Beauvais; Louis, duke of Anjou; and Philip the Bold, duke of

Burgundy.[16] Although not mentioned specifically in the text of the chronicle, the count of Étampes, the count of Flanders, and the duke of Bourbon were peers at the time of the coronation; they were listed as such in both Charles V's *Coronation Book* and in the conflicting list of peers that appeared in the *Traité du sacre*, the commentary on the ceremony of coronation commissioned by Charles from Jean Golein in 1374.[17]

Two of the peers included in these pictures may only have been represented by proxy. Although the county of Toulouse had reverted to the throne by the time of Charles V's reign, it is possible that Charles appointed someone to represent this ancient peerage. Chronicles are silent on this point for Charles V's coronation, but representation by proxy was a practice in the coronations of Charles VII in 1429 and for subsequent kings.[18] If scholars are correct in asserting that Louis of Male, count of Flanders, did not attend Charles's coronation, it may be that he too was represented by a proxy.[19]

Whether the presence of the counts of Flanders and Toulouse in the pictures of the *Grandes Chroniques* and the *Coronation Book* represents reality or a fiction is not germane to this discussion since the counts appear in both manuscripts. More intriguing are the differences between images in these books: the introduction of the duke of Burgundy into the scene of support for the queen and the change of positions of the duke of Bourbon and the count of Étampes in order to place the duke of Bourbon close to the queen.

Since the dukes of Bourbon and Burgundy and the count of Étampes were present at the coronation, pictorial or written accounts of the ceremony cannot explain discrepancies between these pictures. Charles V's concerns for the education of his heir may explain them. Charles V's first child, who became Charles VI, was born in 1368 during the period between the execution of the *Coronation Book* and the *Grandes Chroniques de France*. The birth of a son which had been eagerly anticipated for eighteen years assured the continuity of the Valois line. To safeguard the continuity, Charles V promulgated three ordinances in 1374.[20] One, concerned with the age of majority, was published in the Parlement of Paris in 1375 and was the subject of the last chapter of Charles V's life in this copy of the *Grandes Chroniques*. It thus closed the reign that began with the scene of the peers' support. In many ways the ordinance on the majority was a logical ending for the chronicle when this version of the manuscript was written and painted between 1375 and 1377 while Charles V was still king. Although it did not complete Charles V's life, it did provide a plan for a smooth transition to his son's government.

A consideration of the two ordinances of 1374 that were written simultaneously with the ordinance on majority, yet were not discussed in the chronicle, sheds light on the miniature in the *Grandes Chroniques*. The first ordinance established that Charles's brother, Louis, duke of Anjou, would become regent in the event that Charles died before his son reached his majority. The second may be more significant for understanding the heraldic changes. It charged Jeanne of Bourbon with the education and upbringing of her children and provided her with two major assistants: her brother-in-law, Philip the Bold, duke of Burgundy, and her brother Louis, duke of Bourbon. The association of Philip and Louis with the queen in this special charge must have been sufficient motivation for their inclusion with her in the picture in this manuscript and could be one reason why the scene with the queen was placed by the king's in the first place—to demonstrate visually the provisions for legitimate government.

The choice of a moment of support rather than coronation may also reflect Charles V's concerns with providing a smooth transition to the government of his heirs. A contemporary text, the *Traité du sacre* by Jean Golein, provides insights into the significance of the peers' gestures in the ceremony.[21] Completed in the same year as the ordinance on government and contemporary with the painting of the miniature in the *Grandes Chroniques*, Golein's treatise glossed the events of the coronation with an explanation of their symbolic meaning. In his treatise Golein stressed frequently the peers' role in assisting in the just government of France. The portion of the *Traité du sacre* which described the moment of the ceremony represented in the *Grandes Chroniques* emphasized the peers' role as defenders of king and realm. According to Golein, "the peers surround the king to signify the forces who surround Solomon, all of them expert with the sword, skilled in battle, because if they [the peers] are not presently holding their swords, they are nearby to be taken when it is time to defend the king and realm."[22] Perhaps dual images of baronial support were included here to show that the peers were ready to defend their present king (Charles V) and to uphold the government of his descendants—a government in which the queen and the peers flanking her were supposed to play an important role.

On the most basic level then, this picture is a special commemoration of Charles V's and of Jeanne of Bourbon's coronations in 1364. As such, it derives its iconography from the official commemorative manuscript of the coronation. However, this commemorative function may be less important than a second function that emerges when the picture is considered within the context of the *Grandes Chroniques* as they existed in 1375–1377, after the continuation of the first half of Charles V's reign was added to the book. Within this specific context the picture simultaneously introduces Charles V's reign and alludes to the conclusion of it—to the provisions for government under the young dauphin and to the peers' duty to protect and defend the realm and their king, no matter what his age.

While some may question the validity of this interpretation, support for it is found in an analysis of the baptismal procession (fig. 5.5), the only other large picture of ceremonial from the version of Charles's life that existed in 1375–1377.[23] The theme of dynastic continuity to which the miniature of

Figure 5.5. Baptism procession of Charles VI, *Grandes Chroniques de France*, Paris, B.N., ms. fr. 2813, fol. 446v, c. 1375–1377.

baronial support only alludes is amplified in the representation of the procession that took place in 1368 when Charles's firstborn son was christened. An important part of the ceremony described in the text and highlighted in this image is the role played by queen Jeanne d'Evreux, the last wife of the last Capetian king. Her role carrying the Valois heir must have been seen at the time as an affirmation of the continuity of Capetian to Valois—of the sanction of the Capetian kings for their Valois successors. These two images of ceremonial, coronation and baptism, that are unique to this special copy of the *Grandes Chroniques de France* combine in a sophisticated way with the chronicle's text and with each other to focus on the past and future of the Valois line. In so doing, they provide us with insight into Charles's concerns at a precise moment in history.

Neither the illustrations for the *Grandes Chroniques* nor those from the *Coronation Book* take precedence as accurate representations of history. As a result historians have frequently dismissed them and described the miniature in the *Grandes Chroniques* as a replica of the pictures in the *Coronation Book*. By expecting these images to be pictorial documents, truthful or unchanging in a twentieth-century sense, they misunderstood their function, which in the chronicle depends on a subtle interaction between picture and text.

It is striking that pictures like the scenes of support from the *Coronation Book* and *Grandes Chroniques* are so close in appearance yet are put to such different uses. Within the context of the *Coronation Book*, images depend on the ordo that they supplement, but do not transcend.[24] The scenes of support for the king and queen there are essentially commemorative; they are part of a serial illustration of the ceremony of coronation, sequentially ordered in both space and time. Perhaps because they are removed from the text of the ordo that generated them, the same compositions serve a different purpose in the *Grandes Chroniques*. In that book the double miniature of the king and queen compresses the time that elapsed between the moments of support in the actual ceremony, a passage of time physically experienced by the reader of the *Coronation Book* when he turned the ten folios to proceed from one event to the other. This compression gives singular importance to the queen, particularly in a chronicle where no other events from queens' coronations are reproduced in pictures.[25] In the *Grandes Chroniques* the double miniature does not depend on the text it accompanies. Indeed, its primary meaning only emerges with the reconstruction of its position in the book in 1375–1377. Then it becomes evident that the double miniature simultaneously commemorated a past event and looked forward to the future. At the very least in these scenes of support, the alteration of heraldry updated the model to place near the queen those peers who were especially trusted in 1375–1377. I suspect that the motivation for the changes related more closely to the structure of the chronicle itself. I believe that the placement of this double miniature makes an explicit reference to provisions for succession partially discussed in the text which in 1375–1377 ended the life of Charles V in the *Grandes Chroniques*.

This double miniature is more than a representation or a misrepresentation of fact. It does not expand in any way on knowledge about the ceremony of coronation despite the inclusion of *realia*. Instead, the image associates disparate portions of the chronicle. It and other large images of ceremonial like it are ways of particularizing this special copy of the *Grandes Chroniques de France* and of focusing on Charles V's preoccupation with the continuity of the Valois line.

NOTES

Earlier versions of this paper were presented in March 1981 at the seminar on medieval historiography conducted by M. Bernard Guenée at the Ecole des Hautes-Etudes, Paris, and in January 1985 at the International Conference on Medieval Coronations in Toronto. I am grateful to the Samuel H. Kress Foundation, which funded my reasearch in Europe and to the Research Board at the University of Illinois, Urbana-Champaign, which funded travel to Toronto. For the permission to reproduce illuminations from their manuscripts, I am indebted to the Bibliothèque Nationale, Paris (figs. 5.1, 5.2 and 5.5) and to the Trustees of the British Library, London (figs. 5.3 and 5.4).

1. The pioneer in the study of the French ordines was Percy Schramm who published his findings in "Ordines-Studien 2: Die Krönung bei den Westfranken und die Franzosen," *Archiv für Urkundenforschung* 15 (1938): 3–55; and in *Der König von Frankreich: Das Wesen der Monarchie vom 9. zum 16. Jahrhundert. Ein Kapitel aus der Geschichte des abendländischen Staates*, 2 vols. (Weimar, 1939). For recent research, see Richard Jackson, *Vive le Roi! A History of the French Coronation from Charles V to Charles X* (Chapel Hill/London: University of North Carolina Press, 1984), the collective volume *Le sacre des rois. Actes du Colloque international d'histoire sur les sacres et couronnements royaux (Reims 1975)* (Paris, 1985), and the contributions to this volume.

2. For this, see Claire Sherman, "The Queen in Charles V's *Coronation Book*: Jeanne de Bourbon and the *Ordo ad Reginam Benediendem*," *Viator* 8 (1977): 255–298; and Claire Sherman, "Taking a Second Look: Observations on the Iconography of a French Queen: Jeanne de Bourbon (1338–1378)," in *Feminism and Art History*, ed. by Norma Broude and Mary D. Garrard (New York: Harper & Row, 1982), 101–117. Other early illustrated ordines are now under study. Jean-Claude Bonne is analyzing the illustrations of Paris, B.N. ms. lat. 1246, as part of a comprehensive study of this copy of the ordo with Jacques le Goff, and I have undertaken a study of a fragmentary copy of the last Capetian ordo (University Library, University of Illinois at Urbana-Champaign) which Harry Bober, in "The Coronation Book of Charles IV and Jeanne d'Evreux," *Rare Books: Notes on the History of Old Books and Manuscripts* 8 (1958): 1–12, suggested was used at the coronation of Charles IV.

3. Scheller presented these preliminary findings in a paper entitled, "The French Coronation Ceremony and the Artists, 1365–1520," at the International Conference on Medieval Coronations in Toronto in 1985. For additional discussion of royal imag-

ery by him, see Robert Scheller, "Imperales Königtum in Kunst und Staatsdenken der Französischen Frührenaissance," *Kritische Berichte* 6 (1978): 5–24; Robert Scheller, "Imperial Themes in Art and Literature of the Early French Renaissance: The Period of Charles VIII," *Simiolus* 12 (1981–1982): 5–59; and Robert Scheller, "Enseigns of Authority: French Royal Symbolism in the Age of Louis XII," *Simiolus* 13 (1983): 75–141. For a consideration of genres of narrative in one manuscript, see Anne D. Hedeman, "Restructuring the Narrative: The Function of Ceremonial in Charles V's *Grandes Chroniques de France*," *Studies in the History of Art* 16 (1985): *Pictorial Narrative in Late Antiquity and the Middle Ages*, 171–181.

4. For a critical edition of the *Grandes Chroniques*, see Jules Viard, ed., *Les Grandes Chroniques de France*, Société de l'histoire de France, 10 vols. (Paris, 1920–1953), and Roland Delachenal, ed., *Les Grandes Chroniques de France: Chroniques des règnes de Jean II et de Charles V*, Société de l'histoire de France, 4 vols. (Paris, 1910–1920). Henceforth I shall refer to these volumes by their editor and by the number of the volume. For a summary of the literary sources for the *Grandes Chroniques*, see Gabrielle Spiegel, *The Chronicle Tradition of Saint-Denis: A Survey* (Brookline, Mass. and Leiden: E. J. Brill, 1978).

For a history of Charles V, see Christine de Pizan, *Le livre des fais et bonnes meurs du sage roi Charles V*, ed. S. Solente, 2 vols. (Paris, 1936–1940); Roland Delachenal, *Histoire de Charles V*, 5 vols. (Paris, 1909–1931); Raymond Cazelles, *Société politique, noblesse, et couronne sous Jean le Bon et Charles V*, Mémoires et documents publiés pour la Société de l'Ecole des Chartes, 28 (Geneva-Paris, 1982); Schramm, *Der König von Frankreich* 1: 236–245; and Joseph Calmette, *Charles V* (Paris, 1945).

Previous discussions of Charles V's copy of the chronicle appear in Paris, Bibliothèque Nationale, *La librairie de Charles V*, ed. F. Avril (Paris, 1968), no. 195, pp. 112–113; Paris, Grand Palais, *Les fastes du Gothique: Le siècle de Charles V* (Paris, 1981), no. 284, pp. 329–331; Claire Sherman, *The Portraits of Charles V of France (1338–1380)* (New York: College Art Association, 1969), 41–44; Marcel Thomas, "La visite de l'Empereur Charles IV en France d'après l'exemplaire des *Grandes Chroniques* executé pour le roi Charles V," *Congrès international des bibliophiles, Vienna, 29 septembre à 5 octobre, 1969* (Vienna, 1971), 85–98; Anne D. Hedeman, "Valois Legitimacy: Editorial Changes in Charles V's *Grandes Chroniques de France*," *Art Bulletin* 66 (1984): 97–117; and Hedeman, "Restructuring the Narrative."

5. Delachenal, *Grandes Chroniques* 4: 27–28, identifies the heraldry in the miniatures from the *Grandes Chroniques* and cites the *Coronation Book* as the model for the double picture in the chronicle. In addition, Sherman discusses the artistic relationship between the *Grandes Chroniques* and the *Coronation Book*. She does not note the heraldic discrepancies. See Sherman, *Portraits*, 37.

6. For this and the following, see Hedeman, "Valois Legitimacy," 98–99, and 108–115; and Hedeman, "Restructuring the Narrative," *passim*.

7. A *mandament* of 1377 commissioned bindings for two volumes containing the "Croniques de France and those which Pierre d'Orgement had made." For this, see Delachenal, *Grandes Chroniques* 1: xii. No such order survives for the version of the text ending in the life of Philip of Valois. Nevertheless a codicological study of the manuscript suggests that it was a complete book at that stage as well.

8. The classic analysis of the difficulties faced by the new Valois line remains

Raymond Cazelles, *La société politique et la crise de la royauté sous Philippe de Valois* (Paris, 1958). See also Cazelles, *Jean le Bon et Charles V*. For a summary, see Hedeman, "Valois Legitimacy," 97–98.

9. For the scepter of Charlemagne, see Paris, Bibliothèque Nationale, *Fastes du Gothique*, no. 202, pp. 32 and 249. For the scepter of Dagobert, see Bernard de Montfaucon, *Les monuments de la monarchie françoise*, 5 vols. (Paris, 1729–1733) 1: xxxv and pl. 1.

10. On the *Coronation Book* see E. S. Dewick, ed., *The Coronation Book of Charles V of France (Cottonian Ms. Tiberius B. VIII)*, Henry Bradshaw Society, vol. 16 (London, 1899); R. A. Jackson, ed., "The *Traité du sacre* of Jean Golein," *Proceedings of the American Philosophical Society* 113–114 (1969): 305–324; Jackson, "Les manuscrits des *ordines de courronnement* de la bibliothèque de Charles V, roi de France," *Moyen Age*, vol. 82, ser. 4, f. 31, no. 1 (1976): 76–88; Jackson, *Vive le Roi*, 26–33; Sherman, *The Portraits*, 34–37; and especially, Sherman, "The Queen."

11. For the text, see Delachenal, *Grandes Chroniques* 2: 1–5.

12. Dewick reproduces these images of coronation in *Coronation Book*, pls. 23 and 35.

13. The elimination of the altars together with the juxtaposition of two distinct scenes from the *Coronation Book* in close proximity constitute a transformation, in Scheller's terms, of a factually narrative model into a condensed copy. From this point of view the double miniature in the *Grandes Chroniques* has more in common than first meets the eye with such scenes from Charles V's *Grandes Chroniques* as the Coronation of John the Good (fig. 5.2).

14. Their arms are as follows: count of Flanders—or, a lion rampant sable; duke of Bourbon—azur, semé with fleurs-de-lis or, a bendelet gules; count of Toulouse—gules, a cross argent voided sable; count of Étampes—azur, semé with fleurs-de-lis or, a bendelet company gules and ermine; duke of Anjou—azur semé with fleurs-de-lis or, a border gules; archbishop of Reims—azur semé with fleurs-de-lis or, a cross argent; and bishop of Beauvais—or, a cross between four keys paleways, a ward in chief gules.

15. The arms of the duke of Burgundy are: quarterly 1 and 4—azur, semé with fleurs-de-lis or, a border company white and gules; 2 and 3—banded with or and azur, a border gules.

16. Delachenal, *Grandes Chroniques* 2: 2–3.

17. For the list of peers in the *Coronation Book*, see Dewick, *Coronation Book*, cols. 13–14. For the list in the *Traité du sacre*, see Jackson, "Traité du sacre," 312.

18. Jackson, *Vive le Roi*, 161–162.

19. Delachenal, *Histoire* 3: 88–89.

20. Sherman, "The Queen," 288. Sherman concentrates on the queen's role in the ordinance. For the texts of these documents, see D. F. Secousse, *Ordonnances des roys de France de la trosième race recueillies par ordre chronologique*, 21 vols. (Paris, 1723–1849) 6: 26–32 (the majority), 45–49 (regency conditions), 49–54 (tutelle). For a recent discussion see Cazelles, *Jean le Bon et Charles V*, 579–581.

21. For this and the following, see Jackson, "Traité du sacre," 306–308. See as well Sherman, "The Queen," *passim*, for a discussion of the relationship between the *Traité du sacre* and the representations of the queen in the *Coronation Book*.

22. "... les pers de France qui sont entour en signifiance des fors qui estoit

entour salemon omnes tenentes gladios et ad bella doctissimi. car sil ne tiennent le presentement les espees si sont il pres pour les prendre quant temps en est pour deffendre le Roy et le Royaume en grant hardement." Jackson, "*Traité du sacre*," 317.

23. See Hedeman, "Restructuring the Narrative," 173–174.

24. For a description of the relationship between text and image in the *Coronation Book*, see Sherman, "The Queen," esp. 263–265.

25. Prior to Charles V, Louis VIII (1223), Philip IV (1286), Louis X (1315), Philip V (1317), Philip VI (1328), and John the Good (1350) were crowned with their wives. Despite this, no other dual coronations are represented in Charles V's *Grandes Chroniques*. For a description of these earlier coronations, see Sherman, "The Queen," 268, n. 47.

SIX

The Medieval Entry Ceremony at Paris

Lawrence M. Bryant

The aim of this article is to reconstruct, to the degree that it can be done, the meanings that the medieval entries of rulers into Paris had for the people who staged and acted in them. The base of the study is the Parisian receptions for kings listed in table 6.1.[1] This table represents the "processual units," to take Victor Turner's concept, from which one can analyze the dynamics of the interaction between spontaneous *communitas* and the structural parts of social existence.[2] Each reception and entry of a king was a "social drama," and the sum of these performances over time supplied interested parties with the materials for constructing a ceremonial tradition and for representing models of political society.

The focus of the study is on Parisian entries because the Parisians found the receptions of new kings to be a good place to articulate their claims both to a dominant place in the kingdom and in the king's affection and because the records of the entry celebrations there are relatively continuous and complete. Furthermore, Parisian influences help to illustrate the ways by which a local ceremony, with the king as the symbolic center of civic expression, came to be a manifestation of French Public Law (what in English is called constitutionalism). Historians have pointed out that as a medieval institution the entry formed *"l'occasion d'un dialogue"* between the king and subjects as well as a revelation of a *"sentiment national"* and a *"sentiment monarchique."*[3] In this discussion, the Parisian side and ritual gestures of this "dialogue" with the king are shown both to represent aspects of Parisian political consciousness and to be sources in the development of a monarchical symbolic system.

As a processional, the medieval entry shared a major characteristic with the imperial *adventus* ceremony, with the medieval *jocundus adventus* of the clergy, and with the seventeenth-century absolutist *entrée royale*.[4] However, the medieval entry was unique because its ceremonial gestures directly con-

TABLE 6.1. Ceremonies for Royal Entries into
Paris Considered in this Discussion
(Dates of coronations are in parentheses)

Rulers	Entry Date	Occasion	Festivities or Decorations in City
Louis IX (29 Nov. 1226)	?	Return from coronation	Likely
Philip IV (6 Jan. 1286)	Jan. 1286	Return from coronation	Greeting by University
Philip V (9 Jan. 1317)	Jan. 1317	First entry as king	Likely
Philip VI (29 May 1328)	22 July 1328	First entry as king	Likely
Philip VI	29 Sept. 1328	Triumph at Cassals	Yes
John II (26 Sept. 1350)	12 Nov. 1350	First entry as king	Yes
Charles, duke of Normandy	31 July 1358	Entry as regent and return of royal government to Paris	Likely
John II	13 Dec. 1360	Return from English captivity	Yes
Charles V (19 May 1364)	28 May 1364	First entry as king	Yes
Charles VI (4 Nov. 1380)	11 Nov. 1380	First entry as king	Yes
Charles VI	11 Jan. 1383	Victory of Roosebeke	No
Isabella of Bavaria (21 June 1389)	20 June 1389	Precoronation and signing with England	Yes
Henry V and Charles VI	1 Dec. 1420	Treaty of Troyes	Yes
Duke of Bedford	8 Sept. 1424	Reception as Regent	Yes
Henry VI (16 Dec. 1431)	2 Dec. 1431	Precoronation	Yes
Charles VII (17 July 1429)	12 Nov. 1437	First entry as king	Yes
Louis XI (15 Aug. 1461)	31 Aug. 1461	Postcoronation and first entry as king	Yes
Anne of Beaujeu	19 April 1483	Recognition of right to regency	Yes
Margaret of Austria	2 June 1483	Dauphin bethrothed and peace treaty	Yes
Charles VIII (30 May 1484)	5 July 1484	Postcoronation and first entry	Yes
Anne of Brittany (8 Feb. 1492)	9 Feb. 1492	Postcoronation and first entry	Yes

TABLE 6.1 *Continued*

Rulers	Entry Date	Occasion	Festivities or Decorations in City
Louis XII (27 May 1498)	2 July 1498	Postcoronation and first entry	Yes
Anne of Brittany (18 Nov. 1504)	19 Nov. 1504	Postcoronation and peace treaty	Yes
Mary Tudor (6 Nov. 1514)	6 Nov. 1514	Postcoronation and peace treaty	Yes
Francis I (25 Jan. 1515)	15 Feb. 1515	Postcoronation and first entry	Yes
Claude of France (10 May 1517)	12 May 1517	Postcoronation and signing of Concordet	Yes
Francis I	14 April 1526	Return from Spanish captivity	?
Eleonor of Austria (14 April 1531)	16 April 1531	Postcoronation and peace treaty	Yes
Henry II (26 July 1547)	16 June 1549	First entry as king	Yes
Catherine de' Medici (10 June 1549)	18 June 1549	Postcoronation	Yes
Charles IX (15 May 1561)	6 April 1562	First reception as king	No
Charles IX	16 March 1571	Joyous and triumphant entry	Yes
Elizabeth of Austria	25 March 1571	Postcoronation	Yes
Henry IV (27 Feb. 1594)	15 Sept. 1594	Reduction of the city	No

tained their meaning and statement while the classical and ecclesiastical processionals dramatized rhetorical and written formulae. Only in the production of late medieval entries did textual sources start to prescribe the form for staging an entry. Even this regulation called attention to the demonstrations of reciprocity between two legal personalities: king and city. In distinct and nonconfrontational ways the event balanced between the community's deference to the king as symbol of justice and right order and the urban corporations' assertions of rights and liberties as juridical personalities. Thus, the impulse for staging medieval entries in cities and giving structure to their drama was constitutional as well as social. While in the ceremony we find no direct quotation of *quod omnes tanqit*, we nevertheless see Parisian representation of this romano-canonical maxim in their gestures before the king.[5]

DESCRIPTION

Simply stated, the entry ceremony consisted of processions out of a city to greet a ruler and a procession into the city by the ruler after the greeting. In the Middle Ages, each performance led to additions that augmented and altered the meanings that contemporaries found in the ritual. In Paris, as elsewhere in Europe, the entry took place in the wake of the potentially threatening circumstances caused by the death or collapse of a prince's power and the need to install a new ruler. Like the English progress to the coronation in London and the famous *joyeuse entrée de Brabant*, the Parisian *première, joyeuse*, or *solennelle* entries were in place by the middle of the fourteenth century. Since the twelfth century, townsmen in Flanders, England, Italy, and the empire had greeted new rulers with requests of a legal nature before they escorted them to the place of investiture.[6] However, in France urban receptions followed the coronation at Reims. In the gestures, speeches, entertainments, costume, and processionals staged for the newly crowned king, citizens like those at Paris were anxious to secure old rights and win new favors. Having no part in the rites of making a king, the Parisians looked to defining the duties of the king.

Cities like Paris and London, where the kings were lords, freely asserted their identity when welcoming and giving hospitality to new rulers. Towns were so successful in entertaining lords, that by the late Middle Ages feudal and princely receptions paled in comparison with them. At this time, the word *entrée* came to denote a ritual of welcoming as well as an action, and by the fifteenth century the subject of kings' entries filled chronicles and town registers. Representations of entries also became a genre of manuscript painting, and it is entirely appropriate to start describing the Parisian entry ceremony with the image of one from a medieval manuscript.

Figure 6.1, is a fifteenth-century depiction of Charles V's entry into Paris (28 May 1364). The artist—perhaps Jean Foucquet—has succeeded in condensing into one idealized pictorial frame much of the symbolism that in actual entries extended through time and space. The groups in the picture include the king-in-regalia, uniformly costumed Parisians kneeling reverently before him, and magistrates in robes-of-office in an attitude of submission, as reflected by their downcast eyes. The setting is before the Port St. Denis, the traditional place for living kings to enter Paris for the first time and for dead ones to leave it for the last time. The artist correctly excluded the clergy and Christian images from among the royal and civic groups gathered before the important public space of the gate in 1364, for only after 1431 did the clergy join the citizens in extending extramural greetings to kings, queens, and other dignitaries. In figure 6.2—a fifteenth-century imaginary rendering of Louis IX's entry into Antioch—closely represents the later form for a

Figure 6.1. Charles V's 1364 postcoronation Parisian entry according to a fifteenth-century miniature attributed to Jean Fouquet (B.N., ms. fr. 6465, fol. 417).

Figure 6.2. Louis IX's entry at Antioch as depicted in a fifteenth-century miniature in *Les Passages d'Outre-Mer* (B.N., ms. fr. 5594, fol. 146).

Parisian entry processional: clergy first, then notables on horseback to welcome the king, and costumed citizens before the gate. In contrast to this idealized portrait from *Les Passages d'Outre-Mer* (1472), the first century of Parisian processions for greeting kings remained secular affairs only.[7]

In the first phase of the ceremony, the Parisians marched out of the city to encounter the king. The processions consisted of the *prévôt de marchands*, *échevins*, other officials of the *Hotel-de-ville*, and members of the *corps de métier*. They exited from the Port St. Martin several hundred feet from the point of entry at the Port St. Denis, and after witnessing the greeting of the king most citizens returned via the same route, like the people in the background of figure 6.1. The officials with hooded robes in figure 6.1 probably represent the Parlement of Paris. From 1431 (but not in Charles V's time), these magistrates also participated in the processions in order to make requests and to give reverence to the entering king. The officials kneeling in the foreground probably represent the few Parisians who would march through the Port St. Denis and down the freshly sanded rue St. Denis with the king; that is, the échevins and guildmasters who held the canopy over their lord from the moment of his actual entrance into the city (fig. 6.3).

This miniature with the king riding into the city well illustrates submission of subjects in the entry ceremony, but it offers little hint of another and related feature of the entry productions, the requests by the prévôt des marchands for the preservation of the city's liberties. In figure 6.2, illustrating the first encounter between the king and citizens, the raised drawbridge in the background indicates an important aspect of the dialogue of the ritual of greeting, since for the entry to take place it would be dramatically lowered only after the king acknowledges his escort and responds to their requests. Such a practice would be a secular counterpart of the ecclesiastical rites for a jocundus adventus conducted before Notre Dame Cathedral where the doors closed behind the exiting clergy and only were opened after the king promised to protect the liberties of that church.

The pictorial evidence captures the static aspects of the king-in-regalia before his subjects and the mobile aspects of his entry into the city by combining the movement of the herald's horse with the fixed stance of the king on horseback. However, in an actual performance of an entry, the king and regalia would have been extended in the processional. According to Christine de Pizan (tab. 6.2), the king's ceremonial entry into Paris—where "all ordinance was preserved"—specified that the royal appurtenances go before the king, who entered in "pontifical estate." Among *"les nobles anciennes coustumes royales"* she included the *"fleurs-de-lis en escherps"* (probably the flowered coronet frequently seen on fourteenth-century portraits of Charles V) and the royal sword.[8] Figure 6.1 shows the heralds wearing the hat and carrying the sword, while the king wears the cloak and carries the scepter, rather than having them factored out before him. Christine mentioned that the people

Figure 6.3. Miniature of Charles VII making his 1437 Parisian entry (B.N., ms. fr. 5054, fol. 93v°).

TABLE 6.2. Le chevauchier de Charles V According to Christine de Pizan

1. Gens d'armes
2. Arbalétriers
3. Chevaliers
4. Barons
5. Parement de roy
    i. "les fleurs de lis en escherpe"
    ii. Le Grand Écuyer avec "le mantel d'armines"
    iii. "l'espée et le chappel royal"
6. Le Roy "vestu en habit royal"
7. "Princes de son sang"
8. Destriers de parement

came to greet *leur seigneur*, and that the king, "*en signe d'amour et begninité recevant le salut de tant de gent, il ostoit son chappel.*" Most of the king's companions were to proceed him, but the princes of the blood rode immediately behind him. Figure 6.2 indicates a major change that had taken place by the end of the fifteenth century, since the king is shown entering in military uniform, although he is represented as having changed into royal dress, but not into his ermine robe by the time he entered the city. What is not shown in either miniature is the canopy, and for good reason, since this was a gift of the city to the king. It pertained only to the space within the walls.

Figure 6.4. Modification of Greog Braun's Plan of Paris in *Théâtre des cités du mondes* (Brussels, 1574–1576, 1:8) to indicate the route for the entry and the traditional places for entry pageantry: (1) extramural greeting; (2) St. Denis Gate; (3–7) stagings along the rue St. Denis; (8) Châtelet; (9) Pont-au-change; (10) Notre Dame; (11) Palais de Justice.

TABLE 6.3. Canopy Carriers, and Route for the Entry of Eleanor of Austria, 16 March 1531

Canopy Station	Company in Charge of Canopy	Pageantry Station
		Review stand
Saint Denis Gate	4 Echevins	Saint Denis Gate
		Ponceau Fountain
Church of the Trinty	4 Drappers	Church of the Trinity
Saint Leu and Saint Gilles	4 Grocers	Painters Gate
Church of the Holy Innocents	4 Mercers	Fountain of the Holy Innocents
Sainte Opportune	4 Furriers	
Châtelet	4 Hosiers	Châtelet
Saint Denis-de-la-Chartre	4 Goldsmiths	Notre Dame Bridge
Notre Dame Cathedral		
Palais		Banquet

Royal entry ceremonies at Paris took place in the specific space before the Port St. Denis and down the rue St. Denis and across the Seine to the cathedral. By the fourteenth century it was customary for kings to make their return to Paris from any major undertaking, such as the coronation or going to battle, via the royal necropolis at St. Denis. With the route to Paris so defined, the appropriate rituals for the encounter of king and city appeared in the additions of royal appurtenances and civic gestures expressing reciprocal respect as well as honoring the king.[9]

The specific stations for the pageantry and ritual acts of the entry ceremony are charted on the map in figure 6.4: a set location for encountering the king, the point of entry at the Port St. Denis, stations for the pageantry along the rue St. Denis, a special program at Châtelet, a passage to the Cathedral, the ecclesiastical *jocundus adventus* and oration in the name of the University of Paris, and the conclusion of the entry and banquet at the *palais de justice*. The route carried the king through the heart of the merchant community, and he could have gathered some sense of resident patterns and guild identities in the commercial part of Paris in witnessing the changes of canopy carriers as described in table 6.3.

Only from 1360 was the canopy mentioned in Parisian entries, although its use was well established elsewhere. It appeared to receive the ransomed King John II back from his English captivity. In bringing out the canopy, the Parisians conflated its religious function in the Corpus Christi processions with the extraordinary circumstances that required a ceremony or reunion between the king and the community.[10] The Parisians along with other French towns had paid for the king's return, and he was displayed as a treasure and the agent for restoring order to the kingdom. The canopy became an important device for joining the extramural urban greeting with the intramural monarchical processional; it implied a continuous ceremony. It also framed the king in a particular identity, for his refusal of the greeting and gift of the canopy would have been the equivalent of a refusal to acknowledge the authority and privileges of its carriers—the officials and leaders of the Hotel-de-ville—and, thus, for him to enter the city as a military conqueror rather than as the agent of justice and right order. As it was, the leaders of Paris became his bodyguards at the entrance into the popular sphere; in the streets of the city the king received the shouts of joy and viewed the pageants presented by those whose liberties he had recognized.[11] In 1360, it was also those subjects who had begrudgingly paid a considerable part of his ransom.

The activities along the route of the king's processional mixed religious and secular aspects. Religious dramas were appropriated from the church calendar. Secular presentations were commissioned and they spoke, sometimes in veiled allegories, to contemporary issues. In either case, wherever the king passed urban groups sought to pull him into some action or dialogue. The compilation in table 6.4 gives an overview of the rhetoric and rituals of the medieval Parisian programs. At times, in a spirit of experimentation, the keys of the city were given to the king, refreshment and silver cups were offered, religious instruction presented, and enthroned actors played king and judges from a "lit de justice"—a term pregnant for the future even if only descriptive of stagings at the time.[12] In songs, dances, tableaux vivants, mock battles, play trials, pretended assemblies, and courtly allegories the king witnessed the varieties of Parisian sentiments and was called to acknowledge some maxim or moral pertaining to his office.

The clergy at the cathedral conducted the last act of the Parisian entry. In the account of 1350, the richly habited clerics proceeded out of the cathedral with the treasures of their church. The presiding bishop labeled the rites a *novus et jocundus adventus*, thus connecting the Parisian practice with the traditional form used by religious establishments for greeting dignitaries.[13] However, in Paris the form contained a special request for the king to make a jocundus adventus promise, and John II, with hand on scriptures, swore to preserve the privileges of the cathedral clergy. This juridical rite, and not the religious service, was the only one reported by the notary commissioned to record the event. After the king gave his promise, the cathedral doors opened.

There was a tradition that an orator from the University of Paris address the king on his return from the coronation. In 1286 when Philippe le Bel reached Paris, his former tutor and Parisian theologian, Gilles de Rome, had the honor of speaking for the University. Over time this greeting that included a formal request for renewal of priviliges was joined to the entry cere-

TABLE 6.4. Decorative Motifs on the Rue Saint Denis

Place	Year	Setting	Kingly Image or Dominant Symbol
Châtelet	1389	Lit de Justice	Crowned "Cerf Volant"
Châtelet	1431	Throne and justice	Enthroned king with princely advisors
Châtelet	1437	Lit de Justice	
Châtelet/Butchery	1462	Battlefield	Louis XI's victory over the English
Châtelet	1484	Throne	1. Tree of the commonweal 2. Enthroned king with virtues and three estates
Châtelet	1491	Throne	1. Personified Justice: enthroned king and queen with twelve advisors 2. Solomon's court
Châtelet	1498	Lily	1. Royal portraits of ruler and progenitors 2. King with Justice and Good Counsel
Châtelet	1504	Park of France	
Châtelet	1514	Throne	Justice and "Verité" enthroned with mythological figures and twelve peers
Châtelet	1517	Genealogical tree	King and queen at top of tree, base protected by juridical virtues
Châtelet	1549	Allegory of Rebirth of Justice	Cityscape with New Pandora/Paris
Châtelet	1571	Allegory of Majesty	Majesty enthroned with Justice, Piety, Clemency, and Abundance
Rue	1431	Hunt	Protector/Suzerain
Rue	1437	Jewish history	Herod
Rue	1461	Hunt	
Rue	1484	Jewish history	Herod and the Slaughter of the Innocents
Rue	1491	French history	Charlemagne
Rue	1498	Allegory of Justice	"Cerf Volant" and "Bonne Voulenté"
Rue	1504	Nativity of Christ	Visit of kings
Rue	1514	Park of France	Lily enthroned with Virtues
Rue	1517	Allegory of Love	Examples of Divine, Natural, and Conjugal Love
Rue	1531	Constitutional	Mystery of Four Estates with Peace
Rue	1549	Obelisk monument	"Royal Majesty"
Rue	1571	Classical traits	Dynastic Marriage, Peace, and Empire

mony: first at the exit of the king from Notre Dame Cathedral and next, from 1549, at the extramural reception.[14] In the fifteenth century, this speech for the University completed the series of encounters between the entering king and the receiving urban corporations that constituted an entry ceremony. In the totality of the ceremony, something like a representative description of the body politic had been made.

A banquet at the Palais de Justice followed the jocundus adventus at the cathedral, but it was quite separate from the entry ceremony. At the banquet, princes and great lords claimed back the king given to the citizens for the entry. In later times, when the Parlement of Paris entered into the processionals, it tended to mediate between the Parisians' assembly and the king's entourage; the banquet came to echo a bit more the events of the street. In the sixteenth century the activities of a royal entry were expanded to include tournaments, and even an auto-da-fe in 1549, but these spectacles were alien additions to the popular and legal inspirations that shaped and sustained the medieval Parisian ceremony.[15]

CEREMONIAL AND SYMBOLS

Long before they became formalized into a ceremony, Parisians made demonstrations of support and zeal for new kings. As early as 1226 armed Parisians escorted to Paris the young Louis IX and his regent mother who were threatened by a baronial revolt.[16] Parisians showed equal zeal in welcoming and supporting Philip V in 1316 who also faced a major revolt of the barons.[17] No one reported the rituals or cries such as *Noel!* and *Vive le Roi!* that appeared in the fifteenth century, but one does see the emergence of Paris as a ritual place and as a personality in political dialogue. When the succession to the crown was questioned, as it was in 1316 and 1328, the importance to a king of *"les quiex le rechurent à roy"* was attested to by chroniclers including among the proofs of legitimate right to the French crown the name of the Parisian échevins.[18] Several years after being so received by the Parisians, Philip VI remembered the gesture when he granted them a special favor, noting *"comment les bourgois et tout le peuple de Paris de leur auctorité le rechurent à seigneur."*[19]

In receiving a new lord and king, Paris and its great corporations demonstrated their legal personality in a way comparable to a great lord.[20] By the fifteenth century, heralds of the city went out to the king in advance of the urban processional and reminded the king of the city's virtues and status.[21] Then came the requests of the Parisian authorities in their robes of office. Any gesture of the king, such as going into the city, constituted a response. In reaction to the city's assertion of its identity, the role of the king became more ritualized and remote. In the process the chancellor or some other principal royal official began to speak for the king. The shaping of the ritual can be followed in the evolution of the extramural greeting, the king in the procession, and the rhetoric of the pageantry stations.

The ritual upgrading of the Parisian reception of a king first took place through the symbolism of costumes. In 1350, various Parisian groups donned distinctive uniforms for John II's postcoronation entry. Guildsmen put on identical costumes in order to contrast with the dress of uniformed "Lombards."[22] The échevins took the same cut as the guildsmen, but in a different color. In 1380, two thousand Parisians wore green and white; in 1389, twelve hundred wore green.[23] As other corporations—that is juridical persons—joined the processional, the symbolism of the polity becomes evident: first the clergy, then guildsmen and officials of the Hotel-de-ville, then of the Châtelet, and finally the magistrates of the Parlement of Paris. When the parlementaires first appeared in the processional in 1431, the first president wore what was described as *habit royal* and exercised the prerogative of a powerful lord in having *"son bonnet fourré"* carried in front of him by an usher of the Parlement.[24] The earliest recorded debates about the processional took place over the claim of the Parlement to have a monopoly on the right to wear red robes in entries of kings—a claim that resulted in the Parlement of Paris taking over regulation of the ceremonial performance of entries by urban groups.[25]

Whether or not the costumed Parisian hosts in 1350 made any verbal request is not known. In 1360, they received John II with a gift of plate worth a thousand marks. In 1380, the prévôt des marchands greeted the newly crowned king with a request for tax relief, an item on the agenda of the meeting of the Estates general in Paris the next day.[26] The dominant gesture of the entry in 1383 was submission, and, before the entry, the prévôt des marchands and échevins journeyed over fifty miles to try to placate the king who was angry at the Parisian refusal to support his war with the Flemish cities.[27] Charles VI returned from Flanders victorious, and he prepared to enter Paris in military dress and with his army. Because of the crisis and potential for violence, the ceremonial forms of this entry stand out.

In 1383, the Constable of France—approaching the city in advance of the king's party—encountered armed Parisians who sought to demonstrate both the might of Paris and to submit to the commander of the king's forces. Then the prévôt des marchands with five hundred Parisians went to the king to render reverence and submission and to request his mercy. The king refused to acknowledge the gestures and then proceeded to enter the city with his armed entourage. Nevertheless, even in the strained circumstances, the ceremonial form for the entry balanced between the obvious military might of the king and his juridical obligations; for although Charles VI entered in armor followed by troops, he promised those Parisian leaders who exited to greet him a future hearing before deciding the fate of the city. According to an Italian witness, he replied to the prévôt des marchands: "*Tornate a Parigi, e quand io saro a sedere in luogho di guistizia venite, e domanderete, e parte troverte.*"[28] Over a century later, Louis XII followed the same juridical procedures after defeating and entering in armor his cities of Genoa and Milan and, likewise, Henry II in his dealings with a rebellious Bordeaux.[29]

What was delayed until a hearing and judgment at the Palais de Justice in 1383 had been in previous entries part of the ritual choreography for the first encounter between king and city. In that encounter, the gestures by the city and the ready response by the king dramatized the reciprocity between the two parties. Even when the bond was broken and the rituals for entries refused, any change in the status quo required a juridical process with the king presiding and the citizens seeking justice. Paris lost its independent government and the restoration of Parisian liberties only came about when Charles VI escaped the tutelage of his uncles: an event celebrated in the Parisian entry and coronation of his queen, Isabella of Bavaria (20 June 1389), the best-described entry of the period.[30]

The circumstances of the reign of Charles VI (the madness of the king, the collapse of the French army, religious schism, and the Burgundian and English control of Paris) had an important impact on Parisian ritual symbolism. The number and scale of public processions greatly increased. Parisians more frequently went en masse to attend the king when he visited the city and they often did the same for powerful lords and around religious objects.[31] The more events seemed out of human control, the more civic and religious processionals were conducted to elicit divine intervention in averting disasters. The new civic and religious union in processionals influenced the Parisian conduct of the traditional first entry ceremony, and fourteenth-century symbolism and gestures, which had called attention to the right order of the city and its officials, gave way to calls on the king to be the instrument for bringing prosperity and good government to the city. The request for renewal of specific liberties and offices continued, but the idea was enlarged to include the king as the instrument of all good in the life of the body politic. At this time, the Parlement of Paris joined both processions in the city and the entry processional to greet the king.

The Lancastrian rulers of Paris proved particularly accomplished at using entries to demonstrate their control of government and to legitimize their usurpation of Valois authority. The Parisians received Henry V in the same manner as Charles VI after they had publicly sworn to uphold Henry's right to the crown.[32] In this way, they bound themselves to a treaty and policy rather than to a newly crowned king. After Henry V's death, the reception of the Duke of Bedford as regent was carefully coordinated by "*l'ordannance du conseil du Roy*" and orders were given for the clergy to join the extramural processional.[33] Following the London practice, Henry VI added the new touch of a precoronation entry that was staged on Advent (2 December) 1431. His reception of the urban processionals at the little La-Chapelle-

Figure 6.5. The submission of the town of Troyes to Charles VII with Jeanne d'Arc assisting, in *Vigiler de Charles VII*, c. 1448 (B.N., ms. fr. 5054).

Saint-Denis outside the city's walls altered the synbolism of the entry, and now—in a closed setting—the king first "received" representatives of the corporations residing in Paris before allowing them to receive him. At this moment the Parlement of Paris first acted in the cermonial. It entered because of the Parlement's failure to influence the council of the English king and to obtain security of offices and salaries.[34] In the entry, the parlementaires found a well-established ritual structure to acquire an access to the king and an occasion for freedom of address otherwise closed to them. Their most potent symbol was the first president of the Parlement in the red fur-lined robe that only he, the three other presidents, the chancellor, and the king could wear. Since, in another departure from tradition, the king entered in military dress, the first president's costume also served to remind all— even the English conquerors of France—to do justice and to preserve the highest law court of his French subjects.

The ceremonial improvisations that took place under the Lancastrian kings were continued in the entry rituals of the late Valois rulers. At Charles VII's reception, the gift of the keys of the city first was mentioned for a Parisian entry.[35] The gesture common elsewhere, but not at Paris, was somewhat like that illustrated in the miniature of the submission of Troyes in 1429 (fig. 6.5). Here, the chancellor and Jeanne d'Arc flank the king-in-regalia. Jeanne points to the chancellor and shifts the focus from a rite of submission to a military conqueror to a submission to the chief juridical official of the kingdom. The chancellor gestures with one hand for the magistrates to kneel and, seeing obeisance, indicates with the other hand for him to rise. Figure 6.2 also illustrates the same balance between submission and liberty by having the king gesture for the dignitaries who are in the process of kneeling to rise. In future entry ceremonies at Paris and elsewhere, the king-in-armor replaced Jeanne d'Arc, and the chancellor in robe-of-office carried out the acts of recognition and justice. Over time, the chancellor came to respond for the king to panegyrics and requests; he was the intermediary for justice and peace—the image of reciprocity—over the reserved right of the king to use force.[36]

Louis XI showed sensitivity to the power of symbolism by not renewing parliamentary and other offices in advance of the Parisian entry—including his dismissal of the Chancellor Guillaume Juvenal des Ursins.[37] However, the refusal of the new king to renew offices deprived many civic officials of a legal identity and a ritual place in the ceremony. The splendor of the nobility of France and Burgundy—one of the greatest host of nobility seen in Paris during the century—stood in stark contrast to the civic form of the entry; one chronicler commented, "*la roy et les bourgeois de Paris allèrent au-de-vant du roy, mais ce fust bien peu de chose au regard de la puissance de ladite ville.*"[38] Charles VIII returned the ceremony to the forms of Henry VI and Charles VII. Thereafter, the Parisians and the Parlement de Paris made certain of their places in the ceremony and that in process of the entry kings were reminded of their duty to preserve the city, the kingdom, French laws, and the Parlement.

If to some degree the wave of civic processions compelled the king to act in a juridical manner by granting a hearing to the petitions brought by his subjects, and, at least by tacit gesture, to acquiesce in their requests, the king in entry had more freedom with his entourage in the royal cavalcade. When he started into the city the ranking of his following took place according to the various ways that one could be connected to the king: family or blood relatives, feudal status, military chains of command, position in the royal household, place in the administration of the kingdom, or even by the special favor of the king. As with the Parisian participants, so too with those around the king: to perform ceremonial honors was both to show one's duty and to claim one's rights and privileges. The very nature of the occasion required that each participant in the order of march elicit from those among the audience in the street an anticipation of the arrival of the king. But in calling attention to the king, each also singled out himself and his status. Women did not appear in the kings' entries, nor kings in those of queens.

The presentation of Charles VII in the entry (tab. 6.5) differed from the form prescribed by Christine de Pizan (table 6.2). First, as even a miniature portrait of the time shows, he entered in armor (fig. 6.3). The rich blue tunic with golden fleurs-de-lis, the crown, and the canopy somewhat mitigated the military aspects.[39] The canopy gave the échevins a chance to symbolically

TABLE 6.5. The Cavalcade for the Parisian Entry of Charles VII,
12 November 1437

1. 800 royal archers
2. Great and noble lords
3. Squires with
    i. Great sword with fleurs-de-lis in gold
    ii. Coat of arms on a blue velvet banner with fleurs-de-lis in gold
    iii. Giant fleurs-de-lis on a saddle on a riderless horse
    iv. Crowned helmet with fleurs-de-lis at apex carried on a baton
4. King armed on horse with blue duster
5. Dauphin Louis in silver armor
6. Charles d'Anjou, "contes de Perdriach et de La Marche"
7. Other knights and lords

show their reverence for authority and right order. In what we can not see, but know from the chronicles, the ermine-lined robe and the royal hat had ceased to be among the appurtenances. In their place, there went a riderless horse and a crowned helmet with fleurs-de-lis at the apex.[40] The fleurs-de-lis mark the Valois attention to the French royal cult. The Lancastrian kings first brought the crowned helmet to entries as a sign of conquest, but the Valois kings continued its use as a symbol of authority. Over time it came to represent the *maiestas* of the French kings, as in 1498 when it was described as the mark of imperial authority: "*Et au dessus du heaulme, au millieu de ladicte couronne, avoit une fleur de lys d'or comme empereur.*"[41] Like the change to military costume that the king wore in the entry, the appurtenances asserted the independence of the ruler from juridical limitations—as an emperor—and distanced him from the image of kingship advanced by the Parisian host for over a century of entry ceremonies, that of judge.

Traditionally, kings received the royal sword (another of the preeminent symbols of sovereign magnificence in the entry) at their coronation, and they had it carried in front of them as they left the cathedral at Reims. Christine de Pizan gave it a place of prominence in Charles V's equipage, and the English did not alter a practice already traditional in the London royal progresses. When the Valois ruler returned to Paris, a chronicler took careful notice of Charles VII's exquisite "*grande espee toute semee de fleurs de lis de fin or de orfavrerie.*"[42] Since the death of his father and during the ebb of his fortune, this sword had been carried before Charles VII as symbol of his right to the crown. Louis XI's master of the horse conveyed the royal sword in the 1461 entry, but in 1484 Charles VIII and in 1498 Louis XII had neither the royal sword nor royal robe among their appurtenances. Rather, the chivalric imperial crowned helmet announced their majesty to the crowds. Francis I returned the sword, but not the robe, to the ranks before the king.

Symbols changed or realized their potential for richer meanings, always resident in the atmosphere of the entry ceremony, in response to circumstances. Most striking of all the changes that took place in the late medieval Parisian entry ceremony was the addition of the chancellor and the royal seal to the appurtenances immediately before the king. The practice had been rehearsed in provincial entries at Rouen in 1449 and Bordeaux in 1451. At Bordeaux and elsewhere in the recovery of France, the seal and chancellor substituted for the person of the king who was absent.[43] Only in 1484 were the seal and chancellor added at Paris, but, for the rest of the history of the entry ceremony, the chancellor held the place of honor immediately before the king.

Like the changes in the forms for greeting the king by the urban processionals, the additions to the order of march before the king emphasized his might in the crowned helmet and his right in the fleurs-de-lis. The royal hat and robe of office denoting the kingly duty to justice were transferred to the symbolism of the chancellor and seal. Even if the chancellor entered in armor at Bordeaux, he followed the seal and wore the fur bonnet: the latter being a symbol first brought to the entry ceremony by the first president of the Parlement de Paris in 1431. At Bordeaux in 1451 the chancellor received the submission of the town, its expression of loyalty, its requests, and confirmed its liberties. The seal supplied the symbolic center for the juridical theater and rites of reciprocity. When the king was present in entries, he symbolically gained flexibility in assuming the military role, and he gave a suggestion of his right to rule by conquest. But justice lost little in ritual honors and gained in having the major official for justice securely placed in the entry rituals. The same principle that the parlementaires argued as a fundamental law, that is, that the Parlement of Paris as guardian of law represented "the person of the king," had symbolic statement in the entry treatment of the chancellor.[44]

The retinue of the king greatly expanded after 1431, but other than the addition of symbols of juridical kingship, most changes were of lesser importance. The growth in the royal ranks was such that the great lords continued to have places of honor, but they tended to appear because they held offices of the crown or places in the royal household, particularly after 1484. In this sense, the evolution of the entry ceremony chronicles a shift from an occasion when great lords temporarily gathered around the king in rituals marking the change of suzerains to an occasion projecting the image of a court of servants and officials who permanentlly served the needs of the king. The seal and the chancellor represented the highest duty of traditional kingship: to preserve through justice the entire "body moral" of the kingdom. All the parts of the civic and royal processions of the entry ceremony taken together represented in microcosm the union of such a body politic and moral.[45]

Finally, and briefly, note needs to be taken of how the expressions in the art of the street pageantry relate to the structure of the entry ceremony. The representations, gestures, and rhetoric of the street pageantry produced at stations along the rue St. Denis (as marked out in fig. 6.3) were playful variations inspired by the rituals that the king and Parisian corporations conducted within the entry frame. These productions strike the modern reader as the work of youthful members or even children of the leaders of the corporations and guilds—such as those who formed *abbayes de jeunesse*, the *basoches*, and the *enfants de la ville*—who in miming the acts of their elders and rulers reinforced community values and learned rules of decorum. Thus, although occasionally satires were included, the performances before kings and queens making an entry presented forms of right-rule rather than misrule.[46]

Although almost from the beginning of the ceremonial for an entry Parisians had conducted ritual greetings at St. Denis Gate, decorations and dramatic play at that place only began in 1389. It is no chance occurrence that the Parisians started occasional civic pageantry there at the time when assemblies of estates ceased to be held in conjunction with Parisian entries. The pageants assumed the voice of estates and spoke clearly to the king through their personified representatives (see tab. 6.6). Personifications of the estates appeared in 1431, perhaps in 1437, in 1461, 1483, 1491, as late as 1549. Similarly, the debut of the Parlement of Paris in the entry can be paralleled with the pageant artistry that personified and represented the role of justice in the kingdom. These representations made efforts to reach an increasing remote king in the serious play of entry artistry. The age of organized civic street pageantry developed as kings tended to free themselves from the juridical restraints imposed by institutions, rituals, and customs.

The gesture of actual corporations and officials in the extramural ceremonies found counterparts in the pageantry before the gate and elsewhere. The dominant image of the king at the Port St. Denis was that of the ruler as child. There may be some influence of the popular imagery of great lords kneeling before the Christ Child in these tableaux vivants of submission to the king. More pointedly, the representation of the king as child with his subjects as adult personifications made the statement that the new ruler depended on good counsel and trusted supporters when he took over "France," "the Lily," "Paris," or the "ship of state." Such didactic programs again balanced the necessary act of submission with instruction.[47] All along the ceremonial route, the playful guise of the street pageantry explicitly expressed the meaning of the graver rituals of the entry ceremony; one can gain a sense of the scale and subjects of these dramas from the list in table 6.4. The new patronage and censorship of Renaissance princes ended the artistic playfulness and political inventiveness of their medieval Parisian subjects. Parisian communal control of pageantry space and direct representation

TABLE 6.6. Entry Pageantry at St. Denis Gate

Entry	Central Frame	Image of the Ruler	Companion Figures	Special Features
Isabella of Bavaria (20 June 1389)	Paradise	Christ Child	Virgin Mary	Blazing Sun
Henry VI (2 Dec. 1431)	Ship		University Cathedral Bourgeois	Heart-shaped Bouquets
Charles VII (12 Nov. 1437)	Shield of France	Fleurs-de-lis	Three Angels	Shield of France
Louis XI (31 Aug. 1461)	Ship	Crowned Infant	Nobility Clergy Labor	Equity Justice
Margaret of Austria (2 June 1483)	Three-tiered Stage	Enthroned Sovereign Dauphin Regents	Nobility Clergy Merchants Labor	Royal Family
Charles VIII (5 July 1484)	Giant Lily	Crowned Infant	Peace Love Reason Justice Knowledge Mercy	Anagram Blazing Sun
Anne of Brittany (8 Feb. 1491)	Pavilion/Stage	French Goodwill Secure Alliance	Church Nobility Merchants Labor	Peace/War Hercules
Louis XII (2 July 1498)	Giant Lily	Portrait of Charles V	Nobility Wealth	Ancestral Portrait

Entry			
Anne of Brittany (20 Nov. 1504)	Giant Heart	Power / Humanity / Liberality / Fedelity	
	Sovereign Lady	Clergy / Justice / City	Loyalty / Honor
Mary Tudor (6 Nov. 1514)	Ship		
	Honor Holding Shield of France	Paris / Bacchus / Ceres	Classical Gods
Claude of France (12 May 1517)	Throne		
	Crowned Queen	Justice / Magnaminity / Prudence / Temperance / Biblical Heroines	Descending Dove with Crown
Eleonor of Austria (16 April 1531)			Peace / Concord
Henry II (16 June 1549)	Triumphal Arch		
	Gallic Hercules	Nobility / Clergy / Justice / Labor	Chains of Eloquence
	Francis I		
Charles IX (16 March 1571)	Triumphal Arch		
	Francion / Pharamond / Pepin / Charlemagne	Majesty / Fortune	Crowned Shield of France
Elizabeth of Austria (25 March 1571)	Triumphal Arch	Column of Church / Column of Empire / Gallia / Germania	Crowned Crossed Shields of France and Empire

of political thought vanished before the allegory-filled, but peopleless, arches of wood and plaster favored by new aesthetic values and a new political agenda.[48]

The medieval pageantry stations dramatized political commonplaces such as those expressed in the famous sermon of Jean Gerson on the image of true kingship. In a well-run civic government, he preached, the royal council would maintain Prudence, the nobility would provide Force, the judiciary would ensure Justice, and the people would act with Temperance. As head and symbol of the whole body, "*le Roy doibt estre assis au throne non point quelconque, mais de iustice et de equité.*"[49] In art and reality the king should be shown to make clear that "*il n'est pas personne singuliere mais est une puissance publique ordonnee pour le salut de tout le commun.*" Gerson cautioned against the dangers of flatterers who tell kings that others are beasts to do their bidding, and he warned against portraying the king in any other costume than that of justice and particularly against dressing him as a warrior. Gerson noted that he preached with "*grand franchise et liberté*" because he represented the University of Paris; as he rhetorically asked, "*l'Université ne represente elle pas tout le Royaume de France, voire tout le monde, en tant que de toutes parts viennent ou peuvent venir supposts pour acquerir doctrine et sapience?*"[50]

In the entry ceremony, other Parisians and members of the body politic found an occasion to act, or at least to play, at being a royal counsel. The specific guise of these counselors varied—including the *cerf volant* of the Parlement of Paris, *Fama* as the genius of the city, or the Three Estates—but the message was consistent: the good king ruled to preserve his subjects and he consulted them; the ideal king did not embody but rather brought to his person those whose offices completed his personality as king; the virtues necessary for preserving the common good were in a balance of power such as that visualized in the entry ceremony. The art and ritual of the entry activities clearly attest to both a public consciousness and an arrangement of institutions that emphasized reciprocity and consensus. In consideration of these expressions of their sense of right government, there can be no basis for considering the French Middle Ages weak in constitutional habits of mind and particularly fertile ground for the growth of absolutism. Contrary to arguments such as those put forth by Professor Bryce Lyon that "there was in France no balance of power, all power resided in the king,"[51] balance of power was everywhere evident. The historian's problem is to recognize how it was expressed and by whom.

THE ENTRY CEREMONY AND MEDIEVAL CONSTITUTIONALISM

The image of composite and corporate kingship reveals both the source for the metaphors and models that shaped the medieval entry into a full-scale ceremonial and the key to the symbolism of such rituals as the parlementaire processional and the chancellor's increased importance in the ceremonies. While the groups associated with the cathedral and the Hotel-de-ville marched to assure local liberties, the Parlement de Paris sought to show the continuity of the principal institution for preserving justice. The chancellor and the royal seal in the ceremony acknowledged the legal character of the reciprocal rites between king and corporations and the delicate balance of submission of subjects and recognition of privileges and liberties. Both the chancellor and the Parlement of Paris used this symbolism to remind the king and the kingdom of the great divide between the mortal, error-prone body of the king and his immortal, always just body.[52] Each particular corporation in the entry ceremony deferred to the universal obligation all had to the virtue of justice.

Paolo Emili has the earliest printed account of a king being lectured to in Paris after his return from Reims. He wrote that the eminent political thinker Gilles de Rome told his former student, Philip IV, about the ability that justice had to impart immortal qualities. Whether or not this speech in the name of the University was part of an entry activity can not be established and is not important. It did become part of entry lore after the entry became a Parisian ceremony. Gilles des Rome praised justice commenting *"ut omnia semel complectar—religionis, moderationis, fortitudinis, prudentiae, liberalitatis, justitia parens est; nec diuelli ab Rege potest, incolumi Regio nomine."*[53] The immortality of Philip's name depended on his service to justice, and he urged the new king always to keep this "queen of virtues" in his counsel, to plant its image in his soul, to fashion himself according to it, and to act as it inspired him. Although this speech referred to abstract justice, its myth became such that three hundred years later François Belleforest could comment that the speech had prompted Philip IV *"d'establir celle souveraine et Auguste cour de Parlement de Paris."*[54] At the least, the notion was in the spirit of the later symbolism of the Parlement of Paris in the entry ceremony.

The king gave his explicit assent to the ideal of juridical kingship in the entry ritual when, as a rhymed account reported, after the customary promise to the clergy, Charles VIII

> Aprés jura qu'il soustiendroit
> Les Nobles et les laboureurs
> Et les marchans, en son endroit
> Chascun, sans quelconques faveurs.
> Et non plus aux grands qu'aux mineurs,
> Il ne feroit tort n'injustice;
> Mais en tous leurs droits souteneurs
> Commettroit, pour tenir police.[55]

The jocundus adventus promise, a fourteenth-century Parisian innovation for receptions of new kings, became in the fifteenth century a stage for ceremonial innovation and constitutional statement. As early as 1437 it was popularly believed that the promise pertained to more than the clergy and that the king swore *"qu'il tendroit loyalment et bonnement tout ce que bon roy faire devoit."*[56] The promise became something like a Parisian equivalent to that of the coronation: to preserve the kingdom and its people in their rights, to render justice to all, and to protect the church and clergy. In Paris, the king even came specifically to confirm each order in its privileges.

The creation of tradition was continued in 1498 when Louis XII promised

> *qu'il entretiendroit les nobles, aussi les laboreurs, ensemble les marchans en leurs bonnes loix et coustumes anciennes, et qu'il feroit justice au petit comme au grant au garderoit son peuples des ennemys et adversaires.*[57]

The promise to the estates was on its way to becoming a prescriptive part of the entry activities. The informal-customary definitions of an entry ceremony had acquired a formal-juridical focus.

From the late fifteenth century the Parlement of Paris had experimented with a veriety of rituals to show abstract justice bound to a particular place and inststitution. To the degree that it succeeded in separating justice from the person of the king and associating it with a representative body, the Parlement of Paris made itself more directly subject to the will of the king by mediating for other legal bodies in the name of justice. At the same time, the Parlement made other groups more dependant on its patronage and favor to have their legal voice and petitions heard. This turn of events is exactly what happened to the ordinance of the medieval entry ceremony. The entry promise by the king became a matter for litigation, and sixteenth-century lawyers could even dismiss such promises when made *"du temps des guerres du novel advenement à la coronne."*[58] The strong appearance of reciprocity acted out in the rituals of the entry acquired definitions in the chambers of justice and within the contexts of kingly majesty. However, some French writers of the sixteenth century kept alive the constitutional image of the entry, particularly provincial ones, where the king bound himself directly to his promise rather than through the intermediary of justice and the Parlement. They took the fading side of the medieval entry tradition that corresponded more to the confirmations made by the new duke in the *joyeuse entrée* of Brabant.[59] Even at Paris the sixteenth- and seventeenth-century entry ceremony continued the traditional request for preservation of liberties, but its legal importance and focus were lost in the flattering orations on royal magnificence of which the request formed a small part. The medieval ceremonial had evolved as a *mise en scène* for the union of the body politic; later times transformed the staging and costuming. The setting came to take the form of architectural monuments suitable for the royal majesty. Although rather than in juridical robes the king appeared as conqueror in armor or later as *grand seigneur* in rich fashions of the day, all others in the state ceremony continued to march in robes of office.[60]

The entry ceremony as elaboration of the royal cult called attention to the divinity of the king that through allegory was always part of the atmosphere of royal ceremonies. George Chastellain well illustrates this potential in the medieval entry that was only realized in its fullness in the seventeenth century. In an *allégorie mystique* he paralleled the entry of the new king Louis XI into Paris with the birth of Christ in Bethlehem. The other participants in the entry were given guises appropriate to the analogy: the princes and lords who held *"cure et commission sur la chose publique"* were compared to the shepherds who hastened to Bethlehem *"voir ce que Dieu a fait et manifesté à leurs yeux; certes un roy nouvellement couronné, un roy produit du mot et volenté de Dieu."*[61] Notions of the divine origins of monarchy and of God's design abound in the allegory; the French peers were even labeled the new people of God and the French king *"l'enoint et le souverain christ en terre."* Like the Christ Child, the new king promised peace, social good will, and irrevocably bound all society into a harmonious whole. In the long view this rhetorical image triumphed over the juridical traditions in interpretations of the entry ceremony. Several centuries later the image of the entry was of David and Jerusalem—of Christ and paradise. Along with the demigod Hercules and the god Apollo, these images appear to be part of a revival of late antique and early medieval imagery for *adventus* ceremonies. The focus on peace and justice continued, but not the focus on distinct personalities, legal or otherwise. The ceremony in the ancien régime represented a transcendent moment and an expression of a universal truth rather than the reciprocal rites between a particular king and city. The medieval theme was of the body politic, the absolute one was concord in the state. The celebration turned to defining the king's "messianic-eschatalogical" mission, not the particulars of his government.[62] In this way, the medieval Parisian entries came to appear only as submission to a divine plan and its manifested agent. The *"joyeuse entrée"* in France ceased to be performed and one only spoke of the *"entrée royale."*

NOTES

An earlier version of this article was published in French in: *Annales: E. S. C.* 41, no. 3 (mai-juin 1986): 513–543. Thanks go to the Andrew W. Mellon Faculty Fellowship Program at Harvard University for 1984–1985 for support in writing it and to Ralph E. Giesey, Sarah Hanley, and János Bak for suggestions leading to its final form.

1. See my *The King and the City in the Parisian Royal Entry Ceremony: Politics, Ritual, and Art in the Renaissance* (Geneva, 1986), 66–98.

2. Victor Turner, *Dramas, Fields, and Metaphors: Symbolic Action in Human Society* (Ithaca, N.Y.: Cornell University Press, 1978), 43.

3. Bernard Guenée and Françoise Lehoux, *Les Entrées royale françaises de 1328 à 1515* (Paris, 1968), 7. Guenée calls attention to the importance of the two aspects in his important article, "Histoire de l'Etat en France à la fin du Moyen Age, vue par les historiens français dépuis cent ans," *Revue historique* 236, (1964): 331–360, and in translation in P. S. Lewis, ed., *The Recovery of France in the Fifteenth Century* (New York, 1972), 324–352.

4. Ernst H. Kantorowicz, "The 'King's Advent' and the Enigmatic Panels in the Doors of Santa Sabina," *Art Bulletin* 26 (1944): 207–231, and reprinted in his *Selected Studies* (Locust Valley, New York: J.J. Augustin, 1965), 37–64. Sabine MacCormack, *Art and Ceremony in Late Antiquity* (Berkeley, Los Angeles, London: University of California Press, 1981), 1–92.

5. On the principle, see Gaines Post, "A Romano-Canonical Maxim, *Quod omnes tangit*, in Bracton," *Traditio* 4 (1954): 195–252.

6. For Germany, Winfried Dotzauer has noted "Die Verweigerung oder Gewährung einer feierlichen Einholung war keine Zeremoniellenfrage, sondern eine wichtige Vorentscheidung in der Frage der Anerkennung des Herrschers, denken wir in diesem Zusammenhang an Wahlkandidaten, strittige und Gegenkönige und gebannte Herrsche, denen der Einzug verweigert werden konnte" in "Die Ankunft des Herrschers: Der fürstliche 'Einzug' in die Stadt (bis zum Ende des Alten Reichs)," *Archiv für Kulturgeschichte* 55 (1973): 259. One of the best descriptions of an early civic reception for a French king is that staged by the canons and citizens of Bruges in 1127. Louis VI and William Clitho, his candidate to replace the murdered Count of Flanders, were greeted "in sollempni processu regio more" by the clergy; in an assembly held the next day king and count swore on relics to preserve the liberties of the canons and they promised to preserve the liberties of the citizens granted by the former count. Only then did the citizens give fealty, loyalty, and homage to both king and count: Galbert de Bruges, *Histoire du Meurtre de Charles Le Bon, Comte de Flandre (1127–1128)*, introduction and notes by Henri Pirenne (Paris, 1891), chap. 55, pp. 86–89. Frederick I took great offense at such a request by the Roman citizens before his coronation in 1155: Otto of Freising, *Gesta Frederici*, lib. II, cap. 29, ed. G. Waitz (MGH. SS. rer. germ., 1912), 148 ff.

7. In other places the clergy was prominent in extramural processions, as Noël Coulet makes clear for Provence: "Les Entrées solennelles en Provence," *Ethnologie française* 7 (1977): 63–82.

8. Christine de Pizan, *Livre des fais et bonnes meurs du sage roy Charles V*, éd. S. Solente (Paris, 1936), 50–51 and "Livre de Paix" in Pizan, *Livre des fais*, appendix 5, p. 198. There is no contemporary evidence for the use of the "espée et le chappel royal" in entry ceremonies before the 1420s when Christine was writing her biography.

9. Coulet calls attention to the entry taking shape as a "rite d'honneur" ("Entrées en Province," 70) rather than in feudal obligations such as the "droit de gîte" as suggested by Guenée and Lehoux (*Entrées royales*, 9).

10. In 1437 for Charles VII's entry it was noted: "et à la entrée les bourgeois luy mirent ung ciel sur sa teste que on a la Saint Sauveur à porter Nostre-Seigneur";

Journal d'un Bourgeois de Paris, ed. Jos. Fr. Michaud and J.-J. F. Poujoulat (Paris, 1837, Nouvelle collection des mémoires, 1ᵉsérie, tome 3), 283.

11. The tax payments for 1421, 1423, and 1438 show that the most prosperous guilds carried the canopy: see Jean Favier, *Les Contribuables parisiens à la fin de la guerre de cents ans* (Geneva, 1970), 26–34.

12. On the phrase, Sarah Hanley has the last word: *The Lit de Justice of the Kings of France: Constitutional Ideology in Legend, Ritual, and Discourse* (Princeton University Press: Princeton, 1983), chap. 1, and in *Annales* 37, no. 1 (jan.–fev. 1982): 32–63.

13. Guenée and Leheux, *Entrées royales*, 50.

14. J. B. L. Crevier, *Histoire de l'Université de Paris depuis son origine jusqu'en l'année 1600* (Paris, 1761) 3: 113. The time of the University's reception with the king varied and as late as 1515 was not part of the entry ceremony.

15. See I. D. McFarlane's introduction and notes for the facsimile edition of the 1549 entry: *The Entry of Henri II into Paris, 16 June 1549* (Binghamtom, N.Y.: Medieval and Renaissance Texts and Studies; 1982).

16. Jean, Sire de Joinville, *Mémoires ou Histoire de Saint Louis*, ed. M. Gervais (Paris, 1822), 191. The route that Louis took from Reims to Paris was by way of Montlhery where the Parisians went.

17. Paul Lehugeur, *Histoire de Phillipe le Long, roi de France* (Paris, 1897), 46.

18. *Chronique parisienne anonyme de 1316 à 1339*, ed. A. Hellot, vol. II, Mémoires de la société de l'histoire de Paris et de l'Ile-de-France (Paris, 1984), 175.

19. Ibid., 137: my emphasis.

20. By the end of the thirteenth century, the legal fiction that towns possessed a juridical personality comparable to that of an individual lord was commonly accepted in France primarily, according to Charles Petit-Dutaillis, under the influence of royal office holding and the applications of Roman law; see his *Communes Françaises* (Paris, 1947), 137f.

21. In 1431 the herald, called Loyal Heart, introduced a person portraying the genius of the city in the guise of *Fama*; she was accompanied by "les anciens IX preux et IX preuses" who reminded the new Anglo-French king that "cele ville ainsi fame/ Est digne d'estre bien gouverné." In 1437 he introduced a mock battle of the seven vices with the seven virtues. In 1484 he presented the new king with the five virtues whose first letters formed an anagram for Paris (*"P"aix, "A"mour, "R"aison, "I"oye,* and *"S"urete*). See *The King and the City*, 143.

22. *Chronique des Jean II et de Charles V*, 1: 27.

23. Jean Froissart, *Oeuvres*, ed. Kervyn de Lettenhove (Brussels, 1867–1877) 9: 554 and 14: 10.

24. Guenée and Lehoux, *Entrées royales*, 65.

25. In the mid-fifteenth century the *parlementaire* families began to replace the old merchant elite in major municipal offices: from about one-fifth during the English occupation to about three-fourths of the offices during 1440–1450; see Jean Favier, "Paris, place d'affaires au XVᵉ siècle," *Annales* 28, no. 5 (Sept.–Oct. 1973): 1245–1279.

26. On the tensions of the period and the assembly, see Léon Mirot, *Les Insurrections urbaines au début de règne de Charles VI, 1380–1383* (Paris, 1905), 28–37.

27. Froissart, *Oeuvres* 10: 192–200, 497–500.

28. *Chronica di Buonaccorso Pitti* as printed in Mirot, *Insurrections urbaines*, 180, n. 5. Although the speech may be apocryphal, it both accurately represents events that followed the reception and gained a place in entry lore.

29. The entry ceremony gave structure to reconciliation after rebellion, as described with excellent illustrations in the manuscript of Jean Marot, *La Magnamine victoire du roy très crestien Loys XIIe... contre les Genevoys ses rebelles*, Paris, B.N., ms. franç., ancien fonds, 5091. Robert W. Scheller considers such works of royal propaganda during the last years of Louis XII's reign in "Gallia Cisalpine: Louis XII and Italy, 1499–1508," *Simiolus* (1984–1985): 5–60.

30. See Marcel Thibault, *Isabeau de Baviere, 1370–1405* (Paris, 1903), 109–166.

31. Political crises, religious intensity, and urban processions can quickly be related by a perusal of *"Notes historiques extraites de registres du Parlement, 1340–1640,"* Paris, Arch. Nat., U424. There was a marked increase in processions in which Parlement appeared in the period between 1411 and 1440 and then a tapering off until the period starting in the 1550s.

32. Clement de Fauquembergue, *Journal*, ed. Alexandre Tuetey (Paris, 1903, 1915) 1: 264–269.

33. Fauquembergue, *Journal* 2: 142 and *Journal d'un bourgeois de Paris*, ed. Alexandre Tuetey (Paris, 1981), 144, n. 4.

34. Guenée and Lehoux, *Entrées royales*, 61.

35. In his Parisian entry Charles VII entrusted the keys to the constable: Enguerrand de Monstelet, *Chronique*, ed. L. Douet-d'Arcq (Paris, 1857–1862) 5: 301–302.

36. The miniature reproduced by Guenée and Lehoux (*Entrées royales*) shows a different balance in the submission of Rouen. The kneeling échevin hands the keys to the king, who is on horseback and in armor, while the chancellor, who is also on horseback gestures for the submission. One of the échevins points upward to indicate a desire to rise.

37. See C. Coudevc, "L'Entrée solennelle de Louis XI à Paris" in *Mémoires de la société de l'histoire de Paris et de l'Ile-de-France* (1896) 23: 125–166.

38. Jacques du Clercq, *Mémoires*, ed. J. A. Buchon, in *Chroniques nationales françaises* (Paris, 1826) 39: 155.

39. For descriptions of the kings' costumes in entry ceremonies, see Albert Mirot and Bernare Mahieu, "Cérémonies officielles à Notre Dame en XVe siècle," in *Huitième Centenaire de Notre Dame—Congrès des 30 mai-juin, 1964* (Paris, 1967), 222–290.

40. Guenée and Lehoux, *Entrées royales*, 73. The riderless horse may have echoes of the gift that vassals made at their time of investiture according to the feudal custom of the Ile-de-France and as was practiced in Naples and other places, but no suggestion of such connections is mentioned. René Choppin—*Traité du domaine*, bk. 3, title 13, par. 11, p. 471 from *Oeuvres* (Paris, 1662)—argued that the gifts did not pertain to entries. The horse was a common gift by medieval hosts to honored guests.

41. Guenée and Lehoux, *Entrées royales*, 128. Charles VII (Monstrelet, *Chronique* 5: 305), Louis XI (Du Clercq, *Mémoires*, 153), and Charles VIII (*Entrées royales*, 110) also marched with helmets that were superimposed with a gold crown, but the accounts made no explicit connection between the symbol and imperial rights. On the symbol see Robert W. Scaheller's "Ensigns of Authority: French Royal Absolutism in the Age of Louis XII," *Simiolus* (1983–1984), 103–111 and "Imperial Themes in Art and

Literature of the Early French Renaissance: The Period of Charles VIII," *Simiolus* 12 (1981–1982), 55–63. I would add that from its appearance in the early fifteenth century the crowned helmet quickly came to be seen as a juridical symbol of the superior rights of the king.

42. Guenée and Lehoux, *Entrées royales*, 73.

43. Jean Chartier, *Chronique de Charles VIII*, ed. Auguste Vallet de Viriville (Paris, 1858) 2: 160–172 and 298–310. Scheller notes the seal in substitution for the king in the 1499 oath of fealty by Philip the Handsome: see "Ensigns of Authority," 128–134.

44. E. Maugis, *Histoire du Parlement de Paris de l'avènement des rois Valois à la mort d'Henri VI* (Paris, 1913–1916) 1: 374.

45. On the notion of a political aggregate as a "corpus morale," see Ernst Kantorowicz, *The King's Two Bodies: A Study in Mediaeval Political Theology* (Princeton, N.J. : Princeton University Press, 1957), 210–221.

46. On the actors in the street pageants, see *The King and the City*, 169–172 and 190–192.

47. See ibid., chaps. 5–9. Also, see Elie Konigson, "La Cité de la prince: premières entrées de Charles VIII (1484–1486)" and Michel Reulos, "La Place de la justice dans les fêtes et cérémonies du XVIᵉ siècle" in *Les Fêtes de la renaissance*, ed. Jean Jacquot (Paris, 1975) 3: 55–69 and 71–80. Josephe Chartrou also offers a descriptive survey of the allegorical prsonages and virtues associated with rulers in fifteenth-century entries in *Les Entrées solennelles et triomphales à la renaissance, 1484–1551* (Paris, 1928).

48. On the aesthetic revolution, see V. L. Saulnier, "L'Entrée de Henry II à Paris et la revolution poetic de 1550," *Les Fêtes de la renaissance*, ed. Jean Jacquot (Paris, 1956) 1: 3–59; see also McFarlane, *Entry of Henri II*, "Introduction."

49. Jean Gerson, *Vivat Rex* (Paris, 1559), 13–18.

50. Ibid., 10.

51. "Medieval Constitutionalism: A Balance of Power" in *Album Helen Maud Cam. Studies Presented to the International Commission for the History of Representative and Parliamentary Institutions* (Louvain, 1961) and reprinted in *Studies of West European Medieval Institutions* (London, 1978), 175.

52. On the concept, see Kantorowicz, *The King's Two Bodies*, particularly 360f. On its ritual expression, see my *The King and the City*, 55–56 and 112–115.

53. Emili Paulus, *De Rebus Gestis Francorum* (Paris, 1539), Liber VIII, fo. 165v.

54. François Belleforest, *Harangues militaires et concernant de princes, capitaines, ambassadeurs, et autres manians tant la guerre, que les affaires d'estat* (1595), 2124.

55. Guenée and Lehoux, *Entrées royales*, 116.

56. In 1460, according to Thomas Basin the coronation promise was repeated by Louis XI in his Parisian entry: *Histoire de Louis XI*, ed. Charles Samaran (Paris, 1963), 1: 26–28. Jacques du Clercq only noted that at Notre Dame Louis XI "fit le serment tel que les roys de Franche ont accoustume de faire" (*Mémoires*, 158).

57. Guenée and Lehoux, *Entrées royales*, 134.

58. Matthieu de Vauzelles, *Traicté des péages* (Lyon, 1550), 38.

59. On the subject, see my comments in "Parlementaire Political Theory in the Parisian Entry Ceremony," *Sixteenth Century Journal* 7 (1976): 15–24.

60. Karl Mösenedor, *Zeremoniell und monumentale Poesie: Die "Entrée solennelle" Ludwigs XIV. 1660 in Paris* (Berlin, 1983), 64–80.

61. George Chastellain, *Traité par form d'allégorie mystique sur l'entrée du Roy Loys en nouveau régne in Oeuvres*, Kervyn de Lettenhove (Brussels, 1865) 7: 6, 32.

62. Kantorowicz, "The 'King's Advent'," 72–74 and Mösenedor, *Zeremoniell*, 26–33.

SEVEN

A Note on Viking Age Inaugurations

Elisabeth Vestergaard

Very few details are known about rulership in the Viking Age, but there has been much speculation. In this brief note I shall try to summarize what can be gained about inauguration rites from the written sources, however scarce they may be. An analysis of rituals and social relations connected with the royal office may still provide some insights into early medieval rulership, which I should like to present as preface to and commentary on the much better-documented medieval history of Scandinavian coronations. Laws, chronicles, Snorri's Norwegian kings' sagas as well as scaldic, heroic, and mythological poetry offer some evidence on relations between king, royal office, society, and gods. It is from these aspects of the Viking Age that an inquiry into rituals of rulership should begin. In this project it is important not to assume identy of meaning or function when a cultural feature (object, institution) in one historical context resembles a cultural feature in another.

Three main approaches can be distinguished in the study of Scandinavian kingship: some focus on war kingship (Heerkönigtum), others on folk kingship, yet others on sacred kingship. The description of the war kings by Tacitus is strikingly similar to the image of kings contained in scaldic verse. Taking their cue from Tacitus, many historians aim to understand state formation in Scandinavia and other Germanic societies as based primarily on war.[1] Others concentrate on "democratic" features, emphasizing the folk king who is "taken" to the throne by all free men.[2] The third approach stresses the sacred character of the divinely descended king who bestowed fertility upon the land, who was the priest at the major sacrifices,[3] and whose relation to the gods (especially Odin) brought victory in battle.[4] I believe that, in order to gain proper understanding of Scandinavian rulership, these three characteristics should not be regarded as different types of monarchy but rather as interdependent; together they constituted the institution of kingship. The ritual surrounding the accession of kings reflects this complex character of Viking Age rulership.

The inauguration of rulers is rarely mentioned in any detail in early Scandinavian sources. The most important references are in the Swedish laws, especially in Västgöta Law and Uppland Law and in the Norwegian Hirdskrá; most informative among the sagas is Snorri Sturluson's *Heimskringla*. From the laws we know that the kings had to be "taken" at the popular gatherings at the major courts of the country. Following the taking the king was either deemed (döma) to be king or rejected (vraka).[5] This laconic description accords with the references in the Nowegian royal histories (Heimskringla) and with the narrative accounts in the Danish chronicles.[6] In order to be accepted as a candidate for the royal office, a man had to be a patrilineal member of the royal lineage whose divine origin marked him off from the rest of the population; he also had to be without physical or mental blemish. However, royal descent alone was not sufficient. It needed to be reinforced by the acclamation of free men from whom it also received its limitation for peacetime. Political power of the royal office was further limited because laws had to originate from the popular court (thing) rather than the king. In war and in relation with his *hirdmen*, the king enjoyed a position that was much less limited by the society of freemen: there he was more than first among equals, though less than fully superior to them.

The typical inauguration of a Scandinavian king proceeded as follows: fire was carried around the borders of the court site and a lawman blessed the public court as a sacred place and sacred institution where profane activities of daily life (such as fighting) were forbidden, thereby accentuating the inviolability of the court. This consecration marked off the events at the court site from the time and space of normal activity. The ritual of blessing and consecration took place whenever meetings were held at the *thingðrstaed*. Therefore events superior to social life could take place here. One may call the events in the court, in analogy to the dichotomy "communication–metacommunication," meta-events, for they were actions about actions (events) in society in order to create authority an institution above society is needed.

The next inaugural step in Sweden and Denmark was the candidate king's being led to a stone and placed upon it. The person who led him was a lawman or another high-ranking member of society. In Norway the stone was replaced by a highseat erected on top of a constructed mound,[7] and during the first part of the ritual the candidate may have been sitting on the lowest step of the mound.[8] In each Scandinavian kingdom the placing or seating of the candidate would then be followed by "the people" expressing their approval through clashing arms or raising hands.

In some instances the candidate might have been unacceptable. In such a case, he was probably removed from the stone as an act of rejection. This act implied that the person did not possess the required qualifications and faculties necessary for kingship. In the same way an already reigning ruler could be rejected, if he were found to be unsuitable for office.[9] In such cases the deposition might be followed by the sacrificial killing of the rejected king.[10]

The "taking" of a king was followed by the lawmen's judgment (dóma), whereupon the king would swear oaths to guard peace and law. According to most of the early sources the king had to go through this ritual in all the major *thing*-courts in the realm. Swedish sources record that, before entering a province, the new king had to be granted safe conduct and given hostages lest he be regarded an intruder.[11]

Since the surviving Scandinavian sources say so much less about royal accession than the coronation records of other countries, it has been common to assume that what we know is merely the tip of an iceberg. Consequently, it has been suggested that other rites were also performed and that the king may have received insignia, at least a helmet, a sword, or a shield, even if we have no evidence on these. However, this assumption cannot be validated from any available source. In contrast, I do not consider our knowledge of Viking Age inaugurations deficient, but rather I believe that we do know most of what transpired. One of my reasons for this belief is that in the oldest literature, in the laws, and in the chronicles the only expression used is that "then he was taken king." This is particularly significant, because the same sources describe other rituals quite extensively.[12] Hence, I propose that the placing of the future ruler, with the consent of the people, upon the stone or in the highseat endowed him with regal qualities and royal power. No other ritual was necessary for granting the qualities that belonged to the seated person.

Two examples from literature supply so explicit analogies that I risk to adduce them for the understanding of Scandinavian royal inauguration. The first is in the mythological poem *Fór Scírnis* from the *Poetic Edda*, the second from Snorri's *Haraldz saga ins Hárfagra*. In the eddic poem it is recounted that the god Frey once sat down on the mighty Odin's chair, *Hliðskiálf*, and was immediately able to look into all the worlds. In the world of giants, *Iǫtunheim*, he saw a beautiful girl with whom he fell in love.[13] The mere act of placing himself on the chair of Odin made Frey acquire the faculties of Odin; no further ritual was required. The act itself endowed the one seated on the mighty god's seat with magic power and divine qualities. In the saga we read of King Harald Fairhair fighting minor kings in order to become the supreme ruler of Norway. King Hrollaug of Naumdælafylki had built a mound with a highseat on its summit. Upon hearing that King Harald was approaching with an army, Hrollaug sat down on the highseat on the mound. He then tumbled to the foot of the mound and named himself "earl." Thereafter he went to King Harald and handed over his realm to him.[14] By tumbling down the mound and by assuming the non-royal title of earl, Hrollaug imitated the rejection rite and thus was able to hand over his land to the king. By this act he avoided a defeat, for his land had no longer a king, and Hrollaug could become a retainer of King Harald. Just as placing on the highseat makes a king, so leaving it puts an end of kingship, without any further ritual.

Historians have assumed the existence of more elaborate Scandinavian accession rituals because they started out from the rites introduced to Scandinavia after its conversion to Christianity. Erich Hoffmann, for example, believes that "before their conversion Norwegian Kings did not have crowns, but golden helmets."[15] True, a saga relates that King Hákon the Good was easily recognized by his golden helmet,[16] but this statement does not imply that the king's helmet of gold had a symbolic significance comparable to that of medieval crowns. In the saga episode referred to here, the golden helmet has an epic function. His helmet, glittering in the sunshine, together with his unusual height, made the king highly visible on the battlefield; to reduce his vulnerability as a target to the enemy, Hákon's men covered the king's helmet. The golden helmet cannot be interpreted as a distinct object belonging to Norse kings as rulers, that is, a precursor of crowns. Rather the splendid headgear is a reference to the heroic qualities of the king. When mentioned in eddic or epic poetry, the golden helmet is a symbolic statement: kings, and heroes, are portrayed with golden armor—helmet, sword, shield, or chainmail. Norse descriptions of hoards contain usually such items, in contrast to continental ones, for example, that in the *Nibelungenlied*, where treasures of gold and gems are listed in general, rather than specific pieces.[17] When a person is said to wear golden equipment, we know that he is a great hero, or a mighty king, or, most likely, both.

Although medieval kings received crowns, we ought not project their existence back into the Viking Age; there is no evidence for their presence in scaldic, heroic, and mythological poetry, nor in sagas and chronicles. Crowns, helmets, scepters, and rods cannot be investigated without taking into account the political and symbolic system to which they belong and without considering the transformations that such systems may undergo. Insignia that belong to the royal office are not mentioned in any source from the Viking Age. Nor do the gods, prototypes of the ruler, wear insignia. Insignia symbolize an authority derived from outside society, whereas the "taking" signifies an authority granted by society itself. Hence, insignia belong to the Christian Middle Ages and not to Viking times.

To summarize, with regard to leadership and power, Scandinavian societies were in a way "primitive" until the eleventh or twelfth century; only in a subsequent period was the "primitive" political order transformed into a state in which the king came to be separated from the society of free men. The rulers of the Viking Age were persons of royal descent who were "taken" kings by popular courts and placed upon a stone or highseat. They were both the embodiment of society and agents who stood outside society. The kings were given authority to fulfill a number of functions: they were mediators of relationships with external forces whether human or divine (enemies, bad harvest, chaos) and they were guarantors of peace and social order. However, they did not have power over their seats. Kings could be removed, killed, or sacrificed, should they fail. The king was simultaneously placed above society and kept as its hostage. To put it in terms of social interaction: insiders placed an outsider outside society as a protection against threats from without. The person and the office were distinct entities since, despite the taking, it was yet undecided whether the person would fit the office. Society elevated one of its members to a position, but would deprive him of this authority if he did not suit the office or if he should transgress the limits of his authority by using it to further his private interests as a member of society. Society was the end, the king was its means. With civilization and statehood, the source of royal authority and legitimacy shifted from the inside to the outside; the king became *rex Dei gratia* and society lost control over the king and his office. The state became the end, the society the means.[18]

Although the institution of kingship existed both in prefeudal and semifeudal Scandinavian societies, as well as in the feudal states of Europe, there is a great difference between the meaning of kingship in pagan Scandinavia and Christian societies. Therefore, attempts to trace the rituals and insignia of medieval coronation back to pre-Christian Scandinavia are unwarranted. The traditions that constituted the inaugural ceremonies of medieval Scandinavia were almost entirely of foreign origin, introduced mainly by the Church.[19] Viking Age inauguration—the taking, the seating, and the adjudgment of the king—was, in spite of its simplicity, a ritual as adequate to its social context as was the Christian coronation to its own milieu.

NOTES

1. W. S. Schlesinger, "Über germanisches Heerkönigtum," in *Das Königtum: Seine geistigen und rechtlichen Grundlagen* ed. Th. Mayer, (Vorträge und Forschungen 3, 1955; reprinted Sigmaringen, 1973), 105–141. Based on the results of excavations of Danish military installations (e.g., in Trelleborg) during the past decades, A. E. Christensen, *Vikingetidens Danmark* (Copenhagen, 1977), stresses the military strength and power of the kings.

2. This point of view, which regarded the *thing* and the royal "election" as democratic institutions was prevalent until the 1960s; see, e.g., Hal Koch, *Af Folkets Saga. Dansk Daad* (Copenhagen, 1941); A. E. Christensen, *Kongemagt o Aristokrati* (Copenhagen, 1945; reprinted 1968).

3. O. Höfler, *Germanisches Sakralkönigtum* (Tübingen, 1952); E. Hoffmann, *Die heiligen Könige bei den Angelsachssen* (Neumünster, 1975); E. Hoffmann, *Königserhebung und Thronfolgeordnung in Dänemark bis zum Ausgang des Mittelalters* (Berlin, 1976). J. Fleck, in "Konr-óttar-Geirroðr: A Knowledge Criterion for Succession to the Germanic Sacred Kingship," *Scandinavian Studies* 42 (1970): 41 ff., argues that ritual numinous education (such as runic knowledge) was decisive in succession; see also his

"The 'Knowledge-Criterion' in the Grímnismál: The Case Against 'Shamanism,'" *Arkiv för Nordisk Filologi* 85 (1971): 58–59.

4. Some scholars attempt to combine these approaches; Hoffmann, *Königserhebung*, 7, argues that folk-kingship and war-kingship were successive stages and that the transition took place during the age of the *Völkerwanderung*.

5. See Konungabalken 1–3, in "Upplandslagen," *Svenska Landskaplager* 1 (Stockholm, 1933); Rättegangsbalken 1, in "Äldre Västgötalagan," *Landskapslager*, ed. Å. Holmbäck and E. Wessén, vol. 3 (Stockholm, 1939). "Hirdskrá," chap. 5 in *Norges Gamle Love IV* (Christiania 1846–1895), R. Keyser and P. A. Munch, eds.

6. See, e.g., Saxo Grammaticus, *Gesta Danorum*, ed. F. Winkel Horn (Copenhagen, 1898, reprinted 1975); *Sven Aggesøn historiske skrifter*, ed. M. C. Gertz (Copenhagen, 1916–1917); Adam of Bremen, *Gesta Hammaburgensis ecclesiae pontificum*, ed. C. L. Henriksen (Copenhagen, 1968); Rimbert, *Vita Anskarii*, ed. P. A. Fenger (Copenhagen, 1926).

7. One of the most elaborate descriptions of Norwegian inauguration is found in Snorri Sturluson, "Haraldz saga ins hárfagra," *Heimskringla*, ed. F. Jonsson (Copenhagen, 1911), 45 ff. This corresponds with the rules of private inheritance found in the provincial law, the *Gulathingslovi*, section 115: "Now a man is dead. The heir has to place himself in the highseat." See also A. Taranger, "Om kongevalg i Norge i Sagatiden," *Historisk Tidsskrift* (Oslo, 1934–1936) 30: 120–124. However, we are unable to date when the change from the stone to the highseat took place nor do we have reliable sources on the details.

8. Snorri, "Haraldz saga," 45.

9. As consequence of a long period of bad harvests and famine the Danish king Oluf I Hunger (1086–1095) had to leave office and was succeeded by his brother Erik the Good.

10. See, e.g., Chaps. 15 and 43 of "Ynglinga saga" in the *Heimskringla*, ed. F. Jonsson (Copenhagen, 1911), 12–13, 31.

11. See, e.g., *Upplandlagen enligt Cod. Holm. B 199 och 1607 Års Utgåva*, ed. S. Henning (Uppsala, 1967), 59; G. Hasselberg, "Eriksgata," in *Kulturhistorisk Leksikon for Nordisk Middelalder* (Copenhagen-Stockholm-Oslo, 1959) 4: 22–27.

12. Many references are found, among others, to *blót*, that is "worship," often including sacrifice; for example in *Landnámabók*, ed J. Benediktsson (Reykjavik, 1968, Ízlenzk Fornrit 1), 37, 42 124–126, 163–164, 358. The list could be easily continued.

13. G. Neckel, ed., *Edda. Die Lieder des Codex Regius nebst verwandten Denkmälern*; 5th ed., ed. H. Kuhn (Heidelberg, 1983), 69–70.

14. See above, n. 8

15. See Erich Hoffman in this volume.

16. "Uphaf sogu hákonar góða," chaps. 30–31, *Heimskringla* (as n. 10), 88–90.

17. E. Vestergaard, "The perpetual reconstruction of the past," in *Archaeology as Long-Term History*, ed., Ian Hodder (Cambridge, 1987), 65 f.

18. T. A. Vestergaard, "On Kinship Theory, Clocks, and Steamengines: The Problem of Complex Structures," in *The Future of Structrualism*, ed. J. Osten and A. de Ruijter (Göttingen, 1983), 444–446.

19. See Erich Hoffman in this volume.

EIGHT

Coronation and Coronation Ordines in Medieval Scandinavia

Erich Hoffmann

The Christianization of Scandinavia in the tenth and eleventh centuries helped stabilize royal power in the European North.[1] The king "by the Grace of God"[2] could now regard his office as granted from above; he acquired a legal status that allowed him to become more independent of the popular *thingar* dominated by the great men of the realm. It is not surprising that in all three Nordic kingdoms the Western European practices of anointing and crowning were introduced in addition to traditional and newly developed secular acts of accession. Henceforth only one who had undergone the sacred rites of legitimation was regarded a true king, just as in the rest of Europe.

However, in contrast to the countries to the south, no medieval coronation ordo has come down to us from any of the Scandinavian kingdoms. The present study is an attempt to reconstruct the medieval inaugural rites from scattered pieces of evidence plus the first Protestant coronation ordines in each of the Scandinavian kingdoms.

NORWAY

The earliest Christian royal consecration in Northern Europe was celebrated in Norway.[3] Victorious at the end of a long period of succession struggles, the *jarl* Erling wished to secure the throne for his minor son through sacral legitimation, for Magnus (1162–1184) was related to the royal dynasty only on the female line, not sufficient in the traditional Nordic view. In alliance with the reform-minded archbishop of Trondheim, Eystein,[4] Erling arranged for an ecclesiastical consecration that would raise his son above all other claimants. Magnus was crowned in Bergen in 1163 (or 1164). We know nothing about the procedure or the insignia, only that a law was passed on this occasion, which reserved the right of succession essentially to the oldest legitimate son of Magnus's line and secured considerable influence to the bishops in testing the suitability of each candidate to the throne. Snorri Sturlusson,[5] the chronicler of Norwegian kings, was more interested in the details of the banquet than in the coronation about which he records only that the king was "consecrated" by Archbishop Eystein and five of his suffragans and that the papal legate, who came to negotiate about Norway's obedience to Pope Alexander III, was also present. It is fair to assume that "consecration" implied crowning, anointing, and investiture with other regalia.

However, we know the text of the coronation oath sworn by Magnus,[6] and this is of great value for the reconstruction of medieval coronations. The king promised to be *obediens* and *fidelis* to the Roman Church, acknowledged the papacy of Alexander, and confirmed the arrangements negotiated a few years before with the papal legate Nicholas Breakspeare (later Pope Adrian IV) about the liberties of the church in Norway and the payment of Peter's Pence.[7] After the usual obligations about doing justice to church, clergy, high and low, rich and poor, and above all widows and orphans, a rather unusual clause was added that all this was to be done *secundum patrias leges* and also according to Canon Law. Finally, the king bound himself to demand nothing from the realm of Norway and the church of Trondheim that contradicted divine and human justice or was against the canons of the church.[8] This oath was typical of such professions and specific obligations to the Church which Archbishop Eystein was able to impose on the king in return for political support, but there is also a nod to the traditional laws of the land. The obedience to Rome meant, in the given situation, Magnus's adherence to Alexander III as the legitimate pope and cannot be construed, as Holtzmann argued, as a feudal oath "since no fief is named or implied in the promise."[9] These features lend the oath a certain "singularity": it was clearly formulated for this very occasion. Thus it cannot be used for speculating about the possible ordo used at Magnus's coronation and its probable models. Yet, certain well-known formulations can be recognized in it, including definite hints at the type of *professio* which German kings spoke during their coronations from the twelfth century on.[10]

Either immediately at the coronation in Bergen or, according to other scholars a few years later, Magnus issued a charter for the cathedral church of Trondheim, where St. Olaf was buried, in which he commended his realm to the saint, the ancestor of the royal dynasty, and received it from him as a fief.[11] The connection to the dynastic saint was an additional means for strengthening Magnus's hold on the throne. However, Magnus fell in battle against the pretender Sverre, who followed him on the throne (1177/1184–1202). He, in turn, was anxious to maintain the *honor* of the king vis-à-vis the Church and the papacy[12] and intended to recover the legal advantages acquired by the Church at the foundation of the metropolitan see of Trondheim in 1153 on the prodding of Cardinal Breakspeare and then at the coronation of Magnus. This attempt at reducing ecclesiastical rights led to an open conflict with Archbishop Eirik, whereupon the latter left the country. Yet Sverre, whose royal descent was not beyond doubt, needed sacral legitimation. Since the archbishop refused to crown him, he had to ask the bishop of Oslo to take his place. This coronation in 1194 was also held in Bergen.[13] The Sverre-Saga only records that the king was consecrated and that the main actor was Bishop Nicholas. "Consecration" probably also included anointing, just as in Magnus's case.

The conflict between Sverre and the party of the bishops, which elected its own kings, continued even after the king's death. None of the kings of the two competing parties was ever crowned. Only Sverre's grandson, Haakon Haakonson (1217–1264), succeeded in restoring peace in the realm. His coronation was also intended to enhance his right to the throne, since his birth was illegitimate. In order to win the king's alliance against Emperor Frederick II, Pope Innocent IV granted him dispensation in 1246 and sent William, Cardinal of Sabina, to crown Haakon and have him swear the oath of Magnus.[14] But the king refused to do so. He wanted to promise only that the Church and her servants shall enjoy such rights as they do in countries "in which both holy Church and crown have their freedom and honour," but he did not want to diminish his rights and those of his successors. Finally the cardinal accepted the compromise. At this point one wonders whether the promises Haakon gave were identical with those contained in the *professio* of German kings. If that was so—as suggested by the strong textual resemblances between the oath recorded for Erik Magnusson[15] and the professio of German coronations—then the coronation ordo used at this occasion might have been liturgically dependent on the German one. Haakon's coronation[16] was held on St. Olaf's Day (28 July) 1247 at the largest settlement of the country and the center of the kingship, in Bergen. Unfortunately, Sturla Thórdarson, author of the Haakons-Saga, was mainly interested in the pomp and circumstance and not in liturgical details. Yet we learn from him about the coronation procession and the Norwegian royal insignia. The festive procession included the king's bodyguard (i.e., the immediate retinue), the *sysselmenn* (royal servitors), *skutelsveiner* (table knaves), and those magnates whom the Norwegians regarded as "barons" (lendmenn). Three of the lendmenn carried a table top on which the dress and personal jewels of the king were laid out. The insignia proper were carried by members of the royal family and other high officeholders. Haakon's illegitimate son Sigurd, who according to the new perceptions of the age was not eligible to inherit the throne, and Munan Biskupsson carried royal scepters of silver. The one had a golden cross, the other a golden eagle on its top. Haakon's legitimate son, Haakon, already chosen as coregent, carried the crown, and a nephew of one of King Haakon's predecessors, the sword. The archbishop and two of his suffragans accompanied the king, followed by the other bishops, abbots, and clergy. With the response *Ecce mitto angelum* the procession entered the church. The cardinal legate and two bishops received the king and led him to the altar "whereupon Mass was sung and the coronation performed in the usual way" writes the author of the saga. The "usual way" is thus the only reference to the form and procedure of the crowning. It was obviously the ordo used at the preceding coronations of Magnus and Sverre, about which as noted, we also have no detailed knowledge.

Still, we have a good description of the insignia, and it is worth discussing them at some length. Before their conversion Norwegian kings did not have crowns but golden helmets[17] just as indicated by the Edgar-ordo for Anglo-Saxon England. In his last days the first Christian king, Haakon the Good, still wore such a helmet in the battle of Fitjar (ca. 961).[18] However, the crown might have been introduced to Norway even before the coronation of Magnus Erlingsson. A contemporary stone sculpture of King Eystein Magnusson (1103–1123) from Munkeliv Abbey shows him clearly with a crown on his head, a wide ring-diadem adorned with four crosses.[19] The custom of wearing a crown seems to have prevailed in the Scandinavian kingdoms, just as in the Eastern Frankish-German realm[20] even before the introduction of Christian coronations. Two scepters and a sword are mentioned in the royal procession. The latter is part of the regalia in all Western and Central European kingdoms. The two scepters are reminiscent of the two rods of kingship mentioned by Widukind of Corvey at the 936 coronation of Otto I:[21] *sceptrum* and *baculus* or *virga*. The former may have been derived from Roman, the latter from Germanic traditions, but both symbolized the king's function as judge. Although Sturla Thórdarson does not describe the two scepters, a charter of 1340 containing the inventory of the royal treasures at Castle Bohus gives a hint: *unum ceptrum cum uno rikiswand in quinque partibus*.[22] I agree with Kallström[23] who reads this as a reference to both scepters: a *(s)ceptrum* and a "wand of the realm" which could be taken into five parts, hence a longish rod, a *baculus*. The two signs on the two scepters, cross and eagle, were, of course widespread symbols of rulership all across Europe.

To secure the smooth succession, Haakon had his son, Magnus Lagaböter (1263–1280), elected as coregent and also crowned (on 14 September 1261).[24] Sturla mentions only royal garments and crown and sword as insignia, but it is unlikely that scepter and staff (baculus), as mentioned in the charter quoted above, would not have belonged to them. For Magnus's son, Erik (1280–1299), we have once again the text of the coronation oath,[25] which he swore on 25 July 1280 with his hands on a Gospel-book, at his coronation in Bergen. Of the ceremonies we know only that they included coronation and anointing. The charter containing the oath was the result of a quarrel between the king and the archbishop who seemed to have tried to reintroduce the oath of Magnus Erlingsson; the conflict ended in a compromise formulation, put down in writing for future occasions.

The text of the royal oath contains significant, partially verbatim, parallels to the professio of the German ordo of the twelfth century.[26] However, it is shorter, omitting some parts and thus leaving space for an addition in which the king promises to abolish evil laws and adverse customs, particularly against the freedom of the church (malas leges et consuetudines perversas precipue contra ecclesie libertatem) and to issue, with the counsel of his *fideles* new and good laws. Clearly, these were matters the archbishop wanted to have included in order to secure rights to clerical jurisdiction acquired from Magnus Lagaböter in 1277. The strong dependency of the oath on the German ordo's professio suggests that other parts of the ordo may have also been modeled on German precedent. If this was so, it is possible that parts of the German ordo had already been used both in 1247 and 1261, perhaps with an oath that was quite similar to the continental one.

Erik's oath of 1280 did not, however, become a model. A law about succession and wardship, issued by his brother and successor, King Haakon V (1299–1319), refers to an oath that does not seem to be that of his predecessor. King Haakon wrote that he had promised God at his consecration to hold the laws that were established by St. Olaf and observed by his legitimate successors. These words suggest, instead, an oath that was influenced by the secular oath of Haakon Haakonson's law on succession of 1260[27] and not the German ordo's professio.

Although the sources on the twelfth- and thirteenth-century coronations prove to be laconic, they still contain more than those for the later Middle Ages, which merely record that a king was crowned, occasionally adding the name of the *coronator* and the place of the event. Under Haakon V, who as "duke" had been virtual coregent with his brother, the center of royal power shifted to the south. His coronation may even have been held in Oslo.[28] With him the royal dynasty died out in the male line. His successor, the grandson of Haakon, Magnus Eriksson (1319–1374) was also King of Sweden. Magnus was crowned in 1336 in Stockholm, apparently for both realms; he seems to have worn the Norwegian crown for the first time at a diet in Oslo[29] in 1377. A Swedish source names the archbishop of Uppsala as coronator,[30] but the Lübeck Council's Chronicle (Ratschronik) reports that the king was crowned by the bishop of Dorpat.[31] If that is correct, it is possible that the choice of a "third party" was intended to avoid offending the Norwegians, even if Magnus's main interest remained Sweden. For his son, Haakon VI of Norway (also of Sweden as coregent in 1343 and 1355 and king from 1374–1380) no reports survive about a coronation. This silence may be due to the dearth of sources during the great plague after 1349. Haakon's son, Olaf (1380–1386), died uncrowned, still as a youth. His mother, the great Margaret (regent 1376/1387–1412), who had governed Norway and Denmark for him, now became regent of both countries and acquired Sweden as well.[32] She secured the throne of all three kingdoms for her great-nephew Eric of Pomerania and for a while served as governor in his name. Finally she succeeded in uniting the three northern kingdoms and established a joint coronation ceremony in Kalmar.[33] The king of the Union was crowned conjointly by the Swedish and Danish archbishop, while the Norwegian bishops were absent, with the exception of that of the Faroe Islands. Whether they stayed home because the trip over sea was too dangerous in waters infested by pirates or because they believed that a Norwegian king, an heir to St. Olaf, had to be crowned on Norwegian soil cannot be decided.

No separate Norwegian king was crowned from the time of Eric of Pomerania until the early twentieth century.[34] Christopher III, king of the Union, was crowned in Oslo in 1442 by the archbishop.[35] After his death a struggle broke out between the kings of Sweden and of Denmark for the throne of Norway: both were crowned in Trondheim, Karl Knutsson in 1449, his adversary Christian, who finally won, in 1450.[36] The coronation of Christian's son, Hans, was also in Trondheim (1483), but that of Christian II was moved back to Oslo in 1514.[37] The coronator was always the incumbent metropolitan of Trondheim, and each of the rival kings may have chosen his church in order to win this influential magnate, Archbishop Aslak Bolt, for his cause. Also, both embattled rulers may have found it useful to be consecrated over the grave of St. Olaf, *rex perpetuus Norvegiae*.[38]

In summary then, while the medieval coronation ordo most likely used in Norway resembled the German ordo as developed in the twelfth century, the insignia point to other sources. Besides the most widespread signs of rulership, the sword and the crown, the king was invested as in France and England with two staffs. The absence of an orb parallels French usage. Seals and coins display the kings of Norway with the insignia of their consecration: crown, sword, scepter. But these images are not reliable witnesses, for they usually follow foreign models or pictorial conventions and stylistic fashions.[39] "Correct" insignia, special objects that were to be used at every coronation, were not established in Norway. The regalia were either made for each occasion or older ones used. Neither did a "correct" place for coronations exist, even though it would have been logical for Christ Church in Trondheim, cathedral of the archdiocese and burial site of St. Olaf, to become such a place. In most cases Bergen and later Oslo, centers of royal power and preferential residences of the kings, were chosen for coronations. In three exceptional cases particular reasons suggested the choice of Trondheim. However, the position of the archbishop of Trondheim as coronator in Norway was virtually unchallenged throughout history.

As for the queens, we know only about the wives of Haakon Haakonson and Magnus Lagaböter, who were crowned simultaneously with their husbands.[40] Sverre, Christian I, Karl Knutsson, and Hans were also married at the time of their coronations. Thus their wives may have been crowned together with them. All the other kings married only after their consecrations. There is, unfortunately, no evidence available on the form of the queen's coronation in Norway.

DENMARK

In Denmark[41] King Waldemar I (1154/1157–1182) replaced the kinship-based claims of all male members of the royal house with the rights of the firstborn legitimate son of the Waldemarian line. Following Western and Central European custom, he designated his son Knut (VI) as coregent in order to avoid future succession struggles. The electors had been until the fourteenth century the members of the Danehof, all nobles of the realm as the king's vassals. Then the royal council, representative of the high aristocracy, took their place and the approval of the original electoral bodies, the *landesthingar*, was reduced to mere acclamation. In this process the sacral legitimation of the Waldemarian line, expressed in the simultaneous canonization of Waldemar's father, Knut Lavard, and the crowning[42] and anointing[43] of his seven-year-old son and coregent, Knut VI, on 25 June 1170, played a decisive role. This first Danish coronation was, just like the earliest Norwegian one, the result of a compromise,[44] in this case between Archbishop Eskil of Lund and the king, who in return for his son's coronation declared his obedience to Pope Alexander III. The right to crown a king in Denmark remained till the end of the Middle Ages with the archbishops of Lund,[45] though there were a few exceptions.[46]

A definite site for coronation did not develop in medieval Denmark. Despite the impressive festivities at Ringsted no king was again crowned there even though the cult of Knut Lavard remained important for the dynasty. The cathedral of Lund was chosen for the coronation of Waldemar II (1202)[47] and of Erik Menved (1286).[48] Perhaps it was also here that Erik Ploughpenny (1231) and Abel (1250), for whom no coronation place is recorded, were crowned.[49] Waldemar III (1218) was crowned in Schleswig,[50] Erik Glipping (1259) in Viborg,[51] Christopher II, together with his son and coregent Erik (1324), in Vordingborg,[52] and Christopher III (1443) in Ripen.[53] The late medieval rulers from the Oldenburg dynasty (Christian I in 1448; Hans in 1483; Christian II in 1512; Frederik I in 1524) all chose Copenhagen, the residence of the kings of Denmark[54] since the times of Eric of Pomerania. Thus, as far as one can judge, the coronation took place wherever the king happened to be, but—with the sole exception of the important castle of Vordingborg—always at an episcopal see. The later medieval practice of holding the coronation at the main residence parallels the Norwegian practice of earlier centuries. The coronation of the Union king, Eric of Pomerania, in Kalmar in 1397[55] was a special case for Denmark as well.

From 1170 all kings of Denmark were crowned with the exception of four: Waldemar III, the king placed on the throne by the count of Holstein; Gerhard III, who resigned after three years; Waldemar IV (1340–1375), who decided to forego the ecclesiastical consecration probably because of opposition to the tradition;[56] and his grandson Olaf, who died in 1387, before coming of age.[57] By that time it was considered necessary in Scandinavia for the king to be of age for his coronation. Earlier in the mid-thirteenth century several kings were crowned as minors since only the coronation secured their accession in a time of unsettled inheritance patterns.[58] We may assume that the spouses of the kings were crowned with their husbands, even though explicit reference is made only to the coronations of Queen Mechtild, the wife of Abel in 1250; Margarethe Sambiria the wife of Christopher I in 1252; and Christina, the wife of Hans in 1481.[59] Just as for Norway, we may assume that Danish kings already had some royal insignia, probably a golden helmet, before the coronation of 1170.[60]

No medieval coronation ordo is known from Denmark. The earliest references to details can be found in a festive song (*Carmen*)[61] and a notarial instrument[62] on the coronation of King Christopher III on New Year's Day 1443 in the cathedral church of Ripen. In contrast to his predecessor and uncle on the mother's side (Eric of Pomerania), he was inaugurated by secular acts and ecclesiastically consecrated in every one of his three kingdoms even though he was styled *archirex* by Archbishop Hans Laxman at his Danish one.[63] The two surviving sources on the events of 1443 record a fair number of details of a late medieval Danish coronation.

The complete order for the first Protestant coronation, that of Christian III and his wife Dorothea on 12 August 1537 in St. Mary's in Copenhagen, is so detailed that it can be used to reconstruct medieval ceremonies for which the records are lost.[64] In this ordo new and old ideas and rituals are fused. Large parts of the text, written by the reformer Bugenhagen, reflect the new Lutheran spirit. They include appropriate sermons and prayers and reflect clearly the intended transformation of the mass. On the other hand, the anointing, crowning, and the presentation of the regalia seem to follow long-standing traditions. These two coronation reports, complementing each other, offer sufficient basis for the reconstruction of a late medieval Danish coronation.

In the procession and during the ceremonies the insignia were carried by high dignitaries and displayed for the public. In 1443 these offices were performed by Duke Adolf VIII of Schleswig and three visiting German princes, Dukes William of Brunswick, Waltmar of Silesia, and Frederick of Bavaria.[65] The rule, however, was, as reflected in the reports of 1537 and later, that the main officers of the royal council, the chamberlain, marshall, and chancellor, carried the regalia.[66] In both cases crown, scepter, orb, and sword are listed.[67] In 1537 the queen was invested only with crown and scepter.[68] These, too, were carried by members of the council. In 1443 King Christopher was still unmarried; he did not wear a royal mantle for the oath but only dalmatic and pluvial. In 1537 the king and queen entered St. Mary's Church in Copenhagen not in royal, but in "princely" or "knightly" attire and were received by Bugenhagen who wore *alba* and *pallium*. The royal couple was followed by the councillors who deposited the insignia on the altar. The ordo prescribed the sequence that followed as sermon, prayer, epistle, and the Lord's Prayer. The theological contents of these liturgical elements were purely Lutheran, hence they are of no interest for the reconstruction of the pre-Reformation ordo.

After the *Pater noster* the councillors[69] led the king to a chair in front of the altar, while *Veni sancte spiritus* was sung. The councillors, as "representatives of the realm"—a position they had claimed after the death of Waldemar IV in 1375 and solidified after the fall of Eric of Pomerania in 1438—asked the *ordinator* Bugenhagen to consecrate Christian III. The pastor appealed to the king to lead a good government and to care for peace and prosperity, to protect the church and the new Lutheran faith, to support schools, and to aid the poor. The king swore an oath to perform these duties. Parts of this oath, the protection of church and the poor and the promise to preserve the rights of his *fideles*, that is, the nobility, are reminiscent of medieval formulations. The oath was taken on the New Testament, as could be expected in a Lutheran ceremony. The place of the oath in the ordo, before anointing and coronation, was apparently an innovation. In 1443 Christopher III swore the oath, as was usual at medieval coronations, after the consecration and the reception of the insignia.[70] This change in the sequence can be easily explained. In the German ordo of 1273,[71] even in the older Mainz ordo of 961,[72] this spot was occupied by the *scrutinium*, questions addressed to the king about his intentions to reign justly, protect churches, widows, and orphans, and so on, to which the king replied repeatedly: *volo*. The second explicit and more significant oath, the professio, was introduced in the German ordo of 1273 at the end of all the festive acts, after coronation and anointing. According to the notarial record of 1443,[73] this was also the practice at medieval Danish coronations. In 1537, however, the two sets of promises, scrutinium and professio, were united[74] and placed at the head of the ceremonies, where in the Middle Ages the questions and answers of the scrutinium had been.[75]

The king's oath was followed by that of the queen after the councillors had asked the ordinator to crown and anoint her. This step may have also been inherited from the medieval order. In contrast to the German ordo of 1273, in 1537 only an additional collect and the litany were included at this point. The two prostrations of the king before the altar and the appropriate *benedictio* were left out of the Lutheran ceremony. The anointing,[76] naturally before the coronation, was done with the thumb of the right hand on the lower right arm and between the shoulders of the kneeling king. He was not anointed on the head, no more than was the queen of Christian II in 1515—before the Reformation! Since kings and queens were usually anointed in the same fashion, we may assume that this manner of anointing was the practice in medieval Denmark. Thus the anointing differed from that of the German kings, but resembled that of the emperor in Rome, in which the papacy was anxious to differentiate between clerical unction and imperial anointing.[77] If this feature was borrowed in Denmark from the imperial ordo and the *Pontificale Romanum*, it is likely that medieval kings were also anointed with the oil of catechumenes and not with chrism, just as in Rome. The queen was anointed in 1537 in the same way as her husband, just as in 1515.

After the sacring, king and queen retired to a tent prepared for this purpose where they were dressed in royal attire. The mantle was, therefore, not used in the ceremony of investment with the insignia. Returning to the church, the royal couple listened to the first of the main sermons. The ordinator donned the chasuble before the mass, and Kyrie and Gloria were sung. After another collect and the reading of the Epistle the investiture with regalia began.

The king, kneeling before the altar, received the naked sword from the ordinator into his right hand, with words that resemble the appropriate prayer in the German ordo. He then handed the weapon to the marshal, who sheathed it and returned it to the ordinator. Thereupon he girded the king with the sword. This ritual was different from the German one in which the king girded himself. Now the king drew the sword from its sheath and swung it in the four cardinal directions. The coronation followed, in 1537 apparently of a still kneeling king. The royal councillors helped to place the crown on the king's head, as had been usual at least since the coronation of King Hans in 1483.[78] It was also recorded for 1514,[79] 1537,[80] and several subsequent early modern coronations.[81] The magnates either actually touched the crown while it was being placed on the king's head or at least symbolically extended their hands towards it. The reception of this practice from late medieval England and France suggests the rising constitutional importance of the royal council, which thus demonstrated a status similar to that of the peers of the realm. Since 1376 the council had claimed the right to elect the king, and at least since the fall of Eric of Pomerania this right was taken for granted.

Still kneeling, the king now received the scepter and the orb, which he passed on to the councillors in charge of each of them. This was the place for the royal oath in the medieval German[82] and most likely also in the Danish ceremony. The notary of 1443 records the oath at this point, stating that the archbishop handed the crowned king the text of an oath which he then repeated word for word and swore on, while placing his hand on "a book," a

Bible or a Gospel-book, held by the archbishop. King Christopher's oath follows verbatim the *professio* contained in late medieval German ordines.[83] According to Eichmann and Schramm, this mid-twelfth century text goes back to late Carolingian models and became part of the ordo of 961 under Lothair III or Conrad III.[84] It is most likely that this oath was part of the Danish ordo from 1170 because it had long before been incorporated into its German model. If this was not so (and we have no proof for either assumption), it may have found its way into the Danish coronation during the decline of the kingship under Eric Glipping (1259–1286) or during the minority of his son Erik Menved (1286–1319), or even as late as the invitation of Christopher III to the throne of Denmark.[85]

After the king's coronation the queen was anointed, crowned, and handed a scepter which she too passed on to the councillor in charge of it, just as in 1515. After the choir's singing of *Exaudiat te* and *Et exaudi Deus deprecationem*, the ordinator preached the second main sermon about the meaning of the coronation, and the ceremonies ended with *Te Deum* and the reading of the Gospel.[86]

The king's participation in the Gospel-reading is noted already in the *Carmen* for 1443, but there it is placed before his coronation and this must have had a reason.[87] On the other hand, all early modern coronation ordines place the reading at the very end.[88] Even though the notarial record does not mention this episode for 1443, we may trust the *Carmen* since all the coronations that followed 1537 include this act. Nevertheless, I assume that it was not part of the medieval coronation, but was introduced at the 1443 coronation by Christopher III. References to the king's reading of the Gospel are relatively late in the German Empire as well.[89] We have evidence for Charles IV and his son, Sigismund, having done so, while holding swords in their right hands. This "royal Christmas service" is recorded for several *matutina* of Christmas Day, when the Gospel is Luke 2:1, the passage about the Edict of the Emperor Augustus. The Luxemburg kings-emperors may have been concerned with documenting their Augustus-like imperial position by performing this particular service. It may have reached Denmark through her prelates who attended the Councils of Constance and Basle, especially through Archbishop Hans Laxman, the coronator of 1443, who was present at the latter.[90] Another explanation for this rare innovation, which has its only parallel in Sweden would be to credit it to King Christopher III, a ruler whose political abilities are now recognized, in contrast to earlier negative judgments,[91] and who may very well have ordered the inclusion of the royal Gospel-reading in the ordo.[92] There is good evidence that Rupert of the Palatinate and Sigismund of Luxemburg, kings of the Romans,[93] read the Gospel at their coronations in 1407 and 1414 respectively, "during the Coronation Mass of which the coronation was a part," and not just—as was by then normal—at the Christmas service. Rupert was Christopher III's grandfather through his son John, Palatine of the Oberpfalz, who was married to Katherina, the sister of King Eric of Pomerania. Christopher III could very well have insisted that this act, introduced into the coronation of the king of the Romans by his grandfather should also be included in the Danish and, as we shall see, in the Swedish consecration of the *archirex* of the north. Christopher's intention may have been to demonstrate that the king of the Nordic Union was by no means of lesser estate than the king of the Romans, the future emperor. The dates of the coronations of Rupert (at Epiphany) and Christopher (on New Year's Day) permitted the easy transfer of the Christmas practice into the coronation ordo. To my mind, this was the way in which the Gospel reading was added to the medieval ordo as late as 1443. The concluding liturgy of the Lutheran ordo of 1537 reflects the closing acts of the medieval royal mass: Creed, *Praefatio* of the Trinity, *Sanctus*, another collect, blessing, communion, *Agnus Dei*, another prayer, and the closing blessing.[94]

In summary, then, based on the records of 1443 and 1537, and the considerations presented here, the medieval Danish ordo may be reconstructed as follows:

1. Placing the insignia on the altar.
2. Scrutinium.
3. Anointing the king (kneeling) on the right arm and shoulders.
4. Anointing the queen in the same manner.
5. Handing over the sword.
6. Coronation of the kneeling king.
7. Investiture with scepter.
8. Investiture with orb.
9. Professio of the king.
10. Coronation of the kneeling queen.
11. Handing over the scepter to the queen.
12. The king's reading the Gospel (at least in the late Middle Ages).

We do not know for certain whether there was a regular "enthronement." The 1443 notarial record hints at one, while in 1537 the king merely resumed his seat after the coronation.

The office of the coronator was unchallenged from the first coronation in 1170. It belonged to the archbishop of Lund who was replaced only in extraordinary circumstances. As we have seen, there was no "correct" site for medieval Danish coronations even though the archseat of Lund and later, until 1648, the royal residence in Copenhagen were preferred. If the king was married at his coronation, his queen was crowned with him. The insignia were limited in number—crown, sword, scepter, and orb—resembling more the German and English practice than the French, which did not contain an orb.[95] "Correct" insignia that would have been passed down from ruler to ruler do not seem to have existed in Denmark.[96]

The sequence of acts (unctio, gladius, coronatio, sceptrum, pomum) displays similarities to coronations in England and France.[97] It was the practice there to place the crown on the king's head after the investiture with ring and sword, while scepter and orb followed the crown. Even when some changes were made in England around 1100, the coronation remained in the middle of the ceremony. In contrast, German usage placed the coronation at the climax of the ceremony, the very end. The assistance of royal councillors at the coronation points to Western European models.[98] It is, however, unclear whether this "constitutional" practice originated earlier than the end of the Waldemarian age, during the rise of the *parlamentum* (Danehof), or even as late as 1443, if not 1448, the ascension of the Oldenburg dynasty, the age when the royal council acquired a strong position in the affairs of the realm.

Although a Western European influence can be detected in the sequence of the insignia, the order of the coronation mass seems to have been closer to German practice. Particularly important are the borrowing of scrutinium and professio and their place in the ordo. The adoption of royal Gospel-reading which occasionally appeared in German coronations is an interesting episode; it remained in use from 1443 to 1648, but in the later sixteenth century the chancellor did the reading, while the king stood by with the sword of the realm. The medieval Danish ordo seems, therefore, to have profited from both English and French models on the one hand and the practice of the German Empire on the other.

SWEDEN

Christianity arrived in Sweden[99] later than in the other Scandinavian realms. Succession struggles characterized here, too, the century between 1150 and 1250, fought out mainly among the families of the Sverker and the Erik-clan. Similar to Jarl Erling in Norway, Birger Jarl succeeded in placing his son Waldemar on the throne as an heir, albeit on his mother's side, of the Erik-line and thereby founded the (erroneously) so-called Folkunger dynasty. Just as for the Erik-dynasty before them, the establishment of a cult for the ancestor of the family, St. Erik,[100] was of paramount importance in this process. St. Erik's grandson, Erik Knutsson (1208–1216) was the first King of Sweden to be crowned by the archbishop of Uppsala.[101] The existence of royal insignia, above all, crowns, before the first Christian coronation can be assumed for Sweden as well.[102]

It is most likely that the pre-Christian acts of royal acclamation on the Mora-field near Old Uppsala included some kind of investiture with insignia and, from the twelfth century onwards, probably with a crown. However,

Olivecrona and Thordeman may go too far when they try to deduce a formal Germanic "coronation ceremony" from the Uppland Law of the thirteenth century, which contains a description of the old secular acts of royal inauguration.[103] The crown mentioned here is surely a later interpolation, as Hans Kuhn suggested. The division between secular inauguration on the Mora-field, the subsequent *Eriksgata*, comparable to the German *Königsumritt*[104] as acknowledgment of the new king by the tribes and the final ecclesiastical coronation, is not particularly Swedish, as Thordemann wants to claim. There was a royal circuit to the *landsthinger* also in Denmark, and German kings were often elected in one place and crowned in another, but these are not sufficient grounds to assume a specific secular act of coronation in connection with the nonecclesiastical inauguration.

After 1210 all Swedish kings were crowned. Only for the two sons and coregents of Magnus Eriksson, Erik and Haakon VI (of Norway), do we lack explicit records of their coronation.[105] Apparently the coronator was usually the archbishop of Uppsala[106] even though we have no specific evidence for this between 1210[107] and the coronations of the Union kings Christopher III (1441)[108] and Christian II (1520).[109] However, considering the general dearth of reliable sources for high medieval Sweden, this is by no means a particularly poor record. The assumed prerogative of the see of Uppsala was occasionally overridden, and we have sources for the exceptional cases. As already mentioned, one source credits the bishop of Dorpat with the role of coronator in 1336 at the crowning of Magnus Eriksson.[110] Since this act was meant to be for both Sweden and Norway, the choice of a prelate outside either realm may have been motivated by an attempt to avoid any conflict between Uppsala and Trondheim. In 1448 Karl Knutsson was crowned by the bishop of Linköping,[111] merely an emergency solution, for the archbishop-elect was not yet consecrated. Karl's opponent, Christian I, was crowned by the bishop of Strengnäs in 1457, even though the archbishop was his ally.[112]

Although, like the two other Scandinavian countries, Sweden did not have a definite site for coronation, Uppsala enjoyed a certain preeminence, comparable to Lund in Denmark. Uppsala's position was logical for the early coronations since it counted as the sacral and political centre in pre-Christian Sweden. It was also "practical" since the secular ascension on the Mora-field at the Mora stone (*super lapidem*) was quite close to Old Uppsala where the Christian consecration could take place.[113] After the coronation of Magnus Eriksson in Stockholm (1336)[114] the royal residence frequently also came to be the place for coronations; the Union kings Hans in 1497[115] and Christian II in 1520[116] were crowned there. For the sake of completeness the coronation of the king of the Union in Kalmar (1397)[117] should also be mentioned. As in the rest of Scandinavia, the crowning of the queen seems to have been typical in Sweden as well.[118]

While no medieval coronation ordines survive from Sweden, we have good evidence about the insignia from a charter of King Birger from 1311.[119] The king entrusted a number of signs of rulership and relics to the cathedral chapter of Uppsala and listed the insignia as well the other *ornamenta regalia*: crown, scepter, dalmatica, mantle, tunic, linen garments, sandals, a golden eagle, a silver garter (for the sword), and a *liber de coronacione regis*. Thus we have the "official" list of royal insignia for early fourteenth-century Sweden. It contains, besides the well-known major insignia and the coronation dress, an imperial symbol, the eagle, but lacks the otherwise ever-present royal sword. Most important, the treasure includes a book on the king's coronation which must have contained the coronation ordo, as was usual for other kingdoms in Europe.[120]

Unfortunately no other written source exists about medieval Swedish coronations. The oldest report containing some details concerns the coronation of Christian II in 1520, in the City Church of Stockholm.[121] It informs us that in the course of the consecration the king swore an oath and after the coronation mass partook of the sacrament. The coronation of Gustavus Wasa on 1 December 1528 in the Cathedral of Uppsala should, to my mind, still be seen as a medieval one, and not as the first Protestant ordination. That distinction belongs to the coronation of Christian III in 1537 in Copenhagen, as discussed above. Wasa never unequivocally embraced Lutheranism and only used the religious conflict to reduce the power of bishops and churchmen in Swedish political life. This attitude explains the mixed character of his coronation.[122] Gustavus had the Swedish protagonist of the reformation, Olaus Petri, preach the sermon, but the coronation was entrusted to the senior bishop, Magnus of Skara, since the archbishop, Gustav Trulle, had left the country as a political enemy of the king. Thus the coronation must have followed the traditional, Catholic, and medieval ordo, which we, alas, do not know. We know only that six bishops assisted the coronator and that the insignia were carried by the leading men of the realm: the orb by the imperial master of the court, the sword by the marshal, and the scepter by another member of the royal council.

The Swedish coronation oath, recorded for the first time at this occasion,[123] consists of the first part of the professio known from the German ordo. One may assume that the medieval Swedish ordo contained the entire text and was, therefore, identical with the medieval Danish one. Gustavus Wasa quite consciously halved the text. In this way he retained only a general promise of *lex, iustitia*, and *pax* to the church and his people. The latter half would have bound him specifically to observe the honor, rights, and privileges of clergy and church, of abbots and of counts as vassals, whose counsel he would also have promised to follow. Leaving these out the king avoided swearing on any truly constitutional point which would have limited his attempts to strengthen royal prerogative.

For the first genuine Protestant coronation in Sweden, that of Erik XIV on 19 June 1561, several handwritten and printed sources have come down to us. These permitted Per Janzon[124] to establish, by careful sifting and comparison, two versions of the ordo that were prepared before the coronation. Janzon concluded, just as we did for the first Danish Protestant coronation, that the ordo went back to medieval ordines but was fused with Lutheran ideas, especially in the sermons and the liturgy. The ordo of 1561 existed in two versions before the coronation, represented in a number of variants. Version *A* appears to have been a draft, and hence closer to medieval models, while version *B* displays a stronger influence of Lutheran thought. While *B* represents in all likelihood the ordo that was used in 1561, version *A* is, of course, more important for our enterprise of reconstruction,[125] and we shall follow it in detail.

The king, at this time still unmarried, was received at the church door by the bishops, wearing their *pallia*. After greeting and prayers he was led to the altar while a *reponsorium* is sung. The *ordinator*—in 1561, the Lutheran archbishop of Uppsala—preached a sermon. Following that, the king, now dressed for anointing, knelt on a prayer bench. Then followed the collect, spoken by the archbishop; Epistle, read by one of the leading pastors; and, with the Introit, Kyrie, and Gloria omitted, the scrutiny. Consisting of three main questions by the archbishop, it is clearly discernible, in contrast to the Danish precedent. The king promised to obey God, to hold the right faith, which in Lutheran formulation was called "the pure word of God," to abolish all false teaching and heresy, to protect the church and her servants and the subjects of his realm, and to observe the law of the land and resist injustice. The king replied with "Yes" to all the questions and finally swore a coronation oath that summarized all the preceding points. The oath was similar to the Danish one in the ordo of 1537, but different both from the old professio and the Gustavus Wasa version of it.

The king was then anointed on the forehead, the chest, between the shoulders, on both shoulders, elbows, and wrists. After another prayer, he was given the gloves, the ring, a small sword (girded to his waist), and the mantle. Together with the other bishops, the *ordinator*-archbishop placed the crown on the head of the kneeling king, who was then led to the throne. Seated there, he was given scepter, sword, and orb, and acclaimed as king of Sweden. Subsequently the Swedish king too read the Gospel of the week, holding up the naked sword, while two clerics held the Gospel-book in front of him. The ceremonies ended with the Creed, the king's offertorium, and his partaking of the Lord's Supper for the first time as king. A blessing is the last act noted. The sources do not contain any details about the investiture with the insignia; nothing is said of the swinging of the sword or of secular participation in the placing of the crown, as in Denmark.

The ordo of 1561 shows both parallels with and differences from the 1537

Copenhagen coronation. The combination of scrutinium and professio is the same in both. But the anointing in Sweden is much more elaborate than the Danish and resembles rather the high medieval practice in Germany and Western Europe.[126] Only the anointing of the hands is missing, but this was omitted for a while in thirteenth-century France.[127] The number of the insignia parallels that of the English and German regalia. The duplication of the sword is noteworthy. The place of the coronation in the middle of the ceremony points to Western European models. While an enthronement was only hinted at in Christopher III's coronation in 1443, it is here explictly included. The acclamation of the king in the 1561 ordo (version *B*) refers quite clearly to the medieval practice of the assent of "the people."[128] Here it is noted that after the king has been announced as ruler by a herald, the usual acclamation is given: "God give our king luck and health," or "May he enjoy good luck and a long reign." It is most noteworthy that the king's reading of the Gospel features in the Swedish ordo in the same way as it did in the 1443 coronation in Denmark. I regard this as an additional proof for my hypothesis about Christopher III's introduction of this act to Scandinavian coronation rituals.[129] It is most likely that he proposed it not only for Denmark but also at the coronations for his two other realms, including that in 1441 for Sweden.[130] Thus it is most likely that this German practice did indeed find its way into Scandinavia during the reign of Christopher III.

In summary, coronation and anointing were also introduced to Sweden from the older Christian kingdoms to enhance royal prerogative and state power as well as to secure succession by primogeniture, just as in Norway and Denmark. Here, too, the first coronation was held for a king who claimed the throne as a descendant of a holy king, St. Erik. The office of coronator was from 1210 throughout the Middle Ages with very few exceptions the privilege of the metropolitan of Sweden, the archbishop of Uppsala. Even though a fixed coronation place was not established, the prevalence of Uppsala as archsee and as the church closest to the traditional secular center of ascension, the Mora-field, is obvious. Uppsala's position was unchanged until around 1336 when the principal residence of the kings, Stockholm, moved into first place. The kind and number of the insignia parallel those in Germany and England but lack *baculus* and *armillae* and so surpass the Danish ones. The inclusion of a professio, the insignia, and the form of unction point to German ordines while the sequence of the investiture points rather to English examples. In the light of the above, the medieval Swedish ordo may have had the following structure:

1. Entry of the king.
2. Sermon, prayer for the ruler, collect, Epistle.
3. Scrutinium.
4. Unction (forehead, chest, back, shoulders, elbows, wrists); prayer.

5. Gloves and ring.
6. Small sword.
7. Mantle.
8. Coronation of kneeling king.
9. Enthronement; scepter, orb, large sword.
10. (Since 1441?) Reading of the Gospel with upheld sword by the king.
11. Creed, offertorium, communion.

SUMMARY

The introduction of coronation and anointing was motivated in all three Nordic kingdoms by the same concerns: to narrow the claim to the throne from the entire *stirps regia* to a particular dynasty and even further, to secure the succession right of the oldest legitimate son of the ruler and so secure the stability of the kingship. The relationship of the royal family to a dynastic saint was adduced to give greater weight to these moves.

The position of the coronator was essentially unchallenged in all three realms. Since each consisted of one archdiocese, the metropolitan was unquestionably the prelate who held this right. In contrast to Germany, France, and England, the Scandinavian countries established no fixed rightful place for the coronation, even though Uppsala in Sweden came close to such a position. In Denmark neither the metropolitan's see in Lund nor the burial church of Ringsted managed to acquire such a position. In Norway the centers of royal power and the main residence, locations defined by practical rather than spiritual aspects, came to be the sites for coronation. As the Middle Ages progressed, both Denmark and Sweden moved closer to the older Norwegian model by holding the coronation at the developing royal capitals: Copenhagen and Stockholm.

The most conspicuous difference among the Scandinavian kingdoms is the form of the unction. While the Swedish practice resembled Western and Central European practice, the Danish usage—only arm and back—is closest to the prescriptions of a *decretale* of Innocent III of 1204 which, following the imperial ordo, named these two parts of a king's body as proper places for unction, thus separating the ruler's unction from clerical-episcopal annointing.[131] However, no German or West European king observed these restrictions contained also in the *Pontificale Romanum*. It is equally unlikely that Danish kings would have done so. Danish kingship in 1170 was certainly strong enough to forego any such gesture of humility and even more so the "imperial" kingship of Waldemar II "the Victorious," contemporary of the *decretale*. It is much more likely that the change was introduced as late as 1443 by Christopher III, whose coronation was separated by a hiatus of almost 120 years from the preceeding one. But the exact motive of the king or the archbishop Hans Laxmann of Lund for introducing this change many centuries after the issue of the papal ruling remains a puzzle. A similar development may also be assumed for the difference in regalia between Denmark and Sweden. While in 1537 Christian III definitely wore a royal mantle, gloves, and ring, he was not formally invested with these. In contrast, at the coronation of 1561 all these and other insignia typical of any medieval German or English coronation are listed. Maybe in this respect, too, a simplification was introduced under Christian III for reasons that are not yet known to us.

Norway displays some other peculiarities. There was no orb, as in France, but there was a second staff, the *baculus*, as in both France and England. Western European influence can be assumed for the sequence of the ceremonies in which the placing of the crown was always in the middle of the ceremony, not at the end as in Germany. However, the liturgy, the place, and content of the scrutinium and professio and, as we saw, the unction, point to the German ordines. It was also from German practice, in this case late medieval, that the king's reading of the Gospel with sword upheld found its way into Scandinavia. In all likelihood Christopher III brought it to Denmark and Sweden in 1441 and 1443, respectively, and perhaps also to Norway. Finally, the king's attire, as recorded in the charter of King Birger and the late medieval and early modern records, parallels fully that of Western and Central European rulers.

Thus our inquiry into the coronation practices of the three Nordic realms reveals that the development of these ceremonies reflect neatly the two main cultural and religious influences from abroad, one from Germany, the other from England and France, which affected in many aspects of Scandinavian culture ever since the Christian missions of the tenth and eleventh centuries.

NOTES

1. Cf. E. Hoffmann, *Königserhebung und Thronfolgeordnung in Dänemark bis zum Ausgang des Mittelalters* (Berlin, 1976), 1 ff.; 22 ff.; E. Hoffmann, "Knut der Heilige und die Wende der Dänischen Geschichte im 11. Jahrhundert," *Historische Zeitschrift* 218 (1974): 529 ff.

2. In Norway, Magnus Erlingsson (1162–1184), in Denmark, Niels (1104–1134), and in Sweden, Knut Eriksson (c. 1167–c. 1195) began to use the *Dei gratia* in his royal style.

3. On the general background for Norwegian history in this period see *Vårt Folks Historie*, ed. Th. Dahl et al., vols. 2–4 (Oslo, 1976–1977): K. Helle, *Norge blir en Stat 1130–1319* (Oslo, 1964); K. Helle, *Konge og gode menn* (Bergen, 1971); G. Authén Blom, *Kongemakt og Privilegier i Norge inntil 1387* (Oslo, Bergen, Tronsø 1967), all with bibliography.

4. On these matters, cf. my more detailed study *Die heiligen Könige bei den Angelsachsen und den skandinavischen Völkern: Königsheiliger und Königshaus* (Neumünster, 1975), 156 ff. with bibliography in n. 71, p. 156; also cf. Hoffmann, *Königserhebung* 99, f., with bibliography in n. 99.

5. Snorri Sturluson, *Heimskringla III*, ed. B. Adalbjarnarson (Reykjavik, Izlensk Fornrit 28, 1951), pt. 3, chaps. 21–22, pp. 395–398.

6. *Latinske Dokument til Norsk Historie*, ed. E. Vandvik (Oslo, 1959) no. 10, p. 62; on the analysis of the text cf. W. Holtzmann, "Krone und Kirche in Norwegen im 12. Jahrhundert," *Deutsches Archiv* 2 (1938): 341 ff.; the text is printed, ibid., 376 f.

7. On the mission of Nicholas Breakspeare and the agreements made with him, see *Latinske Dokument* no. 7 (Canones Nidrosienses A.D. 1152); Holtzmann, "Krone," 376 f.; in summary also: W. Seegrün, *Das Papsttum und Skandinavien bis zur Vollendung der nordischen Kirchenorganisation* (Neumünster, 1967), 146 ff. (with bibliography).

8. In contrast to Holtzmann ("Krone," 352 f.) I see in these very much the concern to protect the legal claims of the church of Trondheim.

9. Holtzmann, "Krone," 351 f.

10. Ibid., 352 with n. 1; on the professio, see E. Eichmann, "Die 'formula professionis' Friedrichs I.," *Historisches Jahrbuch* 52 (1932): 137 ff. and P. E. Schramm, *Kaiser, Könige und Päpste* [henceforth: K. K. P.] (Stuttgart, 1969) 3: 65 f.

11. *Latinske Dokument*, no. 9, p. 58.

12. E. Gunnes, *Kongens Aere: Kongemakt og kirke i "En tale mot biskopene"* (Oslo, 1971).

13. On the negotiations before the coronation and the festivities, see *Sverris Saga*, ed. G. Indrebø (Kristiana, 1920), chaps. 122–123, pp. 130–131.

14. *Hǿkonar Saga Hákonarsonar*, ed. M. Mundt (Norsk Historisk Kjeldeskrift-Institutt, Norrone Tekster 2, Kristiana, 1847, 1977), chap. 247, p. 138.

15. *Diplomatarium Norvegicum* [henceforth: DN] I, Oslo, no. 69.

16. On Haakon's coronation, see *Hákonar Saga*, chap. 253–257, pp. 141–145; cf. Blom, *Kongemakt*, 136 f.

17. P. E. Schramm, *Herrschaftszeichen und Staatssymbolik* (Stuttgart, 1955) 2:392; P. E. Schramm, *History of the English Coronation* (Oxford, 1937).

18. Snorri, *Heimskringla* (Reykjavik Islenzk Fornrit 26, 1941) 1:186–189 (chaps. 30–31).

19. B. Thordeman, "Kungakröning och Kungakrona i Medeltidens Sverige," *Arkeologiska Forskningar och Fynd: Studier utg. med. Anlyedning av H. M. Gustaf VI. Adolfs Sjuttioårsdag, 11. 11. 1952.* (Stockholm, 1952), 307 (with tab. 4, p. 314); B. Thordeman, "Erik den Heliges Kungakrona," *Erik den Helige: Historia, Kult, Reliker*, ed. B. Thordeman (Stockholm, 1954), 277 f. with tab. 221, pl. LII.

20. Schramm, K. K. P. (1968) 2:287 ff.

21. *Widukindi res gestae Saxoniae*, II, 1. MGH SS rer. G. 60: II, 1, 65.

22. *Diplomatarium Suecanum* 4, no. 3484.

23. O. Källström on the scepter in Scandinavia, in Schramm, *Herrschaftszeichen* (1956) 3:70 f. Accepting his interpretation, I imply that thus Norway would be the only country, besides France, which retained the *baculus* or *virga* as well as the scepter and did not introduce an orb; cf. P. E. Schramm, *Der König von Frankreich*, 2d ed. (Darmstadt, 1960) 1:211.

24. *Hákonar Saga*, chap. 310, p. 186 f.

25. See above, n. 15.

26. "Protifeor et promitto coram deo et sanctis eius a modo pacem et iusticiam ecclesie dei populoque mihi subiecto obseruare pontificibus et clero prout teneor condignum honorem exhibere *secundum discretionem mihi a deo datam* atque ea que a regibus ecclesiis collata ac reddita sunt *sicut compositum est inter ecclesiam et regnum* inuiolabiliter conseruare *malasque leges et consuetudines peruersas precipue contra ecclesiasticam libertatem facientes abolere et bonas condere prout* de consilio fidelium nostrorum *melius inuenire pote-*

rimus." The nonitalicized passages of this oath formula are borrowed verbatim or in content from the parallal passages of the professio; cf. also G. Carlsson, "Gustav Vasas Kröningsed," *Svensk Historisk Tidskrift* [henceforth: *HT Svensk*], (1946), 324 f. Carlsson detects in the last sentence about the abolition of bad laws and customs a parallel to the English coronation oath of the twelfth and thirteenth centuries; cf. J. Hatschek, *Englische Verfassungsgeschichte bis zum Regierungsantritt der Königin Viktoria* (Munich and Berlin, 1913; Below-Meinecke, *Handb. d. Mittleren und Neueren Gesch.* III/1), 69.

27. *Norske gamla Love* (Kristiana, 1849) 3:45–55.

28. Helle, *Norge*, 187.

29. Ch. Joys "Magnu Eriksson, Norges og Sveriges Konge" in: *Vårt Folks Hist.* 3:264.

30. "Chronologia Svecica 815–1412 ex cod. min. Wisbyensium," *SS rer. Svecicarum* 1 (Uppsala, 1818), 43.

31. *Die Chroniken der niedersächsischen Städte, Lübeck*, vol. 1 (Stuttgart, 1884; Chron. dt. st. 19), 476–477:. . . do war dar komen de vrome biscop Ghiselbert van Darbathe [Dorpat] . . .; den ereden dar de biscop van Upsale unde andere biscope des rikes, dat he sang de mysse unde wyede unde kronede den koning unde de koninhinnen.

32. See Hoffmann, *Königserhebung*, 150–155.

33. Best overview: A. E. Christensen, *Kalmarunionen og nordisk politik 1319–1439* (Copenhagen, 1980), with bibliography.

34. Because from the death of Olaf to 1814 the King of Denmark was also king of Norway.

35. DN 1, no. 783; A. Huitfeldt, *Danmarkis Riges Krønike* (Copenhagen, 1650–1652), 830.

36. "Chronologia vetusta," *SS rer. Svecicarum* 1:97; "Diarium Wazstenense," *SS rer. Svecicarum* 1:166; Chronika Erici Olai, *SS rer. Svecicarum*, 2:158; *Olai Petri Krönika*, ed. G. E. Klemming (Stockholm, 1860), 214 f.

37. A. Huitfeldt, *Danmarkis Riges Krønike: Kong Hans' Historie* (Copenhagen, 1599; reprinted Copenhagen, 1977), 36 (coronation in Norway); A. Huitfeldt, *Kong Christian II.'s Historie* (Copenhagen, 1596; reprinted Copenhagen, 1976), 25 (coronation in Norway).

38. On the significance of the Olaf-cult, as a "national" saint: *St. Olav: Seine Zeit und sein Kult*, Acta Visbyensia VI: Visbysimposiet för historiska vetenskaper 1979, ed. G. Svahnström (Visby, 1981); cf. also, Hoffmann, *Königserhebung*, 58 ff.

39. C. J. Schive, *Norges Mynter i Middelalderen* (Kristiana, 1865); Chr. Brinkmann, *Norske Konge-Sigiller og andre Fyrste-Sigiller* (Kristiana, 1924); Thordemann, "Kungakröning," 306 f., Thordeman, "Erik," 277 ff., Hoffmann, *Königserhebung* 109 f., P. E. Schramm, "Die Grabkrone Erichs von Schweden," *Herrschaftszeichen* 3:769 ff., esp. 773 f.

40. See notes 16 and 24, above.

41. For an overview of Danish history used here, see *Gyldendals Danmarks historie* vols. 1–2, ed. A. E. Christensen et al. (Copenhagen, 1977–1979); N. Skyum Nielsen, *Kvinde og Slave: Danmarkshistorie uden retouche*, vol. 3 (Copenhagen, 1971); Th. Riis, *Les institutions politiques centrales du Danemark 1100–1332* (Odense, 1977).

42. *Saxonis Gesta Danorum*, ed. J. Olrik and H. Raeder (Copenhagen, 1931) vol. 1, XIV, XL; 1, p. 477.

43. "Annales Lundenses," *Annales Danici medii aevi* [henceforth: *Ann. Dan.*], ed.

E. Jørgensen (Copenhagen, 1920), 85; however, mistakenly dated for 1171.

44. Hoffmann, *Königserhebung*, 106–108.

45. The right to coronation was confirmed by Pope John XXII; see *Diplomatarium Danicum* 2. R., 8, no. 182.

46. In 1252, Christopher I was crowned by the Bishop of Schleswig in Lund, because the archbishop had recently died; see Hoffmann, *Königserhebung*, 131 (with a discussion of sources in n. 26); in 1259 the Bishop of Ripen crowned Christopher's son, Erik Glipping, because the archbishop, opposed to the crown, refused to do so; see *Acta processus litium inter regem Danorum et archiepiscopum Lundensem*, ed. A. Krarup and W. Norwin (Copenhagen, 1932), 56. In 1524 Frederick I was crowned, due to the vacancy of the archsee, by the archbishop of Uppsala; see A. Huitfeldt, *Danmarkis Riges Krønike: Friedrich I.'s Historie* (Copenhagen, 1597, reprinted Copenhagen, 1977), 74.

47. Arnold of Lübeck, *Chronica Slavorum*, MG SS rer. G. 14:238.

48. "Chronica Jutensis [henceforth: "Chron. Jut."]," *Scriptores minores historiae Danicae medii aevi* [henceforth: *SS min. Dan.*], ed. M. Cl. Gertz (Copenhagen, 1917–1918) 1:448.

49. For Erik, see the annals in *Ann. Dan.*, 108 f.; for Abel: *Annales Stadenses auctore Alberto*, MGH SS 16:273.

50. "Annales Waldemariani ad a. 1218," *Ann. Dan.*, 104 f.

51. See above, n. 46.

52. "Chron. Jut.," 451; "Chronica archiepiscoporum Lundensium XII," *SS min. Dan.* 2:115.

53. J. A. Cypreaus, "Annales Epsicoporum Slesvicensium" (1634), in *Monumenta inedita rerum Germanicarum*, ed. E. J. von Westphalen (s.l., Leipzig 1793) 3:310–311 (the notarial record); A. Huitfeldt, *Danmarkis Riges Krønike: Chronologia* (reprinted Copenhagen, 1977) 3:656 f. (coronation report and *Carmen*).

54. For Christian I: "Chronica Archiepiscoporum Lundensium," *SS min. Dan.* 2:123; for Hans: A. Huitfeldt, *Danmarkis Riges Krønike. Kong Hans' Historie* (Copenhagen, 1599; reprinted Copenhagen, 1977), 31; for Christian II: Huitfeldt, *Christian II.'s Historie* (Copenhagen, 1596, reprinted Copenhagen, 1976), 23; for Frederick I, see n. 47 above.

55. See n. 33, above.

56. For Waldemar (III), see Hoffmann, *Königserhebung*, 142; for Waldemar IV, ibid., 144 f.

57. Ibid., 152 (but correct the typographical error; Olaf died in 1387!).

58. Ibid., 126 ff.

59. For Mechtild and Abel, see n. 50; for Margarethe and Christopher I, n. 46; and for Christina and Hans, n. 55, above.

60. Obviously, Canute the Great, King of England, must have had a crown (Schramm, *Herrschafstzeichen* 2:633; Hoffmann, *Königserhebung*, 108 f.). The rulers who came to be vassals of the emperor received crowns at their enfeoffment, so *dux* Knut Lavard as *rex Obodritorum* (Helmold of Bosau, *Chronica Slavorum*, chap. XLIX; MGH SS rer. G. 32:97); King Magnus Nielsson (see W. Bernhardi, *Jahrbücher der deutschen Geschichte: Lothar von Supplinburg*, Leipzig, 1879, 404 f.) and King Sven Grathe (*Ottonis et Rahewini Gesta Frederici I. imperatoris* II:5, MGH SS rer. G. 46:105 f.) from Lothair III and Frederick I, respectively. Whether the votive crown displayed by

Bishop Sven in the cathedral of Roskilde was indeed that of St. Canute (1080–1086), as Saxo (XI, XII:6) maintains, cannot be stringently proven. However, Helmold (*Chronica*, 98) explicitly reports about a royal court held in Slesvig c. 1129/1130 that King Niels *sedisset in trono indutus cultu regio*. Danish royal seals display the king with crown and other insignia since the reign of St. Canute, coins since that of Canute the Great, the latter sometimes with helmet. Earlier images have closed and arched crowns, later ones (from the mid-twelfth century onward) open crowns surmounted by lilies or leaves. Additional insignia are usually scepter, orb, and sword, the same ones that are listed in the earliest reports on coronations (1143, 1537). However, it is true for Denmark as well that such images are highly dependent on foreign models and have little value for historical reconstruction; cf. above n. 39; Hoffmann, *Königserhebung*, 108 ff. Further: Th. Riis, *Les institutions politiques centrales du Danemark 1100–1332* (Odense, 1977), 151 ff.; H. Petersen and A. Thiset, *Danske Kongelige Sigiller 1085–1559* (Copenhagen, 1917); P. Hauberg, *Myntforhold og Udmyntninger i Danmark indtil 1146* (Det Kgl. Danske Videnskabernes Skrifter, R. 6, Hist.-fil. Afd. 5, 1906), 51 ff., 106 ff.; Schramm, *Herrschaftszeichen* 1:18 ff.; K. K. P. 1:24.

61. See above, n. 53.
62. See ibid.
63. Hoffmann, *Königserhebung*, 161, with n. 53 (lit.); Hoffman, "Die Krönung Christians III. von Dänemark am 12. August 1537: Die erste protestantische Königkrönung in Europa," *Herrscherweihe und Königskrönung im frühneuzeitlichen Europa*, ed. H. Duchhardt (Schriften der Mainzer Philosophischen Fakultätsgesellschaft 8, Mainz, 1983), esp. 59; N. Skyum. Nielsen, "Aerkekonge og Aekebiskop: Nye Traek i dansk Kirkehistorie 1376–1536," *Scandia* 3 (1955–1957): 1 ff.; J. E. Olesen, *Rigsrad, Kongemagt, Union: Studier over det danske rigsrad og den nordiske kongemagts politik 1434–1449* (Aarhus, 1980), 95–376.
64. There are several records of the Protestant ordo as well as of the actual ceremonies of the coronation. The two main sources, both in German, are a sketchy overview of the coronation, probably compiled for the information of the royal couple and a detailed report about the events of the coronation day. They are printed as: (a) *Aktstykker vedkommende kong Christian den Tredies og Dronning Dorotheas Kroning in Vor Frue Kirke, Kobenhavn, den 12te August 1537 af Dr. Johannes Bogenhagen*, ed. F. Münter [henceforth: Münter], with an intro. by E. C. Werlauff [henceforth: Werlauff] (1831); Werlauff is also available in German, in *Baltische Studien* 5,2 (1838): 1 ff. and (b) *Die Krönung König Christians III. von Dänemark und seiner Gemahlin Dorothea durch Johannes Bugenhagen*, ed. G. Mohnike [henceforth: Mohnike] (Stralsund, 1832). Additional sources in A. G. Hassø, ed. "Kong Kristian III.'s og Dronning Dorotheas Kroning den 12. August 1537," *Kirkehistoriske Samlinger* 6, 2 (1936–38):287 ff.
65. Cf. the *carmen*, as referred to in n. 53.
66. Hassø, "Kong Kristian," 317.
67. For 1443, see n. 53; for 1537, Hassø, "Kong Kristian," 317.
68. Münter, 24 f., Mohnike, 68 f.
69. On the Imperial Council, see Hoffmann, *Königserhebung*, 140 f., 149 f., 151 f., 156 ff., 165 f., and 178 f., Riis, *Institutions*, 252 ff. (cf. also ibid., 236 ff., 256 ff.).
70. Cypräus, "Annales," 311.
71. *Coronatio Aquisgranensis* (24 Oct. 1273), MGH LL 2:386.
72. Schramm, K. K. P. 2:64 f., 95 ff.

73. The text of the professio is in Eichmann, "Friedrich I," 140; cf. Cypräus, "Annales," 311.

74. Münter, 4, 13 f., Mohnike, 36, 51 f.

75. This would point to a relationship to the German ordo.

76. Münter, 5, 16 f.; Mohnike, 37, 55 f.; the oil is described as *kresem* (chrism) or *balsam*. On the coronation and anointing of Queen Elisabeth (Isabella), see Werlauff, xii (or Werlauff, *Baltische Studien*, 14).

77. Schramm, *English Coronation*, 120; K. K. P. 3:153 ff.; E. Eichmann, *Die Kaiserkrönung im Abendland* (Würzburg, 1942), 135, 174, 182 ff. In the light of my present argument, I should like to revise my formulation of 1983 (in "Krönung Christians III.," 64 and 65) about German practice of anointing as to mean "anointing practice following the Imperial usage" and "as far as the anointing is concerned, from the ordo of the imperial coronation," respectively.

78. See n. 54.

79. See ibid.

80. Münter, 6, 21; Mohnike, 38, 64.

81. Hoffmann, "Krönung Christians III," 64; cf. the coronation ceremonies of Christian IV (1588–1648), *Kjøbenhavns Diplomatarium*, ed. O. Nielsen 4 (Copenhagen, 1879), 741 ff., no. 851, esp. 746.

82. MGH LL 2:390.

83. Eichmann, "Friedrich I," 137 ff; the oath formula (140) compares with that of the Danish one very well. In the following text changes from the imperial to the Danish are marked in italics, (om.-omitted in the Danish): Profiteor et promitto coram Deo et angelis eius *amodo et* (om.) deinceps legem et iusticiam pacemque Dei sanctae ecclesiae populoque michi subjecto pro posse et nosse facere et (*ac*) conservare (*servare*) salvo condigno misericordiae respectu sicut cum consilio fidelium nostrorum (*meorum*) melius invenire poterimus (*potero invenire*). Pontificibus quoque ecclesiarum Dei condignum et canonicum honorem exhibere atque ea, quae ab imperatoribus et regibus eclesiis *sibi commissis* (om.) collata et reddita sunt, inviolabiliter conservare (*observare*), abbatibus *etiam* (om.), comitibus et vassis dominicis (*vassallis*) nostris (*meis*) congruum honorem secundum consilium fidelium nostrorum praestare; cf. Hoffman, *Königserhebung*, 168–169, n. 78.

84. Schramm, K. K. P. 3:65 f.; Eichmann, as above.

85. We know of a "coronation oath" of the succesor of Christopher III, the first Oldenburg on the Danish throne, Christian I, which does not follow the professio but rather the "royal oath" of Christian. Royal oaths were usually sworn by late medieval Danish kings at the elevation acts in the three major *landthinger* in Viborg, Ringsted, and Lund. Thus Christian I also swore such an oath in 1448 in Viborg, which is supposed to be almost identical with the alleged "coronation oath." Most likely, tradition mixed up the two different occasions in this case, see Hoffmann, *Königserhebung*, 159–160, 163–164. The royal oath of Christopher III, identical with that of Christian I is printed in *Samling af Danske Kongers Haandfaestninger og andre lignende Acter* (Aarsberetniger fra det kong. Geheimearchiv 2, 1856–1860), 40 ff., no. 12; cf. Christian's royal oath in A. Huitfeld, *Danmarckis Rigis Krønicke, ed. fol.* (Copenhagen, 1652), 844–845; Christian's coronation oath is in *Samling . . . Acter* 45 ff., no. 14.

86. Cf. the royal coronation of Emperor Frederick III in 1442, at which the king

was led after coronation and professio to the throne, whereupon *Te Deum* was sung and the Gospel read; *Deutsche Reichstagsakten* 16:181 f. (no. 102).

87. *Rex Euangelium legit, unctus postea*...

88. See Hoffmann, "Krönung Christians"; P. Janzon, "Erik XIV.'s Kröningsritual," *Kyrkohistorisk Årsskrift* 50 (1959): 175 ff., with the ordines on 213 ff. This sequence was also characteristic for late medieval German coronations (cf. *Deutsche Reichstagsakten*, as above). Even if not mentioned in the notarial record, only in the festive poem for 1443, it is most likely that this event took place, for all early modern coronation report the reading of the Gospel is listed, albeit at the place where it features in the 1537 ordo. There is reason to believe that this act was not part of medieval Danish royal inaugurations, but had been introduced by Christopher III.

89. Cf. H. Heimpel, "Königlicher Weihnachtsgottesdienst auf den Konzilien von Konstanz und Basel," *Tradition als historische Kraft: Interdisziplinäre Forschungen zur Geschichte des früheren Mittelalters*, ed. N. Kamp, J. Wollasch, et al. (Münster, 1982), 388 f.; H. Heimpel, "Weihnachtsdienst im späteren Mittelalter," *Deutsches Archiv* 39 (1983): 131 ff.

90. Hoffmann, "Krönung Christians," 58 f.,

91. Olesen, *Rigsrad*.

92. Hoffmann, "Krönung Christians," 59 f.

93. H. Heimpel, "Königliche Evangelienlesung bei königlicher Krönung," *Aus Kirche und Reich: Studien zur Theologie, Politik und Recht im Mittelalter. Festschrift f. F. Kempf*, ed. H. Mordek (Sigmaringen, 1983), 447 ff.

94. Bugenhagen noted in his instructions that in the Catholic coronation ordo the king and queen, as other rulers of the West, took communion at the end of the ceremony; Münter, 3; Mohnike, 34.

95. On the insignia and their order of investment, see Schramm, *Der König von Frankreich* 1:59 f., 205 ff.; Schramm, K. K. P. 2:140 ff., 169 f., 3:59 ff.

96. However, in the fifteenth century we hear of a royal treasure which Eric of Pomerania, at his deposition was charged with having alienated: "Item heft he ut de rykes trezel to Callingeborch wechbringen laten des rykes schat unde clenode, de to velen jaren van konige unde koninhynnen ghesammelt weren to nutte des rykes...." *Aktstykker vedrorende Erik af Pommerns Afsaettelse som Konge af Danmark*, ed. A. Hude (Copenhagen, 1897; reprinted Copenhagen, 1971), no. 4, p. 14. About Christopher III it is said that he lost the treasure in a shipwreck; Werlauff, "Inledning," xxi; Werlauff, *Baltische Studien*, 14, 26.

97. Hoffmann, *Königserhebung*, 167–168; cf. the writings of Schramm quoted in n. 95 above.

98. Hoffmann, *Königserhebung*, 166.

99. For the history of Sweden in the period under review, see *Sveriges Historia till vara Dagar*, ed. E. Hildebrand, 5 vols. (Stockholm, 1919–1920); *Den Svenska Historien*, ed. St. Carlsson, J. Rosén, and G. Grenholm, 3 vols. (Stockholm, 1966); *Svenska Kyrkens Historia*, ed. H. Holmquist, H. Pleijel, vols. 1–2 (Stockholm, 1941, 1933/1934); *Erik den Helige*, ed. B. Thordeman; S. Carlsson, J. Rosén, *Svensk Historia*, 3d ed., vol. 1 (Stockholm, 1969), all of which contain references to sources and literature.

100. Cf. *Erik den Helige*; Hoffmann, *Die heiligen*, 197 ff., Schramm, *Herrschaftszeichen* 3:769 ff.

101. Thordeman, "Kungakröning," 309; Thordeman, "Kungakrona," 277. Although in the earliest record of this coronation, in Pope Innocent III's letter of 4 April 1216 only anointing is mentioned (*Sveriges Traktater med frümmade Magter*, ed. O. S. Rydberg, vol. 1, no. 64 [Stockholm, 1877], anointing without coronation is not likely to have been performed after the tenth century (cf. Schramm, *Herrschaftszeichen* 3:775, n. 1).

102. Thordeman, "Kungakröning," 308; Thordeman, "Kungakrona," 277f. King Anund Jakob (early eleventh century) is depicted with a golden helmet; later coins and seals display crown, scepter, and orb. Earlier pictures show closed and arched crowns, those from the thirteenth century and later open crowns surmounted with lilies or leaves; however, the source value of these pictures is questionable (see above, n. 60). For the seals see H. Fleetwood, ed., *Svenska medeltidinga Kungasigill*, 2 vols. (Stockholm, 1936–1942); for the coins: B. Thordeman, "Sveriges medeltidsmynt," *Nordisk Kultur* XXIX (1936). The existence of a burial crown for St. Erik suggests, however, that he wore one in life; see Thordeman, "Kungakrona," as above; Schramm, as above.

103. K. H. K. Olivecrona, "Das Werden eines Königs nach Altschwedischem Recht. Der Königsritus als magischer Akt," *Lunds Universitetets Arsskrift* NF 1, 44 (1948); Thordeman, "Kungakröning," 308 f.; Thordeman, "Kungakrona," 278 f.; cf. the review of the latter by K. Olivecrona in *Deutsche Literaturzeitung* 65 (1944): 74–78. See also Hoffmann, *Königskrönung*, 3 f., 12 f., 181 f.

104. R. Schmidt, "Königsumritt und Huldigung in ottonisch-salischer Zeit," *Vorträge und Forschungen* 6 (1961): 97–233.

105. The sources for mid-fourteenth-century Scandinavia are very scant in general, which may be the consequence of repeated waves of the Black Death; hence the silence of the sources cannot be taken as evidence against the possibility of coronations in this period.

106. As the archbishop of Uppsala was the only metropolitan in Sweden, the coronation was his privilege without contest.

107. See above, n. 102.

108. "Chronologia vetusta," *SS rer. Svecicarum* 1 (Uppsala, 1818): 96; "Diarium Wasstenense 1344–1545," ibid., 157 f.

109. *Olai Petri Svenska Krönika*, ed. G. E. Klemming (Stockholm, 1860), 327.

110. See the sources quoted in notes 30–31, above.

111. "Chronologia vetusta," 97.

112. "Annales Holmienses 1457–1468," *SS rer. Svecicarum* 3:27. S. Kraft (in *Sveriges Historia til vara Dagar* 3:2) assumes a brief quarrel between the king and the prelate.

113. G. Holmgren, "Gamla Uppsala och Mora äng in Medeltidslagarnas Valförskrifter," *Upplands Fornminnesförenings Tidsskrift* 45 (1935–1937): 3 ff., esp. 36. Clearly indicated on the sources are only the following coronations in Uppsala: Magnus Ladulas's in 1267 (in "Chronologia..." *SS rer. Svecicarum* 1:25; "Chronologia Anonymi...," ibid., 54; "Chronologia Erici Olai," ibid., 2:59); Christopher III's in 1444 (see above, n. 108); Karl Knutsson's in 1448 (see above, n. 111 Diarium Wasstenense *SS rer. Svericarum* 1:165; chronicon Erici Olai, ibid. 2:155 and n. 112) and Christian I's in 1457 (in: "Chronologia vetusta," *SS rer. Svecicarum* 1:97). There are definite

exceptions from the rule we have assumed: the coronation of Waldemar in 1251 in Linköping (see "Chronologia Anonymi," 1:54, and Chronicon, ibid., 186) and of Birger in 1302 in Sönderköping (see *SS rer. Svecicarum* 1:27, 42, 64, 87, 92, etc.).

114. See notes 30 and 31 above; further *SS rer. Svecicarum* 1:28, 94.
115. *Olai Petri Svenska Krönika* (as n. 109 above), 295.
116. See n. 109, above.
117. See n. 33, above.
118. There is positive evidence for the following coronations only: Margarethe, wife of Birger in 1302 (*SS rer. Svecicarum* 1:27, 64, 87, 92; 2:76); Blanche of Flanders, wife of Magnus Eriksson in 1448 (ibid., 1:28, 43, 94; cf. n. 31 above) and of the wife of Karl Knutsson a few days after the king's coronation in 1448 (ibid., 1:97, 165 and 2:155).
119. *Diplomatarium Suecanum* 3:30–31, no. 1811.
120. Cf. *Deutsche Reichstagsakten* 16:173, no. 100: "... als in dem puch der krönung geschriben steet," 177, no. 101: "... ut in libro coronacionis pretacto...," 178, no. 102. Cf. also G. Carlsson "Gustav Vasas Kröningsed," 323 f.
121. See n. 109, above.
122. Cf. my earlier assessment in "Krönung Christians," 62 and the above (n. 120) quoted article of Carlsson. A contemporary report on the coronation is to be found in: Peder Swart, *Konung Gustaf I.'s Krönika*, ed. N. Edén (Stockholm, 1912), 123.
123. Text in Carlsson, as above, 321: Ego Gotstauus electus rex profiteor et promitto coram Deo et angelis suis, deinceps legem, justiciam et pacem ecclesie Dei populoque michi subiecto pro posse et nosse facere atque seruare, saluo condigno misericordie Dei respectu, sicut in consilio fidelium meorum melius potero inuenire.
124. Janzon, "Erik XIV," 175.
125. Ibid., 206 f.; the two texts are confronted on pp. 213 ff.
126. See above, notes 76 and 77; anointing in the ordo A is in Janzon, as above, p. 218–219.
127. Schramm, *Der König von Frankreich* 1:157.
128. Janzon, "Erik XIV," 223.
129. Ibid., 224 (ordo A), after the acclamation of Eric XIV as king: "När nu alt thz so skiedt ähr, skall Konungen Mtt. ledas fram till Altaret, och their siunga eller läsa Euangelium de tempore, hollandes swerdet i handene bart och vprett, therförinnan holla tuå Ordinarij Euangelij bocken." In ordo B, the one actually used at the coronation of King Erik, this reading of the Gospel is placed between the investiture with cloak and the enthronization and coronation (ibid., 220–221), the king standing by with the imperial sword in his right hand.
130. An additional piece of evidence for this can be found in the Diarium of the Abbey of Vadstena, already noted by Janzon ("Erik XIV," 207, n. 7), where it is reported that the successor of Christopher in Sweden, Karl Knutsson, read the beginning of the Gospel at the mass held for the veiling of his daughter, Brigitta, as nun of the monastery. At this occasion the king wore alba, tunic, and cape.
131. Schramm, *English Coronation*, 120.

NINE

Gesture in the Coronation Ceremonies of Medieval Poland

Aleksander Gieysztor

As a mode of expression at once simple and full of underlying connotations, gestures are a subject worthy of research.[1] The context in which we will be dealing with them in this study, royal ceremony, is in no way defined by any real or pretended spontaneity, but rather by a ritualistic and theatrical geometry that can be demonstrated on particular examples. The anointing and coronation of the kings of Poland, ritual and spectacle at the same time, had been nourished by a centuries-long tradition of programmed dramaturgy of gestures and words appropriate to the sanctifying elevation of a new sovereign. As throughout Europe, these ceremonies transmitted ideas and concepts of a learned and literate elite through the words and gestures of another culture, that of political government, to a popular culture; the receptivity of these transmitted ideas was rooted above all in the logic of symbols. To what extent the culture of the people knew how to adapt, enrich, or select from these concepts and thus influence the initiators of the ideas must remain an open question.

The royal funeral, the consecration of the new king, and his solemn entry form a set of public displays of supreme power. The sacred elements of these demonstrations are expressed in an appropriate liturgy. Sovereign power is most vividly manifest in the coronation and the funeral, but is by no means absent from the royal entry either, even if its French name, *joyeuse*, emphasizes its play-like aspects. All these ceremonies belong to a domain of structured social activities which have been studied by historians for some time but discussed primarily in reference to the symbolism of objects.[2] However, the functioning of these signs and insignia will form a coherent system of communication only if other elements are also considered. To these belong the gestures, the words, the spatial and decorative framework including light and colors, the music, the public—in fact the entire mise en scène of a minutely regulated collective show. All these elements had a role to play in the coronation ceremony in order to express in a kind of synthesis the many relationships that existed in the community. The aim was the preservation of the social order by enacting a symbolic and sociopsychological drama, just as it is sometimes done in our days on similar occasions.

The present study is based on the perception that the entire complex of rituals reveals a latent mental structure far more durable than the more or less rapidly changing social or political situations. Those elements of the Polish ordines which relate to gesture or bodily movement have to be placed in this totality of a ritual context.[3]

A study of these rites is possible from the late thirteenth century onwards when anointing was resumed under King Przemysl I of Great Poland and continued until the last coronation, that of Stanislas Augustus in 1764.[4] Our research is based on different types of evidence: on more or less detailed descriptions; the ordines themselves (compiled in the official version for the coronation of Wladislas III as *Ordo qualiter eligendus in regem induatur*); the ceremonials, of which the oldest dates of 1530; monuments (see fig. 9.1) and objects connected with the rites; and images from the coronations (see figs. 9.2 and 9.3). Analyzed typologically, they permit us to reconstruct the typical procedures of a coronation observed under different reigns. Such an approach appears all the more justified since these rites were part of a cyclic pattern that required that each monarch use the same common stock of words and gestures to assure the legitimacy of his sacred right to power. Certainly, some changes could occur; a major one was the introduction of a political oath, the *Articuli Henriciani et pacta conventa* at the coronation of Henry of Valois in 1575, but we shall not discuss these in the present inquiry.[5]

Following the chronology of the rituals to be studied, our enquiry begins a few days before the coronation ceremony itself. It is noteworthy that Polish custom placed the official royal funeral at a date fairly close to the coronation of the new king, often as close as the Friday preceding the Sunday of the coronation. Actually, the political doctrine in Poland knew the principle of the "king's two bodies," as expressed, for example, by Joachim Bielski in the sixteenth century: *osoba pańska umiera, korona nie umiera* (the royal person dies, the crown dies not).[6] As soon as elected, either from among the members of the dynasty or from another family, the king of Poland was, even before being crowned, entitled to perform a variety of perfectly legitimate political acts. There is, however, one domain that was restricted to a king who had been duly crowned: it is the sphere where the sacred is always present, that of justice. Official, regular jurisdiction went into effect in the name of the king only after his consecration.

In the deliberate juxtaposition of funeral and coronation we may also detect a profound belief in the existence of a connection between the death and the life that succeeds it. Between a man's physical death and his social

Figure 9.1. Cracow, Wawel Cathedral. Holy Cross Chapel. Tombstone of Casimir IV Jagiello, 1492–1494, by Veit Stoss.

Figure 9.2. Cracow, National Museum. Czartoryski Library. Pontifical of Erasmus Ciolek (1507–1510). Coronation scene.

obliteration it is necessary to give him a suitable *pompa funebris*, a ritual farewell and a reconciliation with the dead person, whose stiff body is no more capable of human gestures and is until its burial surrounded by an aura of sacred horror. Before being placed in the crypt of the cathedral, the king's body natural had symbolically to escape its *rigor mortis*. Ever since 1370 when Casimir the Great was solemnly reburied (after a funeral held by the Polish lords and prelates) by his successor Louis of Anjou, King of Hungary, until the last royal funeral, a mounted knight would appear in the cathedral with the visor of his helmet closed. It is specifically stated that he represented the dead king. The horseman then collapsed with great noise on the pavement and broke the wooden shaft of his lance, while at the same time the royal seal was broken. This figure recalls the theme of the living corpse who must be appeased by appropriate rites. This rite of the "faceless knight" was wordless; a mimed drama was sufficient to convey the end of the power of the deceased and move the emotions of the audience.[7]

Figure 9.3. Cracow, National Museum. Czartoryski Library. Pontifical of Erasmus Ciolek (before 1507). The king *in maiestate*.

The Polish ceremony of coronation, elaborate and archaic, stood in a tradition, both European and local, of the magic nature of royal power. On the eve of his consecration, the king had to fast, give alms, and make confession. He also undertook a pilgrimage on foot within Cracow, from the royal castle to the church of St. Stanislas in Rupella, the patron saint of the kingdom. This act, during which the king remained silent and performed only with his body, represented the preparation of the initiate, necessary for his passing from an ordinary lay state to a sacred one, reserved to the initiated. The ritual movement of the king-elect walking from his residence to a sacred place preceding the consecration can be neatly contrasted to his joyful entry into town on horseback on the day after the coronation. The procession on the eve of the coronation, viewed at the time as a gesture of humility and composure, was a highly public display, accessible to the masses and aimed at filling them with amazement through visual contact with the *rex coronandus*. In contrast, the rest of the ceremonies restricted the number of participants: they were selected from the elite, for only they were admitted to the cathedral, just as was the custom elsewhere, for example, in Reims or Westminster.[8]

On the night before the coronation, the king's sleep acquired a symbolic significance as reflected in his ritual waking on the next morning. Sunday morning a procession left the cathedral and made its way to the king's bedroom. The king awaited them lying on his bed, dressed in episcopal vestments: sandals, humeral, alb, maniple, stole, dalmatic, pluvial, gloves, and amice.[9] (In the eighteenth century a mere armchair was used for the king in this ceremony.) The metropolitan *in pontificalibus* approached him, sprinkled him with holy water, and burnt incense. He then stretched out his hand and helped the king to rise. Although a prayer was said in this phase of the royal initiation, it was the series of gestures and not the words which assured its success as a part of the whole complex of ceremonies.[10]

In the subsequent procession from the castle to the cathedral other gestures are to be noted: the king was borne by two bishops; the regalia (scepter, orb, sword) were displayed by secular lords who held them up high on cushions or gilt trays; the grand marshal carried his staff pointing downwards, and the standard-bearer kept the banner of the kingdom still furled, signifying that the king had not yet come into the fullness of his power. This symbolic grammar was simple and effective, without need of any verbal explanation whatsoever.[11]

Like any other spectacle, the liturgy of the coronation required a well-defined scene: there was to be a stage and an audience. The clergy as the primary source of sacred power was on the stage, and the lords, representing political power, were the audience. Once the procession entered the church and the royal insignia were placed on the altar of St. Stanislas, in the center of the cathedral, the king-elect was seated on a low chair next to the altar. The first phase of the rite, in Cracow as elsewhere, was the royal oath with texts both spoken and sung, questions asked by the archbishop and pledges given by the king and completed by the triple acclamation of clergy and people: *Radzi, radzi, radzi!* (We will!) The well-designed choreographic composition, aimed at attracting the attention of the spectators, was performed by the three officiating bishops, who repeatedly removed and replaced their miters blessing the king as he left his seat to kneel before the altar.[12]

The next phase takes us directly to the climax of the ceremony, the anointing itself. It began with a procession of two mitered abbots carrying from a side chapel a large golden chalice filled with holy oils while a canopy was held above them. The gestures of the archbishop were accompanied by formulae of unction and benediction, but the importance of the action derived from the sacred materials and the movements whose magical character is obvious: with a single sway of his right hand (uno contextu) the archbishop anointed the king's head, chest, shoulders, and arms. In modern times anointing was confined to the hands, the right arm, and the shoulders, but the symbolic core of the sacred anatomy was retained. The unction was followed by a brief silence, specifically stipulated in the *ordo coronandi*, accompanied by the absence of any gesture. It was to suggest to the collective imagination the moment of supernatural intervention which transformed a layman into an anointed person, a *christus domini*, in many ways equal to the bishops.[13]

The third phase of the rites, the investiture with the insignia of royal power, was performed between Epistle and Gospel. One of the peculiarities of the Polish coronation was the extent to which it was integrated into the mass in medieval as well as modern times down to the eighteenth century. The archbishop sat in front of the altar; the king was led there by the bishops and knelt at their feet. The coronator first handed him a naked sword. This sword, called Szczerbiec (Jagged), used at all Polish coronations, originates from the late twelfth century and has been preserved to our own days. (After having spent some time in Canada during World War II, it was finally returned to its original home, the royal castle of Wawel in Cracow, in 1962.) The king took the sword from the metropolitan and brandished it, tracing a cross in the air pointing to the four cardinal directions, another aspect of the ceremony which seems to be peculiar to Poland.[14] He then placed it on his left arm, whence it was taken by the sword-bearer, replaced in its sheath, and returned to the archbishop who now girded the king with it while reciting the formula, *Accipe gladium*. While the preceding rites had emphasized the king as judge and as priest (rex et sacerdos), this part highlighted his role as warrior-king. Although the archbishop's actions were accompanied by liturgical texts, it were once again the gestures that seem to have been the most important. The medieval ordo specified in addition the presentation of armillae and a ring, but these had disappeared from the ceremony by the sixteenth century.[15]

In the next phase, the coronation itself, the king knelt down; two bishops held the crown above his head; with their help the archbishop placed it on the king's head. Thereafter the king was given orb and scepter, with the pertinent formulae. Pictorial evidence (see, for example, fig. 9.4) points to the silent participation of the magnates of the realm. They had kept the royal insignia and passed them now in silence from the lay sphere to the sacred, that is, to the officiating archbishop. Since the significance of the gestures and of the symbolic objects was immediately understood, the accompanying explanations in liturgical Latin were, in fact, unnecessary both to participants and witnesses alike. Ritual gesture always has a magical quality, and the memorableness of the ceremony was related to gestures and objects, the crown being the most important among them for the perpetuation of the concept of kingship. Ever since 1320 the crown was considered to be something of a relic attributed to Boleslaw the Brave's coronation in 1025. According to an eighteenth-century text "superstition blames misfortunes of some Polish kings on the fact that they preferred to use other crowns for their coronation."[16]

The fourth and last phase of the coronation ceremony may be called the enthronement. During the mass the king partook of bread and wine, and at the *Pax tecum* kissed a crucifix proffered by the archbishop.[17] After the mass, the king mounted the steps to the throne assisted by the bishops; the archbishop placed him on the throne in majesty, pronouncing the *Sta et retine*, gave him the kiss of peace, and after the Te Deum proclaimed him king by repeating three times *Vivat Rex*, which was echoed in chorus by those present. Then followed the first sovereign act of the new king, the creation of knights, by touching them three times with a drawn sword. Despite the military aspects, knighting should be seen essentially as an act of justice, coming from the throne, which is one of its eminent symbols.[18]

Thus ended the rites performed within the sacred space.[19] Two more important ones took place outside, however. One of these was the coronation feast. The images of the king as judge, as priest, and as warrior were thereby augmented by that of the king as host, the preserver of plenty.[20] A final ceremony led the king, this time on horseback, into the main square of the city, where he sat on a raised seat in front of the town hall and received the homage of the townspeople. According to the fifteenth-century author, Jan Długosz,[21] this mass scene also had its *vetustus ritus*, which regulated the public spectacle of the king's "joyful" entry.[22]

Clearly, all these rites belong to that category of social drama by which, through symbols, gestures, and words, people express their collective experience. Actors and spectators form a unity to accomplish this purpose. Dramas of this kind express and satisfy genuine needs and emotions and address significant problems of the participants. The social drama of the coronation ceremonies focuses on different levels of consciousness: from the principal

Figure 9.4. Benedictine nunnery, Staniatki near Cracow; coronation of King John Casimir, 1640.

one, that of a religious system, which the king reaches during his consecration, to others, even profane ones, which intermingle with the sublime. Besides the immutable magical forms, applied to the raising of the king to the divine order, there are other signifiers and signifieds, such as a mutual contract, something like a marriage of king and people. Other elements, though nonreligious, are not entirely bereft of the sacred, for example, the brandishing of the sword, the knighting, the feast, or the homage of the townspeople in the capital.

What are the implications of all this for the history and anthropology of gesture? The first observation is that the gestures we have been dealing with have to do with ritual in the strict sense of the word, that is with actions intended at directing invisible forces toward a defined goal. In the liturgy gesture was organized in a set and rigorous manner definitively embodied in a coherent language. By way of suggestions for investigation, one need only mention: postures of prayer, standing or kneeling, arms open in the expectation of grace, or hands symbolically tied; the kiss of peace and kissing the crucifix; ritual burning of incense; benediction; the liturgical procession, which has its own rhythm and is composed of people who by their gestures express the sense of being a group engaged in a solemn cultural act; the quasi-divine "epiphany" of the king seated on his throne, resting, yet alert. All these gestures and bodily motions can be found in other ceremonies as well.[23] Their particular importance here, as well as that of the symbolic objects used, is determined by their place in the syntax of the coronation rites. This syntax also contains gestures rarely if ever encountered elsewhere in religious rites, such as the presentation of a symbolic object and its symmetric acceptance; ritual awakening; and ritual anointing.

The second observation concerns the character of the long sequences of gestures which form the totality of the rite and spectacle of a Polish coronation. It is easy to establish parallels to a theatrical representation, inasmuch as their similarities concern the most superficial and external aspects of both. Precisely in the gesture the relationship between the two seems most profound. Unlike other symbols, gesture must be immediately comprehensible. Its relative rapidity does not allow reflection and analysis in contrast to symbolic objects or words, whether spoken or written. Within a framework of fictitious actions, religious or theatrical gestures illustrate things that are not present and do so in a way that is highly visible, comprehensible, emotionally engaging, and instantaneous. Everyday gestures are chosen meticulously for the purpose of the rite or representation, sancified and systematized, and eventually presented over a brief time in specially selected spaces. The consecration and the coronation belong to a global cultural system of royal rites, which, although it may have many connotations, is ultimately based on the central theme of power. In the social environment that produced the actors and directors of this psychodrama, the expression of this theme solely in verbal language would have been unproductive, incomprehensible, even impossible. To understand the fundamental meaning of royalty through gestures and movements, enriched by their auxiliary languages, seems all the more in accord with common sense since, as Aristotle put it in the Poetics, "Man is the animal most given to mime."

NOTES

1. M. Joysse, *L'Anthropologie du geste* (Paris, 1962); R. Brillant, *Gesture and Rank in Roman Art: The Use of Gestures to Denote Status in Roman Sculpture and Coinage* (Copenhagen, 1963); G. Neumann, *Gesten und Gebärden in der griechischen Kunst* (Berlin, 1966); G. Durand, *Les structures anthropologiques de l'imaginaire* (Paris, 1969); *La Communication par le geste. Actes des sessions organisées par la recherche du sacré à l'Abresle 1965–1968* (Paris, 1970); *Gestes et paroles dans les diverses familles liturgiques. Conférences Saint-Serge, XXIVe semaine d'études liturgiques* (Rome, 1978, Bibliotheca Ephemerides liturgicae, Subsidia 14).

2. See, e.g., P. E. Schramm, *A History of English Coronation*, trans. L. G. Wickham Legg (Oxford, 1937); P. E. Schramm, *Herrschaftszeichen und Staatssymbolik*, 3 vols. (Stuttgart, 1954–1956); P. E. Schramm, *Der König von Frankreich...*, 2d ed. (Weimar, 1960). See also: C. A. Bouman, *Sacring and Crowning...* (Groningen, 1957); R. A. Jackson, *Vive le roi! A History of French Coronation from Charles V to Charles X* (Chapel Hill and London: University of North Carolina Press, 1984); H. D. Duncan, *Symbols in Society* (London, 1962); A. M. Hocart, *Kingship* (Oxford, 1927; reprinted 1969).

3. A. Gieysztor, "Non habemus caesarem nisi regem. La couronne fermée des rois de Pologne à la fin du XVe et au XVIe siècle," *Bibliothèque de l'Ecole des chartes* (1969) 127:5–26; "Spektakl i liturgia—polska koronacja królewska [Spectacle and Liturgy: The Polish Royal Coronation]," in *Kultura elitarna a kultura masowa w Polsce późnego średniowiecza* (Wroclaw, 1978), 9–23; "Ornamenta regia w Polsce XV wieku [Royal Insignia in Fifteenth-century Poland]," in *Sztuka i ideologia XV wieku* (Warsaw, 1978), 155–163.

4. S. Ktrzeba, ed., "Ordo coronandi Regis Poloniae," in *Archiwum Komisji Akademia Umiejetności* (1910–1913), vol. 2; S. Ktrzeba, ed. "Zródla polskiego ceremonialu koronacyjnego [Sources of the Polish Coronation Ceremony]," *Przeglad Historiczny* (1911), 12:71–83, 285–307; cf. also his short overview *Koronacja królów i królowych w Polsce* [Coronation of Kings and Queens in Poland] (Warsaw 1918); Schramm, "Das polnische Königtum," in *Herrschaftszeichen* 3:939–962. The Cracow Cathedral MS 35 from the late fourteenth century contains a German ordo with the royal initial W[ladislas]. In the fifteenth century some additions were incorporated from the Durand Pontificale. The ordo in the Cracow MS 17, twice as long as the previous one, linked to the 1434 coronation of Wladislas III, is based on an ordo for the kings of Bohemia from the fourteenth century, which in turn goes back to English ceremonials with borrowings from the German ordo. The "ordo cornandae reginae," edited by Kutrzeba, mentioned above, and also in *Corpus iuris Polonici*, ed. O. Balzer (Warsaw, 1906), 3:208–212 has the same Bohemian-English parentage.

5. Cf. Schramm, *Herrschaftszeichen*, 3:961.

6. M. Bielski, *Kronika polska*, 1st ed. (1597, reprinted Sanok, 1856), 3:1207.

7. E. Sniezynska-Stolot, "Dworski ceremonial pogrzebowy królów polskich w XIV. w. [Courtly Ceremonial at the Funeral of Polish Kings in the fourteenth-century]," in *Sztuka i ideologia XV wieku* (Warsaw, 1978), 89–100; cf. E. M. Hallam, "Royal Burial and the Cult of Kingship in France and England 1060–1330," *Journal of Medieval History* 8 (1982): 359–380.

8. Cf. the ordo of 1434, of c. 1555(?), Kutrzeba, "Ordo," 162, 175. In Westminster Abbey "only an illustrious and select circle could get near" the ceremony, according to Schramm, *English Coronation*, 93.

9. Cf. Kutrzeba, "Ordo," 175, 185; Jan Długosz, "Historia," in *Opera*, ed. A. Przedziecki (Cracow 1873–1878) 13:546. From the sixteenth century to 1764 the king is said to be dressed in *sandalis, tunica, chirotecis, amicto, alba, dalmatica et pallio seu cappa*, according to Kutrzeba, "Ordo," 195.

10. Ordines of 1434, 1530, and the ceremonial of 1764, Kutrzeba, "Ordo," 47, 162, 196.

11. See the ordines and Długosz, *Opera* 13:33.

12. Gieysztor, "Spektakl," 16–17.

13. Ibid., 17–18.

14. In the ordo of 1540: *Et rex accepto ense vibrat illum*; similarly in the ceremonial of 1764 (Kutrzeba, "Ordo," 204). This rite appears also in Wladislas Jagiellonczyk's 1440 Hungarian coronation, see Długosz, *Opera* 13:645. For the history of the regalia, see W. Eliasz Radzikowski, *Korony królóv polskich* [Crowns of Polish Kings] (Poznan, 1899); F. Kopera, *Dzieje skarbca koronnego* [History of the Crown Jewels] (Cracow, 1904); C. Estreicher, *The Mystery of the Polish Crown Jewels* (London, 1945); Schramm, *Herrschaftszeichen* 3:957, 986.

15. The *armilla* in fashion of a stole made of cloth of gold to be put about the king's neck and fastened above and beneath the elbows with silk ribbons is still in use in England, but, like the stole of the kings of Poland, is not handled during the coronation act.

16. Wladislas Jagiello organized in 1412 a solemn entry of the insignia (crown, orb, scepter, and sword) to Cracow after their return from Hungary where they had been since 1382; they were placed in St. Mary's, the main parish church of the city, on public display (Długosz, *Opera* 13:144). This crown, sometimes called the *corona privilegiata* was supplemented in the sixteenth century with two crossed arches surmounted by orb and cross, symbolically underlining the new ideas of Polish sovereignty (Gieysztor, "Non habemus," 5–26). The crown was confiscated by the Prussians in 1795 and secretly melted down in 1811 (Estreicher, *Mystery*). For the metaphorical and political significace of the crown, see J. Dąbrowski, "Die Krone des polnischen Königtums im 14. Jh. Eine Studie aus der Geschichte der Entwiclung der polnischen ständischen Monarchie," in *Corona Regni: Studien über die Krone als Symbol des Staates im späteren Mittelalter*, ed. M. Hellmann (Weimar, 1961), 399–548.

17. The crucufix taken by John Casimir to Paris after his abdication can be still seen in the treasury of Notre Dame, the Holy-Cross reliquary altered in the early nineteenth century; a study by E. Dabrowska is in print.

18. Knighting as the first royal act also seems to be one of the specific features of the Polish coronation with parallels only in Hungary, whence it may have been brought by Wladislas Jagiellonczyk. In England the king conferred knighthood at the Tower two nights before the coronation (Schramm, *English Coronation*, 93–95).

19. If the king was married, his first act after the coronation was to attend the queen's crowning (Kutrzeba, "Ordines," 212–216), just as in England; see J. Wickham Legg, *Three Coronation Orders*, (London, 1900, H. Bradshaw Soc. 19), 62–63.

20. For this aspect, see C. Deptula, "Problema mitu monarchy-dawcyz zywnosci w Polsce sredniowiecznej na przykladzie podania o Piascie [Problem of the Myth of a Food-providing Monarch in Medieval Poland on the Example of the Piast-legend]," *Zeszyty Naukowe Kat. Univ. Lubelski* 18, no. 3 (1975): 41–56; for a Dumézilian approach to sacred kingship cf. D. Dubuisson, "Le roi indo-européen et la synthèse des trois fonctions," *Annales: ESC* 33 (1978): 21–34.

21. *Opera* 13:547.

22. It was followed by a tournament in the main courtyard of Wavel Castle. As Schramm (*English Coronation*, 90) observed, "Men of the late Middle Ages were brought up on courtly and knightly festivities no less than on ecclesiastical, for, there being no antithesis between the, two, the were complementary to one another and encouraged each other."

23. "La prière de l'Eglise est ergon dont la dynamique propre et incessante durant la liturgie," Andronikoff, *Gestes et paroles*, 15.

TEN

The Ordo for the Coronation of King Roger II of Sicily: An Example of Dating from Internal Evidence

Reinhard Elze

Although the edition of an ordo may appear out of place in a collection of papers analyzing rituals, I believe that the present publication can elucidate two very important matters in regard to the study of coronation ordines. The ordo for the coronation of King Roger II of Sicily demonstrates better than any other often-copied—and for centuries unchanged—liturgical document that first, occasionally an ordo can be precisely dated and, second, that changes necessitated by a definite occasion were not as systematically and consistently introduced as the modern historian would like. Both lessons may be of value for future studies of rituals and of their literary reflections in ordines and elsewhere.

THE MANUSCRIPTS

Jacob Schwalm,[1] the first historian who took notice of this text and presented a partial edition, knew of only one manuscript: *C*: Rome, Biblioteca Casanatense, Cod. 614, a pontifical compiled around 1200 A.D., written in Beneventan script coming from the Cathedral Library of Benevento. Our ordo is on ff 22r–30r; on ff 30r–33v it has *Ista est ordinatio de sollempnitate coronationis regis*[2] and on ff 33v–36v the text *Incipit ordo ad reginam noviter benedicendam*.[3] On fol. 36v there is a *Missa pro imperatore*[4] seemingly left over from an *Ordo romanus ad benedicendum imperatorem* included in the register of the manuscript, but later canceled.[5]

In my first article on this ordo[6] I was able to point to three additional manuscripts that might be useful in preparing a text. These are:

  1. *V*: Rome, Bibl. Apost. Vaticana, Cod. Vat. lat. 6748 saec. XIII; a pontifical from Monreale.[7] Our ordo is on ff 103v–111v, followed on ff 111v–112v, 112v–114r, and 114r–115v by the ordines nos. I, II, and III for the coronation of the emperor and the empress.[8]

2. *S*: ibid., Cod. Vat. lat. 4746 saec. XIII; a pontifical coming from Syracuse;[9] Our *ordo* is on ff 17v–22r, followed by OCI III on ff 22r–22v.
3. *M*: Madrid, Bibl. Nacional, Cod. 678, saec. SIV; a pontifical from Messina.[10] Our ordo is written on ff 130v–141r, followed by the three imperial coronation ordines [OCI I–III] on 141r–146r.

I inspected the Roman codices in the Vatican Library and received microfilms of the manuscript in the Madrid National Library. All these liturgical collections are based on the tenth-century Roman-German Pontifical,[11] which from the eleventh century onward was considered the Roman pontifical par excellence (henceforth: PRG). It was later in part replaced by the "Roman Pontifical of the Twelfth Century".[12] As far as the Norman kingdom of Sicily is concerned, it seems that the former was regarded as the authoritative Roman pontifical. Our ordo and the imperial ordines that follow it in three manuscripts are derived from that version of the PRG which we find, for example, in the Monte Cassino Cod. 451 (*C*) or in the Cod. Valicellianus D5 (*D*), both compiled in Beneventan script in the eleventh century. Here we are concerned only with the coronation ordo for Roger II (1130).

THE ORDO

The four manuscripts listed above in which this version of the *Ordo ad regem benedicendum* is included are the only ones from Sicily that contain such an ordo. Two of them have maintained the original disposition of the coronation ordines of the PRG: the one for a royal coronation is followed by two imperial ones and one for the queen or empress, that is, PRG LXII–LXVIII, the German ordo, and OCI I–III. Ms. *C*, retaining from the imperial ordines only the old coronation mass of the emperor, contains the ordo for the queen or empress in a changed form,[13] preceded by an ordo for the festive crownwearings (Festkrönungen).[14] The Syracuse pontifical refers only to king and queen and does not have anything on the emperor or empress. The other parts of the four manuscripts, not examined at this time, follow more or less the model of the PRG.

I have no doubts that the four manuscripts of our ordo derive from a single model and the changes introduced can be explained only by the particular historical situation in 1130. Three major modifications point to this historical conjunction. First, in chapter 21 (of the present edition, which corresponds to the PRG count) the text *Postea sceptrum et baculum accipiat*... was changed to *Postea septrum et regnum accipiat*. The scepter and the staff were thus replaced by scepter and orb. While this change is not exactly borne out by the rather general references in narrative sources to the coronation on Christmas Day 1130, it accords nicely with the Sicilian ordo for crown-wearing (see above), which was probably composed during the reign of Roger II. Second, two of the prescriptions of the ordo in the PRG regarding the heredity of the throne were altered; a third was not. In cap. 7 we read: *Vis regnum tibi a deo concessum iustitia regere...*, while the original had after *concessum* the words: *secundum iustitiam patrum tuorum*. In cap. 25 the formula of the model *Sta et retine amodo locum quem hucusque paterna successione tenuisti hereditario iure tibi delegatum per autoritatem dei omnipotentis* was cut to *Sta et retine amodo locum tibi delegatum per autoritatem dei*.... It is evident, therefore, that the father of the person to be crowned according to this ordo was not the king. Yet the person who rewrote the text may not have been in principle against hereditary succession, since in cap. 14 the words *Reges de lumbris eius egrediantur regnum hoc regere totum* were not changed.

The first change, the replacement of the staff with the globe points to Norman Sicily, where we know that these were the insignia of rulership. The second set of changes suggests that the coronation for which this text was conceived was none other than that Roger II, who was the first Norman king of the kingdom. This assumption is also confirmed by the third change in the text common to all manuscripts: in cap. 13 the passage *ut sis benedictus et constitutus rex in regno tuo* has been abbreviated to *ut sis benedictus et constitutus rex*. Roges had just become king, but up to that moment he was not in possession of a *regnum* in the strict sense of the word.

We can omit the discussion of other, rather slight, variations in this ordo vis-à-vis its model in the PRG, since they do not appear to have any relevance for the coronation of Roger II nor for any analysis of political ideas prevalent in the Norman kingdom of Sicily.

In studies of ordines one of the major problems is always the dating of the text. Here we have one of the rare occasions when this questions can be easily resolved. I believe the arguments sketched above make it clear that this ordo can be linked unequivocally to the coronation of Roger II on Christmas Day 1130 A.D. It was this text that contemporaries saw as the valid *ordo Romanus*. Having inserted some minor ad hoc changes, necessitated by the given conditions—different insignia, new dynasty—they were convinced they had compiled an authoritative version. Whatever was not changed from the tenth-century model (and its eighth-century original) can be interpreted in two ways: either the redactor of 1130 accepted it, or, even if he held it for outdated, he did not find it important enough to alter the text. This, of course, places the historian in a quandary: it is easy to interpret textual changes if found, but much less easy to explain passages which, though obviously obsolete, were not changed sometimes for centuries. The attentive reader of this corrected ordo will find, for example, in paragraph 11 that the new king is supposed to ascend the throne of his father (ad paternum decenter solium... conscendere mereatur). This passage, however inappropriate for the occasion, was not altered, just as the one on the emperor's duty of the governance of the church (ad regendum Ecclesiam) was not changed in the imperial coronation ordines (ordo XXXIX in the MGH edition) after the Investiture Contest, down to 1530.[15]

THE EDITION

I promised some time ago to prepare a critical edition of three ordines that came down to us from the kingdom of Roger II in Sicily. But then I postponed this task, for I was convinced that the *editio minor* published with my brief comments[16] would suffice as a source for the history of the new Sicilian kingdom. In those times there were hardly any historians around who would have cared much for coronation ordines. Those who wrote about medieval *Festkrönungen* overlooked the one from the *regnum Siciliae* or did not regard it important enought to comment upon. The least "peculiar" of the three ordines that I have presented over ten years ago deserves, however, a proper edition, which I now offer in the appendix that follows.

A comparison of our text with the PRG can be made by any reader; in the notes there[17] and in the ones added to our text (below) one will also find the immediate models for the text.

I am following the ms. *C*, with the exception of chapters 31 and 33–35, for which I took the text for *V* and *M*. In the few cases in which *C* differs from the other three or in which two codices do not concord with *C* and with another codex among the three, I have chosen those variants that seem to me the most "Sicilian."[18] Orthographic variants and scribal errors have not been considered.

NOTES

1. J. Schwalm, "Reise nach Italien im Herbst 1894," *Neues Archiv* 23 (1898): 18–22.

2. Ed. in Schwalm, "Reise," 18–20; also in R. Elze "Tre ordines per l'incoronazione di un re e di una regina del regno normanno di Sicilia," reprinted from *Atti del Congresso Internazionale di Studi sulla Sicilia Normanna, 1972* (Palermo, Istituto di Storia Medievale, 1973), 15–18.

3. Schwalm, "Reise," 18–20; Elze, "Tre ordines," 19–20.

4. R. Elze, ed., *Die Ordines für Weihe und Krönung des Kaisers und der Kaiserin*, MGH Font, iur, germ. 9 (Hanover, 1960) [henceforth: *OCI*] II, cap. 6, 7, 9.

5. Schwalm, "Reise," 18.

6. R. Elze, "Zum Königtum Rogers II. von Sizilien," *Festschrift P. E. Schramm* (Wiesbaden, 1964) 1: 102–116.

7. See V. Ehrensberger, *Libri Liturgici Bibl. Apost. Vaticana* (Rome, 1897), 551; Bannister, *Monumenti Vaticani di paleografia musicale latina* (Rome, 1913), 156, n. 520 (with revised dating).

8. Elze, *OCI* I–III.

9. Bannister, *Monumenti*, 157, n. 523*b*; Salmon.

10. Cf. *Inventario general de Mss. de la Biblioteca Nacional* (Madrid, 1956) 2: 115; J. Janini, J. Serrano, and A. M. Mundo, *Manuscriptos liturgicos de la Bibl. Nat.* (Madrid, 1969), 35.

11. C. Vogel and R. Elze, eds. *Le pontifical romano-germanique de Xe siècle.* Vols. 1 and 2, *Le Texte* (Vatican City, 1963; 2d ed. 1966; Studie Testi, 226–227), Vol. 3, *Introduction générale et Tables* (Vatican City, 1972, no. 269) [henceforth: PRG].

12. M. Andrieu, ed. *Le pontifical romain du XIIIe siècle* [= *Le pontifical romain au moyen âge*, 1] (Vatican City, 1938, Studi e Testi, 86).

13. Elze, "Tre ordines," 19–20.

14. Ibid., 15–18.

15. Elze, *OCI*, 171, n. 37.

16. Elze, "Tre ordines," 8–20.

17. Vogel and Elze, PRG, 259–261.

18. Elze, "Königtum," 109.

Appendix

INCIPIT ORDO AD REGEM[a] BENEDICENDUM,
QUANDO NOVUS A CLERO ET POPULO SUBLIMATUR[b] IN REGNUM.

1. Primum[a] exeunte illo thalamum unus episcoporum dicat[b] orationem:
Omnipotens sempiterne deus, qui famulum tuum N. regni fastigio dignatus es sublimare, tribue ei, quesumus, ut ita in huius saeculi cursu cunctorum in commune salutem disponat, quatenus a tue veritatis tramite non recedat. Per.

2. Postea suscipiant illum duo episcopi dextra levaque honorifice parati habentes sanctorum reliquias collo pendentes, ceteri[a] autem clerici sint casulis adornati, precedentes[a] cum sancto[b] evangelio et duabus crucibus cum incenso boni odoris ducant illum ad ecclesiam canentes responsorium[c]:
Ecce mitto angelum meum. Vers.: *Israel si me audieris,* cuncto eum vulgo sequente ad[d] hostium ecclesie.

3. Clerus[a] subsistat et archiepiscopus dicat hanc[b] orationem:
Deus, qui scis genus humanum nulla virtute posse subsistere, concede propitius, ut famulus tuus[c] quem populo tuo voluisti preferri ita tuo fulciatur adiutorio, quatenus quibus potuit preesse valeat et prodesse. Per.

4. Introeuntes autem precedentes[a] clerici decantent[b]: *Domine salvum fac regem*, usque introitum[c] chori.

Lemma. a) reg. ben.] ben. reg. MV. b) sullimatur S.
1. a) Primo MV. b) dicit S.
2. a) ceteri—precedentes *om*. MV. b) sancto *om*. S. c) resp. *om*. S. d) ad hostium eccl.*om*.S.
3. a) Ad hostium ecclesie clerus S. b) dicit hanc S; dicat hanc sequentem MV. c) tuus N. C.
4. a) procedentes V. b) dicant MV; decantent responsorium C. c) ad introitum S; in introitum *corr*. M.

5. Tunc episcopus metropolitanus dicat[a] hanc sequentem orationem:
Omnipotens sempiterne deus, celestium terrestriumque moderator, qui famulum tuum N. ad regni fastigium dignatus es provehere, concede, quesumus, ut a cunctis adversitatibus liberatus et ecclesiatice pacis[c] dono muniatur et ad eterne pacis gaudia te donante pervenire mereatur. Per.

6. Ibi autem ante chorum designatus rex pallium et arma deponat atque inter manus episcoporum perductus in chorum usque ad altaris gradus incedat, cunctoque pavimento tapetibus[a] et palliolis contecto, ibi humiliter totus in cruce prostratus iaceat una cum episcopis et presbyteris psallentibus letaniam[b], duodecim apostolos[c] ac totidem martyres, confessores et virgines. Et inter cetera inferenda sunt ista:
Ut[d] hunc famulum tuum N. in regem eligere digneris. Te rogamus.
Ut eum benedicere et sublimare digneris. Te rogamus.
Ut eum ad imperii fastigium perducere digneris. Te rogamus.

7. Sublimatus autem princeps interrogetur ab episcopo metropolitano[a]:
Vis sanctam fidem a[b] catholicis viris tibi traditam tenere et operibus observare?[c] Resp. *Volo.*
Int. *Vis sanctis ecclesiis ecclesiarumque ministris tutor ac defensor esse?* Resp. *Volo.*
Int. *Vis regnum tibi a deo concessum[d] iusticia regere et defendere?* Resp. *Volo, et in quantum divino fultus adiutorio ac solacio omnium sanctorum[e] valuero, ita me per omnia fideliter acturum promitto.*

8. Deinde ipse domnus metropolitanus affatur populum his[a] verbis:
Tali principi ac rectori vos subicere ipsiusque regnum firmare, firma fide stabilire atque iussionibus illius obtemperare debetis iuxta apostolum: Omnis anima potestatibus sublimioribus subdita sit regi quasi precellenti:

9. Tunc ergo a[a] circumstante clero et populo unanimiter dicatur[b]:
Fiat. Fiat. Amen.[c]

10. Postea vero, eo devote inclinato, dicatur ab uno episcopo[a] oratio[b]:
Benedic, domine, hunc regem nostrum, qui regna omnium moderaris a seculo, et tali eum benedictione glorifica, ut davitice teneat sublimitatis sceptrum et glorificatus in eius protinus reperiatur merito. Da ei, te inspirante[c], cum mansuetudine ita regere populum, sicut Salomonem fecisti regnum optinere pacificum. Tibi semper cum timore sit subditus,

---

5. a) dicit S.   b) sequ. *om.* C.   c) paucis M.
6. a) tapetis MV.   b) letaniam id est C.   c) apostolos—virgines] apostolorum ac totidem martirum confessorum virginum MV.   d) Et CS.
7. a) metr. *om.* C.   b) a. c. v.] catholicam iuris C.   c) obs.] exercere MV.   d) traditum et concessum MV.   e) suorum C.
8. a) his verbis] ita MV.
9. a) a *om.* CS.   b) dicitur SV; dicant C.   c) Amen] Fiat C.
10. a) ep. or. *om.* C;   b) hec or. S.   c) inspiramine S.   d) providens S.   e) tribuat MV.   f) Per *om.* CS.

tibique militet cum quiete. Sit tuo clipeo protectus cum proceribus, et ubique tua gratia victor existat. Honorifica eum pre cunctis regibus gentium. Felix populis dominetur, et feliciter eum naciones adornent. Vivat inter gencium catervas magnanimus. Sit individue equitatis singularis protector. Locupletet eum tua previdens[d] *dextera. Frugiferam optineat patriam, et eius liberis tribuas*[e] *profuturam. Presta ei prolixitatem vite per tempora, et in diebus eius oriatur iusticia et eterno glorietur in regno. Per.*[f]

11. Oratio[a]:

Omnipotens eterne deus, creator omnium, imperator angelorum, rex[b] *regnancium dominusque dominancium, qui Abraham fidelem famulum tuum de hostibus triumphare fecisti, Moysi et Iosue populo prelatis multiplicem victoriam tribuisti, humilemque David puerum tuum regni fastigio sublimasti, et Salomonem sapiencie pacisque ineffabili munere ditasti, repice, quesumus, ad preces humilitatis nostre, et super hunc famulum tuum N.*[c] *quem supplici devotione in regem eligimus benedictionum tuarum dona multiplica, eumque dextere tue potentia*[d] *semper ubique circumda, quatenus predicti Abrahe fidelitate firmatus, Moysi mansuetudine fretus, Iosue fortitudine munitus, Salomonis sapiencia decoratus, tibi in omnibus placeat, et per tramitem iusticie inoffenso gressu semper incedat, ecclesiamque tuam deinceps cum plebibus sibi annexis ita enutriat ac doceat, muniat et instruat, contraque*[e] *visibiles et invisibiles hostes*[f] *eiusdem potenter regaliterque tue virtutis regimen administret, et ad vere*[g] *fidei pacisque concordiam eorum animos, te opitulante, reformet*[h]*, ut horum populorum debita subiectione fultus, cum digno amore glorificatus, ad paternum decenter solium tua miseracione conscendere mereatur. Tue quoque proteccionis galea munitus, et scuto insuperabili iugiter protectus, armisque celestibus circumdautus, optabilis victorie triumphum feliciter capiat, terroremque sue potencie infidelibus inferat, et pacem tibi militantibus letanter reportet. Per dominum nostrum qui virtute sancte crucis tartara destruxit, regnoque diaboli superato ad celos victor ascendit, in quo potestas omnisque regni consistit victoria, qui est gloria*[i] *humilium et vita salusque populorum. Qui tecum.*

12. Deinde ab altero episcopo dicatur hec oratio:

Deus inenarrabilis auctor mundi, conditior humani[a] *generis, gubernator imperii, qui ex utero fidelis amici tui patriarche nostri Abrahe preelegisti reges seculi profuturos, tu presentem regem hunc*[b] *cum exercitu suo per intercessionem omnium sanctorum uberi benedictione locupleta et in solium regni firma stabilitate conecte. Visita eum sicut Moysen in rubo, Iesu Nave in prelio, Gedeon in agro, Samuelem in templo, et illa eum benedictione syderea ac sapiencie tue rore perfunde, quam beatus David in psalterio Salomonem filium eius te remunerante percepisse decantat e celo. Sis ei contra acies inimicorum lorica, in adversis galea, in prosperis paciencia, in proteccione clipeus sempiternus, et presta, ut gentes illi teneant fidem, proceres sui habeant pacem, diligant caritatem, abstineant*[c] *se a*

---

11. a) Or. *om.* MV; Deinde ab altero episcopo hec dicatur or. S.   b) rex *om*, C.   c) N. *om.* C.   d) potentie CS.   e) contraque hostes MV; c. omnes S.   f) hostes *om.* MSV.   g) vere] nostre S.   h) informet MV.   i) gloria] victoria C.

12. a) hum. gen.] gen. hum. C.   b) hunc *om.* V; hunc N. C.   c) abstineant—veritatem *om.* C.

cupiditate, loquantur iustituam, custodiant veritatem.[c] *Et ita populus iste sub eius imperio pullulet coalitus benedictione eternitatis, ut semper maneant tripudiantes in pace atque victores. Quod ipse.*

13. Tunc ab episcopo metropolitano ungantur[a] manus de oleo sanctificato:

Unguantur manus iste de oleo sanctificato[b], *unde uncti fuerunt reges et prophete, et sicut unxit Samuel David in regem, ut sis benedictus et constitutus rex super populum istum quem dominus deus tuus*[c] *dedit tibi ad regendum et*[d] *gubernandum. Quod ipse.*

14. Sequitur[a] oratio:

Respice, omnipotens deus, hunc gloriosum regem N. a[b] *serenis obtutibus, et sicut benedixisti Abraham, Ysaac et Iacob, sic illum largis benediccionibus spiritualis*[c] *gracie cum omni plenitudine tue potencie irrigare atque perfundere dignare.*[d] *Habundanciam frumenti, vini et olei, et omnium frugum opulenciam, ex largitate divini muneris longa per tempora tribue, ut illo regnante sit sanitas corporum in patria, et pax inviolata sit in regno, et dignitas gloriosa regalis palacii, maximo*[e] *splendore regie potestatis oculis omnium fulgeat, luce clarissima clarescat, atque splendere*[f] *quasi splendidissima fulgura, maximo perfusa lumine, videatur. Tribue ei, omnipotens deus, ut sit fortissimus protector patrie et consolator*[g] *ecclesiarum atque cenobiorum sanctorum, maxime cum pietate regalis munificentie, atque ut sit*[h] *fortissimus regum, triumphator hostium, ad opprimendas rebelles et paganas naciones. Sitque suis inimicis satis*[i] *terribilis, pre maxima fortitudine regalis potencie, optimatibus quoque ac precelsis proceribus*[k] *ac fidelibus sui regni sit magnificus et amabilis et pius, ut ab omnibus timeatur atque diligatur. Reges quoque de lumbis eius per successiones temporum futurorum egrediantur regnum hoc regere totum, et post gloriosa tempora atque felicia presentis vite gaudia sempiterna in perpetua beatitudine habere mereatur.*[l] *Quod ipse.*

15. Postea ab[a] episcopo metropolitano unguantur[b] de oleo sanctificato caput pectus scapule ambeque compages brachiorum[c]:

Ungo te in regem de oleo sanctificato. In nomine patris et filii et spiritus sancti. Amen.

16. *Spiritus*[a] *sancti gratia humilitati nostre officio in te copiosa*[b] *descendat, ut sicut manibus nostris indignis oleo materiali pinguescis exterius oblitus, ita eius invisibili unguedine delibutus impinguari merearis interius, eiusque spirituali*[c] *unccione perfectissime semper imbutus et inlicita declinare tota mente et spernere discas et utilia anime tue iugiter*[d] *cogitare optare atque operari queas. Auxiliante domino nostro Iesu Christo, qui cum*[e] *deo.*

13. a) ungatur CS.   b) sacrato MV.   c) tuus *om.* C.   d) et ad MV.
14. a) S. o. *om.* MV.   b) a *om.* MV.   c) spiritualibus C.   d) digneris MV.   e) max. *om.* S.   f) splendore MV.   g) consolatorum MV.   h) sit *om.* C.   i) satis *om.* C.   k) proceribusque V.   l) mereantur C.
15. a) ab ep.] a MV.   b) ungantur M; ungatur C.   c) br. et dicat MV; br] membrorum S.
16. a) *Lemma*: Oracio C.   b) gloriosa S.   c) speciali V.   d) iug. cog. opt.] cogitare iugiter et optare MV.   e) cum deo] tecum V.

17. Deinde[a] dicatur hec oracio:

Deus qui es iustorum gloria et misericordia peccatorum, qui misisti filium tuum preciosissimo sanguine suo genus humanum redimere, qui conteris[b] *bella et propugnator es in te sperancium, et sub cuius arbitrio omnium regnorum continetur potestas, te humiliter deprecamur, ut presentem famulum tuum N. in tua misericordia confidentem in presenti*[c] *sede regali benedicas eique propicius adesse digneris, ut qui tua expetit proteccione defendi omnibus sit hostibus fortior. Fac eum, domine, beatum esse et victorem de inimicis suis. Corona eum corona iusticie et pietatis, ut ex toto corde et ex tota mente in te credens tibi deserviat*[d], *sanctam tuam ecclesiam defendat et sublimet, populumque*[e] *a te sibi commissum iuste regat; nullis insidiantibus malis eum in*[f] *iniusticiam*[g] *vertat. Accende, domine, cor eius ad amorem gracie tue*[h] *per hoc unccionis oleum, unde unxisti sacerdotes, reges et prophetas, quatinus iusticiam diligens per*[i] *tramitem familiariter iusticie populum ducens post*[i] *peracta*[k] *a te disposita in regna excellencia annorum curricula pervenire ad eterna gaudia mereatur. Per eundem.*

18. Alia[a]:

Deus, dei filius, Iesus Christus, dominus noster, qui a patre oleo exultacionis unctus est pre participibus suis, ipse per presentem sacre[b] *unguedinis infusionem spiritus paracliti super caput tuum infundat benediccionem eademque usque ad interiora cordis tui penetrare faciat, quatenus hoc visibili et tractabili dono invisibilia percipere et temporali regno iustis moderaminibus exsecuto eternaliter cum eo regnare merearis. Qui solus sine peccato rex regum vivit et gloriatur cum deo patre in unitate.*

19. Postea[a] ab episcopis ensem accipiat et cum ense totum sibi regnum fideliter ad regendum secundum supradicta verba sciat esse commendatum dicente metropolitano:

Accipe gladium per manus episcoporum licet indignas vice tamen et auctoritate sanctorum apostolorum consecratas tibi regaliter impositum nostreque benediccionis officio in defensionem sancte dei ecclesie divinitus ordinatum. Et esto memor de quo psalmista[b] *dicit: Accingere gladio tuo super femur tuum, potentissime, ut in*[c] *hoc per eundem vim equitatis exerceas, molem iniquitatis potenter*[d] *destruas et sanctam dei ecclesiam eiusque fideles propugnes atque protegas, nec minus sub fide falsos quam christiani nominis hostes execres ac destruas, viduas et pupillos clementer adiuves ac defendas, desolata restaures, restaurata conserves, ulciscaris iniusta, confirmes bene disposita, quatenus hec in*[e] *agendo virtutum triumpho gloriosus iusticieque cultor egregius cum mundi salvatore, cuius tipum geris in nomine, sine fine merearis regnare. Qui cum.*[f]

20. Accinctus autem ense similiter ab illis armillas et pallium et anulum accipiat dicente metropolitano:

17. a) D.d.h.] Sequitur MV. b) ceteris C. c) presente CS. d) serviat C. e) populumque tuum MV. f) in *om.* C. g) iusticiam S. h) tue] eius S. i) per—post *om.* C. k) acta S.
18. a) Alia *om.* MV; Alia oratio S. b) sacri S.
19. a) Postea] post hec C. b) psalmista propheta CS. c) in *om.* S. d) conteras potenter destruas MV. e) in *om.* V. f) cum deo C; cum patre S.
20. a) perseverabilis MV. b) locuples C. c) cui S; cuius C.

Accipe regie dignitatis anulum et per hunc in te catholice fidei cognosce signaculum, quia ut hodie ordinaris caput et princeps regni ac populi, ita perseverabis[a] *auctor ac stabilitor christianitatis et christiane fidei, ut felix in opere, locuplex*[b] *in fide cum rege regum glorieris. Per eundem qui*[c] *est honor.*

21. Postea sceptrum et[a] regnum accipiat dicente sibi ordinatore:
Accipe virgam virtutis atque equitatis qua intelligas mulcere pios et[b] *terrere reprobos, errantibus viam pandere, lapsis manum porrigere, disperdasque superbos et*[c] *releves*[d] *humiles, et aperiat tibi hostium Iesus Christus, dominus noster, qui de se ipso ait: Ego sum hostium, per me si quis introierit, salvabitur; et ipse, qui est clavis David et sceptrum domus Israel, qui aperit et nemo claudit, claudit et nemo aperit. Sitque tibi auctor, qui educit vinctum de domo carceris, et umbra mortis, et in omnibus sequi merearis eum, de quo David propheta cecinit: Sedes tua, deus, in seculum seculi, virga equitatis virga regni tui. Et imitando ipsum*[e] *diligas iusticiam et hodio habeas iniquitatem, quia propterea unxit te deus deus tuus ad exemplum illius quem ante secula unxerat oleo exultacionis pre participibus suis, Iesum Christum dominum nostrum.*

22. Postea metropolitanus reverenter coronam capiti regis imponat dicens:
Accipe coronam regni que licet ab indignis, episcoporum tamen manibus capiti tuo umponitur quamque sanctitatis gloriam et honorem et opus fortitudinis expresse signare intelligas, et per hanc te participem ministerii nostri non ignores, ita ut, sicut nos in interioribus pastores rectoresque animarum intelligimur, tu quoque in exterioribus verus dei cultor strenuusque contra omnes adversitates ecclesie defensor regnique a deo tibi dati[a] *et per officium nostre benedictionis in vice apostolorum omniumque sanctorum tuo regimini commissi utilis executor regnatorque proficuus semper appareas, ut inter gloriosos adletas virtutum gemmis ornatus et premio sempiterne felicitatis coronatus cum redemptore ac salvatore Iesu Christo cuius nomen vicemque gestare crederis sine fine glorieris. Qui vivit et imperat deus cum deo patre in unitate.*

23. Et ab eo statim dicatur benediccio super eum, que et tempore synodi super regem dicenda est[a]:
Benedicat tibi deus[b] *custodiatque te et, sicut te voluit super populum suum esse regem, ita in presenti seculo felicem et eterne felicitatis tribuat esse consortem. Amen.*[c]

Clerum ac populum, quem sua voluit opitulatione in tua sanccione congregari, sua dispensacione et tua amministracione per diuturna tempora faciat feliciter grubernari. Amen.[c]

Quatenus divinis monitis parentes, adversitatibus carentes, bonis omnibus exuberantes, tuo imperio fideli amore obsequentes[d], *et in presenti seculo tranquillitate fruantur, et tecum eternorum civium consorcio potiri mereantur. Amen.*[c]

Quod ipse prestare.

21. a) et *om.* MV.   b) ac C.   c) et *om.* C.   d) reveles V.   e) illum V.
22. a) traditi MV.
23. a) sit C.   b) dominus MV.   c) Resp. Amen C.   d) exequentes MV.

24. Deinde coronatus honorifice per chorum ducatur de altari ab episcopis usque ad solium canente clero[a] reponsorium[b]: *Desiderium anime eius.*[c]

25. Deinde dicat[a] sibi metropolitanus:

Sta[b] *et retine amodo locum, tibi delegatum per auctoritatem dei omnipotentis et presentem tradicionem nostram, omnium scilicet episcoporum ceterorumque dei servorum. Et quanto clerum sacris altaribus propinquiorem perpicis*[c], *tanto ei*[d] *pociorem in locis congruis honorem impendere memineris, quatinus mediator dei et hominum te mediatorem cleri*[e] *et plebis permanere faciat.*

Hoc in loco sedere eum faciat domnus metropolitanus super sedem dicendot:

In hoc regni solio confirment[g] *et in regno eterno secum regnare faciat Iesus Christus*[h] *dominus noster rex regum et*[i] *dominus dominancium. Qui cum deo patre et spiritu sancto.*

26. Tunc det illis[a] oscula[b] pacis.

27. Cunctus autem cetus clericorum tali rectore gratulans sonantibus hymnis alta voce concinat: *Te deum laudamus.*

28. Tunc metropolitanus[a] missam celebret[b] plena processione.

29. Sequitur ordo missarum, si in feria evenerit, sed melius et honorabilius die dominico. Oracio:

Deus qui miro ordine universa disponis et ineffabiliter gubernas, presta, quesumus, ut famulus tuus rex N. hec in huius seculi cursu implenda decernat, unde tibi in perpetuum placere valeat.[a] *Per.*

30. Secreta:

Concede, quesumus, omnipotens dues, in salutaribus sacrificiis placatus, ut famulus tuus N. ad peragendum regalis dignitatis officium inveniatur semper idoneus et celesti patrie reddatur acceptus. Per.

31. Benedictio pontificis:

Omnipotens deus, qui te populi sui voluit esse rectorem, ipse celesti benedictione sanctificans eterni regni faciat esse consortem. Amen.

Concedatque tibi contra omnes fidei christiane hostes visibiles victoriam triumphalem et pacis equitatisque ecclesiastice felicissimum te fieri longe lateque fundatorem. Amen.

Quatenus, te gubernacula regni tenente, populus tibi subiectus christiane religionis

---

24. a) choro S.   b) resp. *om.* C.   c) eius *om.* M.
25. a) dicit SV.   b) Ita S.   c) prospicis S.   d) eis S.   e) clerici CS.   f) dicens C.   g) te confirmet C.   h) Christus *om.* S.   i) et *om.* C.
26. a) illi CS.   b) osculum V.
28. *om.* S.   a) episcopus metr. C.   b) cel. pl. proc. *om.* C.
29. *om.* S.   a) prevaleat C.
30. *om.* S.
31. *om.* CS.

curam custodiens undique tutus pace tranquilla perfruatur et te in concilio regum beatorum collocato eterna felicitate ibidem tecum pariter gaudere mereatur. Amen.
Quod ipse.

32. Ad complendum[a]:
Hec[b], *domine, salutaris sacrificii percepcio*[c] *famuli tui N. peccatorum maculas diluat*[d] *et ad regendum secundum tuam voluntatem populum idoneum illum*[e] *reddat, ut*[f] *hoc salutari misterio contra visibiles atque*[g] *invisibiles hostes reddatur invictus, per quod mundus est divina dispensacione redemptus. Per.*

33. Alia missa:
Deus cuius regnum est omnium seculorum, supplicationes nostras clementer exaudi et christianissimi regis nostri protege principatum, ut in tua virtute confidens et tibi placeat et super omnia regna precellat. Per.

34. Secreta[a]:
Sacrificiis, domine, placatus oblatis pacem tuam nostris temporibus clementer indulge. Per.[b]

35. Ad complendum:
Deus qui diligentibus te facis cuncta prodesse, da cordi regis nostri inviolabilem caritatis affectum, ut desideria de tua inspiracione concepta nulla possint temptacione mutari. Per.

Concordance:
1 = PRG LXXII 1, Sp 2393.
2 = PRG LXXII 2; cf. R.-J. Hesbert, *Corpus Antiphonalium Officii* 4 (1970).
3 = PRG LXXII 3, Sp 1276.
4 = PRG LXXII 4, cf. Ps. 19, 10.
5 = PRG LXXII 5, Sp 1275.
6 = PRG LXXII 6 (codd. CDRTV).
7 = PRG LXXII 7 (codd. CDV).
8 = PRG LXXII 8 (codd. CDRTV).
9 = PRG LXXII 9.
10 = PRG LXXII 10; GeA 2317.
11 = PRG LXXII 11.
12 = PRG LXXII 12; G 2029; KO 188.
13 = PRG LXXII 13 (codd. CDV).
14 = PRG LXXII 14 (codd. CDRTV); KO 191.

32. *om.* S.   a) Ad compl.] Post comm. C.   b) Hec/Te V.   c) percepcio *om.* MV   d) diluas C.   e) illud C.   f) et C.   g) atque invisibiles *om.* MV.
33. *om.* CS.
34. *om.* CS.   a) Secr. *om.* V.   b) Per *om.* M.
35. *om.* CS.

15 = PRG LXXII 15 (codd. CDV).
16 = PRG LXXII 16 (codd. CDRTV); KO 191.
17 = PRG LXXII 17 (codd. CDRTV); KO 189.
18 = PRG LXXII 18; KO 188.
19 = PRG LXXII 19; KO 187.
20 = PRG LXXII 20; KO 187.
21 = PRG LXXII 21; KO 187.
22 = PRG LXXII 22.
23 = PRG LXXII 23; Moeller, *Corpus ben. pont.* No. 143 (vol. 1, p. 62f).
24 = PRG LXXII 24 (codd. CDRTV); cf. Hesbert, *Corpus*, 4 p. 106, no. 6412.
25 = PRG LXXII 25.
26 = PRG LXXII 26.
27 = PRG LXXII 27.
28 = PRG LXXII 28.
29 = PRG LXXIII 1, Sp 1277.
30 = PRG LXXIII 2, Sp 1278.
31 = PRG LXXIII 3; Moeller, *Corpus* no. 1667 (vol. 2, p. 682f).
32 = PRG LXXIII 4, Sp 1279.
33 = PRG LXXIV 1; V 2745, Sp 1331.
34 = PRG LXXIV 2; V 1395; G 918, 2713, Sp 1350.

ELEVEN

Papal Coronations in Avignon

Bernhard Schimmelpfennig

The Avignon period brought about significant changes in papal ceremonial, just as it did in many other aspects of the papacy. These changes were to a great extent connected with the fact that from 1316 the popes resided for six decades (if we add the Avignonian popes of the Schism, even for eight) in the selfsame town. Usually the Renaissance popes are believed to have started the tradition of papal "immobility," which lasted for centuries—actually, until the many travels of Pope John Paul II and his predecessor Paul VI—but in fact it is older: it goes back to Avignon.[1] The palaces in Rome were ever since the early Middle Ages important residences and places for papal ceremonial: until the twelfth century the Lateran and from the thirteenth onward the Vatican.[2] Papal ceremonies also emphasized the bishop of Rome's close connection with the clergy and people of the City through services in the town and processions in its streets. However, the frequent absences of popes from their see during and after the Investiture Contest reduced significantly their association with the city of Rome and even more with one specific palace. In this respect the Avignon epoch was a definite break and had long-lasting consequences.

The longer the return to Rome was delayed the more efforts were made to build a palace along the Rhône. While John XXII (1316–1334) seems to have been satisfied with the episcopal palace, in 1335 Benedict XII (1334–1342) began the construction of a new residence.[3] With additions under Clement VI (1342–1352) the Avignon palace received essentially the form in which we see it today. The long construction time explains why some of the most important spheres of papal government, such as the Chamber and the courts, did not move into the new palace until the late years of Clement VI. From that time onward the papal ceremonies came to be even more concentrated in the palace. Beginning with Innocent VI's (1352), papal coronations were also moved here from the Dominican convent, where they had been held in 1335 and 1342.

There are, alas, no liturgical sources for this development. We have good information about the events surrounding papal coronations of the second half of the century from authors of papal lives[4] and from accounts of the Apostolic Chamber.[5] The latter also contain many interesting details, such as the fact that in 1352 six new locks were ordered for the doors behind which the wine for the coronation was kept to secure it from premature consumption.[6] But a coronation ordo that could be dated with certainty between 1352 and 1395 (Benedict XIII) had not been known to exist in the fairly rich collection of ceremonial texts from Avignon. All relevant texts that have survived are in collections that either predate the mid-fourteenth century or are later than the popes' stay in Avignon. It is, therefore, necessary to utilize the ordines from the age of the Great Schism, confront them with data from *vitae* and accounts[7] and thus try to reconstruct the sequence of events at an Avignon coronation.

Before turning to this enterprise, it might be useful to summarize the characteristics of pre-Avignonese papal coronations, so that continuities and changes can be more precisely analyzed.[8] Traditionally the ritual of the ascension of a new pope in Rome consisted of three stages: possession (*possesso*) of the Lateran; consecration or benediction in St. Peter's, including enthronization; coronation in front of the church with the subsequent procession to the Lateran. However, the events of the Investiture Contest, the frequent need for the elevation of a pope outside of Rome, the III Lateran Council, and new ideas about church hierarchy under Innocent III changed the sequence and significance of these traditional acts.

One of the most consequential decisions for the universal Church was Canon 1 of the III Lateranum. It prescribes that the person who receives the votes of at least two-thirds of the cardinals present should be regarded the legitimate pope. With the establishment of this quorum future schisms were to be avoided and the exclusive right of the cardinals to elect the pope assured. Another passage, which granted the pope-elect full pontifical powers in the moment he accepted the legitimate election, minimized the significance of all subsequent acts. Even though this strict ruling was not immediately accepted without opposition,[9] it survived into present-day canon law and, gradually, reduced all ceremonies connected with the inauguration of the pope to mere pomp and circumstance, without any legal significance.

Soon after the III Lateranum the sequence of the acts was also changed. While traditionally the possesso of the Lateran Palace and Basilica had been the first act, signifying the close connection of the pope to the town whose lord and bishop he was, this act was now moved to the end of the ceremonies, after consecration in and coronation in front of St. Peter's. This change can be seen as underlining the pope's universal position as successor of the apostle Peter, while relegating his urban role to second place. The same trend was enhanced under Innocent III by the order of the procession: the pope was followed and accompanied by representatives of the Church universal—abbots, bishops, archbishops, patriarchs, cardinals—instead of the secular and clerical officers of his palace, as was the rule in the earlier centuries.

Besides the universalist emphasis, the popes' frequent absence from Rome had obvious impacts on the ceremonies. The *possesso* of the Lateran and the consecration in St. Peter's was often not possible because the new pope took office outside of Rome. After the Investiture Contest mostly bishops, who did not need to be consecrated, but received merely the sacramentally irrelevant *benedictio* were made popes. The inaugural rites were increasingly connected to portable insignia: the *pallium*, as sign of the *plenitudo pontificalis officii*, and the tiara tended to acquire the most important role among the insignia, and the coronation became the most significant act. Hence it is no wonder that, from the times of Innocent III on, a pope, to be identified as such, was usually depicted with the tiara on his head, even when shown as undressed and asleep. From the late thirteenth century onward, all events surrounding the papal ascension were termed, perhaps in emulation of the imperial inauguration, as *coronatio*.[10] This double meaning of the term—that is, the actual placing of the tiara on the new pope's head as well as the entire set of rites following the election—tended to confuse even near-contemporary historians. Papal lives from the fourteenth century[11] describe that their subject was "crowned" by the cardinal bishop of Ostia "in" the church, although in fact the Ostiensis was the main actor of the consecration or benediction inside the church, while the actual crowning, in front of the church, was done by the prior of the cardinal deacons.

These kinds of transformations are reflected in the ordines, compiled in the late thirteenth and early fourteenth centuries, which came to be of great importance for the Avignon inaugurations. Among these an ordo formulated on the behest of Pope Gregory X is most instructive[12] and should be introduced here. It contains seven parts that older texts (see fig. 11.1) mention only briefly or not at all: (1) acts immediately following the election; (2) administration of higher orders (deacon and priest) if the pope-elect did not have them; (3) consecration as bishop of Rome, without much notice about the benediction of a bishop elected to the papacy; (4) coronation in front of the church and procession to the palace; (5) entry to the papal palace, payment of the so-called *presbyterium* to cardinals and prelates, and coronation banquet. All these acts are designed to take place when the inauguration is not in Rome. Additional clauses include: (6) changes if the acts are performed in the City, including the ordination in St. Peter's, the procession through Rome, and the possesso of the Lateran; or, alternatively, (7) the entry of a pope in Rome who had been elected and consecrated elsewhere.

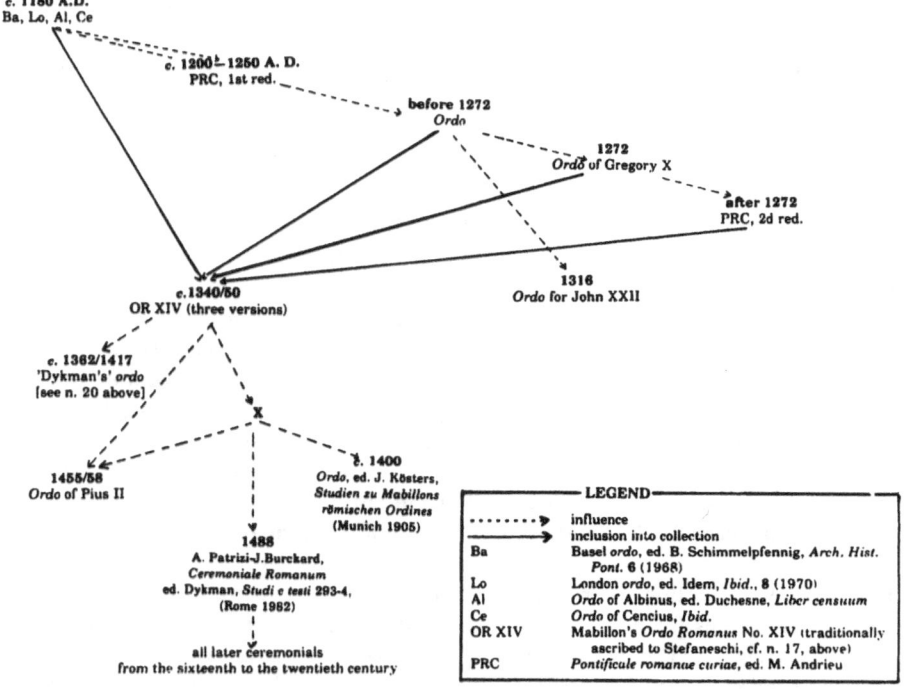

Figure 11.1. PAPAL CORONATION ORDINES

The detailed prescriptions for parts one to five and seven suggest that it was seen as usual that a pope would be elected and ordained at some place other than Rome. This assumption reflected the reality of the thirteenth century, since most of the successors of Innocent III were in fact elected and inaugurated elsewhere: Honorius III in Perugia (1216); Innocent IV in Anagni (1243); Alexander IV in Naples (1254); Urban IV in Viterbo (1261); and Clement IV in Perugia (1265).[13] Actually the patron of this ordo, Gregory X, was elected in absentia in Viterbo in 1271, even though he was consecrated and crowned in Rome on 27 March 1272. The emphasis on the acts outside of Rome suggest that the ordo was composed after Greogry's arrival in Viterbo on 10 February 1272[14] but before the decision to proceed to Rome for the consecration ceremony. More important than the date is that for the first time an ordo had been compiled that prescribed inaugural acts as taking place outside of Rome. This does not mean, of course, that all passages were modeled on actual conditions; rather a series of sentences were borrowed from older ordines, mainly of the twelfth century. A point in case is the procession[15] in which such office holders are listed as the *prefecti navales, scriniarii, advocati, iudices*, offices that had long before ceased to play any role even in Rome. This dichotomy between literary tradition and actual reality is typical for most ordines, even those written after 1272.

One of the models for Gregory's ordo was of relatively recent origin.[16] It had been transmitted independently after 1272 and thus found its way in two versions into the Avignon ceremonials, the great compilation traditionally called since Mabillon *Ordo Romanus XIV* (see fig. 11.1).[17] It prescribed the rites in Rome from the benediction in St. Peter's down to the banquet in the Lateran. Because of its multiple transmission it had a greater influence on the knowledge of city-Roman traditions in Avignon than its derivate, the Gregory X ordo, which found its way in a third version into the *Ordo Romanus XIV*. Its importance is documented by an ordo that follows it to a great extent, written for the coronation of John XXII on 5 September 1316 in Lyons.[18] Although, as we have seen in the Gregory X ordo, the titles of the participants in the procession are usually left unaltered, this ordo is very much geared to the local conditions in Lyons. The entire ordo found its way into the compilation of the *Ordo Romanus XIV*, in all three of its versions, and shall be adduced for the Avignon coronations, especially for those of 1335 and 1342, because it is a fine example of how a text based on Roman conditions could be adapted for another location. Actually because these first two events took place before the completion of the papal palace, the Lyons ordo fitted well, its last passages even unchanged, for the banquet was held in both places in a Dominican convent.[19]

This ordo could also be used for coronations in the papal palace, as evidenced in an ordo recently published for the first time by Marc Dykmans.[20] While a note in this unique manuscript suggests that it was used for the coronation of Pope Martin V on 21 December 1417 in Constance, in contrast to Dykmans, I believe that it was not written for this occasion but rather compiled still in Avignon. Let me present my reason for the alternative dating, which would mean that this is the only known ordo written during the period when the popes were crowned in the new palace of Avignon. That it was not composed for a specific occasion but written before 1417 is indicated by the fact that no name is used in most of the formulae and only in a single instance[21] has the name *Martinus* been inserted above the usual "N." For the acts following the investiture with the *pallium*[22] the order of 1316 was copied almost verbatim, but the references to locations in Lyons[23] are incomplete, suggesting that the ordo was to be amended for every particular situation. Only once are the Constance conditions considered: it was there that the pope resided not, as in Lyons, in the Dominican, but in the Augustinian convent.[24] However, this reference proves merely that the version retained in the only known manuscript was prepared for 1417, but not that its original text was of that date. Indeed, several corrupt and misunderstood words in the extant manuscript point to a lost, older original.

The possibility exists that the text originated in Rome during the Great Schism, but the first thirty-nine paragraphs contradict such a hypothesis: they are only marginally related to the older, above mentioned ordines and contain much new material. The most telling are the first few paragraphs, according to which the pope leaves his chambers and enters the palace chapel called *capella magna*, where he receives liturgical dress.[25] The subsequent acts are also performed in this chapel. Although there was such a chapel in the Vatican Palace since Urban V,[26] it was not used in the papal coronation; the Roman popes of the Schism were consecrated or blessed in St. Peter's and crowned on its steps, following old Roman tradition.[27] The architecture implied in the ordo—procession from living quarters through a door to the altar of the chapel and then across to the end of it—conforms best with that of the Avignon palace (see fig. 11.2). The ordo foresaw a pope who was a priest but not a bishop; hence no priestly ordination (as in 1371 for Gregory XI) but an episcopal consecration is contained in it. These facts point to the consecration and coronation of Urban V (on 6 November 1362) who indeed was a priest but not a bishop. Even if the exact date is not stringently proven by these considerations, I hope to have demonstrated that this ordo should be seriously considered in the reconstruction of Avignonese coronations.

It is best to start with the coronation before 1352 and then examine the changes that were caused by the transfer of the ceremonies into the new palace. As already mentioned, Benedict XII and Clement VI were crowned in 1335 and 1342, respectively, not in and in front of the cathedral, but in the convent of the Dominicans. This location is surprising since their predecessors, Clement V in 1305 and John XXII in 1316, chose the cathedral church

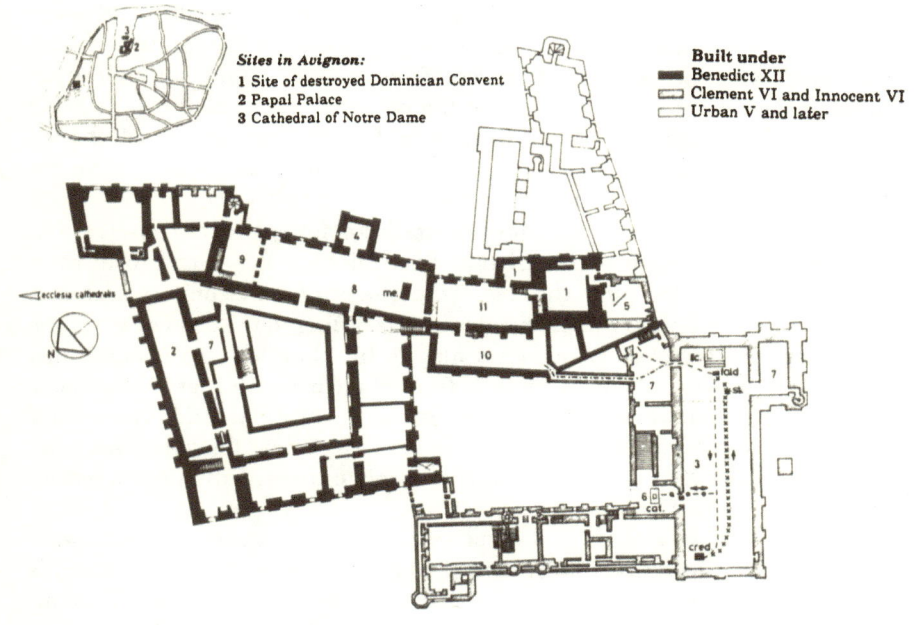

LEGEND

Parts of the papal palace:
1. Camera papae
2. Capella magna of Benedict XII (Chapel of St. John)
3. Capella magna of Clement VI (Chapel of St. Peter)
4. Capella parva (c. consistorii), capella tinelli
5. [upper floor] Capella secreta (Chapel of St. Michael)
6. Indulgence window
7. Sacristies
8. Tinellus magnus
9. Dressatorium
10. Tinellus parvus
11. Camera paramenti

Procession routes:
- - - - - ingressus capelle (Innocentii VI)
-·-·-·- ingressus capelle (Urbani V et al.)
▪▪▪▪▪▪ processio ad altare
-o-o-o- processio ad coronandum papam

Places mentioned in the ordines:
c.   cathedra papae
cat.   catafalcus ad coronandum papam
fald.   faldistorium papae
me.   mensa papae
st.   locus ad imburendum stupam

Figure 11.2. THE PAPAL PALACE IN AVIGNON
(by B. Schimmelpfennig after the plan of S. Gagnières)

of Lyons for their coronations. The cathedral in Avignon with the adjacent episcopal-papal palace would have nicely paralleled the Roman set-up with St. Peter's and the Vatican. The size of the convent could not have been decisive, as we are told that parts of the convent were torn down to make room for the events and had to be restored later.[28] Also, the papal chapel, used after 1352, was by no means larger than the cathedral. With our present knowledge we cannot explain this choice.

Following the centuries-old liturgical tradition for episcopal consecration, both popes received their benediction on a Sunday. Benedict had already moved the day before[29] into the convent, perhaps for mere comfort, and thus had made it a temporary papal residence. According to the ordo of 1316, the pope-elect proceeded on Sunday morning to the church of the Dominicans. After a first prayer on a *faldistorium*, in front of the main altar or in the center of the church, he received the first reverence of the cardinals and prelates and subsequently prayed the tierce with the *capellani*. While the chaplains sang the closing psalms, a subdeacon and an acolyte dressed the pope's feet in socks and sandals.

At this point we already find ourselves asking a few questions. Who were the *capellani*? Benedict XII had founded a new college at the beginning of his pontificate: the *capella intrinseca*. The new chaplains were to concern themselves above all with the private divine services of the pope.[30] Hence, it is possible that the tierce was sung by this new college in 1342 or perhaps already in 1335. A second question relates to the pope's footgear, which has not been sufficiently researched for the Middle Ages.[31] Third, it would be important to know which psalter was used: Psalm 83, regularly sung at tierce, is quoted in the traditional texts, including the ordo of 1316, as *Quam amabilia* according to the Psalterium Romanum, but since about 1340 as *Quam dilecta*, following the *Psalterium gallicanum*.[32] The change of the psalter suggests the same kind of Gallicanization of papal liturgy as the growing influence of the *Pontificale* of Guillaume Durand,[33] an important process that remained characteristic also after the Schism.

After the tierce the pope, assisted by the senior of the cardinal bishops, washed his hands and donned a particularly precious liturgical dress, the color of which reflected the actual day in the church calendar. He was helped by the senior cardinal deacon and a subdeacon supported by acolytes. The cardinal deacon finally placed a *mitra pretiosa* on the pope's head; the cardinal bishop, who in the meanwhile had similarly taken liturgical vestments, put the bishop's ring, and a *cubicularius* the Ring of the Fisherman on the pope's finger. A brief note on this cardinal deacon (prior of the cardinal deacons): he plays a decisive role in the ceremonies, for he, successor of the archdeacon, organizes the different processions and, just as he places the miter on the pope's head before, he also crowns him after the mass with the tiara. At the accession of Benedict XII this office was held by the old Napoleon Orsini, who had also crowned Clement V and John XXII, having been very influential in their elections as well.[34]

The first procession arranged by the cardinal deacon led from the dressing area to the main altar. In contrast to the later coronation procession, this time only clergy participated. Their arrangement still reflected Roman conditions of pre-Investiture Contest times. They were clearly divided in two groups. The first consisted of the representatives of the Church universal: behind the subdeacon carrying the processional cross followed the abbots, bishops, and archbishops in pluviale and simple miter and, behind them, in similar regalia, the cardinal priests and bishops. In the second group we find the pope's liturgical servants and his spiritual court (the cardinal deacons): first two acolytes with censer and incense boat, then seven subdeacons with candles, surrounding the two subdeacons in charge of the Greek and Latin Epistle, followed by the deacon of the Greek Gospel, the cardinal deacon of the Latin Gospel accompanied by two cardinal deacons, and finally the pope under a baldachine, flanked by two other cardinal deacons. At the altar he was received by three cardinal priests with whom he exchange the kiss of peace. They kissed the pope's chest and one of them straightened his chasuble.

Before we turn to the mass that was to follow, a digression is in order about the question of the famous burning of the flax (stupa). It has been customary down to our own times that at the papal coronation mass a cleric burns flax in front of the pope, at the alter or at three different places, with the words: *Pater sancte, sic transit gloria mundi*, which is supposed to remind the pontiff of the temporality of even his power. The question is, since when has this practice been part of the coronation mass? It is not only that all ordines usually quoted for this practice originate from the times of the Great Schism,[35] but the first papal coronation at which it is explicitly mentioned was that of Gregory XII on 19 December 1406,[36] also during the Schism. According to these data, the burning of the flax would go back no further than to early fifteenth-century Rome. However, we know that the pope himself burnt flax ever since the twelfth century upon entering the presbytery of St. Peter's on feast days.[37] The so called "Ordination of the Roman curia," probably from the pontificate of Innocent III, mentions this act.[38] The pope lit the flax himself at the beginning of feast-day masses, and the symbology was understood as pointing to the passing of this world. The meaning began to be transferred to the mortality of papal power as early as the late thirteenth century, for example by Alexander of Roes, and was referred to in this sense by Alvaro Pelayo, a favorite theologian of John XXII.[39] It is, therefore, possible that in consequence of this reinterpretation the act was restricted to the pope's first festive mass, namely that of his coronation; logically, the candidate could not light the fire himself any more. Although the ordines of the *Ordo Romanus XIV* do not mention it, the new practice may very well have started in Avignon. There is a hint at this change in the ordo dated by Dykmans to 1417 (but most likely from the pontificate of Urban V), which contains the description of the burning of *stupa* at the altar of the papal chapel and reports the "opinion of some" that greater impact could be achieved if it were done outside the chapel at the catafalque (to be discussed below). If my dating of Dykmans's ordo and my identification of the chapel are correct, than the burning of flax at the coronation mass began in Avignon, in 1352 at the latest. But if we read Pelayo's comment as a reference to this act, then the famous sentence may have first been uttered much earlier, while flax was being burned, when the consecration still took place in the Dominican church.

The reception of the pope by the three cardinal priests followed the burning of the flax. While Introit and Kyrie were sung—maybe already in polyphony—the pope took off the miter, said the *Confiteor*, received again the miter, and took his seat on a faldistorium, close to the altar, facing it. Now the three cardinal bishops of Albano, Porto, and Ostia approached him and spoke, in this order, three prayers of benediction over him. The text of these were traditional long before, fixed at least since the twelfth century. Benediction, in contrast to consecration, has no sacramental character; hence the bishops did not hold their hands over the pope's head. They asked for him in three prayers, first, God's blessing; second, God's *pietas* and the grace of the Holy Ghost; and third, that he, who, as successor of St. Peter, held the primate be granted to his high office rich blessings of virtues so that he might bear the burden of the church universal, with God's help. Clearly, there is a crescendo in these supplications, which explains why the senior suburban bishop, that of Ostia, spoke the last one, just as he did at a consecration. Subsequently the pope received the cardinals and prelates to do the second reverence consisting this time of a kiss on the mouth and on the foot.

Meanwhile the prior of the chaplains had laid out the pallium on the altar. After the reverence the pope ascended the altar where the two most senior cardinal deacons held the pall. The senior one—in 1334 Orsini—placed it around the neck of the pope and called upon him to take with this sign also the plenitude of episcopal office on him. Whereupon, assisted by a subdeacon, he fastened the pallium with three golden pins to the chasuble of the pope.

This vesting of the pope concluded for the time being the constitutive acts. At the altar the pope burned incense and then retired to the throne in the apse. In St. Peter's this was the marble throne placed there by Gregory the Great. For 1335 and 1342 we have to imagine that a special *cathedra* was placed under the arch of the choir, decorated with precious cloths.[41] Here the pope received the cardinals and prelates to do the third reverence, once more a kiss on the mouth and foot. Then, standing up, he intoned the *Gloria*, followed by the *oratio* which the pope usually augmented by a silent prayer.

Having resumed his seat on the throne, the pope received the festive *laudes* sung under the lead of the prior of the cardinal deacons. Probably borrowed from the imperial coronation,[42] these acclamations belonged since the twelfth century to every festive papal mass, including the coronation. The names of saints, such as the inclusion of St. Basil and St. Sabas, suggest an even older origin in the ninth or tenth centuries. The laudes hailed the pontiff as the lord of the diocese and city of Rome. As an acclamation by his clerical subjects, these were originally presented by the pope's staff: the deacons, subdeacons, *scriniarii*, and *iudices*. Just like the old saint's names, these titles also survived to the end of the Middle Ages. Only rarely were attempts made at updating them, as for example in a text probably prepared for the coronation of Celestine V (1294) according to which[43] the laudes were to be sung by *capellani et alii*. In reference to Avignon that would have meant that the two groups of chaplains, the *commensales* and the *intrinseci*, who would have offered the laudes standing in two rows in front of the altar.

Since the coronation mass essentially followed the general practice of papal festive masses, including the reading of Gospel and Epistle in Greek and Latin, we may leave it aside and continue with the acts following it. All participants changed their vestments to precious white ones, according to their rank; the pope wore not only the *mitra pretiosa*, pallium, and bishop's ring, but also gloves. This "white procession" moved now to the portal of the church in front of which the pope, flanked by the cardinals and high secular dignitaries, took his place on a profusely decorated seat on a temporary wooden structure, the catafalque. Older texts[44] speak of a folding chair covered with velvet on a small pedestal. A higher construction, the red catafalque, is first mentioned in the ordo of 1316. It may have become necessary because the papal seat was not, as in Rome, on the top of steps, and the pontiff would have otherwise not been seen by the multitude. That was why such a construction was built in 1335 and in 1342 and became even more necessary after 1352, when the people gathered in the court of the new palace could not behold the enthroned pope unless he was seated on such a contraption. The cameral accounts dutifully register the expenses for the catafalque.[45]

It was on the catafalque that the coronation proper took place: the oft-mentioned prior of the cardinal deacons took the miter off the pope's head and replaced it by a tiara, accompanied by the "Kyrie eleison" of the assembled *populus* thus acclaiming on its part the new sovereign. Subsequently the prior of the cardinal bishops announced a pardon granted by the pope the extent of which was chosen by the pontiff. Aside from the relatively new addition of the indulgence, the papal coronation was in comparison to that of an emperor a short and liturgically not particularly elaborate matter.[46] The difference is understandable if one considers that traditionally the crowning had been merely the opening of the great papal procession from St. Peter's to the Lateran which presented the new pontiff as ruler and lord of Rome and of the Patrimony of St. Peter. Hence it sounds only logical that in the ninth century it was a lay official, the Master of the Stables, who placed the crown on the pope's head. The coronation became gradually sacralized after the Investiture Contest, beginning with Nicholas II who had been crowned at a synod by the archdeacon Hildebrand with a *corona regalis*. This function remained in the hands of the archdeacon and his successor, the prior of the cardinal deacons, into modern times. It is unclear how old the acclamation of "the people" was; the first record comes from the ordo of Gregory X. A more elaborate liturgy was added to the coronation in the sixteenth century. Perhaps in response to challenges from secular rulers and Protestant churches, a prayer was added, in which the tiara was interpreted as the sign of the pope's being not only Vicar of Christ but also *pater principum et regum* and thus *rector orbis*.

The actual appearance of the tiara is rather uncertain save that it had three crown bands since Benedict XII's pontificate. It is therefore most likely that Clement VI was crowned in 1342 with such a tiara. However, we do not know whether the new type of papal crown was a newly made headgear or merely a middle crown-ring was added to the traditional tiara that already had a kind of diadem at the bottom and a crown-like band at the top. The solution to this problem would be important because, although the popes seem to have owned several tiaras, one of them enjoyed a privileged position and was seen as late as the fifteenth century as the crown granted to Pope Sylvester I. This one was specifically taken to Lyons in 1305 for the coronation of Clement V; was stolen from Pope Urban VI in 1378 by the Chamberlain Pierre de Cros who handed it to Clement VII; and finally in 1429 reluctantly was released by the last Avignon pope, Clement VIII, in favor of the new universal pope, Martin V.[47] It was this very tiara the crowning ruby of which was lost in 1305 and seen as a bad omen for Clement V. That Clement VI in 1342 was crowned with this insigne or with one modeled after it is implicitly mentioned in two *vitae*.[48] According to these, the pope crowned on Sunday of Pentecost rode on the next day in a festive cortège back to the papal palace wearing a tiara which had a *carbunculus* on its top radiating like fire.

Both reports and an additional source for 1335 suggest that Benedict XII and Clement VI, in contravention of all ordines, postponed the coronation procession to the following day. Since the coronation banquet was to be held in the Dominican convent, a procession through town between coronation and feast may have been seen as too cumbersome and difficult.[49]

At the banquet the pope sat alone at a table, dressed in mass vestments without chasuble, *pallium* and gloves, miter on his head. Cardinal bishops and priests sat at a table to his right, cardinal deacons to his left. Other high guests dined further away or in adjacent rooms, while "the people" were served in the courtyard of the convent. The pope was waited upon by the highest noblemen present; Clement VI, for example, by Jean Dauphin of France. The highest ranking served the first course to the pontiff and then took his assigned place, other lay dignitaries poured his wine, cut the meat, and served the other dishes. Charging Christian princes, even kings, with table service was to indicate, just as at the coronation banquet of the emperor, the high status of the patron, that is of the pope, as being above all clergy and even secular rulers. This elevated status of the pontiff was also demonstrated by the seating order of the laymen, for even the highest of them—the emperor or kings—were placed below the senior cardinals.[50] The cameral accounts for the banquet of Clement VI suggest[51] that the rank of the guests defined even their menu: sweet mustard was served only to the pope; of fruits, the higher ranks received pears, others only apples. (The menus would be worth a special study.)

The next morning, after having had a restful night, the pope set out on his ride to the palace. The subordination of the universal Church and the whole Christian society to the *summus pontifex* is more apparent here than anywhere else. This procession, too, was arranged by the prior of the cardinal deacons, but it was much more elaborate than the previous one, for now the laity was also included. The emphasis on the pope as head of the Church universal was most conspicuous.[52] According to the ordo of 1316, one of the pope's richly decorated riderless horses and the cross-bearing subdeacon were to be followed by the first group: twelve flagbearers, reminding us of the twelve regions of Rome, and two men carrying the standards with cherubim. A miniature from the fifteenth century[53] suggests that these were purple banners with cherubim painted in gold; the twelve flags displayed the coat of arms of the Roman Church,[54] tiara and crossed keys, similarly in gold on purple. They were probably made anew for every coronation.[55] The second group comprised the representatives of spiritual and secular Rome and the papal court. Just as with the laudes, the titles of the participants were traditional. We cannot tell who in fact rode under the obsolete titles of *iudices*, *advocati*, and *scriniarii*, probably middle-rank officers of the Curia, members of the papal familia, such as clerics of the Chamber, auditors, and the like. The mysterious *prefecti navales* may have been replaced by two noblemen. The third group consisted of the liturgical personnel of the coronation mass: the choir with the subdeacons who had read the Gospel and Epistle. They were followed by the fourth detachment, clergy representing the universal and the Roman Church: abbots, bishops, archbishops, patriarchs, cardinal bishops, cardinal priests, and cardinal deacons. That the latter rode immediately in front of the pope reflects in their traditional position as the initially highest group of papal clerics.

The pope rode on a grey horse, covered by a scarlet caprison. A *serviens* (*armorum*) carried behind him the ceremonial umbrella, a subdeacon held a towel ready, to dry off sweat and dust. Probably already in Avignon, the pope was followed by the highest officers of his staff who were not cardinals: chamberlain, *corrector, auditor contradictarum*, marshal of justice. As noted for the coronation of Clement VI, this group also included high-ranking laymen, among them the Dauphin.[55] The marshal of justice was in charge of throwing coins among the people at certain spots, but it is uncertain whether this was done in Avignon.

The route of the coronation procession in Rome is fairly well known,[57] and the ordo of 1316 suggests that in Lyons the stations were neatly adjusted to the city's topography. But there is no information available for the processions of 1335 and 1342. We know only the final stop, the papal palace; it is, however, likely that the cathedral was one of the stations, as it was Innocent's in 1352.[58] Also, probably somewhere along the route, as foreseen for 1316, the pope met the Jewish community, received their laudes in grace, and damned their teachings as obsolete. It is also likely that the streets through which the pope and his entourage rode had been well cleaned in advance, as recorded for 1352. But since we have no details, we had best let the pope enter the palace and rest from the fatigue of the ride through the throngs. Our ride through the ceremonial history is also about to end.

As a last point, let us establish what changed in 1352, once the main buildings of the palace were completed. Most significant, all acts with the exception of the coronation procession were held within the palace complex.[59] If, as in the case of Urban V, the procession was cancelled because the pope wanted to avoid untoward events (fastum vitens), the entire sequence of events was held behind the palace walls. In that case the pope was seen only during the short coronation with the tiara, on the height of the catafalque. The palace chapel, built by Clement VI, was used for the coronation because of its size and perhaps also because of its dedication to St. Peter, just as the coronation church in Rome was. As mentioned before, and noted in figure 11.2, the new ordo[60] prescribed that the pope enter the Clementine chapel from his living quarters and receive benediction or consecration and pallium there. The catafalque was now placed in front of the main portal of the palace chapel, and the crowned pontiff was visible through the so-called indulgence window. The coronation procession went to the cathedral and other unknown stations in town, while the banquet was held in the halls of the palace, all decorated, some even remodeled, for the event. The pope, the cardinals, and high-ranking guests were served in the large dining hall, the entries to which were fenced so that no uninvited person might enter. All other large halls, including even the older palace chapel built by Benedict XII, were used to feed the guests on benches and tables. The huge kitchen built under Clement VI, the size of which still impresses the visitor, was not sufficient; the courtyard was also used to prepare the food, with 126 men working at the spits alone.

Henceforth the palace served almost fully as the frame for the popes' lives. This arrangement was retained by the Roman successors of the Avignonese popes as well, with the exception of the coronation[61] which was again held in and in front of St. Peter's with the procession crossing the town to the Lateran. However, the heritage of Avignon was quite conspicuous: the ever-increasing number of *curiales* and, even more, of noble laymen and bodyguards gradually pushed back the representatives of the universal Church, whom Innocent III had placed so conspicuously up front in the ceremonies, to second place. The pope was shown first and foremost as a monarch, and his people were guarded by arms. Just as the coronation procession in Avignon remained often unmentioned—or even canceled, as by Urban V—it began to lose significance in Rome as well. Julius II (1503–1512), for example, postponed it for two days after his coronation. Thus in Rome, too, the ceremonies tended to concentrate on the Vatican Palace and on St. Peter's, as palace church. The alienation of the pope from Church and people, as demonstrated in the Avignonese ceremonial, was in this way transmitted to the Renaissance popes and their successors, to be broken down only in our own day.[62]

NOTES

1. Cf. B. Schimmelpfennig, "Die Funktion des Papstpalastes und der kurialen Gesellschaft im päpstlichen Zeremoniell vor und während des Großen Schismas," in *Genèse et débuts du Grand Schisme d'Occident: Colloques internat. du CNRS* 586 (Paris, 1980), 317–328.

2. For the Lateran, see Ph. Lauer, *Le palais du Latran* (Paris, 1911); for the Vatican, most recently, K. B. Steinke, *Die mittelalterlichen Vatikanpaläste und ihre Kapellen* (Vatican City, 1984, Studi e documenti per la storia del palazzo apostolico Vaticano 5).

3. F. Piola Caselli, *La construzione del palazzo dei papi di Avignone*: 1316–1367 (Milan, 1981); cf. also L.-H. Labande, *Le Palais des Papes et les monuments d'Avignon*, 2 vols. (Marseille, 1925); S. Gagnière, *Le Palais des Papes d'Avignon* (Paris, 1965).

4. E. Baluze and G. Mollat, eds. *Vitae paparum Avenionensium* (Paris, 1914) 1:309, 330, 343 (for Innocent VI); 349, 384, 394–395, 398–399 (for Urban V); 415, 439 (for Gregory XI).

5. P. Guidi, "La coronazione d'Innocenzo VI," in *Papsttum und Kaisertum. Forschungen... Paul Kehr... dargebracht* (Munich, 1926), 571–590.

6. Guidi, "La coronazione," 587.

7. Besides the references in notes 4 and 5, see Baluze and Mollat, *Vitae* 1:195, 210, 217, 226 (for Benedict XII); 241, 263, 276, 289 (for Clement VI); further, see K. H. Schäfer, ed. *Die Ausgaben der Apostolischen Kammer unter den Päpsten Benedikt XII., Klemens VI., und Innozenz VI* (Paderborn, 1914, Vatikanische Quellen... 3) [henceforth: Schäfer, *Ausgaben*], 33, 184–191.

8. For the following cf. B. Schimmelpfennig, "Die Krönung des Papstes im Mit-

telalter dargestellt am Beispiel der Krönung Pius II (3. 9. 1458)," *QFIAB* 54 (1974): 192–270; B. Schimmelpfennig, "Papal Coronation," *Dictionary of the Middle Ages* (New York, 1983) 3:602–605; N. Gussone, *Thron und Inthronisation des Papstes von den Anfängen bis zum 12. Jahrhundert* (Bonn, 1978).

9. Schimmelpfennig, "Krönung," 250–255; C. G. Fürst, "'Statim ordinetur episcopus,'" in *Ex aequo et bono: Willibald M. Plöchl zum 70. Geburtstag* (Innsbruck, 1977), 45–65.

10. Schimmelpfennig, "Krönung," 210, 241; to the tiara, last G. B. Ladner, "Der Ursprung und die mittelalterliche Entwicklung der päpstlichen Tiara," in *Tainia: Festschr. f. Roland Hampe* (Mainz, 1979), 449–481; now also his *Die Papstbildnisse des Altertums und des Mittelalters 3* (Vatican City, 1984, Monumenti di antichità cristinana II, 4), 270–307.

11. Baluze and Mollat, *Vitae* 1:210, 226, 384, 394–395, 398–399; G, Melville, "Quellenkundliche Beiträge zum Pontifikat Benedikts XII. anhand von neu aufgefundenen 'Gesta'. I," *Historisches Jahrbuch* 102 (1982): 176 (verbatim as Baluze and Mollat 1:226).

12. The *ordo Romanus XIII*, so called ever since Mabillon, was last edited by M. Dykmans in his *La cérémonial papal de la fin du moyen âge à la Renaissance 1* [henceforth: Dykmans, *Cérémonial* 1] (Brussels-Rome, 1977, Bibl. de l'Institut historique belge de Rome 24), 155–218.

13. K. Eubel, ed. *Hierarchia catholica medii aevi*, 2d ed. (Münster, 1913) 1:5–8; to the elections and the places cf. P. Herde, "Die Entwicklung der Papstwahl im dreizehnten Jahrhundert," *Österreichisches Archiv für Kirchenrecht* 32 (1981): 11–41.

14. Cf. the Prooemium of the ordo (Dykmans, *Cérémonial* 1:158): *...sanctissimus pater et communis dominus, dominus Gregorius papa decimus, qui olim...electus extitit,...ad cautelam presentium...hec que sequuntur fecit redigi.* Thus only the election, not the consecration is implied to have taken place. Dykmans (*Cérémonial* 1:16–17) dates the text to c. 1272/1273.

15. Dykmans, *Cérémonial* 1:173, cap. 49. To the sources, cf. *ibid.*, 155–218 and B. Schimmelpfennig, *Die Zeremonienbücher der römischen Kurie im Mittelalter* (Tübingen, 1973, Bibl. d. Dt. Hist. Inst. in Rom, 40), 31.

16. Schimmelpfennig, *Zeremonienbücher*, 66.

17. Most recent edition: M. Dykmans, "De Rome en Avignon ou Le cérémonial de Jacques Stefaneschi," in his *Le cérémonial papal &c. 2* [henceforth: Dykmans, *Cérémonial 2*] (Brussels-Rome, 1981, Bibl. de l'Institu...25), 2:275–87. Dykmans (*Cérémonial* 2:168) dates the text after 1303; to the ascription to Stefaneschi, cf. Schimmelpfennig, *Zeremonienbücher*, 89–95; to election and coronation, *ibid.*, 66–71.

18. Schimmelpfennig, *Zeremonienbücher*, 69; recent ed., Dykmans, *Cérémonial* 2:290–305.

19. Cf. the literature cited above in notes 7 and 11.

20. M. Dykmans, "Les textes avignonnais jusqu'à la fin du grand schisme d'occident," in *Le Cérémonial...3* (Brussels-Rome, 1983 Bibl. de l'Institut...26), 462–473; to the dating, *ibid.*, 141–144.

21. Dykmans, *Cérémonial* 3, 468, para. 46.

22. Ibid., 467, para. 40.

23. Ibid., 470–471, paras. 63, 65, 66.

24. Ibid., 471, para. 69.
25. Ibid., 462, paras. 1 and 3. That the subsequent paragraphs refer also to the palace chapel is, to my mind, obvious from the reference to *altare* and not to *altare maius* as it would be in a large church with several altars.
26. Steinke, *Vatikanpaläste* (see n. 2), 99–105.
27. Cf., for example, the description at the occasion of Gergory XII's coronation, in H. Finke, "Eine Papstchronik des XV. Jahrhunderts," *Römische Quartalschrift* 4 (1890): 361.
28. Schäfer, *Ausgaben* 2:33 and 191.
29. Baluze and Mollat, *Vitae* 1:217.
30. B. Schimmelpfennig, "Die Organisation der päpstlichen Kapelle in Avignon", *QFIAB* 50 (1970): 80–111.
31. J. Braun, *Die liturgische Gewandung im Occident und Orient* (Freiburg/B., 1907; reprinted Darmstadt, 1964), esp. 399–410; more detailed is G. Pouyard, *Dissertazione sopra l'anteriorità del bacio de' piedi de' sommi pontifici* (Rome, 1807).
32. Cf. Schimmelpfennig, *Zeremonienbücher*, 466b: Index s. v. "*Quam amabilia,*" and "*Quam dilecta.*"
33. M. Andrieu, *Le pontifical de Guillaume Durand* (*Le pontifical romain au moyen âge* 3, Vatican City, 1940, Studi e testi 88).
34. C. A. Willemsen, *Kardinal Napoleon Orsini (1263–1342)* (Berlin, 1927); the cardinal is named explicitly for 1335 in a *vita*, see Baluze and Mollat, *Vitae*, 1:217.
35. Schimmelpfennig, *Krönung* (see n. 8), 207–208; Dykmans, *Cérémonial* 3:143.
36. Finke, "Papstchronik," 361.
37. P. Fabre, L. Duchesne, eds., *Le Liber censuum de l'église romaine* (Paris, 1910, Bibl. de l'Ecole Française 2:6) 2:145b, para. 17; and 153a, para. 47.
38. St. J. P. Van Dijk, *The Ordinal of the Papal Court from Innocent III to Boniface VIII and Related Documents* (Fribourg, 1975, Specilegium Friburgense 22), 291.
39. Schimmelpfennig, *Krönung*, 207, n. 77.
40. Dykmans, *Cérémonial* 3:464, para. 14.
41. Schäfer, *Ausgaben* 2:185; fourty-five fl spent by Clement VI at his coronation *pro 2 pannis pro 2 cathedris papae*.
42. R. Elze, "Das 'Sacrum Palatium Lateranense' im 10. und 11. Jahrhundert," *Studi Gregoriani* 4 (1952): 27–54; now also in his *Päste-Kaiser-Könige und die mittelalterliche Herrschaftssymbolik* (London, 1982, CS 152), R. Elze, "Die Herrscherlaudes im Mittelalter," *ZSRG Kan. Abt.* 40 (1954): 214–226; also in *Päpste &c.*, no. X.
43. Dykmans, *Cérémonial* 2:329, para. 15.
44. Ibid., 319, para 30: . . . *sedet in faldistorio super pulvinar, coopertum de samito rubeo, et scabello ad pedes posito, in medio eiusdem* [= St. Peter] *platee, super gradus prefatos, unde ab omnibus videri possit*. Since this passage was also included in the Ordo Roman VIX, the prescriptions about the fabrics may have been observed in Avignon as well; cf., however, the passage quoted in the next note.
45. Schäfer, *Ausgaben* 2:190 (for Clement VI) on timber bought *pro cadafalco, ubi papa coronatus fuit*. Guidi, "Coronazione" (see n. 5), 583–584 records expenses for mason's work at Innocent VI's coronation *in muro cadafalli ad ponendum fustas saumeriorum ubi dominus noster papa fuit coronatus*, and (on p. 587) for fabric to be draped over the catafalque *pro pannis aureis* (!!) . . . *cathedre, ubi, fuit facta coronatio*.

46. To this and the following cf. Schimmelpfennig, *Krönung*, 214–219; the lit. cited there is to be augmented now by Ladner, "Ursprung," and *Papstbildnisse* (as n. 10, above).
47. Schimmelpfennig, *Krönung*, 214–219.
48. Baluze and Mollat, *Vitae* 1:263, 276.
49. Ibid., 217.
50. Schimmelpfennig, *Krönung*, 246, 248.
51. Schäfer, *Ausgaben* 2:184–191.
52. Schimmelpfennig, *Krönung*, 219–231.
53. Reproduced from Cod. Vat. lat. 1145, fol. 36v in M. Dykmans, "D'Avignon à Rome. Martin V et la cortège apostolique," *Bulletin de l'Institut historique belge* 43 (1986): pl. I–II.
54. C. Erdmann, "Das Wappen und die Fahnen der römischen Kiche," *QFIAB* 22 (1931): 227–255.
55. Schäfer, *Ausgaben* 2:190; Guidi, "Coronazione," 589.
56. Baluze and Mollat, *Vitae* 1:263, 276.
57. Schimmelpfennig, *Krönung*, 231–238.
58. Guidi, "Coronazione," 584, records expenses for a catafalque *supra cancellum, quod est iuxta ecclesiam beate Marie de Domps*.
59. For the following, see Baluze and Mollat, *Vitae* 1:330, 334 (Innocent VI); 384, 394, 398 (Urban V); 439 (Gergroy XI); and Guidi, "Coronazione," 571–590.
60. Dykmans, *Cérémonial* 3:462–473; cf. n. 20 above.
61. Schimmelpfennig, *Krönung*, passim; Schimmelpfennig, "Fuktion," (as n. 1).
62. For the later developments, cf. Schimmelpfennig, *Krönung*, 196 ff.

TWELVE

The Origins and Descent of the Fourth Recension of the English Coronation

Andrew Hughes

An essential part of the evidence that must be assessed to determine fully the ancestry and evolution of liturgical services as a whole is usually ignored: much can be learned, by any scholar, from the chants and notation of the items sung in the services (that is, if reciting-tones are also included, most items), and from some of the ancillary liturgical and musical texts such as alleluya extensions for Easter time, and psalm terminations. For the coronation of Edward II in 1308, the consecration service and mass were substantially revised to produce the fourth recension of the English coronation ordo. Several items omitted from the previous recension, used in the twelfth and thirteenth centuries, were reinstated, and others were moved from their original position to elsewhere in the ceremony. Changes of this kind, and some lesser modifications of text, were no doubt significant, since the coronation was not merely an important service in which new liturgical or political circumstances could be reflected but was also a possible occasion for the symbolic prior assertion of ecclesiastical and political messages.

Several features suggest that the fourth recension may have been revised for the latter purpose.[1] *Vivat rex . . .* , the acclamation by popular recognition, was reinstated after two centuries of absence, and placed prominently at the beginning of the service. It was reinforced, too, in the antiphon sung at the anointing, *Unxerunt Salomonem*, also reinstated after omission in the previous recension. Only a comparison of the chant of this antiphon reveals that, although the text was revived, its plainsong was replaced by what is apparently a totally new tune, unique to the English coronation. Because it borrows part of the melody of the Magnificat antiphon for St. Edmund, king and martyr, the tune seems deliberately contrived to stress that the king had a saint as a predecessor, perhaps a reminder that the canonization of Louis IX in 1297 did not confer a greater holiness on the French monarchy. More important, the chant of *Unxerunt* emphasized the king's divine status by pointedly recalling the chant of the consecration of the Paschal Candle to compare the baptism of Christ the King with the anointing of Edward the King. *Confortare*, another antiphon in the fourth recension, was moved, this time perhaps to draw greater attention to the crowning.

Here we have the three pillars of the coronation; popular acclaim, divine anointing, and investiture with the symbols of temporal authority. Strengthening of the English monarchy with respect to the French may have been one reason for these changes; another may have been the need for a "categorical affirmation of the sovereign rights of the Crown" in response to Pope Boniface VIII's "unheard-of demands" and "arrogant declarations" in his recent bulls, especially *Unam sanctam* of 1302.[2] In another revision of the coronation ceremonies, the introit specified for the mass was *Protector noster*, which "usurped" the text used in papal consecrations. These changes, and others in this version of the ceremony, are relatively substantial and may be motivated by important political events, making the fourth recension boldly different from earlier ones.

Table 12.1 shows briefly the English antecedents to the fourth recension, with respect to the items of the consecration ceremony discussed here; numerous interactions with continental orders are not shown in this table.

TABLE 12.1. English Recensions of the Coronation ordo

Recension	I	II				III	IV
Ms	1	2	3	4	5	6	
Date	1000					1100	1308
Firmetur	—	si	st	m	si	m	m
Confortare	—	st	st	st	—	x	(New chant?)
Vivat rex (Shouted at end)	t	st	—	—	st	x	(Shouted at beginning)
Unexerunt (Ending with *Vivat rex* once)	m	st	st	st	—	x	(New chant, ending with *Vivat rex* three times)

In this table the letters signify
i: incipit only
m: music given complete
x: item omitted from this recension
s: sung, no music given
t: text given complete

Some twenty manuscripts transmit the first, second, and third recensions: the few relevant ones are listed here, corresponding to the columns in table 12.1. Their dates are approximate and the ordines are often earlier than the date assigned to the manuscripts.

RECENSION I

1. *The Lanalet Pontifical*, Rouen, Bibl. mun., ms. A 27 (368), c. 980–1000: coronation order ff. 88–93, ed. (1) Legg (*LGW*), 3–9 and (2) Doble, 59–63.

RECENSION II

2. *The Pontifical of Robert of Jumièges*, Rouen, Bibl. mun., ms. Y 6 (369), between 1016 and 1051: coronation order ff. 126–171, ed. Wilson (1903), 140–148.
3. *Pontifical*, Cambridge, Corpus Christi College MS 146, early eleventh century: coronation order pp. 138–150, ed. Legg (*LGW*), 14–23. This is the Edgar ordo.
4. *The Pontifical of St. Dunstan*, Paris, B. N. ms. lat. 943, late tenth century: coronation order ff. 67–75v, variants noted in Legg (*JW*, 1900), 162–173.
5. *Pontifical*, Cambridge, Corpus Christi College MS 44, possibly used for the coronation of William the Conqueror: coronation order pp. 278–308, ed. Legg (*JW*, 1900), 53–61.

RECENSION III

6. *Pontifical*, Oxford, Magdalen College MS 226 (now in the Bodleian Library), second half of the twelfth century: coronation order ff. 99–110, ed. Wilson (1910), 89–97.

With respect to the origins of *Vivat rex* and *Unxerunt*, on the one hand, I need add nothing to what was said above. *Unxerunt* and other items, on the other hand, can profitably be traced through the manuscripts of the fourth recension. To discuss these sources it is necessary to distinguish the date of the manuscript from the date of the order it contains. John Brückmann identified those giving the ordo for Edward II's coronation, 1308.[3] It is generally agreed that the order in manuscripts *a–d* below was written prior to the coronation of Edward II, and that the order in manuscripts *g–i* was prior to the coronation of Richard II, 1377. Brückmann thinks there is little direct evidence to associate the intervening manuscripts with the intervening coronation of Edward III, 1327. The occasion and purpose of manuscripts *j* and *k*, fifteenth-century copies or conflations of earlier orders, is uncertain.[4] Although agreeing that the orders of *a–d* and *g–i* were drawn up prior to specific coronations, Brückmann questions whether ordines were necessarily prepared directly for specific ceremonies. I shall confirm this important point.

RECENSION IV

Of the numerous sources that transmit the texts of the fourth recension, the following manuscripts also give the chants.

1. **Prior to the coronation of Edward I, 1308:**
   a: London, B. L., Harley 2901, early fourteenth century: ed. Brückmann (1964), 455–542. This manuscript contains only the coronation ordo and some other material relevant to the ceremony. Because of its large, clear script, it may have been used in the coronation of Edward II, possibly carried by the king's monk.[5]
   b: Oxford, Bodleian Library, Rawl. c 425, early fourteenth century: coronation order ff. 60v–83v, variants noted in Brückmann (1964), 455–542. This is a Pontifical that seems to be of Westminster provenance and which probably belonged to the abbot of Westminster. As with *a*, its neat and clear hand suggests that it was used.[6]
   c and **d:** Oxford, Bodleian Library, Ashmole 842 and 863, seventeenth century: coronation order ff. 64–73 and pp. 401–423 respectively. These are late and careless copies.

2. **Perhaps prior to the coronation of Edward III, 1327:**
   e: London, B. L., Lansdowne 451, fourteenth century: coronation order ff. 96v–110v. This unedited order is in a Pontifical of Exeter, written in a clear liturgical hand.[7]
   f: Cambridge, University Library, Mm III 21, fifteenth century: coronation order ff. 196v–210, ed. Maskell, 3–48. This is a Pontifical of Lincoln, perhaps copied from the Pontifical of a bishop who participated in the coronation of Edward III, 1327.[8] Unlike the preceding sources, this manuscript gives only the music for the Prefaces, needed in practice by no one but the archbishop of Canterbury.

3. **Prior to the coronation of Richard II, 1377:**
   g: *The Lytlington Missal* or *The Westminster Missal*, Westminster Abbey MS 34, compiled by abbot Lytlington, 1362–1386: coronation order ff. 206–224, ed. Legg (*JW*, 1891), 2:673–735. At the beginning of volume 2 are twelve plates showing facsimiles of the plainsongs of the coronation as given in the Missal. This order is almost identical with the *Liber regalis* (Westminster Abbey MS 37), which does not contain the music, ed. Legg (*JW*), 81–130. The date of composition of this order, whether before or after the coronation of Richard II, 1377, is still not certainly established. The Missal was written by the year 1384;[9] Sandquist produces some evidence suggesting the composition of the ordo between 1362 and 1368 but later decides on 1383–1384.[10] Schramm[11] and most authorities now generally agree on the earlier date. By opting for the later date, Sandquist links the order with the coronation of either Anne, 1382, or Isabella, 1397. I do not recollect, in descriptions of this

FOURTH RECENSION OF THE ENGLISH CORONATION

Figure 12.1. *Westminster Missal* (f. 219v) Preface tone: cadences, reciting notes, intonations, and feminine terminations

source, any reference to the feminine terminations that are interlineated in the Preface of the mass and would suggest that the Missal was indeed used for the coronation of a queen (see fig. 12.1). Even in preparing for the coronation of a queen a compiler might tend to use the more frequently needed masculine terminations. This piece of evidence, then, does not further the establishment of the date for the ordo. The earlier date is adopted here. The order is again clearly written and beautifully decorated.

h: Cambridge, Corpus Christi College MS 79, between 1400 and 1426:[12] coronation order ff. 102v–127. The order in this unedited Pontifical is a copy of an earlier source.

i: London, B. L., Add. 6157, fifteenth century: the coronation order is fragmentary, beginning just before the Secret of the mass. The Preface is set to the solemn tone. The Communion is not given music.

j: London. B. L., Arundel 149, fifteenth century: coronation order ff. 9–22. Brückmann thinks this copy of an earlier order is a conflation of the 1308 and 1327 forms.[13]

k: London, B. L., Harley 561, fifteenth century: coronation order ff. 24v–37v. This manuscript consists of fragments of a Pontifical, clearly for English use. Beginning the coronation order, the scribe himself records that it is *secundum cronicas et registra in abbathia Westymonasterii inventa*. Wilkinson[14] and Brückmann agree that it is heavily dependent on the Lytlington ordo and the former scholar suggests that the compiler inserted parts of the order of MS *f* into the conflation. As I shall describe later, it seems to me that the Lytlington ordo and MS *f* belong to somewhat distinct streams, and that Harley 561 agrees more with MS *f*. It is musically distinctive, in a manner which suggests fifteenth-century revision.[15]

John Brückmann identified the ordo for Edward II's coronation through conventional textual analysis. I shall point to other features, in all the sources listed above, which need to be considered. As well as identifying or confirming for whose coronation a particular manuscript was prepared or used, it may perhaps be possible even to deduce some hints as to who used it.

Useful information can be obtained from the notation of the chants, for instance. Such an investigation need involve little or no musical expertise and is largely a matter of comparing the shapes of each symbol. Although some variants are probably no more than different "letter-forms," others are clearly significant. Excluding the later copies, manuscripts *a*, *b*, *e*, *g*, *h*, *j*, and *k* above transmit the chant of *Unxerunt*. At seven points, *h*, *j*, and *e* agree on a particular variant in musical notation, usually against all of the other four; these variants are, for instance, ♫ against ♫, where the omission of a symbol (and pitch) makes it certain that a change is involved rather than an alternative shape. Manuscript *k* agrees with *h*, *j*, and *e* in four of these variants, although it is in general rather different from all the other manuscripts. Slightly more knowledge of musical symbols would be required to examine the clefs in the seven manuscripts of this chant. The total absence of clef changes in manuscript *g* suggests that it was carefully prepared by an experienced scribe. It is the Westminster Missal. The other six sources have at least one change of clef, always at the end of manuscript lines, except in manuscripts *e* and *j*, where inattention or inexperience has made it necessary for the scribe to change clefs in the middle of a line. These manuscripts, too, are alike in another respect. In place of the final words

Vivat rex, vivat rex, vivat rex in eternum,

manuscript *j* has

Vivat rex, vivat rex in eternum. Alleluya,

with the rubric *In tempore paschali* preceding the Alleluya; manuscript *k*, like *j* a fifteenth-century copy, agrees with *j* on this variant. Manuscript *e* has the same, but omits the rubric and follows the chant with *Infra Septuagesima finiatur hoc modo: in eternum*, distributing these two words over a restatement of the chant from *in* to *-ya*. This last manuscript is unique in assigning the Ps. *Eructavit* rather than *Domine in virtute*. From these points, we might be tempted to conclude that manuscripts *e*, *j*, and *k* reflected a coronation held during Easter, but that *e* takes into account the possibility of a coronation in a

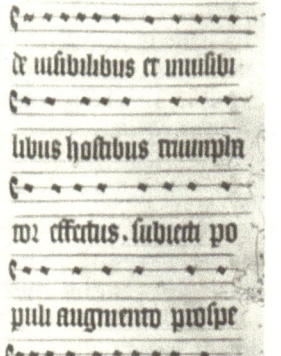

Figure 12.3a. *Oxford, Bodleian Library ms Rawl. c 425 a*, f. 60v Intonation of *Firmetur*

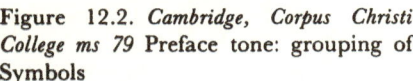

Figure 12.2. *Cambridge, Corpus Christi College ms 79* Preface tone: grouping of Symbols

Figure 12.3b. ibid., f. 61r. Shortened intonation of *Firmetur*

penitential season. Such information might seem to be useful in assigning the sources to particular events.

Firmetur manus, in both continental and English uses, is normally associated with the coronation or reception of a bishop,[16] and under the rubric *in adventu episcopi* it appears with music in the Winchester troper of ca. 1037.[17] The coronation chant in MS 4 of table 12.1, the only ordo of this recension to give the music,[18] is considerably different from the episcopal chant of the Winchester source. It corresponds substantially, however, with the next record of it, in the Magdalen Pontifical, MS 6.[19] This late twelfth-century book gives a third recension coronation order immediately followed by the litany for the consecration of a bishop. For Firmetur, then, we have an episcopal tune in the Winchester Troper and a coronation tune continuing from the second into the third recension. This tune, too, continues into the fourth recension chant, which is different only in being more elaborate musically.[20] Second recension rubrics indicate that the chant is to be started by two bishops: *clerus hanc decantet antiphonam duobus episcopis precinentibus* [or *initiantibus*].[21] This directive is omitted in some manuscripts of the fourth recension. A possible reason for this subsequent failure to specify who begins the antiphon may lie in the extent of the incipit, graphically quite obvious (fig. 12.3a). Musically, the incipit corresponds to none of the traditional intonations for antiphons, and its great length extends to an unreasonable length the normally brief solo beginning. How far this incipit should be sung by the soloist(s) is a practical problem that some manuscripts of the fourth recension help to solve. The earliest ordines of the fourth recension omit the reference to two bishops and thus by implication leave the incipit for the precentor, more musically qualified to deal with its special difficulty: *et [regem] processive in ecclesiam ducant, ipsoque introducto atque in pulpito in sede sibi apta collocato, hec antiphona ab omnibus decantetur.*[22] A few later orders of this recension keep the reference to two bishops but are less specific about their musical function: *Moxque missi duo presules a metropolitano cum parte cleri cum cereis et crucibus introducant in ecclesiam consecrandum regem electum, cum vocis emissione hanc concinentes antiphonam.*[23] One fourth recension manuscript (*b*) indicates a suitable solution, by repeating the word Firmetur after the psalm with the opening of the chant slightly modified to bring the incipit to a close on the tenth note[24] (fig. 12.3*b*). The two seventeenth-century copies (MSS *c* and *d*) also include this essential information for cantor and choir but shorten the incipit even more.[25] The extra musical information supplied in MS *b* suggests that it is a manuscript more closely associated with the musical personnel involved in the ceremonies.

Firmetur traditionally accompanies the procession into the church: *Incipit consecratio regis, quem de conventu seniorum per manus perducant duo episcopi and ecclesiam.*[26] In the fourth recension manuscripts dating from the 1370s, the processional function of Firmetur is removed and the antiphon is delayed until later in the ceremony. The antiphon now accompanies only the movement of the king, his canopy, the bishops of Bath and Durham, and others from the scaffold in the crossing to the high altar.[27] Henceforth until the fifteenth century, no provision is made for the procession into the church. We must therefore turn to the *Liber regie capelle* where it is specified that the elaborate responsory *Ecce mitto* shall accompany the king to the church, and the psalm-antiphon *Domine in virtute* his movement, with monks, clergy, and nobles, down the nave.[28] Ecce mitto is also given in the ordo for the coronation of Henry VI as king of France, in Paris, 1431. Despite its absence from ordines of the later part of the fourteenth century, we need not assume that its use to accompany the procession into the coronation was new in 1431.[29] Neither Ecce mitto nor Domine in virtute is in any way peculiar, and both are used elsewhere in the Sarum rite, *Ecce* on the fourth Sunday of Advent, Domine on Sundays throughout the year. Furthermore, Ecce occurs as an antiphon in the Roman Pontifical *ad recipiendum processionaliter Imperatorem* and as a responsory for regal or imperial processions in thirteenth-century Pontificals.[30] No direct evidence suggests that Ecce was actually used in the fourteenth-century coronation but, in view of its use in continental processions of the same kind and the strong dependence of the orders of 1377 on a wide variety of English and continental models, it is likely to have been introduced when Firmetur relinquished its processional function, in the 1377 coronation, when the later and most influential ordines of the fourth recension were compiled.[31] (See table 12.2).

From Firmetur, then, we can gain several pieces of evidence about the

TABLE 12.2. Alleluya Terminations and Tracts

Coronation year:	1308				1327?		1377		?	
Ms:	a	b	c	d	e	f	g	h	j	k
(Ms. *i* is fragmentary, and has been omitted)										
Firmetur	processional						nonproc.			
alleluya	m	m	m	m	m	t	m	m	x	*
(Ms. e makes the *alleluya* specifically optional)										
Unxerunt	m	m	m	m			m	m		
alleluya					m	t			m	m
(Ms. e has an alternative for *infra Septuagesima*)										
Confortare	m	m	m	m		t	m	m		
alleluya					m				m	m
MASS										
int. *Protector*	m	m	m	m		t	m	m	t	t
alleluya					m					
gr. *Dirigatur*	m	m	m	m	m	t	m	m	t	t
Alleluya V. *Domine*	m	m	m	m	m	t	m	m	t	t
tr. *Desiderium*	—	—	—	—	—	t	m	m	t	t
off. *Intende*	m	m	m	m		t	m	m	t	t
alleluya					m					
ocomm. *Intellige*	m	m	m	m		t	m	m	t	t
alleluya					m					

m: music provided complete
t: text only provided complete
x: fragmentary (item not extant)

*This manuscript gives a totally different tune.

fourth recension manuscripts: their possible origin before or after the coronation of 1377, and a possible destination of those that transmitted information essential to very important participants in the ritual, the precentors and choir.

The remaining antiphon of the coronation ceremonies is *Confortare et esto vir*. It first appears in ordines of the second recension, without music. Like Unxerunt, it is dropped from the third and reintroduced into the fourth recension, and like Unxerunt also, its chant in that recension does not appear to be the same as the one in earlier sources, which are difficult to interpret. In fact, the chant is drawn from the responsory *Regnum mundi*. Transference of responsory chant to an antiphon involves some musical difficulty of a kind that is similar to that of Firmetur; the chant does not correspond to those described in the Tonary, and uncertainty as to how to classify it for purposes of performance is reflected in scribal variants and errors that confirm, in a general way, the groupings already outlined.

With respect to the musical items of the Proper of the mass which follows the consecration service, similar musical details could be elucidated in a comprehensive study. Here, it is necessary to draw attention only to the presence or absence of material suitable for Easter, since it will complement material already discussed. All manuscripts include the Alleluya at mass, performed during Easter time and in some other seasons. Only one, however, manuscript *e*, gives optional alleluya terminations appropriate only for Easter time; these terminations conclude the introit, offertory, and communion chants. The Alleluya, of course, does not need them, and the gradual would be omitted during most of Easter.[32] Only MS *e*, then, allows for an Easter-time ceremony. More interesting is the presence or absence of the tract, necessary for Lent and other penitential seasons. Of all the manuscripts listed above, *a–e* lack and *f–k* contain the tract. One might be tempted again to think that this abrupt change was the result of necessity. The situation is shown in table 12.2, which provides some new details.

In the consecration ceremony, Firmetur has the word *alleluya* in every source. This discrepancy can be explained easily; unlike the other items, Firmetur, as we saw earlier, is present in the third recension, where the Easter termination also occurs.[33] It was simply copied, with the termination, from that recension. Manuscripts *j* and *k*, the fifteenth-century copies, give the music and alleluya terminations for the consecration ceremonies but only the text and no terminations for the mass. Since these sources share common variants with *e*, we should consider whether they are copies of the ordo in *e*. With Unxerunt, manuscript *e*, it will be recalled, gives the termination, together with an option for Septuagesima, but it does not provide the tract. From Septuagesima to Easter, the tract is generally sung on Sunday, Monday, Wednesday, and Friday, the usual penitential days, but not on Tuesday, Thursday, or Saturday.[34] But whether liturgical assignations can be considered consistent enough to direct us firmly to a coronation on one of those days is questionable.

The items discussed so far are those sung to melodic chants. Much can also be learned from those items such as prayers and Prefaces which are sung only to reciting-tones, that is, largely on a single pitch with inflexions for cadences to emphasise the phrase structure of the text.

In the normal Litany of the saints, a special clause is inserted, to be sung as a dramatic although restrained interruption by the archbishop. The text of this clause is recorded with a rubric in the ordines, but its musical setting appears only in manuscript *k*, already mentioned for its musical peculiarities. Can we infer that this book, and none of the others, was either used by the archbishop or as an exemplar for the book he would have used? The special phrase is also appended to the Litany in the Worcester Antiphonal.[35] The recitation in manuscript *k* is on C. In the Worcester and probably correct version the archbishop recites not on the C, which characterizes the rest of the Litany, but on the D a pitch higher, falling to C only toward the end. The dramatic and surely deliberate effect of this subtle change is difficult to comprehend except when heard in context.

A dramatic function is even more relevant to the other Litany used for coronations. This is the *Laudes regie*, assertive rather than submissive. Nothing can be added here to Kantorowitz and Bukofzer's comprehensive investigation of text and music.[36] As crown-wearing and the concept of liturgical kingship waned, from the thirteenth to the fourteenth century, so did the use of Laudes,[37] and in the fourth recension they are recorded in only manuscript *a*, for Edward II's coronation in 1308, and in *g*, the Westminster Missal, reflecting Richard II's in 1377. In both the reference is no more than a marginal afterthought. Although after Richard II's coronation the Laudes recede "into complete obscurity,"[38] surely neither Henry IV, a usurper who used every means including a resuscitation of the special consecration oil of Thomas Becket[39] to strengthen his claim to the throne, nor Henry V, also faced very quickly with challenges to his right, would have failed to use these significant acclamations of power.

As political or temporal approval is demonstrated by the assembled people in the acclamations and Laudes, divine authority is bestowed in the Prefaces, one in the consecration ceremony, the other in the subsequent mass for the king. Those manuscripts of the fourth recension which give the tone give it complete. Several features may offer the researcher interesting clues. To my knowledge there is no comprehensive study of the music of the medieval Preface nor of medieval rules, if any, for the correct pointing (that is, the correct distribution of the syllables of text to the inflexions of the reciting-tone). If there were rules for the tone or for pointing they are certainly not evident from the coronation manuscripts. We can collate the settings of the two Prefaces in nine different sources. The exact form of the tone and its inflexions need not be described in detail;[40] several different intonations lead to the reciting pitch, two different reciting pitches, and a medial and final cadence are combined in various ways. Figures 12.1 and 12.2 show several of these features. The placing of cadences, and the use of medial or final forms, agrees in most sources, although a few consistently continue reciting at several points where others use medial cadences or, alternatively, one or two present medial cadences where most recite. Five manuscripts direct that in the consecration Preface the final formula *Per Christum dominum* . . . should be said *submisse*, and these therefore place a final rather than a medial cadence at the end of the proper text. There is a considerable discrepancy in the placing of intonations and where recitation begins or ends. Some sources adopt one

      Sursum corda.   Habemus ad Dominum.   Gracias agamus Domino Deo...

Figure 12.4.
a: Cambridge, Corpus Christi College Ms. 79 [Ms *h* of Table 12.2]
b: Westminster Missal [Ms. *g* of Table 12.2]

symbol for most of the recitation but use a different symbol on accented syllables, or at the beginning of words, or on monosyllables. These may be merely different "letter-shapes" with no significance. All this suggests that the pointing was quite flexible. In this case (as perhaps in others) the fact that material appears in written form does not guarantee that anything can be learned from the variants about the way manuscripts are related.

If the exact form of the Preface tones was sufficiently well known that only a reminder was required in the manuscripts, one might ask why the scribes bothered to write the whole item out in full. One might also ask whether another feature differentiating the Prefaces in the manuscripts is significant. According to the Sarum Missal, and said to be true of Missals in general,[41] there was no distinction, in the mass, between the tones used on feasts and ferias. The exemplars given for both feasts and daily use agree in following the solemn tone, which has elaborate cadences with several notes to a syllable. According to Birkbeck, the simpler tone, strictly one note to a syllable, was not used at mass but at other ceremonies such as the blessing of the candles on Candlemas Day and of the fonts before Easter.[42] Presumably the simple tone for the opening versicles and responses, *Sursum corda*..., preceded the simple one for such Prefaces, but I have not been able to confirm this from a manuscript that gives the music. Interestingly, however, the simple tone is frequently used for the sentence *Gratias agamus*... even though the other versicles use the solemn version.[43] This musical oddity, which needs explanation, is to be found also in many of the sources giving the coronation Prefaces. Example *a* in figure 12.4 shows the simple clause within a solemn context; example 1*b* shows the more musically consistent alternative. Table 12.3 summarizes the way the Preface is presented.

The Preface in the *consecratio* begins explicitly with the responses set to the solemn tone. Since only that tone was used for mass,[44] the Prefaces for the coronation mass omit the responses and begin immediately with the proper text. Manuscript *h* alone includes them, in solemn form. In view of this solemn opening, it is a surprise to find that for the proper continuation of

FOURTH RECENSION OF THE ENGLISH CORONATION 209

TABLE 12.3. Prefaces

Coronation year:	1308				1327?		1377			?	
Ms.:	a	b	c	d	e	f	g	h	i	j	k
CONSECRATION											
Responses	S	S	S	S	S	S	S	S	x	S	S
Tone	s	s	s	s	s	s	s	s	x	s	s
MASS											
Responses	—	—	—	—	—	—	—	S	—	—	—
Tone	s	s	s	s.	*	S	s	s	S	S	x

S: Solemn tone   s: simple tone
x: fragmentary (item not extant)

*This Preface omitted, although the manuscript is otherwise complete.

both Prefaces almost all sources adopt the simple tone. The combination of solemn responses with simple tone is something of a musical solecism and the presence, in three manuscripts (but not manuscript h),[45] of the solemn tone for the Preface in the mass puts in some doubt the value of comparing these features. One possibility is that those documents presenting the solemn tone may have been used by the archbishop himself, or may have been copied from such sources, and that where the exact complex form was not required it was abbreviated. This argument does not fit well with other conclusions about the sources. Those showing the solemn form, for example, are not the best documents for the coronation in general, since all date from the fifteenth century. No sources give the solemn tone for the proper text of the Preface in the *consecratio*.

If the notational symbols and the form of the tone may not be reliable clues to assessing the manuscripts, another aspect of the notation may be of more significance. Manuscript e, for example, in the *consecratio*, and manuscripts h and f in the mass Preface, group the symbols so that the words are separated visually in the music (see fig. 12.2). This aid to correct performance of the text suggests that these sources were used by the celebrant, that is, the archbishop of Canterbury. The presence or absence of benediction signs at *sanctificare* may also help in identifying the user of a particular book. Manuscripts e, f, and h are pontificals, probably written for specific bishops; in the coronation, however, all the bishops of the realm were present, many with active roles, and the abbot of Westminster had equivalent status. If we can say that a particular item in the ceremony was performed by the user of a certain book and can assign the book to a particular bishop, we may be able to bring together the bishop and his particular role in the ceremony. An example will be given below.

The following remarks, based on only a small part of the evidence, are intended to complement the results of more comprehensive study of the sources.

Edward II was crowned on February 23, 1308, the Saturday of Sexagesima week. If the liturgical information presented earlier is reliable, no tract was necessary, and none appears in the manuscripts conventionally assigned to this event. The alleluya termination retained in Firmetur as the item was copied from the third recension can easily be omitted and was not provided with the other items. John Brückmann demonstrates that the order "must have been compiled considerably before the... coronation."[46] But either the compilers knew the date of the event or were fortunate, since neither tract or alleluya was required. The celebration in a season when tracts were often needed may have brought the liturgical omission to notice for remedy in a future order, when alleluya terminations could also be added to accommodate the possibility of a ceremony during Easter time. Manuscripts *e* and *f* show signs of such revisions.

Edward III was crowned on 29 January 1327, a Wednesday during Epiphany. Neither tract nor alleluya was necessary, and in this respect the order for his predecessor could have served. Manuscripts *e* and *f*, sometimes tentatively assigned to this coronation, provide unnecessary revisions. Manuscript *e* deals with the case of Easter time, providing terminations and making the termination of Firmetur optional (as it surely always was) with the rubric *in tempore paschali*; it does not provide the tract, although Unxerunt, uniquely, has a special ending for Septuagesima and a different psalm.[47] Manuscript *f* revises only by supplying the tract and an alleluya for Unxerunt. Neither manuscript is relevant to this particular coronation. Each seems like an incomplete attempt to generalize the service for all seasons of the year; manuscript *e* is a more successful and professional revision.

Manuscripts *g* and *h*, for the coronation of Richard II, 1377, celebrated after Pentecost, do not provide the Easter terminations (unnecessary for this season); the mass does include a tract (also unnecessary) and thus cannot have been prepared specifically for this coronation, although it may reflect earlier revisions. Manuscripts *j* and *k*, as we have seen, are copies; they provide for all circumstances in the consecration ceremony, but not in the Mass.

The sequence of events and the way the manuscripts reflect them are not consistent. As stated earlier, the impetus for revision of the ordo was possibly the preparation of a pontifical, unrelated to a specific coronation. In such circumstances, the motive for revision may have been to provide a ritual usable at all times, pentitential or joyful. Sometimes, coronation followed so soon after the accession, twenty days in the case of Edward III, that the production of carefully thought-out revisions and well-executed books would have been out of the question. We may say that a specific ordo was compiled before but not necessarily for a particular coronation.

Divorcing the ordo from the event allows us to consider it as a transmitted text. No doubt later ordines were to some extent copied from earlier ones. But the compiler may have recalled that his exemplar had proved to be inadequate for the previous coronation and may have tried to anticipate future difficulties. If ordines are based on, rather than copied from, earlier ones, then transmission is quite different from that of other kinds of books. In general, liturgical books, and other books that are for practical use, are transmitted in a manner inherently different from that of literary texts. Conventional methods of textual analysis are quite inappropriate for dealing with this kind of material, and appropriate methods have not been evolved. At the most, conventional methods can apply only to the texts of individual items and not to rubrics or optional adaptations or to details of layout or to services as whole. John Brückmann, admitting the dangers, gives a filiation of the 1308 manuscripts, based only on the texts.[48] The relevant part of his *stemma* is:

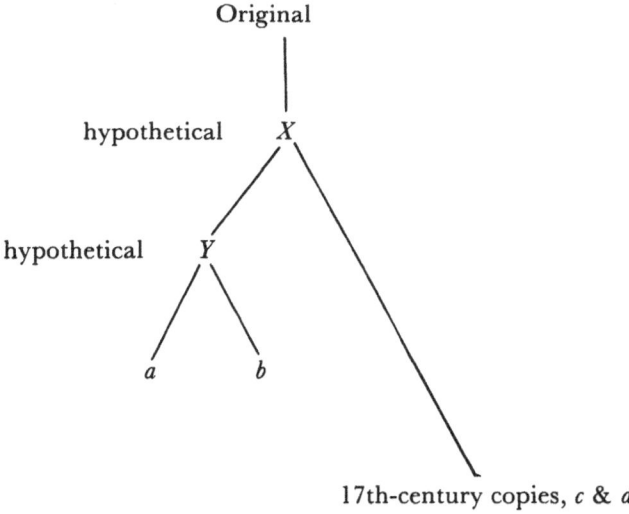

The ordo in the Westminster Missal, reflecting the coronation of 1377, manuscript *g*, is clearly related to *a* and *b*.[49] In the mass Preface, *a*, *b*, *c*, and *d* agree on the erroneous form *honorum*;[50] we can probably assume that the correct form, *bonorum*, in the Missal is a scribal emendation, so that it may descend from *a* or *b*. It is perhaps somewhat closer to *b* or *X* since manuscript *a* is isolated with some musical variants from the forms shared by the Missal *g*, and by *b*, *c*, and *d*.[51] The other source with music for the 1377 coronation, manuscript *h*, is much closer to manuscripts *e* and *f*. In all of them, the Prefaces show the musical notation separated into word groups, and the same is probably though less clearly true of manuscript *i* (also 1377). Numerous other musical and textual variants link these documents, but manuscripts *e* and *f* show variants not followed by *h* and *i*.⁵² The unplaced manuscripts *j* and *k* probably belong to this group also, judging partly by their agreement on melodic variants for the Preface responses, which are not shared by the Westminster Missal group, and on the distribution of other differences.⁵³

Two broad groups therefore emerge. One culminates in the Westminster Missal (manuscripts *a*, *b*, *g*), with seventeenth-century copies in *c* and *d*, and links the 1377 coronation with that of 1308; the other links it with the revised orders in pontificals *e* and *f* and includes manuscripts *h*, *i*, *j*, *k*. An important feature separating *g*, *h*, *i*, *j*, and *k* from the others is their removal of Firmetur from the entrance procession to a position later in the service. Thus, if we consider the manuscripts relating to the coronation of 1377 as a group, the information in them derives from at least three different "sources": from physical ancestors *a* and *b*, associated with a specific earlier coronation; from physical ancestors *e* and *f*, pontificals from Exeter and Lincoln respectively, and not closely associated with a specific coronation; and from two separate liturgical decisions regarding the tract and the status of Firmetur as a procession.

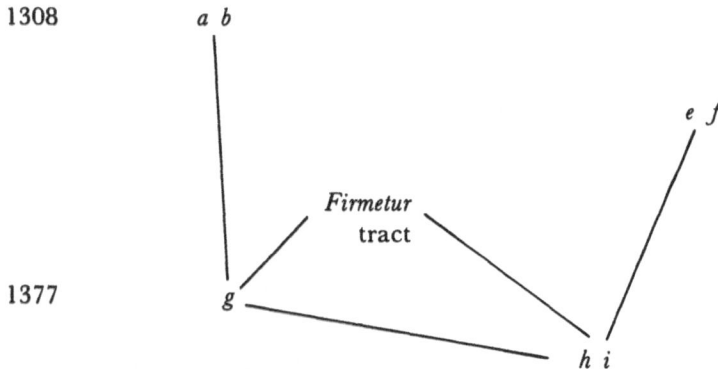

The point hardly needs to be stressed; texts for living, practical uses are likely to be conflated and "contaminated" to an extent rare in the transmission of a dead text. Each coronation is different, and the manuscripts that represent it will differ in content and presentation. What is more, even for the same event, each role within the service is different and manuscripts may differ according to the requirements of specific users.

John Brückmann stated that the music in the coronation manuscripts was added "where necessary." This begs the question. A source giving additional material helpful mainly to the choir or precentor may have been destined for their use. Pontifical *b*, clarifying the incipit of Firmetur, would seem at that point to be most useful for the precentor, or whoever began this antiphon, not the archbishop. Brückmann concludes that the manuscript probably belonged to the abbot of Westminster and was indeed for actual use.[54] Its large letters and clear script point to an active participant. Did the abbot intone Firmetur? A document grouping the reciting tones of the Prefaces carefully, or giving the music of the archbishop's clause in the Litany and the incipits of *Veni creator* and the *Te Deum*, may have been used by the archbishop, who needs such information while others do not. Most of the documents considered here give the music indiscriminately, regardless of need, and seem to be more in the nature of "reference" copies, aiming for completeness. A more thorough discussion is not possible; we do not know, for example, who actually performed the music, which of the participating bishops intoned the incipits (if indeed this earlier practice was continued), nor what part the clerks of the Chapel Royal and the monks of Westminster played in the musical items.[55]

Not one published edition of any coronation text includes the chant. A large proportion of the evidence has thus been disregarded. What has been demonstrated here with respect to some simple musical matters in one recension of the English ceremonies should be expanded into a general consideration of all European coronations. Many of the dependencies and interrelationships between various national ordines will be strengthened; some will be weakened; new relations may emerge. A study of the music, with its political and liturgical emphasis, its implications of liturgical season and practical destination, and its assistance for the dating and grouping of sources, is essential for fully understanding both the origin of the ordines and their documents and the dramatic and symbolic meaning of the coronation.[56]

NOTES

This study came about as a result of a reenactment of the coronation of Henry V, organized, edited, and musically directed by me, and produced as authentically as possible by the *Poculi Ludique Societas* and the Medieval Music Group of the University of Toronto. A shortened version of the production was videotaped in color for distribution by the media center of the university. I should like to thank all those who made that reenactment possible. In particular I should like to remember gratefully John Brückmann, who generously loaned me many films for long periods and willingly gave much of his time advising me.

For permission to publish the facsimiles, I should like to acknowledge the Bodleian Library (fig. 12.3) the Dean and Chapter of Westminster Abbey (fig. 12.1) and the Master and Fellows of Corpus Christi College, Cambridge (fig. 12.2).

1. A companion article entitled "Antiphons and Acclamations: The Politics of Music in the Coronation Service of Edward II, 1308," *The Journal of Musicology* 6 (1988): 150–68, documents and exemplifies the discussion summarized in the follow-

ing paragraphs. A third article, "The Music of the Late Medieval English Coronation Ceremonies," for which a place of publication has yet to be found, deals with general matters of musical style and performance of the chants in the coronation, including those discussed in the remainder of the present study.

2. H. Pirenne, *A History of Europe*, trans. B. Miall (Garden City, N.Y.: 1958) 2:85, 90.

3. J. Brückmann, "English Coronations, 1216–1308: The Edition of the Coronation Ordines," doctoral dissertation, Toronto 1964, table XIV (following p. 384).

4. Compare the groupings in H. G. Richardson and G. O Sayles, "Early Coronation Records," *Bulletin of the Institute of Historical Research* 13 (1935–1936), 129–45 and 14 (1936–1937), 1–9, 145–148, and in P. E. Schramm, "Ordines-Studien III: Die Krönung in England vom 10. Jh. bis zur Neuzeit," *Archiv für Urkundenforschung* 15 (1938): 305–91 and 16 (1939): 279–286.

5. H. G. Richardson, "The Coronation of Edward II," *Bulletin of the Institute of Historical Research* 16 (1938–1939), 7, 11; Brückmann, "English Coronations," 335–337.

6. Brückmann, as above, 337–339.

7. L. B. Wilkinson, "Notes on the Coronations Records of the Fourteenth Century," *English Historical Review* 70 (1955): 581–600, here 591–592.

8. Ibid.

9. J. Wickham Legg, ed., *Missale ad usum ecclesie Westmonasteriensis*, 3 vols. (London, 1891–97; Henry Bradshaw Soc. 1, 5, 12), here: addendum preceding vol. 3, describing the Accompt roll of 1384 which lists charges incurred for preparing Lytlington's Missal. Cf. Richardson and Sayles, "Early Coronation," 138–139.

10. T. A Sandquist, "English Coronations," doctoral dissertation, Toronto 1962, 7–10.

11. P. E. Schramm, *A History of the English Coronation*, trans. L. G. Wickham Legg (Oxford, 1937), 80.

12. Schramm, "Ordines-Studien," 345.

13. Personal communication.

14. Wilkinson, "Notes," 591, 596.

15. See my "Music...," as in n. 1, above.

16. M. Andrieu, *Le pontifical romain au moyen-âge*, 4 vols. (Vatican City, 1938–1941, Studi e testi, 86–88, 99), here: 2:367 and 3:391; H. A. Wilson, ed., *The Pontifical of Magdalen College* (London, 1910; Henry Bradshaw Soc. 39), 89; here 249 and 251.

17. W. H. Frere, ed., *The Winchester Troper* (London, 1894; Henry Bradshaw Soc. 8), f. 53v in the manuscript.

18. MS 4 of table 1, f. 67; L. G. Wickham Legg, *Three Coronation Orders* (London, 1900; Henry Bradshaw Soc. 19), 163–164.

19. Wilson, *Pontifical*, 89.

20. The Ms Harley 561 (MS *k* of table 2, a fifteenth-century copy of the Fourth Recension which has a very peculiar position in the transmission of the music) gives a chant different from either English version and from that in fifteenth-century French sources.

21. MS 5 of table 12.1, p. 279; Legg, *Three*, 53; MS 3 of table 1, p. 138; L. G. Wickham Legg, *English Coronation Records* (Westminster, 1901), 15 (with *chorus* for *clerus*).

22. Brückmann, "English Coronations," 457.

23. MS *f* on table 12.2, f. 196v; MS *e* of table 12.2, f. 97, gives *hec* for *hanc*.
24. MS *b* of table 12.2, f. 62.
25. MSS *c* and *d* of table 12.2, f. 64 and p. 402 respectively.
26. W. G. Henderson, ed., *Liber Pontificalis Chr. Bainbridge* (Durham, 1875; Surtees Soc. 61), 270; Legg, *English*, 15; Legg, *Three*, 53; Brückmann, "English Coronations," 412.
27. Legg, *English*, 86–87.
28. ... *capella regia solemniter decantat sequens responsorium* ... *"Ecce mitto"*... *Introeuntibus autem illis in ecclesiam usque ad introitum chori cantet predicta capella hanc antiphonam "Domine in virtute,"* see D. H. Turner's note on music in W. Ullmann, ed., *Liber regie capelle* (London, 1961; Henry Bradshaw Soc. 92), 50.
29. See F. Ll. Harrison, *Music in Medieval Britain* (London, 1958), 244.
30. C. Marbach, ed. *Carmina scripturarum* (Strassburg, 1907; repr. Hildesheim 1963), 371; Andrieu, *Le pontifical* 2:386, 3:427.
31. Ullmann, *Liber*, 26–27.
32. Andrew Hughes, *Medieval Manuscripts for Mass and Office: A Guide to their Organization and Terminology* (Toronto 1982), 86.
33. I refer only to the source with music, the Magdalen Pontifical (as n. 16 above), MS 6 of table 12.1. The Second Recension Order with music does not give the Alleluya; this may provide a clue about the coronation for which the Magdalen Pontifical was used.
34. See above, n. 32.
35. *Antiphonaire monastique, XIIIe siècle, Codex F. 160 de la Bibl. de la cathédrale de Worcester* (Tournai, 1922, Paléographie musicale, I:12), pl. 201.
36. E. H. Kantorowicz, *Laudes Regiae. A Study in Liturgical Acclamations and Medieval Ruler Worship* (with a Study of the Music of the Laudes and Musical Transcriptions by M. F. Bukofzer) (Berkeley: University of California Press, 1946), passim.
37. Ibid., 101, 174, 180.
38. I. Bent, "The English Chapel Royal Before 1300," *Proc. of the Royal Musical Association* 90 (1983–1984), 77–95, here 89.
39. Legg, *English*, 69–76.
40. See B. Stäblein, "Prefätion," *Die Musik in Geschichte und Gegenwart*; P. Wagner, *Einführung in die gregorianische Melodien*, Gregorianische Formenlehre (Leipzig 1921; repr. Hildesheim, 1970) 3:69–82; F. H. Dickinson, ed. *Missale ad usum...ecclesie Sarum* (Oxford, 1861–1883), 597–610.
41. W. J. Birkbeck, in Legg, *Miss. Westmon.* 3:1401.
42. Ibid.
43. Henderson, *Liber*, 98, 118, 130, 144, 161.
44. *Hoc modo incipiantur omnes Prefationes ad missam per totum annum tam in feriis quam in festis*, Dickinson, *Missale...Sarum*, 607.
45. MS *i* in table 12.2, f. 1–1; MS *j* f. 18v–19; MS *f* f. 204v–5 (or 205v–6).
46. Brückmann, "English Coronations," 160.
47. Psalm 44, *Eructavit cor meum*, contains almost as many regal references as Psalm 20 and provides texts for parts of the service.
48. Brückmann, "English Coronations," 384.
49. See, for example, the *differentia* of *Unxerunt*, the melody of *Firmetur* at *et exal-, prece-,* and *Alle-*, and numerous melodic and textual variants in the responses of the

coronation Preface, and in the same Preface variants at *Electorum, fortitudo, redditam, iterumque, predixisti, ut per, et exempla, tuamque, benedictione. habere facias.*

50. Not just MS *b*, as Brückmann states.

51. MS *a* stands alone in the *differentia* and *flexa* of *Firmetur*, in the gradual at *sicut incensum* and *Elevatio*, and in the coronation Preface at *Deo nostro* and *Dignum et justum.*

52. MS *e* stands alone in omitting the choral responses in the coronation Preface and at *et humilium, diluvi,* and *David vocem* in the same item; MS *f* stands alone in the coronation Preface at *servicio, imitari, adiuvante,* and *exhill-.*

53. Many of the variants in n. 49, as well as linking MS *g* with *a, b, c,* and *d,* may be used to demonstrate the unanimity of *e, f, h, i, j,* and *k.*

54. Brückmann, "English Coronations," 337-9.

55. Some evidence on these matters is assembled in Bent, "Chapel Royal", Kantorowicz, *Laudes* (esp. Bukofzer's Study), 98, and elsewhere; Sandquist, "English coronations," 56, 307; Ullmann, *Liber,* esp. in Turner's appendix.

56. Other citations of interest but not used for anything specific are as follows:

Bailey, Terence *The Processions of Sarum and the Western Church*, (Toronto, Pontifical Institute of Medieval Studies 1971 Studies and Texts, 21).

Brückmann, John, "Latin Manuscript Pontificals and Benedictionals in England and Wales," *Traditio* 29 (1973): 391-458.

Doble, G. H., ed., *Pontificale Lanalet*, (London, 1937 Henry Bradshaw Society 74).

Frere, Walter H., ed., *The Use of Sarum*, 2 vols. (Cambridge, 1898, 1901; reprint 1969).

———, ed., *Antiphonale Sarisburiense* (London: 1901-1924; reprint 1966).

Greenwell, W., ed., *The Pontifical of Egbert, Archbishop of York*, (Durham, 1853 Surtees Society 27).

Hesbert, René-Jean, "Les manuscrits liturgiques de l'église de Rouen," *Bulletin Philologique et Historique* (1955-1956): 441-483.

———, *Corpus antiphonalium officii*, 4 vols., Rerum Ecclesiasticarum Documenta, ser. major, Fontes 7, 8, 9, 10 (Rome, 1963, 1965, 1968, 1970).

Leroquais, Victor, *Les pontificaux manuscrits des bibliothèques publiques de France*, 4 vols. (Paris, 1937).

Maskell, William, ed., *Monumenta ritualia ecclesie Anglicanae*, 3 vols. (London, 1846, 1847).

Richardson, H. G., "The Coronation of Edward I," *Bulletin of the Institute of Historical Research* 15 (1937-1938): 94-99.

Turner, Derek H., ed., *The Claudius Pontificals*, Henry Bradshaw Society 97 (London, 1971).

Vogel, Cyrille, and Reinhard Elze, eds., *Le Pontifical romano-germanique du dixième siècle*, 2 vols., (Vatican City, 1963 Studi e Testi 226, 227).

Wordsworth, Christopher, *Salisbury Ceremonies and Processions* (Cambridge, 1901).

THIRTEEN

"The Wonderfull Spectacle"
The Civic Progress of Elizabeth I and the Troublesome Coronation

Richard C. McCoy

Henry VIII won his crown by force on Bosworth field, but when the time came to solemnize its acquisition, the founder of the Tudor line carefully emulated the coronation ordo of his vanquished predecessor. Indeed he simply made it his own. The manuscript of Henry's "little devise of the coronacion" was originally Richard III's, but the heralds crossed out the names of the old monarch and inserted those of the new.[1] The sense of ceremonial continuity was preserved and deepened through the more orderly succession of Henry VIII, whose own "device for the maner and order of the Coronation" closely followed his father's.[2]

Nevertheless, the stability of these rites and their sacramental force was inevitably shaken by the Tudor Reformation. Although the coronation rite could easily accommodate political conflicts and crises, religious controversy struck at its vital heart. Henry's new status as supreme head of the church prompted him to tamper with the coronation oath, making several corrections in his own hand in order to assert "his dygnite ryall and fredommes of the crowne of Englond in all maner hole w[i]t[h]out any maner of mynyshement."[3] Henry's autocratic version of the oath was never officially adopted by his successors, but his conflicted religious settlement and tangled succession dramatically altered the relationship between church and royal authority while disrupting the coronation's ceremonial continuity. At their accessions, his heirs faced grave liturgical problems, and their solutions varied widely. Edward's mentors sought to desacralize the event, by affirming a Protestant view of ceremony and kingship, whereas Mary tried to restore the coronation's sacramental status. Elizabeth I faced far more challenging ecclesiastical and liturgical difficulties than either of her predecessors, and yet, characteristically, her solution was more adroit and more oblique. Her considerable theatrical skills diverted attention from the problematic religious ritual to secular civic pageantry. By examining her somewhat confusing conduct during the coronation mass and comparing it with her skilled performance during the civic progress the day before, I hope to illuminate the increasingly theatrical and secular nature of Tudor power and its rites.

Henry's first successor, Edward VI, was handicapped by his youth and weakness, and, throughout his brief reign, Edward remained dependent on more powerful subjects to affirm and execute his authority. At his coronation, the task of asserting his supremacy over the church fell paradoxically to the archbishop of Canterbury, Thomas Cranmer. Cranmer took an essentially moderate but functional view of religious ceremonies, and, in his coronation sermon, he preached a thoroughly Protestant view of the liturgy and kingship:

> The solemn rites of coronation have their ends and utility, yet neither direct force or necessity: they be good admonitions to put kings in mind of their duty to God, but no increasement of their dignity: for they be God's anointed, not in respect of the oil, which the bishop useth, but in consideration of their power, which is ordained, of the sword, which is authorized, of their persons, which are elected by God, and endued with gifts of his Spirit, for the better ruling and guiding of his people.
>
> The oil, if added, is but a ceremony: if it be wanting, that king is yet a perfect monarch notwithstanding, and God's anointed, as well as if he was inoiled.[4]

For Cranmer, the monarch's supremacy was inherent and absolute, and the ceremony had only a weak, admonitory force.

Within a few years, Mary Tudor came to the throne determined to restore Rome's authority and to resacralize the coronation no less paradoxically by royal fiat. She assembled a large and properly outfitted clerical procession in order to bring her "from Westmyster hall with iij crosses with a gret qweer and many byshoppes with their myteres on their heddes and crose stavys in ther honddes."[5] Her coronation Mass was London's main liturgical event, requiring all the priests from St. Paul's "save only them that ware maryd, that in so moch that the day was no servyss in Powlles, nother matins nor masse nor evensonge [nor] sermon at the crosse."[6] In addition to surrounding herself with as many bishops and priests as she could assemble, Mary also sought to restore the coronation's sacramental efficacy by sending to the emperor for newly consecrated oil. The pope was informed of this and was also assured that she had made her own changes in the coronation oath while promptly undertaking measures "for the re-establishment of all the due Ceremonies relating to the honourable dignity of that Order [of the Garter] which consist in the saying of certain masses, and confessing themselves at certain seasons, and celebrating the festival of St. George, according to the original institution." In doing so she was trying to reverse changes made by Protestants under Edward VI designed to purge "the statutes of this fellowship" of its "many doubtefull, superstitious, and repugnant opinions" including the veneration of St. George and his images.[7] Mary wanted to restore Catholicism to the rites of the English monarchy as well as to the English church, but she was finally thwarted by her own fanaticism.

When Elizabeth Tudor ascended to the throne not long afterward, she displayed none of her half-sister's reverence toward the clergy or their solemnities. When greeted by the abbot of Westminster who was "robed pontifically, with all his monks carrying lighted torches," she brusquely dismissed them, saying "Away with those torches, for we see very well."[8] As for the bishops, their ranks were already depleted at Mary's death by the death of ten of their number, including the archbishop of Canterbury, Cardinal Pole, who had obligingly died shortly after Elizabeth I's accession. Elizabeth I diminished the number attending on her even further by excluding the staunchly Catholic primates such as Heath and Bonner from the coronation service. There were also several distinctly Protestant changes in the ceremony held on the eve of her coronation, the creation of the Knights of the Bath: the all-night vigil was eliminated, prayers were said in English, and, during the Mass, the Queen's chaplain "heavyd not up the osty"—that is, the host was not elevated.[9] To confirmed Protestants, the elevation of the host was the essence of popish idolatry. In a "Sermon concerning the Right Use of the Lordes Supper," the Marian exile, John Ponet, had preached that "it is an unreverente and ungodly opinion and voyd of all Godlye religion to saye or thynke, that we muste eate and chawe with our corporall teeth, or that we must swallow with our corporal throte, Christes blessed fleshe and bones"; those who believe in such a literal communion "woulde feed of Christe, as ye woulde feed of a pece of motton." In Ponet's view, such absurdities should be rejected along with the liturgical practices that accompany them: the host should not "be holden up in the handes of the priest over his hed" or "hanged up in ye church to be worshipped."[10] Contemporary hostility to this gesture is graphically illustrated in the frontispiece of Foxe's *Booke of Martyrs* in which a priest raises a host to Lucifer and all the devils in hell hovering above the altar.

Elizabeth I's position on this controversy was thoroughly enigmatic. Having excluded the higher-ranking primates from her coronation, Elizabeth I still demanded that a Catholic bishop anoint her, and she settled on Owen Oglethorpe, bishop of Carlisle and suffragan of the archbishop of York, requiring Bishop Bonner of London to lend this subordinate his own splendid vestments for the occasion. Yet Oglethorpe proved intractable on the matter of the elevation. A few weeks before the coronation, "on Christmas day, the Bishop of Carlisle sang high mass, and her majesty sent to tell him not to elevate the host; to which the good Bishop replied that thus had he learnt the mass, and that she must pardon him as he could not do otherwise."[11] Offended by this intransigence, Elizabeth I walked out after the reading of the gospel. At the next day's service Bishop Oglethorpe was replaced by a more pliant royal chaplain. Elizabeth's extraordinary reaction to the elevation would seem to confirm her strong Protestant sympathies, and yet her irritation at this affront to her stated preferences may have been as important as any deeply held convictions on the transubstantiation. Indeed, she reacted similarly to a Protestant attack on Catholic doctrine a few years later. A group of Cambridge scholars tried to entertain her with a farce in which one actor masqueraded as the hated Bonner gnawing on a lamb while another portrayed a dog with a host in his mouth: such was the folly of believing, in Ponet's words, "that we must eate and chawe with our corporall teeth- ...Christes blessed fleshe and bones" as we would a "pece of motton." Unfortunately for the actors, Elizabeth I was so offended by these antics, that she stalked out again, this time taking her torchbearers and leaving the performers in the dark.[12]

How then did Elizabeth conduct herself at her coronation, and what solution did she devise for these fierce liturgical controversies? We finally cannot say, for although there are tantalizing hints in the records of scandalous irregularities, the records' inconsistencies only compound the confusion surrounding the event. Elizabeth I's coronation is one of those events that recede from view as one learns more about it. The written records consist of an usually cryptic and fragmentary heraldic proclamation, the only official account, plus a letter from the Mantuan resident, Il Schifanoya, and finally a report by an anonymous English eyewitness.[13] The first two accounts indicate that, while Bishop Oglethorpe crowned and anointed the Queen, the Mass was celebrated by the dean of the Chapel Royal, George Carew, a man who could be trusted to refrain from elevating the host or any other unseemly displays of clerical independence. The Spanish ambassador was so horrified by the prospect of such a sacrilege that he refused to attend the mass as did several other Catholic residents, including, apparently, Il Schifanoya; his description of events certainly gives the impression of being secondhand, for it is filled with mistakes.[14] The anonymous English report suggests an even more scandalous possibility. This version says that a bishop celebrated mass, and, during its course, "her Grace retorned unto her Clossett hearing the Consecration of the Mass."[15] The heralds' proclamation also attributes some rather unusual movements to the Queen, recording her withdrawal after the Collect "to her traverse," a curtained pew or closet; afterward, "the masse proceeds and ended the Queene went into Saint Edwards Chapelle to shift her."[16]

All these clues and enigmas have inspired, in David Sturdy's words, "much ingenious detective work," but scholars have had difficulty establishing the facts.[17] C. G. Bayne was the first to conclude that Oglethorpe said the mass and repeated his offense of elevating the host, thus prompting Elizabeth I to walk out again, this time withdrawing from her throne before the high altar to a curtained closet or traverse in St. Edward's Chapel.[18] There, completely hidden from view for the duration of the mass, she abstained from receiving communion. After carefully reviewing the evidence available, Bayne charged the queen with committing "a striking breach of the ritual of centuries."[19] Bayne later changed his mind on the basis of a Spanish Jesuit's claim that the elevation was omitted and the other records' ambiguity concerning the location of the traverse, but A. F. Pollard pressed the case for her withdrawal by citing Elizabeth I's remark to the French ambassador, Fénelon, in 1571 that "she had been crowned and anointed according to the ceremonies of the Catholic church, and by Catholic bishops without, however, attending the mass."[20] Pollard also points out the inaccuracy of the Spanish ambassador's initial apprehensions, an inacuracy Feria admitted: "By last post I wrote your Majesty that I had been told that the Queen took the holy sacrament *sub utraque specie* on the day of the coronation, but it was all nonsense. She did not take it at all."[21] A. L. Rowse's discovery of a heraldic illustration used for planning the event seemed to clinch the case for her withdrawal.[22] It clearly shows that "the Queen's Travers" was behind the high altar and sanctuary wall, and the note says that the traverse was intended "to make her reydy in after the ceremonyes and Service [were] doon," but if this is the same traverse mentioned in the Heralds' report, she went there midway throught the Mass.[23]

Nevertheless, those conclusions have been disputed by scholars emphasizing the cryptic ambiguity of the records, the possibility of a second traverse, and the implausibility of such behaviour exciting so little remark. H. A. Wilson raises several of these objections, pointing out that both the anonymous account and the heralds' proclamation imply some sort of distinction between the "closett" or "traverse" to which Elizabeth I withdrew during the mass and the place she went to "behind the high Aulter" in "Sanit Edwards Chapelle" after its conclusion.[24] A memorandum on religious policy written before the coronation anticipates Elizabeth I hearing the mass from her traverse and the omission of the elevation. After asserting that the English litany of Henry's time could be used, the document affirms that "her Ma-[jes] tie in her closett may use the Masse without lyfting up above the Host according to the Ancient customs and may have also at every masse some communicants with the Ministers to be usyd in both kynds."[25] Thus, her withdrawal to the traverse during the consecration could have been planned rather than resulting from offended impulse. In his review of the evidence, William Haugaard concludes that Elizabeth I's chaplain probably celebrated a "moderately Protestant" Mass after Bishop Oglethorpe presided over the traditionally Catholic coronation. The service thus represented a liturgical compromise, "in which allowance had been made for conflicting consciences," in Haugaard's view, "Elizabeth was crowned according to the rites of the Latin liturgy . . . but the minor changes on which she insisted gave warning of her intention to reassert the independence of the English Church."[26]

Elizabeth I's coronation was indeed a compromise of sorts, but her intentions were hardly clear, and her subjects conflicting consciences were, in many cases, more alarmed than reassured by the service's ambiguities. Catholics were distressed by her omission of the elevation and reports of her irreverence toward the clergy and their ceremonies. Nicholas Sanders recounted her brusque treatment of Bishop Oglethorpe during the Christmas mass and claimed that, although she was anointed, "she disliked the ceremony and ridiculed it; for when she withdrew, according to the custom, to put on the royal garments, it is reported that she said to the noble ladies in attendance upon her. 'Away with you, the oil is stinking.' "[27] At the same time, the Genevan exiles were so shocked by her adherence to traditional Latin rites that some resolved to stay away "until directed by Calvin himself to return."[28] The coronation was a typical Elizabethan compromise with something to confuse and offend everyone. It anticipated the inconsistencies of her early religious settlement, which was less often a *Via media* than an erratic "mingle-mangle": the elevation of the host continued to be omitted, but the use of communion wafers, "eucharistic vestments," and kneeling during communion was prescribed despite strenuous Protestant opposition.[29] During the first year of her reign, even as rood-lofts, crucifixes, and altars were being destroyed or dismantled, Elizabeth I retained a small silver crucifix and two burning candles "standing altar-wise" in her own Chapel Royal. By February of 1560 some of her newly appointed bishops were threatening to resign over this "offendicle," and the ambassador to France, Sir Nicholas Throckmorton, wrote with alarm that the Guise "made their advantage of the cross and candles in your chapel, saying you were not yet resolved of what religion you should be."[30] Her coronation presented the same confusing inconsistencies, but their disturbing implications were finally muted by the event's essential obscurity. It was a rite muddled by liturgical controversy, witnessed by a small number, and inadequately recorded.

By contrast, the civic progress the day before was a far more harmonious, popular, and better-documented event. Elizabeth I's dazzling performance in the pageants staged by the city guilds was seen by all of London, and the prompt publication of the tract, *The Quenes Maiesties Passage through the Citie of London to Westminster the Day before her Coronacion*, expanded the audience and perpetuated the memory of the glorious events, overshadowing the coronation and its difficulties. According to this tract, the queen was of the people received merveylous entierly, as appeared by thassemblie, prayers, wishes, welcomminges, cryes, tender woordes, and all other signes, which argue a wonderfull earnest love of most obedient subiects towarde theyr soveraygne. And on thother syde her grace by holding up her handes, and merie countenaunce to such as stoode farre of, and most tender and gentle language to those that stode nigh to her grace, did declare her selfe no lesse thankefullye to receive her people's good wille, than they lovingly offred it unto her.[31]

The progress enacted a drama of stylized reciprocity and affection. As Jonathan Goldberg has noted, the illusion of "intimate give-and-take" and "the air of spontaneity" were partly factitious, but no less convincing for all that.[32] Elizabeth helped to subsidize these spectacles by loaning costumes from the Revels Office to the city guilds, as David Bergeron has shown, and she undoubtedly saw the pageants' scripts beforehand.[33] She was an inspired actress who knew from the beginning of her reign that "We princes... are set on stages, in the sight and view of all the world duly observed."[34] Her progress transformed the entire city of London, according to the tract, into "a stage wherin was shewed the wonderfull spectacle, of a noble hearted princes toward her most loving people, and the peoples excading comfort in beholding so worthy a soveraign."[35]

Significantly there are several pictures of Elizabeth's civic progress, and these also project an image of hierarchy and harmony. These heraldic drawings include one set that is fairly crude and which was probably used as a planning device. The archbishops of Canterbury and York are included in the procession, despite the death of the first and the exclusion of the second, but there are *x*s and lines beneath them that probably indicate their absence as well as indicating that their places should be taken by the Norroy and Clarenceux Kings of Arms. Elizabeth's problems with her bishops are simply ignored in the other two drawings. In these, the two primates assume their proper places, arrayed in the respectably academic square cap of Protestant bishops.[36] By contrast, in the drawing of the church procession, they had been described as "bishops in their pontificalibus," and shown with their miters and crosiers. These two drawings are more elaborate and visually detailed. In the original sketch, the queen's litter is indicated by a rectangle and the words "the Queens most excellent majesty," but in these the queen is shown in her litter preceded by her throng of noble and courtly attendants. More attention is paid to ornaments and clothing and the effect is one of sumptuous display. Their function was partly prescriptive since a similar order of precedence was to be observed, according to a note, at "procydyng to ye parlement or coronation," but the drawings were also commemorative and celebratory, serving the same purposes as the tract, *The Quenes Maiesties Passage*.

Elizabeth I keenly appreciated the theatrical power of secular pageantry and shrewdly exploited its more flexible and popular features. The great historian of English coronation rites, Percy Schramm, deplored these same features because they threatened the exalted status of the sacred ritual. In fact, the coronation was jeopardized by its privileged sacramental character since "only an illustrious and select circle could get near it, and so it became a question whether it would not lose its central position and become a mere episode in a long sequence of festivities."[37] The civic progress had always been more of a crowd-pleaser, and it included "manifestations of royal power that could be abandoned, changed, or devised anew. After the close of the Middle Ages the danger threatening the coronation was precisely that it might be degraded into a pageant of this sort."[38] These dangers hardly bothered Elizabeth I, for she used secular pageantry to eclipse sacred ritual. In his introduction to *To Quenes Maiesties Passage*, J. E. Neale says that the Tudor civic progress "became increasingly important until with Queen Elizabeth, it was finally transformed from an introit to the coronation into an occasion in its own right—a popular and secular companion for the subsequent solemn sacrament worthy of commemoration, as commemorated it was, in print."[39] Yet even this understates the impact of the progress and the publication because they were more than mere companions. The progress became the main event, reducing the vexatious coronation to an obscure side-show whose troublesome irregularities have faded from sight and mind.

The civic progress and the commemorative pamphlet were the opening scenes of an enormously successful and long-running stageshow with Elizabeth I as its star. The "cult of Elizabeth" could be nearly idolatrous, but it was almost always artfully so: it was an essentially theatrical enterprise in which secular ceremony and the printed word affirmed royal authority more effectively than sacred ritual. There were, of course, problems with such techniques. The "divinity [that] doth hedge a king" was inevitably diminished by the desacralization of royal ceremony.[40] Nevertheless, the trend was irreversible as the eventual failure of the Stuart monarchy indicated.

After James I's accession, an outbreak of the plague made it necessary to postpone the civic progress. James I would have happily dispensed with it completely, given his aversion to the populace. For him, the ecclesiastical, sacred rite was the critical event, and the secular progress superfluous. The royal proclamation affirmed that "we have thought it best to forbeare of that Solemnitie, whatsoever is not Essentiall to it, and to deferre all shewe of State and Pompe accustomed by our Progenitors, which is not necessitie to be done within the Church at the time of our Coronation."[41] The king eventually submitted to the progress, but grudgingly enough, "for naturally he did not love to be looked on; and those Formalities of State, which set a Lustre upon Princes in the Peoples Eyes, were but so many Burthens to him." Unlike

Elizabeth I, he remained silent and detached throughout, grimly enduring the civic speeches

> wherein he must give his Ears leave to suck in their gilded Oratory, though never so nauceous to the Stomach. He was not like his Predecessor, the late Queen, of famous Memory, that with a well-pleased Affection, met her People's Acclamation, thinking most highly of her self when she was born upon the Wings of their humble Supplications. He endured this Day's Brunt with Patience, being assured he should never have such another.[42]

The Stuarts' contempt for popular pageantry, along with their ecclesiastical conservatism and ideas of rule by divine right, eroded rather than enhanced their authority during the course of the seventeenth century. The last Stuart king, James II, also canceled the civic progress, spending the money on the queen's jewels instead. In criticizing this folly, Macaulay wrote "If pageantry is to be of any use in politics, it is of use as a means of striking the imagination of the multitude."[43] The Stuarts never grasped this essential principle of modern politics, but their successor did: William III set out to dazzle the citizens of London with a magnificent and carefully planned progress in order to enhance his shaky claims to the throne.[44] yet few of her successors displayed the same assured personal skill and understanding of pageantry's impact on "the imagination of the multitude" as Elizabeth I.

NOTES

1. B. L. Egerton MS 985, f. 1. The text is reproduced in Leopold G. Wickham Legg, *English Coronation Records* (Westminster, 1901), 220–239.

2. B. L. Tiberius E, viii, ff. 90–100.

3. Ibid., f. 89. The text is reproduced in Legg, *English Coronation Records*, 240–241.

4. John Strype, *Memorials of Archbishop Cranmer* (Oxford, 1848) 2:8.

5. *Chronicle of the Greyfriars of London*, ed. John Gough Nichols (London, 1852), 84.

6. *Calendar of State Papers, Venetian*, (1534–1554), ed. Rawdon Brown (London, 1873) 5:432.

7. Edward M. Thompson, "The Revision of the Statutes of the Order of the Garter by King Edward the Sixth," *Archaeologia* 54 (1894): 184.

8. J. E. Neale, *Elizabeth I and Her Parliaments* (1559–1581) (New York: St. Martin's Press, 1958) 2:42.

9. B. L. Ashmole MS 862, f. 299. The text is reproduced and discussed by C. G. Bayne in a brief article, "The Coronation of Queen Elizabeth," *English Historical Review* 25 (1910): 550–553.

10. John Ponet, "A Notable Sermon concerninge the Right Use of the Lordes Supper... preached before the Kynges Most Excellent Mayesty" (1550), C. iiii; C. iii; and D. iii.

11. *Calendar of State Papers, Venetian*, (1558–1580), ed. Rawdon Brown and G. Cavendish Bentinck (London, 1890) 7:2.

12. *Calendar of State Papers, Spanish*, (1558–1567), ed. Martin A. S. Hume (London, 1892–1899) 1:375.

13. C. G. Bayne reproduces and discusses the texts of all three in an earlier and lengthier article, also entitled "The Coronation of Queen Elizabeth," *EHR* 22 (1907): 650–673.

14. See ibid., 656–657; A. F. Pollard, "The Coronation of Queen Elizabeth," *EHR* 25 (1910): 125–126; and William P. Haugaard, "The Coronation of Elizabeth I," *Journal of Ecclesiastical History* 19 (1968): 163–165.

15. Bayne (1907), 670.

16. Ibid., 671.

17. See below in this volume.

18. Bayne (1907), 663.

19. Ibid., 661.

20. Bayne, "The Coronation of Queen Elizabeth," *EHR* 24 (1909): 332–323; and Pollard (1910), 125.

21. *Calendar of State Papers, Spanish*, (1558–1567) 1:25.

22. A. L. Rowse, "The Coronation of Queen Elizabeth I," *An Elizabethan Garland* (London: Macmillan, 1954), 21.

23. B. L. Egerton MS 3320. I saw this same illustration before reading Rowse's article and leapt to the same conclusion, but the objections raised by H. A. Wilson and Haugaard make certainty on these matters very difficult.

24. H. A. Wilson, "The Coronation of Queen Elizabeth," *EHR* 23 (1908): 87–91. See also Haugaard, 168.

25. Public Record Office, State Papers Domestic, Elizabeth, I, 68. The memorandum goes on to say, "I thynke it most necessary that before any p[ar]on published after the old manner, at the Coronation, that certain of the Principall Prelats be comytted to the Tower."

26. Haugaard, 166 and 170. David Sturdy (below) briefly reviews both versions of the event and abstains from choosing between them, but he arrives at a conclusion similar to Haugaard's: "Whichever version is preferred, however, the outcome is the same: Elizabeth introduced a dramatic gesture into her coronation in order to publicise a statement on the religious ethos of the coming reign." I am arguing that unlike either of her predecessors, she effectively obscured rather than publicized the nature of her religious settlement for some time.

27. Nicholas Sanders, *The Rise and Growth of the Anglican Schism* (1585), trans. David Lewis (London, 1877), 242–243.

28. Patrick Collinson, *The Elizabethan Puritan Movement* (Berkeley and Los Angeles: University of California Press, 1967), 31.

29. See Collinson (ibid.) who discusses the Prayerbook's equivocation between the Puritans' "memorialist emphasis" and formulations "which could be construed as an affirmation of the real presence in the consecrated elements" (p. 34). See also M. M. Knappen, *Tudor Puritanism* (1939; reprint Chicago: University of Chicago Press, 1970), 169–170; and G. J. Cuming, *The Anglican Liturgy* (London, 1969), 132–133.

30. Collinson, *The Elizabethan Puritan Movement*, 35.

31. *The Quenes Maiesties Passage through the Citie of London to Westminster the Day before her Coronacion*, ed. James M. Osborn (New Haven: Yale University Press, 1960), 27.

32. Jonathan Goldberg, *James I and the Politics of Literature* (Baltimore: Johns Hopkins University Press, 1983), 29.

33. David Bergeron, "Elizabeth's Coronation Entry (1559): New Manuscript Evidence," *ELR* 8 (1978): 3–8. Goldberg makes the plausible suggestion that Elizabeth I saw and approved the scripts beforehand (p. 31).

34. J. E. Neale, *Elizabeth I and Her Parliaments, 1584–1601* 2:119.

35. *The Quenes Maiesties Passage*, 28.

36. These drawings are included in B. L. Egerton MS 3320 and College of Arms MS. M6.

37. Percy Ernst Schramm, *A History of the English Coronation*, trans. L. G. W. Legg (Oxford, 1937), 93. Ceremonial innovation and the shift from sacred rite to secular pageant is not necessarily a degradation. See David Cannadine's discussion of the very successful adaptations of the Victorian and modern monarchy in "The Context, Performance, and Meaning of Ritual: The British Monarchy and the 'Invention of Tradition,'" c. 1820–1977," *The Invention of Tradition*, ed. Eric Hobsbawm and Terence Ranger (Cambridge, 1983), 101–165.

38. Schramm, *A History of English Coronation*, 10.

39. *The Quenes Maiesties Passage*, 7.

40. *Hamlet*, IV.v.124. For a discussion of the problems of a power dependent on theatrical artifice, see Stephen Orgel's essay, "Making Greatness Familiar," *Genre* 15 (1982): 41–48; and my "'Thou Idol Ceremony': Elizabeth I, Henry V, and the Rites of the British Monarchy" (forthcoming).

41. J. Wickham Legg, ed., *The Coronation Order of King James I* (London, 1902), lxiii.

42. Arthur Wilson, *Life and Reign of James the First*, quoted in *James I by His Contemporaries*, ed. Robert Ashton (London, 1969), 63–64.

43. Thomas Babington Macaulay, *The History of English from the Accession of James II*, ed. C. H. Firth (London, 1913–1914) 1;468–469.

44. See Lois G. Schwoerer, "The Glorious Revolution as Spectacle: A New Perspective," in *England's Rise to Greatness, 1660–1763* ed. Stephen B. Baxter (Berkeley, Los Angeles, London: University of California Press, 1983), 109–149; and "Propaganda in the Revolution of 1688–89," *The American Historical Review* 82 (1977): 843–874.

FOURTEEN

"Continuity" versus "Change": Historians and English Coronations of the Medieval and Early Modern Periods

David J. Sturdy

English coronations have received their due share of scholarly attention over the last hundred years or so. The essay that comprises this chapter traces one theme in the historiography of the subject: the tendency for some writers to emphasize "continuity" between coronations, whereas others stressed change, innovation, departure from tradition. The title of the essay may seem to threaten a mere chronicle of those historians who favored the one approach as against those who adopted the second. But something more ambitious is intended: an attempt to assess how far the broader mental interests and preoccupations of certain scholars could draw them to a particular position vis-à-vis "continuity" or "change." Further, the essay intends to say something of the interpretation of English medieval coronations current when John Joseph Brückmann began his researches, and to comment on his own contribution to the debate on "continuity" or "change."

THE HENRY BRADSHAW CIRCLE

A controversy over continuity or change flourished at the turn of the nineteenth century into the twentieth. Serious studies of the English coronation first appeared in the 1800s; there were published such classics as Arthur Taylor, *The Glory of Regality: An Historical Treatise of the Anointing and Crowning of the Kings and Queens of England* (London, 1820); T. C. Banks, *An Historical Account of the Ancient and Modern Forms, Pageantry and Ceremony, of the Coronations of the Kings of England* (London, 1820); and William Maskell, *Monumenta Ritualia Ecclesiae Anglicanae*, 3 vols. (London, 1846–1847). It is this last work that introduces the origins of the controversy, for Maskell wrote not as a restrained, dispassionate scholar, but as one possessing deep religious convictions that gave his writing a strongly teleological quality. He was steeped in that High Anglicanism that found rich expression in the Oxford Movement and which set some of its adherents, including Maskell himself, on the spiritual road to Rome. At this juncture a few words on the Oxford Movement are appropriate.[1] Led in its early stages by John Keble (1792–1868), John Henry Newman (1801–1890), and Edmund Pusey (1800–1882), and destined to exert a profound influence upon nineteenth-century Anglicanism, the movement first bloomed in the 1830s and 1840s. It sought to elevate certain principles in the struggle to restore High Anglicanism to preeminence in the church; those principles included veneration for ancient liturgical practices. The main thesis advanced by the Oxford Movement may be summarized as follows, although with much simplification and therefore distortion: the Anglican Church was the depository of "authentic" or "pure" Catholicism, which Rome had foresaken. It had preserved Catholicism through many trials and tribulations, but now stood in danger of betraying its mission: in the late eighteenth and nineteenth centuries the Evangelical wing of the church had acquired excessive influence, while the church as a whole was tending to slip into an easy-going Latitudinarianism. If the Anglican church were to remain faithful to its calling it must diminish the influence of the Evangelicals and restore High Anglicanism with its stresses upon tradition, apostolic succession, authority, and a liturgy based on ancient ritual.

Maskell (c. 1814–1890) found in High Anglicanism a religious ethos conducive to his own spiritual development; indeed, like John Henry Newman he was to evolve beyond High Anglicanism to become a convert to Roman Catholicism, in his case in 1850. Before that he acquired public notoriety in 1840 when he attacked the bishop of Norwich, Edward Stanley, for his Latitudinarianism. Maskell, who had entered holy orders, was appointed rector of Coscombe in Devon in 1842; he resigned on his conversion in 1850 but spent the rest of his life in the west country writing upon matters of antiquarian interest. Many of his works dealt with aspects of liturgy, including his *Monumenta Ritualia*. Its pages contain abundant material on English coronations and remained a standard work of reference on the subject into the twentieth century.

His interpretation of the coronation was to help initiate the late nineteenth-century debate in two respects. First, the general proposition (which runs through many of his early compositions) that the Anglican church had preserved authentic Catholicism over the centuries, incorporated a subsiduary thesis that the church likewise had preserved authentic coronation ritual. The one followed from the other; and just as the ceremonial of Anglican worship stretched back across the centuries in magnificently uniform prospect (admittedly with some lapses along the way!), so did that of the English coronation whose purity and consistency in essentials had been defended by the church. "Continuity" was the hallmark of the coronation.

Second, Maskell's presentation of the coronation suggested that the "protection" given to the ceremony by the Anglican church both symbolized and helped to create a uniquely "English" association between church and state. From at least the tenth century a form of "national synthesis" between church and state existed, which had no exact parallel anywhere in Europe. The association served both parties immaculately: the king, possessing certain ecclesiastical attributes, helped the church to defend itself against heresy or deviation, while the church helped to preserve the legitimacy of monarchy and the purity of the coronation. This tradition of mutual aid helped to explain the capacity of the Anglican church to avoid the errors into which Rome had fallen; it also saved the monarchy from degenerating into the absolutism and despotism that afflicted so many continental dynasties. Viewed from this perspective, that most controversial of episodes, the "Henrician Reformation," ceased to represent a major rupture in traditional relations between church and state; it became a restatement or reinterpretation of those relations, even if the minutiae of Henry's conduct (especially his matrimonial escapades) hardly commended themselves to a sensitive High Anglican of the Victorian age!

A modern commentator doubtless would find much that was defective in the implications of Maskell's work; but this scholar found general support among a group of remarkable writers who studied coronations in the 1890s and early 1900s. Serious coronation studies in English rarely have flourished as they did at the turn of the century. To appreciate how abundant in scholarship those years were one has but to recall such names as Wickham Legg, Wordsworth, Macleane, Dewick, and others who brought to the subject minds of high caliber and a historical methodology based on the newest ideas. Although these writers published a variety of books and articles, the medium through which they announced some of their most original propositions, and the one which served to define them as a "school," was the *Proceedings* of the Henry Bradshaw Society. Bradshaw (1831–1886) spent most of his career at Cambridge University Library, where he was librarian from 1867 until his death.[2] He too was High Anglican, although he repudiated some of the more extreme views of some of his associates. He also tempered his regard for ancient liturgy with a desire to submit liturgy to historical analysis. He conveyed his enthusiasm to other scholars, who formed the society and journal named after him. The aim of the Henry Bradshaw Society was to track down old liturgical texts chiefly, although by no means exclusively, deriving from the church in England (coronation records were considered to come within their purview), to publish them, and to accompany the printed texts with explanatory introductions and annotation. The *Proceedings* of the society are representative of the late-Victorian penchant for basing historical research as much as possible on original sources. The late 1800s were a time when in England as on the continent the great official archival collections were being organized, important private collections were being made available to scholars, and when documents of many types were being printed in bulk so as to distribute the "raw material" of history as widely as possible.[3] The Henry Bradshaw Society conformed to the age as it published an impressive corpus of annotated texts. The *Proceedings* included ample material on coronations of the medieval and early-modern periods; every student of English coronations has cause to feel a whole-hearted gratitude to the Henry Bradshaw circle whose scholarly labors laid the foundations of later coronation studies.

The publications of the Bradshaw group nevertheless did not go unquestioned either in their method or in their import. For all the apparent objectivity with which members of the group undertook their research, critics discerned a tendentious character in their writing: a strong desire to vindicate the High Anglicanism of the Oxford Movement and its latter-day disciples. Those who deprecated the work of the Henry Bradshaw group held that the "disinterestedness" of much of its research was putative; they chided Bradshaw scholars for having employed methods that appeared to be "scientific" but which in practice were leading to predetermined conclusions. When such charges were applied specifically to coronations, they reproached the Bradshawists for having reinforced without discrimination the thesis suggested by Maskell: English coronation ritual maintained its consistency save in peripheral or unimportant detail, this continuity exemplifying the unbroken association between church and state which underpinned English liberty in politics and right belief in matters of religion.

The most comprehensive assault on the Bradshaw group came from the pen of a Jesuit, Herbert Thurston, whose book, *The Coronation Ceremonial* (London, 1902),[4] attempted to set the record straight. He stated his objections to the Henry Bradshaw scholars:

> But I must confess that while paying tribute to the pains spent by some of the Bradshaw Society editors in editing texts, the net result of all that was then written seems to me profoundly disappointing. Of scholarly and impartial discussion of the many complicated problems suggested by the Coronation Service there is hardly a trace. The whole effort of the writers engaged was to make this question of ritual subservient to a highly controversial purpose, bolstering up a set of highly disputable propositions regarding the ecclesiastical character of the Sovereign, and the supposed independence of the English Church before the Reformation, which no Continental scholar, or for the matter of that no English scholar outside the Ritualist camp, could for a moment regard as established. The *mot d'ordre* seems to have been given in certain articles of Dr. Wickham Legg, and writer has followed writer echoing his words, quoting his proofs, even exaggerating his conclusions, without contributing a single new fact and hardly so much as a new illustration. Practically speaking, the history of our Coronation Orders still stands where Mr. Maskell's *Monumenta Ritualia*

left it years ago. . . . The one aim of all concerned has seemed to be to ignore all the connections and parallels which link the English *Ordines* to Rome and Germany, except in so far as a reference to foreign usages might occasionally be made useful to enforce some pet Anglican theory.[5]

Thurston's general broadside included some specific targets. One was the historian Henry Wakeman whose *Introduction to the Church of England* (London, 1896) vigorously expounded a self-confident, High Anglican interpretation of the history of the church (the final chapter of the book—"The Oxford Movement, 1833–1896"—was nothing less than an apologia; it defined the movement as, "the complete reaction against the Protestant movement of the sixteenth century"[6]). Another was F. C. Eeles, author of *The English Coronation Service: Its History and Teaching* (Oxford, 1902), who stressed the "Englishness" of the coronation ceremony, and the "priestly" nature of the king. But the Jesuit was not merely negative in his remarks; he attempted to correct these Anglicans in three principal areas.

First, Thurston conceded that the "continuity" thesis regarding the ritual of the coronation was tenable with tolerable justification as far as Charles II. But the coronation of James II and even more so that of William III and Mary, included such striking deviation from tradition that a neutral observer surely would conclude that a change of character had indeed taken place; and further, that no English coronation since then had fully restored pre-1685 ritual and meaning.[7]

Second, at no stage could the pre-1685 ceremony be said to have been wholly "English"; that is, immune from outside influences. Thurston examined the four known recensions of the medieval coronation Order. The first or "Egbertine" (fragments of which he traced to the ninth century, the main copies coming in the tenth) he considered to reveal some Scottish or Gallic influences, although no Roman.[8] The second, or "Order of King Ethelred," he placed in the tenth century as having been used at the coronation of Edgar in 973. This recension augmented the first by drawing upon ritual of the coronation of Emperor Otto the Great. Thurston's source on this point was Anton Diemand, *Das Ceremoniell der Kaiserkrönungen von Otto I bis Friedrich II* (Munich, 1894), who indicated the links with the coronation of Edgar: "But of all this our liturgiologists tell us nothing. It would involve the suggestion that, when the English Churchmen before the Conquest wanted to enhance the dignity of their liturgical forms, they turned their eyes Romewards and borrowed Rome prayers. So Dr. Diemand is left out in the cold. There is not one of the Henry Bradshaw editors, so far as I can make out, who so much as condescends even to mention his book."[9] Of the third Order Thurston has little to say; he devotes only one paragraph to it, asserting that Norman influences are traceable in the prayers.[10] The fourth and most important recension, copied in the *Liber Regalis* preserved in Westminster

Abbey, contains, he says, "fresh prayers which seem to be borrowed from the Roman Coronation rituals."[11] This was the recension used at the coronation of Edward II and which was the model for all other coronations to 1685.

The third respect in which Thurston sought to remedy the "shortcomings" of the Bradshaw editors concerned those qualities of the king attested by the coronation. Here the objects of his displeasure were Wickham Legg, Eeles, but especially Douglas Macleane's *The Great Solemnity of the Coronation of the King and Queen of England* (London, 1902). These authors, he protested, alleged that pre-Reformation coronations portrayed the king as a priestly figure who in certain senses shared spiritual authority with the ecclesiastical hierarchy. Thereby, Macleane and others were able to construct the elaborate but erroneous fiction that when Henry VIII assumed headship of the church no revolutionary change was implied, doctrine was unaffected, the king was doing little more than refining a traditional relationship. Here, argued Thurston, the High Anglicans most grievously were at fault. In their desire to expound their understanding of the Anglican church, and in the interests of communicating their vision to others, they were guilty of abusing historical truth. Thurston devoted a whole chapter of his book to a demonstration that the English coronation never recognized spiritual authority of the king within the church.[12] For Thurston the Reformation emphatically marked a breach with the past; the post-Reformation Church of England was not that of the pre-Reformation era. In this, as in the history of the coronation, the Henry Bradshaw group had contrived a continuity not borne out by the facts.

It is no part of the present exercise to attempt a detailed assessment of the tenability of Thurston's objections to the content and implications of the publications of the Bradshaw circle. It can be noted, nevertheless, that even a writer broadly sympathetic to his position—Dom C. Smith in an article published in 1953[13]—conceded that Thurston overstated his case. For one thing the Bradshaw group did not take continuity as implying immutability. Dewick, Wickham Legg and others were aware—indeed, they had demonstrated—that coronation ritual evolved over the centuries. In a somewhat rough-and-ready simile, coronation ritual may be likened to a plant: it grows, produces new foliage, buds and flowers, shedding dead leaves in the process, but it remains the same plant. Similarly, it would be naive to pretend that English coronation ritual did not change during the course of the Middle Ages; but the essence of the ceremony remained unimpaired; it was still the "English" coronation. In short, the concept of continuity was capable of comprehending change of a certain order. An example of this mode of reasoning is an article by H. A. Wilson in 1901 in which he surveyed the four recensions of the coronation Order,[14] drawing heavily on Henry Bradshaw Society publications for his material. His conclusion was that, "The general tendency in the development of the service down to the formation of the fourth order is towards accretion."[15] From coronation to coronation the ceremony grew in complexity, some features being discarded; yet in all essentials it remained the same down to the early-modern period.[16] Change in ritual was reconcilable with the concept of the continuity of the coronation. Again, the Bradshaw group was by no means ignorant of, or blind to, interaction between English and continental coronations. A publication such as E. S. Dewick (ed.) *The Coronation Book of Charles V of France*, (London: Henry Bradshaw Society, vol. 16 1899) was at pains to acknowledge the similarities between the English and French ceremonies. It is possible to query the manner in which the Bradshaw editors treated cross-currents between English and the continent, but it would be false to suppose that they depicted English coronations as the product solely of native traditions untouched by outside influences.

English coronations, and that part of their history related to the question of continuity or change, were absorbed into a campaign for the "soul" of the Anglican church. We would do well to avoid an attitude of censoriousness toward scholars involved in the controversy. For all the lip-service paid to Ranke and his disciples with their call for "objectivity" in the writing of history, and for all the meticulous attention paid by scholars to primary sources, most historians in late-Victorian England sensed a duty to seek moral, religious, political laws in history which would raise English civilization to ever more splendid heights. Even the greatest scholars were inveterate searchers after "Truth" in their study of the past, being ever prepared to point to a moral or to read into history signs of the present times.[17] Inasmuch as the Bradshaw circle derived certain lessons from history, lessons that confirmed their own religious convictions, they were typical of the age. It should occasion no surprise that they used their scholarship as they did.

THE CORONATION AND KINGSHIP

Since the early decades of the twentieth century our knowledge and understanding of English coronations have been greatly augmented and corrected. New material has been unearthed, the comparative analysis of coronations has proceeded apace, the relations between coronations and their political or social circumstances have been explored, while documents that have long been well known have been reassessed or reinterpreted in more variegated ways than in the past. That is not to say that the potential for differences of opinion among scholars has appreciably diminished; quite the contrary. To take but the years since the 1940s, the study of English coronations has engendered stimulating, productive debates freed from cloying religious or political piety. Over the last forty years or so coronation studies have attracted first-rate scholars who have maintained the subject in the forefront of research into the Middle Ages. It must be said that much credit for this healthy state of affairs is owned to non-British scholars among whom such names as Schramm and Kantorowicz are, of course, especially notable. In the case of Schramm it was his general history of the English coronation (the English translation appeared in 1937) that supplied the synthesis of the subject against which further research could be measured. The theme of "continuity" or "change" was given a new lease of life not so much in connection with the internal study of coronations, as with regard to the implications of coronation studies for other branches of medieval history. This is well illustrated in the case of works on the evolution of English kingship. The ritual of the coronation may not have been designed as a comprehensive embodiment of the medieval constitution, but the ceremony was not without significance as a statement on the relation between the king and his subjects.

It was H. G. Richardson who observed that while contemporaries in the thirteenth and fourteenth centuries regarded unction as the climax to the coronation, for present-day scholars it was the oath that inspired most interest.[18] During the 1940s and 1950s there developed a far-reaching debate on the oath, in which there loomed large the question of whether the oath remained unchanged, thus sustaining forces of continuity in the concept of kingship, or whether it had undergone amendment in accordance with shifting ideas on monarchy. Paradoxically, historians had at once too much and too little material with which to work. Too much in the sense that, as regards those coronations for which the terms of the oath were extant (such as those of 1308 and 1327), several versions in Latin and in French were available, each displaying individual traits. By what criteria, therefore, could greater or lesser authenticity or authority be attributed to one as against another? How were differences between them to be explained? Of what significance were those differences? But too little in the sense that for many coronations no text of the oath had been discovered. In such cases how far was it safe to depend on the continuity principle and to take for granted that no changes of substance had occured? Thus, while it was conceivable that the coronation oath potentially was a valuable aid to medieval constitutional history, there was an intricate task of textual criticism to be undertaken as a preliminary.

Many articles of the 1940s and 1950s were devoted to that end.[19] It emerged that the oaths taken at two coronations deserved special attention. The first was that taken by Edward I in 1274. It was accepted by scholars that royal coronation oaths normally contained three promises: to preserve peace and to defend the church; to uphold just laws and to abrogate the unjust; to dispense justice to all without favor. But H. G. Richardson argued that a fourth clause was inserted into the oath of Edward I: "that the king would preserve the rights of the kingship—*iura regni*—unimpaired, and that nothing affecting the rights of the crown would be done without the counsel of the prelates and great men of the realm."[20] The evidence for the fourth clause was circumstantial, for the actual words of Edward I's oath had never been discovered; nevertheless, Richardson considered that the indications were so convincing that the existence of an extra clause in 1274 could not be doubted. If he was right, what were the constitutional implications of the new clause? To this question Richardson was unable to provide a clear-out answer; but whatever the thinking behind the clause there were, he suggested, remarkable short-term consequences. The king used the clause to ward off papal intervention in English affairs, to resist incursions by barons upon royal rights, and to overcome resistance by the clergy to certain royal nominations to benefices.[21] The fourth clause, in other words, served to dilate royal power. It must be said, however, that skillfully as Richardson argued his case, he had inferred rather than demonstrated the existence of the clause. If the inference was sound then the constitutional implications were truly prodigious: rejection by the crown of almost any unbidden limitations on its actions; a triumphant Erastianism redolent of the sixteenth century; and a drive toward absolute monarchy that portended conflicts of the seventeenth century.

The second oath to merit scrutiny was that of Edward II. Historians reacted with more confidence in this instance, for the coronation of 1308 is exceedingly well documented: this was the ceremony at which the fourth recension of the Order was first employed, while the terms of the oath are available in Latin and in French. Moreover, the context within which the coronation took place is intriguing on several counts. The fact that late in the day the coronation was postponed from 18 February to 25 February invites explanation; was there a serious breach between the king and the archbishop of Canterbury who was out of the country? The disordered state of relations between Edward II and the barons hints at implications for the coronation, as does the ill-grace displayed by earls resentful of the honors bestowed upon the parvenu Piers de Gaveston. These and other possibilities have been countenanced by scholars, whose assembled works make the 1308 coronation the most closely scrutinized of English medieval crowning ceremonies.[22]

The oath taken by Edward II contrasted with that of his predecessors in that it did include a fourth clause; even if it is conceded that an additional clause had been inserted in 1274, again that of 1308 was different. In this new clause (which was administered and responded to in French, not in Latin; it is the French version that is authoritative), the king was asked: "Sire, grauntez vous a tenir et garder les leys et les custumes droitureles les quiels la communaute de vostre roiaume aura eslu, et les defendrez et efforcerez al honour de Dieu, a vostre poer?"[23] The key phrase is: "les quiels la communaute de vostre roiaume aura eslu." Did it imply that the king not only bound himself to rule within the confines of existing law but covenanted to subject himself to future and thus unpredictable law shaped, perhaps, by the caprice of hostile fortune? If so, are we not confronted by a dramatic contrast with 1274 when English monarchy appeared poised to roll back limitations on its power? In 1308 are we presented with the spectacle of a king whose power is strictly circumscribed, and whose relations with the "community of the realm" have undergone thorough revision?

Not necessarily so, according to one line of argument.[24] When the circumstances immediately surrounding the coronation are taken into account, the fourth clause palpably excites less controversy. Edward II, in an attempt to foster an atmosphere of political amity and cooperation at the beginning of his reign, sought means to restore the rapport between crown and magnates which had been eroded under Edward I. The coronation was useful to achieve that end. Contrary to what has sometimes been maintained, it is certain that the terms of the oath were not concocted in haste; they were composed with the utmost care, the king and his advisers consenting to them only after painstaking analysis of their implications. The oath stands as a genuine statement of the royal position, and as such ought not to be depicted as a form of "surrender" to magnates. The fourth clause in no sense justifies the proposition that the king's will was subordinated to that of his subjects. Its purpose was to reassure them, to placate them, to remove any fears that Edward II later would violate promises taken in 1308. As regards the phrase concerning laws yet to be enacted, even here there was no radical intent or meaning. Once more the king was aiming to be conciliatory. The point of the phrase was not that a new method of creating law was envisaged, or that law might be enacted in opposition to royal will, rather that the customary procedures for creating law would be followed, but that once law passed the king would abide by its provisions and rule according to its prescriptions, just as he promised to rule within existing law. If anything the fourth clause is consistent with the thesis of the growth of royal power: Edward II was prepared to take such an oath precisely because he was confident of his ability to control legislation and to determine that normally it would coincide with royal interest.

These were among the more controversial issues treated by the scholar whose premature death left such a deep sense of loss, personal and professional, among his friends and colleagues: John Joseph Brückmann. It was in his doctoral dissertation, *English Coronations, 1216–1308: The Edition of the Coronation "Ordines"* (University of Toronto, 1964) that he advanced his own thoughts on the oath. Those thoughts did not entirely confirm the views of Richardson. For Brückmann the oath may have indicated changes in the patern of kingship, but in a different sense from that advocated by Richardson. It should be stressed that the principal contribution of the thesis to coronations studies is textual. Brückmann took the four known recensions of the English coronation Order and presented them in a critical edition. In itself this was an achievement of the first magnitude. The recensions, of course, had long been known to and used by scholars; but the absence of a reliable, thoroughly annotated text of these essential documents had hampered research for many decades. Brückmann produced a text that was masterly in its accuracy, in the sophistication of its analysis, and in the amplitude of its critical commentary. But the dissertation involved more than an exercise in textual presentation and criticism: it included a general history of English coronations from the twelfth to the fourteenth centuries. In these pages he delved into some of the more knotty problems facing historians; especially was he interested in investigating changes in the coronation oath and the extent to which those changes were of constitutional significance.

Brückmann argued that although the oath taken at some coronations has been lost, and that where texts have survived it is in several versions, there is sufficient evidence to indicate that the oath as actually spoken by the king in the thirteenth century varied only marginally in wording and not at all in meaning. He disputed Richardson's claim that during the thirteenth century the traditional threefold oath was augmented by a fourth wherein the monarch swore to defend the rights and privileges attaching to kingship. He considered the evidence to be too circumstantial to be convincing. For Brückmann the thirteenth-century oath remained traditional and lends no support to the idea of innovation. He also queried Richardson's interpretation of the 1308 oath with its fourth clause. Even when the political background to the coronation of Edward II is taken into account, however, even admitting that the king on the eve of his crowning was seeking to placate his magnates, the constitutional principles involved in the proposition that the king will observe not only the established laws and customs of England, but in addition those which the community of the realm might elect in future, can only be deemed revolutionary. Brückmann saw the oath of 1308 as imposing severe limitations on the power of the king. It foreshadowed a monarchy subjected to unprecedented restrictions since the community of the realm at any time might impose legal constraints on royal action, constraints to which Edward II already had committed himself under oath. In the development of English monarchy, said Brückmann, the coronation of 1308 occupies a position of pivotal importance. Whereas Richardson perceived "change" in the coronation of 1274 and "continuity" in that of 1308, Brückmann saw the opposite.

THE CORONATION AND LEGITIMATION

So far this essay has considered the theme of continuity and change as it affected the ceremony of the coronation. In this last section it is proposed to adopted an "external" perspective—that of "legitimation"—and to consider the manner in which early-modern regimes in England contrived to used coronations to define and to propagate their legitimacy. There is no need to labor the point that one of the distinguishing features of the early-modern period, in English as well as in continental European history, is that the state as we now understand it was beginning to emerge as a recognizable historical phenomenon. The interlocking themes that normally are considered to constitute the growth of the state are fully treated in literature on the subject:[25] the cult of monarchy, the development of new machinery of central and provincial government and administration, intervention in the economy, the creation of more powers of coercion and control of society, the steady expansion and management of the armed forces, and so forth. But it is also instructive to inquire whether coronations of the sixteenth and seventeenth centuries shed any light on the process whereby regimes legitimized themselves; especially in the case of England where dynasties came and went with comparative frequency, either through natural causes or revolution.

The theme of legitimation calls to mind, of course, the theories of Max Weber and his disciples. For Weber the legitimation process focuses on three categories: tradition and custom, the charisma of leadership, and the legality of a regime, that is, the extent to which it conforms to its statutory obligations.[26] Weber's model is an ideal-type concept useful for organizing the results of empirical research. How far is it of assistance in examining English coronations as instruments in the legitimation process?

There were occasions in the sixteenth and seventeenth centuries when the legitimacy of a regime in a fundamental sense was at stake: was a particular monarch a rightful sovereign? A cloud of doubt hung over Henry VII. Later, Pius V's condemnation of Elizabeth I as heretic and his release of her subjects from obedience to the queen raised the specter of assassination attempts. The aftermath of the 1688 revolution saw the emergence of a Jacobite movement that, in spite of its tendencies toward internal division, was capable of mounting a serious challenge to the Orange and Hanoverian dynasties. In this regard the early modern period witnessed the revival of conditions that the Yorkist kings struggled against in the fifteenth century.[27] Then, Edward IV and Richard III, sensitive to the tenuous nature of their incumbency, exploited all ceremonials in the drive to validate the legitimacy of their rule. For them the coronation was indispensable to legitimation; hence the emphasis they placed on unction, that visible sign of divine approval of the "chosen one." In an age when poison, the dagger thrust, and on one celebrated occasion a hogshead of wine, were liable to be employed to dispatch pretenders or monarchs suspected of usurpation, no ceremony was too stagy, no myth too implausible to be availed of in the process of legitimation. And so Yorkist kings showed no compunction about circulating the story that the oil used at their coronations was none other than that transmitted miraculously to Thomas Becket by the Virgin by virtue of her special regard for the kings of England![28]

Early-modern coronations, at least up to 1685, were based on the fourth recension of the Order. The only change of note, which in no sense modified the meaning of the ceremony, was the use of English in place of Latin from

1603 onward. To this extent, therefore, the retention of the traditional Order even after the Reformation conforms to two of Weber's three criteria for legitimation: tradition and custom, and legality. But on closer inspection it appears that those parts of the coronation that did not carry implications for the actual crowning and unction could be amended if the regime wished to affirm a certain political or social point. The coronation of Elizabeth I provides a case in point. The ceremony followed the conventions until the mass. Then, according to some sources, when the host was about to be elevated the queen temporarily withdrew, dramatically exposing her rejection of transubstantiation.[29] Striking as this version of events is, it rests on the supposition that the host was indeed elevated. Other witnesses assert that the elevation was omitted from the mass, that the representatives of Catholic states withdrew from this part of the ceremony as an act of protest, and that Elizabeth I did not retire. At the time of the coronation of James I the Venetian ambassador even came up with a third version: that the host was elevated, that Elizabeth I remained in position, but that she covered her face with a handkerchief so as not to observe this objectionable act! Much ingenious detective work has been undertaken in an attempt to establish the facts, but questions remain. Who officiated at the mass? Was it George Carew, dean of Windsor, an egregious pluralist and opportunist who would comply with every whim of the queen, or was it Owen Oglethorpe, bishop of Carlisle, who performed the act of crowning Elizabeth I but was no time-server, and who on one occasion had elevated the host against her express command? Again, if Elizabeth I did withdraw, did she remain in the sanctuary or did she go elsewhere? Whichever version is preferred, however, the outcome is the same: Elizabeth I introduced a dramatic gesture into her coronation in order to publicize a statement on the religious ethos of the coming reign.

Religious matters were equally prominent at the coronation of James II, although in a contrary sense: every effort had to be made to concoct a ceremony that remained faithful to tradition but which would disguise the Catholicism of the new king. By resorting to the pretence that the conventional ceremony was too long and that it imposed inordinate physical strains on the monarch, James II's coronation was purged of potentially controversial material with the essence of the ceremony left untouched. More than any other aspect of the crowning ceremony, this was the one that brought from the pen of Macaulay the cynical but celebrated passage:

> James had ordered Sancroft [archbishop of Canterbury] to abridge the ritual. The reason publicly assigned was that the day was too short for all that was to be done. But whoever examines the changes which were made will see that the real object was to remove some things highly offensive to the religious feelings of a zealous Roman Catholic. The Communion Service was not read. The ceremony of presenting the sovereign with a richly bound copy of the English Bible, and of exhorting him to prize above all earthly treasures a

volume which he had been taught to regard as adulterated with false doctrine, was omitted. What remained, however, after all this curtailment, might well have raised scruples in the mind of a man who sincerely believed the Church of England to be a heretical society, within the pale of which salvation was not to be found. The King made an oblation on the altar. He appeared to join in the petitions of the Litany which was chaunted by the Bishops. He received from those false prophets the unction typical of a divine influence, and knelt with the semblance of devotion while they called down upon him that Holy Spirit of which they were, in his estimation, the malignant and obdurate foes. Such are the inconsistencies of human nature that this man, who, from a fanatical zeal for his religion, threw away three kingdoms, yet chose to commit what was little short of an act of apostasy, rather than forego the childish pleasure of being invested with the gewgaws symbolical of kingly power.[30]

The coronations of Elizabeth I and James II should cause us to be cautious about the extent to which Weber's legitimation thesis can be applied without qualification. Insofar as the actual acts of crowning and unction remained orthodox they conform to his propositions on tradition and custom and on legality. But around these two essential features of the coronation was a penumbra of associated ritual which could be changed in the interests of legitimation; legitimation could require a departure from tradition and custom.

There is one aspect of the coronation that bears close scrutiny vis-à-vis the theme of legitimation: the sermon.[31] It gave to the church, one of the great and distinctive institutions of the state, the opportunity to address the king and "community of the realm" jointly just before the monarch was crowned. Indeed, it exemplified that association between church and state which stood at the center of the view of coronations advocated by the Henry Bradshaw group. The sermon was preached at an early stage of the coronation, coming after the Procession and Recognition, but before the Oath. It sought to convey to those assembled and others beyond (the sermon was printed and given wide distribution) the church's statement on the condition of society, on the tasks facing the monarch, and on the guiding principles that he ought to adopt. The sermon was no inconsequential diversion peripheral to the more serious proceedings; it was an integral part of the ceremony when the voice of the church spoke prophetically. Although the evidence is circumstantial, it is probable that those who preached the coronation sermons were selected both because their views on the state matched those of monarch and because they had earned royal favor or gratitude in the past; the honor of preaching the sermon was a reward for service. Nevertheless, it would be misguided to suppose that preachers were nothing other than servile mouthpieces for the monarch, or that their sermons aimed simply to propagate a message agreeable to the regime. Early-modern coronation sermons contain outspoken passages on the obligations of kingship and on the penalties of their nonobservance. They seek to instruct the king as well as to counsel his subjects; to urge him to great tasks; frankly to warn him against the dangers and temptations ahead. Even so, coronation sermons glorified the monarch, dwelt upon the divine origins of the institution of monarchy, railed against rebellion, and sustained every proposition with copious references, biblical, classical, and historical. As a exercise in legitimation the sermon's contribution to the coronation could be of firstrate importance: the voice of the church affirmed to the community at large that divine approbation rested on the monarch.

Among Weber's three themes of legitimation, that of the charisma of the leader surely finds extravagant illustration in early-modern coronations, as well as those of the medieval period. It is a theme capable of much deeper analysis than it has received hitherto. The crowning of a new monarch occasioned a veritable profusion of pageants, balls, processions, private festivities, poems, encomiastic prose, songs, plays, sermons, prophecies, horoscopes, paintings, drawings, engraving, natural signs and portents, miraculour healings (not least by kings who "touched"), and a host of other celebratory or wondrous events. The publication of comprehensive editions of the journals and correspondence of such perspicacious observers as Evelyn, Pepys, or Horace Walpole (a sharp-witted and detailed source on the coronation of George III) have placed at our disposal eyewitness accounts of coronation celebrations that can be exploited to great effect. Here is a field of research that still has many rich results to yield. Already we are indebted to scholars who have published essays in this collection, and to others such as Sydney Anglo and Father Reedy.[32] Their work suggests profitable lines of inquiry: the significance of the themes, often classical or mythological, chosen for pageants or for literary and musical works; the use of symbolism and the meanings it was intended to convey; the qualities of the monarch singled out for special emphasis. Of exceptional importance is the royal procession traditionally held in London on the day before the coronation.[33] It was the event that drew together into a carefully contrived manifestation of civic pageantry many diverse festivities and celebrations. Whatever merit attaches to the thesis that in early-modern England "courtly culture" and "popular culture" were drifting apart into distinct forms,[34] the coronation was an occasion that united all the cultural and celebratory impulses of society into one great carnival with a single point or focus: the king or queen. The ceremony of crowning and anointing the monarch served the legitimation process in respect of tradition and custom and of legality; its attendant festivities served the cult of the charismatic leader.

The conclusions to be drawn from this discussion by now are apparent. The first is uncontroversial but has emerged with some force: even the most distinguished historians of medieval and early-modern English coronations have had difficulty in deciding whether the forces of continuity or of change have been the more characteristic of their subject. This is scarcely surprising.

To the question "what happened?" in the case of an individual coronation, rarely is it possible to supply a precise and detailed answer. The surviving evidence often is too fragmentary or self-contradictory to sustain dogmatic interpretations. Those historians who have been drawn toward all-embracing theories of the history of the coronation often have been inspired by aspirations other than a dispassionate pursuit of historical research. This leads to the second conclusion: as a topic for historical inquiry coronations have a significance above and beyond the minutiae of the ritual itself. Without in any sense straining their possibilities, coronations and their history can augment and refine our understanding of themes in constitutional, political, and social history. If a somewhat rough-and-ready simile may be used, a coronation is rather like a blood test: it may provide essential clues as to the condition and general health of the patient. Thus, coronations, especially if they are understood in the widest sense of comprising processions and festivities as well as the crowning of the monarch, can inform us as to the temper of a community, even of a nation. In this sense coronations both restate those permanent principles that are considered central to monarchy and give expression, either consciously or unconsciously, to current aspirations and concerns. Third, the "blood test" approach to coronations is probably relevant up to and including the crowning of William III and Mary. Thereafter (although this is outside the period covered by this essay) coronations tended to become but shadows of the great ceremonies of earlier periods. Several hypotheses can be advanced as an explanation. The 1688 Revolution greatly advanced the power of Parliament at the expense of that of the crown; eighteenth- and nineteenth-century monarchs reigned in a political atmosphere and according to a constitutional theory very different from that of the middle ages or early-modern period. Again, coronation ceremonial itself was treated in cavalier fashion in the 1700s and 1800s: Hanoverian coronations lacked the attention to detail that characterized those of earlier periods, the nadir probably being reached with the crowning of George III whose coronation was reduced almost to a shambles as one mishap followed another; on that occasion even the sermon scarcely could be heard above the clatter of cutlery and popping of corks as the congregation used the opportunity to take lunch! The coronations of George VI and William IV were mean affairs; that of Victoria only marginally better. In short, after 1685 the constitutional and social significance of the coronation went into decline. By the time of Victoria's coronation, however, there were signs of a desire for the revival of a ceremony of some splendor. In a debate in the House of Lords on 28 May 1838, the Marquess of Londonderry was at the head of those who badgered the government, accusing it of a parsimonious attitude toward what ought to be an occasion of national rejoicing. The debate resulted in some prickly exchanges. Earl Fitzwilliam expressed the opinion that, "coronations were fit only for barbarous, or semi-barbarous ages; for periods when crowns were won and lost by unruly violence and ferocious contests."[35] The sober tones of *Hansard* record the response: "The Marquess of Londonderry asked whether the noble Earl opposite was of the opinion that there ought to be no coronation at all? Earl Fitzwilliam answered in the affirmative. The Marquess of Londonderry said that he supposed that the noble Earl was prepared to follow up the proposition by moving that there ought to be no Lord Fitzwilliam at all."[36] And quite right too!

NOTES

1. The literature on the Oxford Movement is profuse; a good summary of the movement and its aims is in O. Chadwick, *The Victorian Church*, pt. 1, 2d. ed., (London, 1970), chap. 3; for a survey of recent publications see S. Gilley, "The Oxford Movement," *History* 69, no. 226.
2. On Bradshaw, see A. C. Benson, "Henry Bradshaw," *The Cornhill Magazine* 30 (1911): 814–824.
3. See J. P. Kenyon, *The History Men: The Historical Profession in England Since the Renaissance* (London, 1983), 85–97.
4. His thoughts on the Coronation are available in brief form in two articles that he wrote: "The English Coronation Ceremonial," *The Month* 99 (1920): 561–576, and "The Coronation," *The Dublin Review* 149 (1911): 1–22.
5. Herbert Thurston, *The Coronation Ceremonial*, 2d ed. (London, 1911), 4–50.
6. Ibid., 492.
7. Ibid., 12–13, chap. 4.
8. Ibid., 13–18.
9. Ibid., 18–22.
10. Ibid., 22.
11. Ibid., 22–23.
12. Ibid., chap. 5.
13. "The Origins and Development of the Coronation Liturgy," *The Clergy Review*, new series, 38, no. 4 (1953): 193–202.
14. "The Coronation Orders," *The Journal of Theological Studies* (July, 1909): 481–504.
15. Ibid., 495.
16. Nevertheless, he doubted whether it could be said that the traditional ceremony survived the seventeenth century.
17. Kenyon, *The History Men*, 97–143.
18. "The Coronation in Medieval England," *Traditio* 16 (1960): 116.
19. R. S. Hoyt, "The Coronation Oath of 1308," *English Historical Review*, 81–280 (1956): 354, n. 2, contains a comprehensive bibliography on the subject.
20. H. G. Richardson, "The English Coronation Oath," *Transactions of the Royal Historical Society*, 4th series, 23 (1941): 131.
21. Ibid., 133–135.
22. See especially, Hoyt "The Coronation Oath of 1308"; Richardson, "The English Coronation Oath"; "The Coronation in Medieval England," 138–140; "Early

Coronation Records: The Coronation of Edward II," *Bulletin of the Institute of Historical Research* 16 (1938–1939): 1–11; "The English Coronation Oath," *Speculum* 24, no. 1 (1949): 44–75; L. B. Wilkinson, "Notes on the Coronation Records of the Fourteenth Century," *English Historical Review* 70, no. 277 (1955): 581–600.

23. Hoyt, "The Coronation Oath of 1308," 356.

24. Hoyt and Richardson reach similar conclusions on this point.

25. J. H. Shennan, *The Origins of the Modern European State, 1450–1725* (London, 1974), contains essential bibiographical references.

26. H. H. Gerth and C. Wright Mills, eds., *Max Weber* (London, 1970), 77–79.

27. C. A. J. Armstrong, "The Inauguration Ceremonies of the Yorkist Kings and the Title to the Throne," *Transactions of the Royal Historical Society*, 4th series, 30 (1948): 51–73.

28. J. W. McKebba, "The Coronation Oil of the Yorkist Kings," *English Historical Review* 82, no. 322 (1967): 102–104.

29. This paragraph on Elizabeth's coronation is based on: C. G. Bayne, "The Coronation of Queen Elizabeth," *English Historical Review* 22, no. 87 (1907): 650–673; Ibid., 24, no. 94 (1909): 322–323; Ibid., 25, no. 99 (1910): 550–553; W. P. Haugaard, "The Coronation of "Elizabeth I," *Journal of Ecclesiastical History* 19, no. 2 (1968): "Elizabeth." *English Historical Review* 25, no. 97 (1910): 125–126; G. L. Ross, "Il Schifanoya's Account of the Coronation of Queen Elizabeth," *English Historical Review* 23, no. 91 (1908): 533–534; H. A. Wilson, "The Coronation of Queen Elizabeth," *English Historical Review* 23, no. 89 (1908): 87–91. See also R. C. McCoy's contribution to this volume.

30. Lord Macaulay, *The History of England from the Accession of James II*, ed. C. H. Firth, 6 vols. (London, 1913–1914), i, 469.

31. D. J. Sturdy, "English Coronations in the Seventeenth Century," in *Herrscherweihe und Königskrönung im Frühneuzeitlichen Europa*, ed. H. Duchhardt (Wiesbaden, 1983), 69–71.

32. S. Anglo. *Spectacle, Pageantry, and Early Tudor Policy* (Oxford, 1969); G. Reedy, S. J., "Mystical Politics: The Imagery of Charles II's Coronation," in *Studies in Change and Revolution: Aspects of English Intellectual History, 1640–1800*, ed. P. Korshin (Menston, 1972), 19–42.

33. The procession was not held before the coronation of Charles I because of plague, nor was it held before that of James II because of the costs involved; Macaulay saw the omission as a grave error on the part of James II (*History*, i, 468–469).

34. See C. Hill, *The Century of Revolution, 1603–1714* (London, 1961), *passim*; A. Hughes and W. R. Owens, eds., *Seventeenth-Century England: a Changing Culture*, 2 vols. (London, 1980).

35. Hansard, 43 (1838), 350.

36. Ibid., 351.

CONTRIBUTORS

Bak, János M. Department of History, University of British Columbia, Vancouver, British Columbia, V6T 1W5, Canada.

Bonne, Jean-Claude. Ecole des Hautes Etudes en Sciences Sociales, Groupe d'anthropologie historique de l'occident médiéval, 54 Boulevard Raspail, F-7006 Paris, France.

Bryant, Lawrence. Department of History, California State University, Chico, California, 95929–0735.

Elze, Reinhard. Münchener Freiheit 16, D-8000 München 40, German Federal Republic.

Giesey, Ralph E. Department of History, University of Iowa, Iowa City, Iowa, 52242.

Gieysztor, Aleksander. Dyrektor zamku królewskiego w Warszawie, PL 00277 Warszawa, pl. Zamkowy 4, Poland.

Hedeman, Anne D. School of Art and Design, University of Illinois at Urbana-Champaign, Champaign, Illinois, 61820.

Hoffmann, Erich. Historisches Seminar, Universität Kiel, D 2300 Kiel, German Federal Republic.

Hughes, Andrew. Faculty of Music, University of Toronto, Toronto, Ontario, M5S 1A1, Canada.

Le Goff, Jacques. Ecole des Hautes Etudes en Sciences Sociales, Groupe d'anthropologie historique de l'occident médiéval, 54 Boulevard Raspail, F-7006 Paris, France.

McCoy, Richard C. Department of English, Queens College, City University of New York, Flushing, New York, 11367.

Nelson, Janet L. Department of History, King's College, London, WC2R 2LS, United Kingdom.

Schimmelpfennig, Bernhard. Lehrstuhl für mittelalterliche Geschichte, Universität Augsburg, Universitätsstr. 10, D-8900 Augsburg, German Federal Republic.

Sturdy, David J. University of Ulster at Coleraine, Coleraine, County Londonderry, BT52 1SH, Northern Ireland.

Vestergaard, Elisabeth. Middelalterlaboratoriet, Universitet Odense, DK-5230 Odense M, Denmark.

GENERAL INDEX

Aachen (Aix-la-Chapelle), 53
Abel, king of Denmark, 131
acclamation (incl. *laudes*), 6, 50, 53–54, 65, 141, 158, 171, 189, 190, 197, 198, 207
accounts, papal (cameral), 180, 189
Adrian IV, pope, 126, 127
Adventius, bishop of Metz, 23
Alexander III, pope, 126, 131
Alexander IV, pope, 183
allegory (allegorical interpretation), 3, 5, 99, 107–109, 112
Alleluya terminations and tracts, 206–207, 210
Anglican church, 229–231 passim, 233
Anjou, duke of, 79, 80
Annals of St. Bertin, 16–34 passim
Anne of Beaujeu, regent of France, 89
Anne of Brittany, queen of France, 89, 90, 108, 109, 198. See also *sacre*
Ansegis, archbishop of Sens, 21
archirex, 132, 136
aristocracy (magnates, *primores*), 18, 21–22, 23, 24, 25, 38, 139; role in coronations, 49, 50, 67, 77–81 passim, 134. See also peers of France
Aristotle, 162
armillae, 158, 174
Avignon, 8, 179–196 passim; papal cathedral, 186; palace, 184–185, 192
Avril, François, 46, 61

Banks, T. C., 228
banquet (royal, papal), 55, 100, 159, 190–191, 192

baptism, 51–52, 65, 81–83, 198
Bayne, C. G., 221
Beauvais, bishop of, 79
Bedford, duke of, regent of France, 89, 102
Belleforest, François, 111
Below, Georg von, 3
Benedict XII, pope, 179, 184, 186, 190, 192
Benedict XIII, pope, 180
Bergen (Norway), 125, 127
Bergeron, David, 223
Berkeley, "school of," 5
Birger, king of Sweden, 139, 143
Birger Jarl, 137
Birkbeck, W. J., 208
bishops, 23, 49, 65, 159, 170–171, 218, 219, 223; as king-makers, 21, 23–24
Bloch, Marc, 3, 4, 5, 6, 8
Boleslaw the Brave, king of Poland, 159
Boniface VIII, pope, 198
Bonne, Jean-Claude, 7, 46–47
Bonner, bishop of London, 219
Bordeaux, 102, 106
Boso (of Vienne), king of Lower Burgundy, 21–22, 26
Bouman, Cornelius, 6
Bourbon, duke of, 79, 80, 81
Brabant, *joyeuse entrée* of, 91, 112
Bradshaw, Henry, 230. See also Henry Bradshaw Society
Branner, Robert, 46, 61
Breakspear, Cardinal Nicholas. See Adrian IV, pope
Bruges, treaty of, 74

249

Brückmann, John, vii, 7, 199–202 passim, 210–213 passim, 228, 237–238
Bryant, Lawrence, 7, 8
Bugenhagen, Johannes, 132, 133
Bukofzer, M. F., 207
Burgundy, duke of, 54, 66, 79–81 passim. *See also* individual rulers
Byzantium, 5, 11 n. 2, 13 n. 17

Cambridge, "school of," 5
Canada, 158
canopy, 65, 67, 95, 97–98, 204
Capetian, dynasty, 36
cappella, papal, 186, 189
cardinals (bishops, deacons), 187–189 passim
Carew, George, dean of the Chapel Royal, Windsor, 220, 240
Carloman, son of Charles the Bald, 19–20
Carloman, son of Louis the Stammerer, 20–21
Carmen de coronacione (1443), 132, 135
Carolingians, 18–26 passim
Casimir III (the Great), king of Poland, 155
Casimir IV Jagiello, king of Poland, 154
catafalque, 189–190, 192
Catherine de' Medici, queen of France, 90
Catholicism, Roman, 219, 220, 221
Celestine V, pope, 189
Châlons-sur Marne, 46, 58
chancellor of France, 106
chant, 197–216 passim; melodic, 203–206; notation, 2, 202–203, 209
charisma, 242
Charlemagne, 75
Charles, duke of Normandy, 89
Charles the Bald, king of the Franks, emperor, 19–20; king of Lotharingia, 22–26 passim
Charles the Fat, king of the Eastern Franks, 20
Charles II, king of England, 232
Charles III, grand duke of Lorraine, 40
Charles IV, king of Bohemia, emperor, 135
Charles V, king of France, 73, 74, 75, 89, 91, 92. *See also* Coronation Book
Charles VI, king of France, 80, 89, 101, 102
Charles VII, king of France, 89, 95, 103, 104, 108
Charles VIII, king of France, 89, 104, 105, 108, 111
Charles IX, king of France, 42, 43, 90, 108
Chastellain, George, 113
Châtelet (Paris), 41, 96–97

Christian I, king of Denmark, 131
Christian II, king of the (Scandinavian) Union, 130, 131, 138, 139
Christian III, king of the (Scandinavian) Union, 132–134 passim, 139
Christina, queen of Denmark, 132
Christine de Pizan, 94–95
Christopher II, king of the (Scandinavian) Union, 131
Christopher III, king of the (Scandinavian) Union, 130, 131, 135–136 passim, 138, 142, 143
civic progress, 222–225 passim
Claude of France, queen, 90, 109
Clement IV, pope, 183
Clement V, pope, 184, 190
Clement VI, pope, 179, 184, 190, 191, 192
Clement VII, pope, 190
clergy, 48–49, 63, 66, 69, 94, 98, 112, 139
Clovis, king of the Franks, 24; anointing of, 24, 49, 65
coat of arms. *See* heraldry
color, symbolic value of, 54, 60, 101, 152, 186
consecration (*sacre, Weihe*), 10 n. 1, 17, 37, 70, 120; episcopal, 181. *See also* anointing; coronation; inauguration; *sacre et couronnement*
constable of France, 101
contract, 48, 66
Copenhagen, 131, 132, 136, 142
Coronation Book of Charles V, 72–87 passim, 234
coronation: Anglo-Saxon, 53; in Denmark, 132–137 passim; English, 5, 197–245 passim; French (*see* sacre et couronnement); in general, 10 n. 1, 35, 181; mass, 55, 135, 139, 157–159 passim, 176, 218, 220, 221; modern, 1, 234–238 passim; in Norway, 125–131 passim; oath, 35, 53, 126, 128, 129, 133, 134, 139, 140, 148 n. 83, 148 n. 85, 157–158, 235–238 passim; papal, 179–196 passim, 198; in Poland, 152–164 passim; Protestant, 125, 140, 220–222; as social drama, 159; studies, medieval 3–4; in Sweden, 137–142 passim
Corpus Christi procession, 97
courtly culture, 242. *See also* tournament
Cracow, 154–158 passim
Cranmer, Thomas, archbishop of Canterbury, 218
crown, 55, 67, 127, 133, 137–138, 139, 140, 159, 175

crown-wearing (*coronamentum, Festkrönung*), 9, 166, 168
crusade, 61

Danehof (parliament), 137
David, king of Israel, 16, 54, 60, 113
Denmark, 120, 131–137 passim, 142. *See also* individual rulers
deposition (of ruler), 120–121
Dewick, E. S., 230, 233, 234
Diemand, Anton, 232
Długosz, Jan, canon of Cracow, 159
Dorothea, queen of Denmark, 132
Dorpat, bishop of, 129, 138
Du Tillet, Jean, clerc of the Parlement de Paris, 42
Durand, Guillaume. *See* Pontifical of Durandus
Dykmans, Marc, 182–184 passim

Eales, F. C., 232, 233
Edda, Poetic, 121
Edgar, king of the Anglo-Saxons. *See ordines*, English
Edward I, king of England, 200, 235, 237
Edward II, king of England, 197, 199, 202, 207, 210, 233, 236, 237, 238
Edward III, king of England, 199, 200, 210
Edward IV, king of England, 239
Edward VI, king of England, 218, 219
effigy (funeral), 39, 41, 43
Egbert, king of the Anglo-Saxons. *See ordines*, English
Eichmann, Eduard, 5
Eirik, archbishop of Trondheim, 127
Eleanor of Austria, queen of France, 90, 109
Elisabeth of Austria, queen of France, 90, 109
Elizabeth I, queen of England, 217–227 passim, 239–241 passim
Elze, Reinhard, 1, 6, 7, 10
Emili, Paulus, 111
England, 134, 137, 143, 197–245 passim. *See also* individual rulers
entry (*entrée*): ducal (Brabant), 41; papal, 181; royal, 36, 40–41, 43, 88–118 passim, 152. *See also* civic progress
Erdmann, Carl, 5, 6
Erik-clan (Sweden), 137
Eric of Pomerania, king of the (Scandinavian) Union, 130, 131, 132
Erik Glipping, king of Denmark, 131, 135
Erik Knutsson, king of Sweden, 137
Erik Menved, king of Denmark, 131, 135
Erik Ploughpenny, king of Denmark, 131
Eriksgata, 138
Erik XIV, king of Sweden, 140
Erling, Norwegian jarl, 125
Eskil, archbishop of Lund, 131
estates (general), 101, 110
Étampes, count of, 79–80
Eystein, archbishop of Trondheim, 125, 126
Eystein Magnusson, king of Norway, 128

"faceless knight," rite of, 155
fealty. *See* homage
Fénot, Pierre, 46, 59
Firmetur tracts (music), 204–206
Fitzwilliam, Earl, 243–244
flag, flagbearer (banner), 38, 137, 191
Flanders, count of, 79, 80
flax, burning of (*stupa*), 187–188
fleurs-de-lis, 50, 54, 55, 94, 95, 105
footgear (sandals or slippers, royal, papal), 50, 66, 186
Fortes, Meyer, 10, 47
Fouquet, Jean, 91
France, 3, 7, 35–118 passim, 134, 137, 141, 143. *See also* individual rulers
Francis I, king of France, 90
Franks, kingdom of, 17–34 passim. *See also* individual rulers
Frederick II, king of Sicily, emperor, 6, 127
Frey, Germanic god, 121
funeral; ducal, 39–40; royal, 9, 36, 38–40 passim, 41, 152, 153, 155

Gauzlin, abbot of St. Denis, 21
Geertz, Clifford, 10, 15 n. 35, 47
Gennep, Arnold van, 10, 52, 55
Genoa, 102
George III (of Hanover), king of England, 242–243
George V, king of England, 5
George VI, king of England, 243
Germany, 11 n. 2, 137, 143; Holy Roman Empire, 3; Second Reich (1871), 3
Gerson, Jean, 110
gestures, 7, 8, 9, 63, 152–164 passim
Giesebrecht, Wilhelm, 3
Giesey, Ralph, 1, 47
Gieysztor, Aleksander, 7
Gilles de Rome, 98

gloves (papal, royal), 189
Godefroy, Thedore, and Denis, 11 n. 12, 47
Goldberg, Jonathan, 223
Golein, Jean, 80, 81
Gospel-reading, royal, 135–136 passim, 137, 141, 142
Göttingen, 3, 4; "school of," 5
Gottschalk, monk in Orbais, 25
grand chamberlain of France, 50, 66
Grandes Chroniques de France, 72–87 passim
Great Schism, 180, 184, 187
Gregory X, pope, 181, 183. See also *ordo* of Gregory X
Gregory XI, pope, 184
Gregory XII, pope, 187
Gustavus Wasa, king of Sweden, 139

Haakon Haakonson, king of Norway, 127, 129
Haakon the Good, king of Norway, 122, 128
Haakon V, king of Norway, 129
Haakon VI, king of Norway and Sweden, 129
Hanley, Sarah, 7, 44, 47
Hans, king of the (Scandinavian) Union, 130
Harald Fairhair, king of Norway, 121–122
Haugaard, William, 221
helmet, 121, 122, 128, 132, 150 n. 102
Henry Bradshaw Society, 5, 230–234 passim
Henry II, king of France, 42, 90, 102, 109
Henry IV, king of France, 37, 42, 44, 90
Henry V, king of England, 89, 102
Henry VI, king of England, 89, 102, 108, 204
Henry VII, king of England, 239
herald, 94
heraldry, 67, 79, 86 n. 14
Heusch, Luc de, 69
highseat (royal), 120, 122–123
Hildebrand, archdeacon (= Gregory VII, pope), 190
Hincmar, archbishop of Reims, 2, 8, 16–34 passim
historical anthropology, 9–10
Hoffmann, Erich, 7
Holtzmann, Robert, 126
Holy Ampulla (Holy Chrism), 24, 49, 53, 54, 55, 60, 64, 65, 69
homage, fealty, 49, 55, 159, 161
Honorius Augustodunensis, 12 n. 6
Hrollaug, king of Naumdælafylki, 121–122
Hugh of St. Victor, 9
Hugh, abbot of Tours, 21
Hugh, son of Lothar II, king of the Franks, 22

Hughes, Andrew, 7
Hungary, 163 n. 16, 163 n. 18

iconography, 2. See also illumination; text and image
illumination, 2, 58–87 passim, 153, 155, 156
inauguration, 35–45 passim, 52. See also consecration; coronation; *sacre et couronnement*
India, ancient, 53
Innocent III, pope, 142, 180, 181, 187
Innocent IV, pope, 127, 183
Innocent VI, pope, 179, 192
interregnum, ceremonial, 38
Investiture Contest, 168, 180, 181, 190
Isabella of Bavaria, queen of France, 89, 102, 108
Ivrea Sacramentary, 61

Jackson, Richard, 7, 35, 44, 46, 47, 51
Jacobite movement, 239
James I, king of England, 224, 240
James II, king of England, 225, 232, 240–241 passim
Janzon, Per, 140
Jeanne d'Arc, 103–104
Jeanne d'Evreux, queen of France, 83
Jeanne of Bourbon, queen of France, 74, 75, 81
Jews, of Avignon, 192
John Casimir, king of Poland, 160
John II (the Good), king of France, 75, 76, 89, 97, 98, 101
John XXII, pope, 179, 183, 184, 187
John Paul II, pope, 179
Joshua, 16
Josias, 16
Julius II, pope, 193
Juvenal des Ursins, Guillaume, chancellor of France, 104

Kallstöm, Olle, 128
Kalmar, 130, 132
Kantorowicz, Ernst H., 4, 6, 207, 235
Karl Knutsson, king of the (Scandinavian) Union, 130, 138
Keble, John, 229
"king's two bodies," 6, 39, 153
kiss of peace, 49, 56, 67, 160, 176, 187
knighting, 50, 51, 54, 159, 219
Knights of the Bath, 219
Knut Lavard, 131
Knut VI, king of Denmark, 131

GENERAL INDEX

Ladner, Gerhard, 6
Lancastrian, dynasty, 102–103 passim, 105
Lateran palace (Rome), 179–181 passim, 190, 193; Council, Third, 180; *possesso* of, 180–181
laudes. See acclamation
law (incl. constitution), 16, 35, 106, 111, 119–120, 125, 126, 236, 237
Laxman, Hans, archbishop, 132, 135
Le Goff, Jacques, 6, 8, 9, 61, 69
Le roi est mort!, 39
Leach, Edmund, 10
legitimacy: of birth, 19–20, 142; by divine intervention, 60; of succession, 17
legitimation, 2, 9, 238–243
Leroquais, Canon V., 47, 58
L'Hopital, Michel de, chancellor of France, 42
Liber regie capelle, 204
lit de justice, 36, 41–44 passim, 98
liturgy, liturgical texts, 3, 7, 8, 180. *See also* acclamation (*laudes*); chant; *ordines*
London, 91, 102, 105, 242
Londonderry, marquess of, 243–244
Lothar II, king of the Franks, 16–17, 19
Lotharingia, 22–23. *See also* individual rulers
Louis, duke of Anjou, brother of Charles V, 80
Louis, duke of Bourbon, 81
Louis of Male, count of Flanders, 80
Louis the Younger, king of East Francia, 21
Louis (I) the Pious, king and emperor of the Franks, 24
Louis I of Anjou, king of Hungary and Poland, 155
Louis II, king of the Franks, son of Louis the Stammerer, 20–21, 23
Louis VI, king of France, 37
Louis VIII, king of France, 47, 49
Louis IX (St. Louis), king of France, 37–38, 43, 46, 49, 55, 61, 69, 89, 91, 93, 100, 197
Louis XI, king of France, 89, 104, 105, 108, 113
Louis XII, king of France, 90, 102, 105, 108, 112
Louis XIII, king of France, 43, 44
Lund, 136, 142
Lyon, Bryce, 110
Lyons, 41, 183, 184, 186, 192

Mabillon, Dom Jean, 3
Macleane, Douglas, 230, 233
McCoy, Richard, 8

Magnus, bishop of Skara, 139
Magnus Eriksson, king of Norway, 129, 138
Magnus Erlingsson, king of Norway, 125–126
Magnus Lagaböter, king of Norway, 128, 129
main de justice, 55
Margaret, regent of Norway, Denmark and Sweden, 130
Margaret of Austria, queen of France, 89, 108
Margarethe Sambria, queen of Denmark, 132
Marie de Médicis, queen of France, 42
Martin V, pope, 184, 190
Mary Tudor, queen of England, 90, 109, 217, 218
Maskell, William, 228–232 passim
Mechtild, queen of Denmark, 132
mentalité, history of, 6
Metz, 23–25 passim
Milan, 102
minority/majority (of ruler), 42, 74, 80, 132, 135
Mora-field (and stone), 137, 138, 141
Moses, 6
music. *See* chant

Napoleon Orsini, cardinal deacon, 186–187, 188
narrative sources (annals, chronicles), 2, 17–34 passim
Nathan the priest, 16
Neale, J. E., 225
Nelson, Janet, 3, 7, 47
Newman, John Henry, cardinal, 229
Nibelungenlied, 122
Nicholas I, pope, 18
Norway, 120, 125–131 passim, 143. *See also* individual rulers
notation of music. *See* chant
Notre Dame, cathedral of (Paris), 94, 97
numerical symbology, 49–50

oath, royal. *See* coronation oath
Odin (Wotan), Germanic god, 119, 121
Oglethorpe, Owen, bishop of Carlisle, 219–222 passim, 240
"oil of Thomas Becket," 207, 239
Olaf (Haakonsson), king of Norway, 129
Oldenburg, dynasty, 131, 137
Olivecrona, 138
orb (*pomum*), 133, 141, 157, 159, 167
ordines (coronation orders), 1, 2, 3, 7, 17, 18, 72; Anglo-Saxon (Egbert, Edgar), 232;

ordines (continued)
  English (First to Fourth Recension), 197–216 passim, 232–233, 237–238, 239–240; papal, 181–184, 190; Polish, 153
ordo, Bohemian (14th C.), 162 n. 4
ordo, Danish (reconstructed), 136
ordo, Dykmans's, 183–184, 188. See also *ordines,* papal
ordo, Erdmann's, 53
ordo, German of 1273, 133, 162
ordo, German of the twelfth century, 129, 130
ordo, last Capetian, 47, 59
ordo, Sicilian (1130), 165–178; for crown-wearing, 166
ordo of Charles IV, 65
ordo of Charles V, 59, 65
ordo of Gregory X, 182–183. See also *ordines,* papal
ordo of Mainz (961), 133, 135
ordo of Reims, 46, 47, 50, 51, 52, 55, 65
ordo of 1250, 46–71 passim
ordo of 1316. See *ordines,* papal
ordo of 1530 (Poland), 153
ordo of 1561 (Sweden), 140–141 passim
Ordo Romanus XIV, 182–183, 187
Oslo, 129, 130
Oxford Movement, 229, 231

pageantry, 8, 40, 100, 102–110 passim, 222–225 passim, 242
pallium, 181, 188, 189, 190
papacy, 8, 179–196 passim. See also individual pontiffs
Paris, 40–43 passim, 88–118 passim; Parlement of, 74, 80, 94, 100, 102–112 passim; University of, 98–100, 110
Parliament, British, 243
participants (in rituals), 8, 9, 48–51 passim, 66, 106, 141, 157–159 passim, 189, 191
Paul VI, pope, 179
peers of France, 49, 74, 77, 79, 80, 81
Pelayo, Alvaro, 187–188
Pepin the Short, king of the Franks, 55
Petri, Olaus, 139
Philip the Bold, duke of Burgundy, 79–80, 81
Philip II, king of France, 37
Philip III, king of France, 37, 38, 47
Philip IV (le Bel), king of France, 89, 98, 111
Philip V, king of France, 89, 100
Philip VI, king of France, 89, 100
Pius V, pope, 239

Poland, 7, 8, 152–164 passim
Pole, Reginald, cardinal archbishop of Canterbury, 219
Pollard, A. F., 221
Ponet, John, 219
Pontificale Romano-Germanicum, 166, 169 passim, 177–178
Pontificale Romanum, 134, 142, 166, 204
Pontifical of Durandus, 186
Pontifical of Mainz (960), 61
pontificals, English. See Index of Mss.
popular culture, 152, 242
populus, 8, 48, 50, 189
Port St. Denis (Paris), 91, 96, 97
possesso. See Lateran
Preface, liturgical, 207–209
presuccession initiation, 37
prévôt des marchands (Paris), 94
processions, 52, 53, 67, 69, 81, 157, 161, 187, 189, 191, 192, 204, 205, 223, 242, 243
professio (in coronation *ordines*), 53, 126, 127, 133, 135, 139, 141
promises (royal), 50, 53, 98, 111–112 passim, 141
Przemysl I, king of Poland, 153
Psalterium Romanum, 186
Pusey, Edmund, 229

queens: French, 48, 67, 75, 78–83 passim, 87 n. 25; Scandinavian, 131, 133, 139, 151 n. 118. See also individual rulers and consorts

Ranke, Leopold von, 234
Reedy, G., S. J., 242
regnum et sacerdotium ("state" and "church"), 5, 46, 55–56, 61, 70, 127, 157, 158, 191, 217, 242
Reims, 37–38, 41, 44, 48, 50; cathedral, 50–51; palace, 51. See also Hincmar, archbishop of Reims
René II, duke of Lorraine, 67
Richard II, king of England, 199, 200, 207, 210
Richard III, king of England, 217, 239
Richardson, H. G., 235–238 passim
Riefenstahl, Leni, 30–31 n. 42
ring (as royal insigne), 54, 67, 143, 159, 174; episcopal, 189; of Fisherman, 186
Ringsted (Denmark), 142
rites of passage, 47, 48, 52
rod (staff, *baculus*), 54, 128, 143, 167

GENERAL INDEX

Roes, Alexander of, cardinal, 187
Roger II, king of Sicily, 165–178 passim
Rome, 179–196 passim
Rouen, 41
Rowse, A. L., 221
rulers and subjects, relations between, 10, 88, 94, 102–103, 111, 122–123, 223–225 passim
Rupert of the Palatinate, king of the Romans, 135

sacre et couronnement (French coronation), 10 n. 1, 36–38 passim, 44, 45, 53–55, 65–67, 72–87 passim
sacred (sacral) kingship, 3, 119, 153
St. Denis, abbey of, 39, 65, 74; abbot of, 49, 55
St. Edmund, king and martyr, 197
St. Edward's Chapel, 220–221
St. Erik, 141
St. George, 218–219
St. Louis. *See* Louis IX, king of France
St. Olaf, 126, 127, 129, 130
St. Peter, 192; Basilica of (Rome), 180–184 passim, 193; Patrimony of, 190
St. Remigius, bishop of Reims, 24, 53
St. Rémi, abbey in Reims, 49, 55, 65, 66
Samuel, prophet, 54
Sandquist, T. A., 200
Sancroft, William, archbishop of Canterbury, 240
Sarum Missal, 208
Scandinavia, 119–151 passim. *See also* individual rulers
scepter, 54, 67, 75, 127, 128, 130, 133, 139, 140, 142, 157, 159, 175; of Dagobert, 75
Scheller, Robert, 62–63 passim
Schimmelpfenning, Berhard, 8
Schramm, Percy Ernst, 3–8 passim, 200, 224, 235
Schwalm, Jacob, 165
scrutinium (in coronation orders), 53, 133, 141, 171, 236
seal, royal, 106, 130
Selden, John, 3
sermon (coronation), 135, 141, 241–242
Sherman, Claire, 72–73 passim
Sicardus of Cremona, 11 n. 6
Sicily, 8, 165–178 passim
sic transit gloria mundi, 187–188
Sigismund of Luxemburg, emperor, 135
"sleeping king," 44, 51–52, 157, 170

Smith, Dom C., 233
Snorri Sturlusson, 119, 120, 121, 126
Solomon, king of Israel, 16
Spain, 11 n. 2
Stanislas Augustus, king of Poland, 153
Stanley, Edward, bishop of Norwich, 229
Stockholm, 138
stone, sacred, 120, 121. *See also* Mora stone
Sturdy, David, 4, 221
Sturla Thórdarson, 127, 128, 129
succession: divided/undivided 20, 26; elective, 18, 35, 48, 120, 153; filial, dynastic, 17, 35–36, 48, 81, 120, 125, 141; law of, 129
Sverker, royal clan in Sweden, 132
Sverre, king of Norway, 126–127
Sweden, 120, 129, 130, 135, 137–143 passim. *See also* individual rulers
sword, royal, 38, 40, 50, 56, 66, 67, 94, 105, 121, 127, 128, 130, 133, 134, 139, 157, 174; brandishing of, 158

Tacitus, 119
"taking a king," 120–122 passim
Taylor, Arthur, 228
text and image, 7, 58, 59, 73, 83
thing, 120, 121, 125, 131
Thordeman, B., 138
Thorston, Herbert, S. J., 231–232, 233
Throckmorton, Sir Nicholas, 222
throne (enthronement), 48, 49, 51, 53, 141, 161, 176, 188, 189
tiara, papal, 181, 190
tournament, 164 n. 22
Trondheim, 125, 130
Turner, Victor, 10, 52, 88
tyrant, 17

Ullmann, Walter, 4, 5, 6, 8
umbrella, ceremonial, 191
unction, *unctio*. *See* anointing
Uppland Law, 120, 138
Uppsala, 129, 137, 141, 142
Urban IV, pope, 183
Urban V, pope, 184, 193
Urban VI, pope, 190

Valois, dynasty, 74, 83
Vatican, palace (Rome), 179, 184, 186, 193
Västgöta Law, 120
Verdun, treaty of, 26
Vestergaard, Elisabeth, 7

Victoria, queen and empress, 243
Viking Age, 119–123 passim
Viterbo, 183
Vordingborg (Denmark), castle, 131

Waitz, Georg, 3, 5
Wakeman, Henry, 232
Waldemar, king of Sweden, 137
Waldemar I, king of Denmark, 131
Waldemar II, king of Denmark, 131, 142
Waldemar III, king of Denmark, 132
Waldemar IV, king of Denmark, 132
Walpole, Horace, 242
Ward, Paul, 4, 6

Weber, Max, 239–242 passim
Westminster, 200, 213, 219; Missal (*see* Index of Mss.)
Wickham Legg, J., 230, 233
Wilkinson, Bertie, 201
William III, king of England, 225
William IV, king of England, 243
Wilson, H. A., 221, 233
Winchester Troper, 203
Wladisias III, king of Poland, 153
women (in royal ceremonials), 69, 104
Wordsworth, Ch. 230

Zadoch the prophet, 16

INDEX OF MANUSCRIPTS

Cambridge
  Corpus Christi College
    Ms. 44, 198–199, 203
    Ms. 79, 201–213 passim (incl. fig. 12.2 on p. 203)
    Ms. 146, 198–199
  University Library
    Ms. Mm III 21, 200–213 passim

Cracow
  National Museum, Czartoryski Library
    Pontifical of Erasmucs Ciolek, 155–156 (fig. 9.2–3)

London
  British Library
    Ms. Add. 6157, 201–213 passim
    Ms. Arundel 149, 200–213 passim
    Ms. Cotton Tiberius B. VIII, 72–87 passim (incl. figs. 5.3–4 on p. 77–78), 24
    Ms. Harley 561, 200–213 passim
    Ms. Harley 2901, 200–213 passim
    Ms. Landsdowne 451, 200–213 passim
  Westminster Abbey
    Ms. 34 ("Lytlington/Westminster Missal"), 200–201, 203; fig. 12.1, 207, 211, 212

Madrid
  Biblioteca Nacional
    Cod. 678, 166–177 passim

Oxford
  Bodleian Library
    Ms. Rawl. c 425, 200–213 passim (incl. fig. 12.3 a/b on p. 203)
    Ms. Ashmole 842, 200–213 passim
    Ms. Ashmole 863, 200–213 passim
  Magdalen College
    Ms. 226 (now in Bodleian Library), 198–199, 203

Paris
  Bibliothèque Nationale,
    ms. fr. 2813, 73–86 passim (incl. figs. 5.1–2 on p. 74, 75)
    ms. fr. 5054, 94–95, 103–104 (incl. figs. 6.3, 6.5)
    ms. fr. 5594, 93 (fig. 6.2)
    ms. fr. 6465, 92 (fig. 6.1)
    ms. lat. 943, 198–199, 203
    ms. lat. 246, 46–71 passim (incl. figs. 4.1–3 on p. 62, 64, 68)
    ms. nouv. acq. lat 1202, 59

Rome
  Bibl. Apost. Vaticana
    Cod. Vat. lat. 4746, 165–177 passim
    Cod. Vat. lat. 6748, 166–177 passim
  Bibl. Casanatense
    Cod. 614, 165–177 passim

Rouen
  Bibliothèque municipale
    ms. A 27 (368), 198–199
    ms. Y 6 (369), 198–199

Designer:	U.C. Press Staff
Compositor:	Asco Trade Typesetting Ltd
Text:	10/12 Baskerville
Display:	Baskerville

www.ingramcontent.com/pod-product-compliance
Lightning Source LLC
Chambersburg PA
CBHW021700230426
43668CB00008B/678